lonely planet

ITALY'S
BEST TRIPS
40 AMAZING ROAD TRIPS

This edition written and researched by

**Duncan Garwood,
Paula Hardy**

SYMBOLS IN THIS BOOK

✓ Top Tips

📖 History & Culture

📷 Essential Photo

⑤ Link Your Trips

👪 Family

🏃 Walking Tour

💬 Tips from Locals

🍷 Food & Drink

✗ Eating

↩ Trip Detour

🌳 Outdoors

🛏 Sleeping

☎ Telephone Number

@ Internet Access

⛱ Swimming Pool

🕙 Opening Hours

📶 Wi-Fi Access

👶 Family-Friendly

P Parking

🥗 Vegetarian Selection

❄ Air-Conditioning

MAP LEGEND

Routes
▨▨ Trip Route
▨▨ Trip Detour
▨▨ Linked Trip
▨▨ Walk Route
Tollway
Freeway
Primary
Secondary
Tertiary
Lane
Unsealed Road
Plaza/Mall
Steps
)(Tunnel
Pedestrian Overpass
Walk Track/Path

Boundaries
— — International
— — — State/Province
━━ Cliff

Hydrography
River/Creek
Intermittent River
Swamp/Mangrove
Canal
Water
Dry/Salt/ Intermittent Lake
Glacier

Highway Markers
① Highway Marker

Trips
1 Trip Numbers
9 Trip Stop
🏃 Walking tour
↩ Trip Detour

Population
◉ Capital (National)
◉ Capital (State/Province)
● City/Large Town
● Town/Village

Areas
Beach
Cemetery (Christian)
Cemetery (Other)
Park
Forest
Reservation
Urban Area
Sportsground

Transport
✈ Airport
🚠 Cable Car/ Funicular
P Parking
🚆 Train/Railway
🚊 Tram

Note: Not all symbols displayed above appear on the maps in this book

CONTENTS

Northern Italy
p63

Central Italy
p209

Southern Italy
p293

Contents cont.

ROAD TRIP ESSENTIALS

Venice Gondola on the Grand Canal in front of the Basilica di Santa Maria della Salute

Rome Piazza Navona with the Chiesa di Sant'Agnese in Agone and the Fontana dei Quattro Fiumi

WELCOME TO
ITALY

Few countries can rival Italy's wealth of riches. Its historic cities boast iconic monuments and masterpieces at every turn, its food is imitated the world over and its landscape is a majestic patchwork of snow-capped peaks, plunging coastlines, lakes and remote valleys. And with many thrilling roads to explore, it offers plenty of epic driving.

The 40 trips outlined in this book run the length of the country, leading from Alpine summits to southern volcanoes, from hilltop towns in Tuscany to fishing villages on the Amalfi Coast, from Venetian canals to Pompeii's ghostly ruins. They take in heavyweight cities and little-known gems, and cover a wide range of experiences.

So whether you want to tour gourmet towns and historic vineyards, idyllic coastlines or pristine national parks, we have a route for you. And if you've only got time for one trip, make it one of our eight Classic Trips, which take you to the very best of Italy.

→

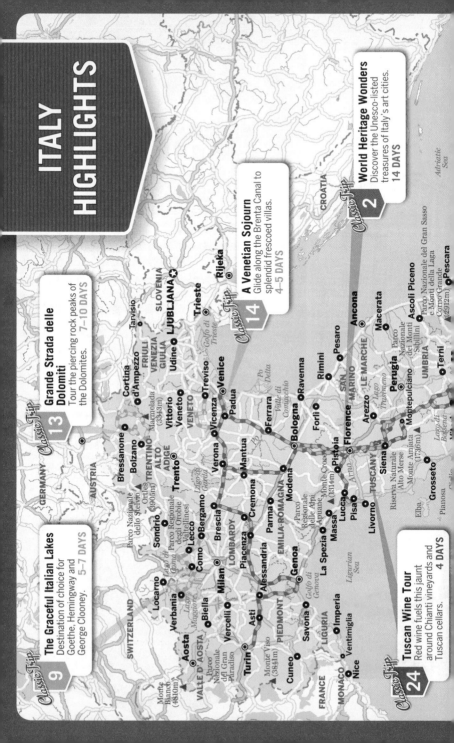

ITALY HIGHLIGHTS

Classic Trip

9 The Graceful Italian Lakes
Destination of choice for Goethe, Hemingway and George Clooney. 5–7 DAYS

Classic Trip

13 Grande Strada delle Dolomiti
Tour the piercing rock peaks of the Dolomites. 7–10 DAYS

Classic Trip

14 A Venetian Sojourn
Glide along the Brenta Canal to splendid frescoed villas. 4–5 DAYS

Classic Trip

2 World Heritage Wonders
Discover the Unesco-listed treasures of Italy's art cities. 14 DAYS

Classic Trip

24 Tuscan Wine Tour
Red wine fuels this jaunt around Chianti vineyards and Tuscan cellars. 4 DAYS

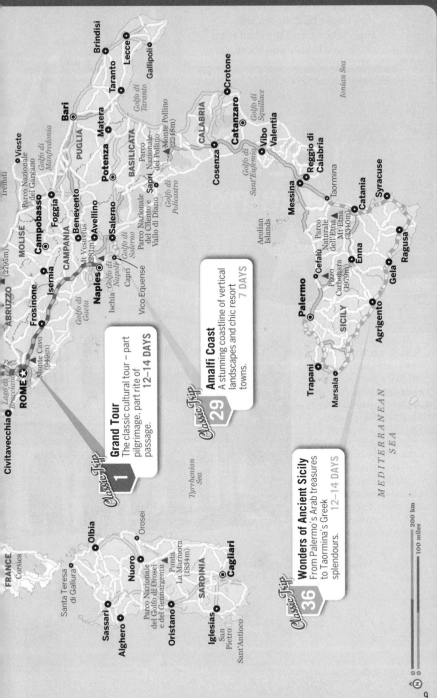

FRANCE

Corsica

Santa Teresa
di Gallura

Olbia

Sassari

Alghero

Nuoro

Oristano

Parco Nazionale
del Golfo di Orosei
e del Gennargentu

Punta
La Marmora
(1834m)

Iglesias

San
Pietro

Sant'Antioco

SARDINIA

Cagliari

Classic Trip

36

Wonders of Ancient Sicily

From Palermo's Arab treasures
to Taormina's Greek
splendours.   12–14 DAYS

*MEDITERRANEAN
SEA*

100 miles

200 km

Civitavecchia

Lago di
Bracciano

ABRUZZO ▲ (2795m)

Tremiti

ROME ✪

Monte Cavo
(949m)

Frosinone

Isernia

MOLISE

Campobasso

Parco Nazionale
del Gargano

Golfo di
Manfredonia

Vieste

Classic Trip

1

Grand Tour

The classic cultural tour – part
pilgrimage, part rite of
passage.   12–14 DAYS

CAMPANIA

Mt Vesuvius
(1281m)

Benevento

Avellino

Foggia

Bari

PUGLIA

Matera

Potenza

Salerno

BASILICATA

Golfo di
Napoli

Naples

Ischia

Capri

Golfo di
Salerno

Parco Nazionale
del Cilento e
Vallo di Diano

Sapri

Golfo di
Policastro

Parco
Nazionale
del Pollino

Monte Pollino
(2248m)

Classic Trip

29

Amalfi Coast

A stunning coastline of vertical
landscapes and chic resort
towns.   7 DAYS

Vico Equense

Golfo di
Gaeta

*Tyrrhenian
Sea*

Cosenza

Golfo di
Sant'Eugemia

CALABRIA

Catanzaro

Golfo di
Squillace

Crotone

Golfo di
Taranto

Taranto

Brindisi

Lecce

Gallipoli

Ionian Sea

Vibo
Valentia

Reggio di
Calabria

Messina

Aeolian
Islands

Parco
Naturale
dell'Etna

Mt Etna
(3340m)

Taormina

Catania

Syracuse

Cefalù

Pizzo
Carbonara
(1979m)

Enna

Ragusa

Palermo

SICILY

Agrigento

Gela

Trapani

Marsala

9

> Italy's best sights and experiences, and the road trips that will take you there.

ITALY
HIGHLIGHTS

★

Rome

All roads lead to Rome (Roma) and **Trip 1: Grand Tour** is one such, stopping off at the Eternal City en route from Turin (Torino) to Naples (Napoli). The one-time *caput mundi* (capital of the world) is a mesmerising city, home to celebrated icons – the Colosseum, Pantheon, Trevi Fountain, Michelangelo's Sistine Chapel – and spectacular works of art. Even strolling its romantic lanes and operatic piazzas is a thrill to remember.

Trips

Rome Colosseum

Venice Ponte delle Guglie

Venice

Drive **Trip 2: World Heritage Wonders** and the road runs out in Venice (Venezia), where highways give way to waterways. Venice is absolutely unique and it's a soul-lifting experience to explore its backstreets and piazzas, revelling in East-meets-West architecture. Art treasures abound, but for sheer 'wow' factor little can compare with the Basilica di San Marco and its 24-carat-gold mosaics.

Trips 1 2 8 14

Pompeii

A once-thriving Roman port frozen in its 2000-year-old death throes, Pompeii is an electrifying spectacle. Head down on **Trip 27: Shadow of Vesuvius** and wander its fantastically preserved streets, exploring the forum, the city brothel, the 5000-seat theatre and the frescoed Villa dei Misteri. Body casts of victims add a sense of menace as Vesuvius looms darkly on the horizon.

Trips 1 27

The Dolomites

One of the inspiring sights of northern Italy, the Dolomites are the stars of **Trip 13: Grande Strada delle Dolomiti**. Their pink-hued granite summits form the majestic backdrop for this drive along Italy's most famous mountain road between Bolzano and Cortina d'Ampezzo. Stop off en route to admire sweeping panoramas and explore the Alpine villages of the Alta Badia and Alpe di Siusi.

Trip 13

Dolomites Santa Maddalena village and the Gruppo di Odle

BEST ROADS FOR DRIVING

Grande Strada delle Dolomiti Epic road through exhilarating Alpine scenery. **Trip**

SS17bis Traverses Abruzzo's awe-inspiring Campo Imperatore plateau in the shadow of the Gran Sasso. **Trip** 19

SP146 A panoramic drive through classic landscapes in Tuscany's Unesco-listed Val d'Orcia. **Trips** 24 25

SS163 Also known as the Nastro Azzurro, this road weaves along the precipitous Amalfi Coast. **Trip** 29

Cinque Terre

Tackle the Unesco-listed Cinque Terre on **Trip 7: Cinematic Cinque Terre**. An idyllic stretch of coastline named after five villages – Riomaggiore, Manarola, Corniglia, Vernazza and Monterosso al Mare – the Cinque Terre offers superb walking. A coastal path snakes along cliffs and hills, while up above, trails traverse shrub-covered mountains as they lead to ancient sanctuaries and heavenly views.

Trip 7

13

Florence Duomo

Florence

From Brunelleschi's red-capped Duomo to Michelangelo's *David* and Botticelli's *The Birth of Venus*, Florence (Firenze) boasts priceless masterpieces and a historic centre that looks much as it did in Renaissance times. Art aside, the city sets the perfect scene for al fresco dining and relaxed wine drinking. Lap it all up on **Trip 2: World Heritage Wonders** and **Trip 23: Piero della Francesca Trail**.

Trips

BEST MUSEUMS & GALLERIES

Vatican Museums Michelangelo's Sistine Chapel, Raphael frescoes and much, much more. **Trips** 1 2

Galleria degli Uffizi Florence gallery housing Italy's finest collection of Renaissance art. **Trips** 1 2 23 24

Peggy Guggenheim Collection Striking modern art in a classic Venetian setting. **Trips** 1 2 8 14

Museo Archeologico Nazionale Naples' premier museum with breathtaking classical sculpture and mosaics from Pompeii. **Trips** 1 27

15

HIGHLIGHTS ★

Amalfi Coast Atrani

Valle d'Aosta Valpelline valley

Amalfi Coast

The quintessential Mediterranean coastline, the Amalfi Coast is Italy's most dazzling seafront stretch. Its coastal road – detailed in **Trip 29: Amalfi Coast** – curves sinuously, linking the area's steeply stacked towns and rocky inlets. All around, cliffs sheer down into sparkling blue waters, lemons grow on hillside terraces, and towering *fichi d'India* (prickly pears) guard silent mountain paths.

Trip 29

Lago di Como

The most picturesque and least visited of Italy's main northern lakes, Lago di Como (Lake Como) is a highlight of **Trip 9: The Graceful Italian Lakes**, a scenic jaunt around Lakes Maggiore, Orta and Como. Set in the shadow of the Rhaetian Alps, Lago di Como's banks are speckled with Liberty-style villas and fabulous landscaped gardens that burst into blushing colour in April and May.

Trip 9

Valle d'Aosta

Italy's smallest and least populous region is also one of its most beautiful. Follow **Trip 12: Valle d'Aosta** as it inches up a narrow mountain valley ringed by the icy peaks of Europe's highest mountains, including Mont Blanc (Monte Bianco), the Matterhorn (Monte Cervino), Monte Rosa and Gran Paradiso. Leave your car and take to the slopes for exhilarating hiking and hair-raising skiing.

Trip 12

Syracuse

An ancient metropolis turned model baroque town, Syracuse (Siracusa) is one of Sicily's most enchanting cities. Its wonderfully intact 5th-century BC amphitheatre is one of the many memorable Greek ruins on **Trip 36: Wonders of Ancient Sicily,** while its baroque centre is a vision of 17th-century urban design. At its heart, Piazza del Duomo is a glorious spot for an evening *aperitivo*.

Trips 36 37

Tuscan Landscapes

Picture in your mind's eye the ideal Italian landscape – golden fields, haughty cypress trees, hills capped by medieval towns. You're imagining Tuscany, a region whose fabled panoramas have inspired everybody from Renaissance artists to overwrought poets and modern motorists. Drive **Trip 24: Tuscan Wine Tour** or **Trip 25: Tuscan Landscapes** and give yourself up to its soothing beauty and delicious *vino*.

Trips 24 25

(left) **Tuscany** Val d'Orcia

(below) **Milan** Galleria Vittorio Emanuele II

BORUT TRDINA/GETTY IMAGES ©

JUSTIN FOULKES/LONELY PLANET ©

Milan

With its designer boutiques, cool *aperitivi* bars and chic restaurants, Italy's fashion and financial capital is a city for urbanites with a sense of style. Milan (Milano) is also a cultural heavyweight, home to Europe's most famous opera house, a gloriously fairy-tale Gothic cathedral and da Vinci's celebrated mural *The Last Supper*. Discover all this on **Trip 1: Grand Tour** or **Trip 8: Northern Cities**.

Trips

BEST HILLTOP TOWNS

Matera Basilicata town famous for its primitive *sassi* (cave houses). **Trip** 34

Urbino A Renaissance gem in off-the-radar Le Marche. **Trip** 23

Orvieto Proud clifftop home of a stunning Gothic cathedral. **Trip** 25

Montalcino Tuscan producer of Brunello di Montalcino, one of Italy's top red wines. **Trip** 24

19

IF YOU LIKE...

Piedmont Cheese for sale in the Langhe Valley

Food & Wine

With its superb produce, culinary traditions and world-beating wine, Italy is a food- and wine-lover's dream destination. Whether it's tasting white truffles in Alba, dining al fresco on a medieval piazza, or tasting Chianti at a Tuscan vineyard, great foodie experiences await at every turn.

4 Gourmet Piedmont
Feast on chocolate, cheese and wine in Italy's Slow Food heartland.

15 Valpolicella Wine Country Sample bold wines at historic wineries in the vine-clad hills west of Verona.

24 Tuscan Wine Tour
Savour Tuscany's great reds in Chianti vineyards.

26 Foodie Emilia-Romagna Discover the towns that put the Parma into ham and the Bolognese into spag bol.

Art & Architecture

Boasting an unparalleled artistic and architectural legacy, Italy is home to some of the Western world's most celebrated masterpieces. Works by Renaissance heroes and baroque maestros grace the country's churches, museums and galleries, many of which are works of art in their own right.

1 Grand Tour Take in the Cappella degli Scrovegni, The Last Supper, the Galleria dell'Accademia et al.

8 Northern Cities Admire Giotto frescoes, medieval cityscapes.

23 Piero della Francesca Trail From Urbino to Florence, follow the trail of frescoes left by the great Renaissance master.

37 Sicilian Baroque
Swoon over extravagant baroque architecture in southeastern Sicily.

Ancient Relics

Everywhere you go in Italy you're reminded of the country's long and tumultuous past. Etruscan tombs and Greek temples stand testament to pre-Roman civilisations, while amphitheatres, aqueducts, even whole towns, testify to the ambition of ancient Rome's rulers and the genius of its architects.

2 World Heritage Wonders Rome's Colosseum and Verona's Arena headline on this classic cross-country drive.

20 Etruscan Tuscany & Lazio Duck into tombs decorated with ancient frescoes.

27 Shadow of Vesuvius Wander around Pompeii and Herculaneum, the most celebrated victims of Vesuvius' volcanic fury.

36 Wonders of Ancient Sicily Sicily's ancient Greek temples are the best you'll see outside of Greece.

Cinque Terre Vernazza

Beaches & Coastal Scenery

From the cliffs of the Amalfi Coast to the villages of the Cinque Terre, and from Sicily's volcanic seascapes to Sardinia's dreamy beaches, Italy's 7600km-long coastline is as varied as it is enticing. Add crystal-clear waters in a thousand shades of blue and you've got the perfect summer recipe.

7 Cinematic Cinque Terre Cruise one of Italy's most picture-perfect coastal stretches.

29 Amalfi Coast Italy's most celebrated coastline is a classic Mediterranean pin-up.

33 Salento Surprises Join Italian beach-goers in Puglia's summer hotspot.

39 Emerald Coast Sardinia's northern coast boasts dazzling beaches and heavenly waters.

Mountains

For a taste of the high life take to Italy's mountains. From the northern Alps to the lesser-trodden Apennines, stunning roads snake past mighty, snow-capped peaks, over hair-raising passes and through silent valleys swathed in ancient forests. Outdoor enthusiasts will find superb skiing, hiking, climbing and cycling.

11 Roof of Italy Drive the fabled Stelvio Pass as you explore northern Italy's high-altitude borderlands.

12 Valle d'Aosta A spectacular Alpine region overlooked by Italy's highest mountains.

19 Abruzzo's Wild Landscapes Look out for wolves and bears in Abruzzo's remote national parks.

34 Across the Lucanian Apennines Go off-piste in the dramatic mountains of southern Basilicata.

Villas & Palaces

Ever since the days of the Roman Empire, Italy's ruling dynasties have employed the top artists and architects of their day to design their homes. The results are imperial palaces and royal residences, Renaissance mansions and aristocratic villas.

2 World Heritage Wonders Explore imperial palaces and art-filled palazzi (mansions) in Rome, Siena, Florence and Venice.

3 Savoy Palace Circuit Tour the Savoy family's royal palaces in Turin and the Piedmont countryside.

9 The Graceful Italian Lakes For grace, style and floral exuberance, head to the villas and gardens of Italy's northern lakes.

14 A Venetian Sojourn Stop at Unesco-protected Palladian villas as you drive through Veneto's wine country.

NEED ᵀᴼ KNOW

CURRENCY
Euro (€)

LANGUAGE
Italian

VISAS
Generally not required for stays of up to 90 days (or at all for EU nationals); some nationalities need a Schengen visa.

FUEL
You'll find filling stations on autostradas and major roads. Reckon on €1.49 for a litre of unleaded petrol and €1.33 for diesel.

HIRE CARS
Avis (www.avis.com)

Europcar (www.europcar.com)

Hertz (www.hertz.it)

Maggiore (www.maggiore.it)

IMPORTANT NUMBERS
Ambulance (☏118)

Emergency (☏112)

Police (☏113)

Roadside Assistance (☏803 116; ☏800 116 800 from a foreign mobile phone)

Climate

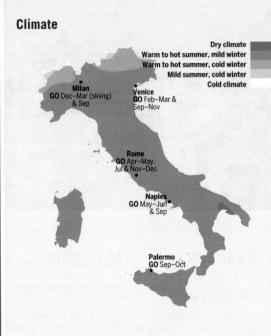

Dry climate
Warm to hot summer, mild winter
Warm to hot summer, cold winter
Mild summer, cold winter
Cold climate

Milan
GO Dec–Mar (skiing) & Sep

Venice
GO Feb–Mar & Sep–Nov

Rome
GO Apr–May, Jul & Nov–Dec

Naples
GO May–Jun & Sep

Palermo
GO Sep–Oct

When to Go

High Season (Jul–Aug)
» Queues at big sights and on the road, especially in August.

» Prices also rocket for Christmas, New Year and Easter.

» Late December to March is high season in the Alps and Dolomites.

Shoulder (Apr–Jun & Sep–Oct)
» Good deals on accommodation, especially in the south.

» Spring is best for festivals, flowers and local produce.

» Autumn provides warm weather and the grape harvest.

Low Season (Nov–Mar)
» Prices up to 30% less than in high season.

» Many sights and hotels closed in coastal areas.

» A good period for cultural events in large cities.

Daily Costs

Budget: Less than €100
» Dorm bed: €15–30

» Double room in a budget hotel: €50–110

» Pizza or pasta: €6–12

Midrange: €100–250
» Double room in a hotel: €110–200

» Local restaurant dinner: €25–50

» Admission to museum: €4–15

Top End: More than €250
» Double room in a four- or five-star hotel: €200–450

» Top restaurant dinner: €50–150

» Opera ticket: €40–200

Eating

Restaurants (Ristoranti) Formal service and refined dishes, with prices to match.

Trattorias Informal, often family-run, places with classic regional cooking.

Vegetarians Most places offer good vegetable starters and side dishes.

Price indicators for a two-course meal with a glass of house wine and *coperto* (cover charge).

€	less than €25
€€	€25–45
€€€	more than €45

Sleeping

Hotels From luxury boutique palaces to modest family-run *pensioni* (small hotels).

B&Bs Rooms in restored farmhouses, city townhouses or seaside bungalows.

Agriturismi Farmstays range from working farms to luxury rural retreats.

Room Tax A nightly occupancy tax is charged on top of room rates.

Price indicators for a double room with private bathroom (breakfast included) in high season:

€	less than €110
€€	€110–200
€€€	more than €200

Arriving in Italy

Leonardo da Vinci (Fiumicino) Airport (Rome)

Rental cars Agencies are located near the multilevel car park.

Trains & buses Run every 30 minutes from 6.23am to 11.23pm.

Night buses Departures at 1.15am, 2.15am, 3.30am and 5am.

Taxis Set fare to centre €48; 45 minutes.

Malpensa Airport (Milan)

Rental cars Agencies in the Arrivals sections of Terminals 1 and 2.

Trains & buses Run every 30 minutes from 5.45am to 11.30pm.

Night buses Limited services from 12.15am to 5am.

Taxis Set fare €90; 50 minutes.

Capodichino Airport (Naples)

Rental cars Contact agencies via an intercom in the Arrivals hall.

Buses Run every 20 minutes from 6am to 11.40pm.

Taxis Set fare €16 to €23; 30 minutes.

Mobile Phones (Cell Phones)

Local SIM cards can be used in European, Australian and some unlocked US phones. Other phones must be set to roaming.

Internet Access

Free wi-fi is available in most hotels, B&Bs, *pensioni* etc and in many bars and cafes.

Money

ATMs at every airport, most train stations and widely available in towns and cities. Credit cards accepted in most hotels and restaurants.

Tipping

Not obligatory but round up the bill in pizzerias and trattorias; 10% is normal in upmarket restaurants.

Useful Websites

Italia (www.italia.it) Comprehensive tourism site.

Michelin (www.viamichelin.it) A useful route planner.

Agriturismi (www.agriturismi. it) Guide to farmstays.

Lonely Planet (www. lonelyplanet.com/italy) Destination lowdown.

For more, see Italy Driving Guide (p421).

CITY GUIDE

ROME

Even in a country of exquisite cities, Rome (Roma) is special. Epic, hot-blooded and utterly disarming, it's a heady mix of ancient ruins, awe-inspiring art, iconic monuments and vibrant street life. If your road leads to Rome, give yourself a couple of days to explore its headline sights.

Rome St Peter's Square

Getting Around

Driving is not the best way to get around Rome. Traffic can be chaotic and much of the *centro storico* (historic centre) is closed to non-authorised traffic on weekdays and weekend evenings. You're better off using public transport; a 24-hour pass is €7.

Parking

On-street parking, which is expensive and scarce, is denoted by blue lines. There are a few car parks in the centre, which charge about €2.20 per hour or €15 to €20 per day. Some top-end hotels offer parking, usually at an extra charge.

Discover the Taste of Rome

For authentic nose-to-tail Roman cooking check out the trattorias in Testaccio, and for traditional Roman-Jewish cuisine head to the atmospheric Jewish Ghetto.

Live Like a Local

The most atmospheric place to stay is the *centro storico*, where you'll have everything on your doorstep. Night owls will enjoy Trastevere, while Tridente offers refined accommodation and designer shopping. The Vatican is also popular.

Useful Websites

060608 (www.060608.it) Rome's official tourist website.

Coopculture (www.coopculture.it) Information and ticket booking for Rome's monuments.

Lonely Planet (www.lonelyplanet.com/rome) Destination lowdown, hotel bookings and traveller forum.

Trips Through Rome 🚋 🚌

For more, check out our city and country guides.
www.lonelyplanet.com

TOP EXPERIENCES

➡ Get to the Heart of the Ancient City

Thrill to the sight of the Colosseum, Roman Forum and Palatino, where Romulus and Remus supposedly founded the city in 753 BC.

➡ Gaze Heavenwards in the Sistine Chapel

File past kilometres of priceless art at the Vatican Museums to arrive at the Sistine Chapel and Michelangelo's fabled frescoes. (www.museivaticani.va)

➡ Villa Borghese's Baroque Treasures

Head to the Museo e Galleria Borghese to marvel at a series of exhilarating sculptures by baroque maestro Gian Lorenzo Bernini. (www.galleriaborghese.it)

➡ Admire the Pantheon's Dome

The Pantheon is the best preserved of Rome's ancient monuments, but it's only when you get inside that you get the full measure of the place as its dome soars above you.

➡ Pay Homage at St Peter's Basilica

Capped by Michelangelo's landmark dome, the Vatican's showpiece church is a masterpiece of Renaissance architecture and baroque decor.

➡ Live the Trastevere Dolce Vita

Join the evening crowds in Trastevere to eat earthy Roman food, drink in the many bars and pubs, and parade up and down the streets.

➡ Hang Out on the Piazzas

Hanging out on Rome's piazzas is part and parcel of Roman life – having a gelato on Piazza Navona, people-watching on Piazza del Popolo and posing on Piazza di Spagna.

CITY GUIDE

Florence View over rooftops to the Duomo

FLORENCE

An essential stop on every Italian itinerary, Florence (Firenze) is one of the world's great art cities, boasting Renaissance icons and a wonderfully intact medieval centre. Beyond the Michelangelo masterpieces and Medici *palazzi* (mansions), there's a buzzing bar scene and great shopping in artisanal workshops and designer boutiques.

Getting Around

Non-resident traffic is banned from much of central Florence, and if you enter the Limited Traffic Zone (ZTL) you risk a fine of around €150. Rather than drive, walk or use the city buses; tickets cost €1.20 or €2 on board.

Parking

There is street parking around Piazzale Michelangelo and car parks (about €20 per day) at Fortezza da Basso and Piazzale di Porta Romana. Otherwise, ask if your hotel can arrange parking.

Discover the Taste of Florence

Florence teems with restaurants, trattorias, *osterie* (casual taverns) and wine bars catering to all budgets. Top neighbourhoods include hip Santa Croce, home to some of the city's best restaurants, and the increasingly gentrified Oltrarno.

Live Like a Local

To stay right in the heart of the action, the Duomo and Piazza della Signoria areas are a good bet with some excellent budget options. Near the train station, Santa Maria Novella has some good midrange boutique/design hotels.

Useful Websites

Firenze Turismo (www. firenzeturismo.it) Official tourist site; comprehensive and up-to-date.

Visit Florence (www. visitflorence.com) Practical advice and info on accommodation, sights and tours.

Firenze Musei (www. firenzemusei.it) Book tickets for the Uffizi and Accademia.

Trips Through Florence 1 2 23 24

NAPLES

Naples (Napoli) is an exhilarating sprawl of bombastic baroque churches, Dickensian alleyways and electrifying street life. Its in-your-face vitality can be overwhelming, but once you've found your feet you'll discover a city of regal palaces, world-renowned museums, superb pizzerias and sweeping seascapes.

Getting Around

Driving is not the best way of getting around Naples – the roads are anarchic and much of the city centre is off-limits to non-resident traffic. You'll be better off leaving your car as soon as you can and using public transport (bus, metro and funicular); a day pass costs €3.50.

Parking

Street parking is not a good idea – car theft is a problem – and few hotels offer it. There's a 24-hour car park east of the city centre at Via Brin, otherwise ask your hotel for advice.

Discover the Taste of Naples

To taste authentic wood-fired pizza, head to the *centro storico* where you'll find a number of hard-core pizzerias serving the genuine article. For a more refined meal, make for seafront Santa Lucia and the cobbled lanes of Chiaia.

Live Like a Local

For maximum atmosphere, consider staying in the *centro storico* where you'll have many sights on your doorstep. Seaside Santa Lucia is home to some of the city's most prestigious hotels, and Chiaia is cool and chic.

Useful Websites

I Naples (www.inaples.it) The city's official tourist-board site.

Napoli Unplugged (www. napoliunplugged.com) Attractions, up-to-date listings, news and blog entries.

Campania Artecard (www. campaniartecard.it) Details discount cards covering museum admission and transport.

Trips Through Naples

1 **27**

VENICE

A magnificent, unforgettable spectacle, Venice (Venezia) is a hauntingly beautiful city. For 1000 years it was one of Europe's great sea powers and its unique cityscape reflects this, with golden Byzantine domes and great Gothic churches, noble *palazzi* and busy waterways.

Getting Around

Venice is off-limits to cars, leaving you to walk or take a boat. You'll inevitably get lost at some point but directions to Piazza San Marco, the Rialto and Accademia are posted on yellow signs. *Vaporetti* (small ferries) ply the city's waterways; a one-way ticket costs €7.50.

Parking

Once you've crossed the Ponte della Libertà bridge from Mestre, you'll have to park at Piazzale Roma or Tronchetto car parks; bank on €21 to €29 for 24 hours.

Venice Gondolas on the lagoon

TOP EXPERIENCES

➡ Cruise the Grand Canal
Take a *vaporetto* (small ferry) down the Grand Canal for an uplifting introduction to the city's extraordinary sights.

➡ Marvel at Mosaics at the Basilica di San Marco
Step inside Venice's signature basilica, an architectural hybrid of Byzantine domes, Gothic windows and Egyptian walls, to gape at golden dome mosaics. (www.basilicasanmarco.it)

➡ Compare Titian and Tintoretto
Soaring I Frari is home to Titian's masterpiece, *Assunta*. Nearby, the Scuola Grande di San Rocco boasts stunning frescoes by Tintoretto. (www.scuolagrandesanrocco.it)

➡ Enjoy Modern Art at the Guggenheim
Step inside the canal-side home of Peggy Guggenheim to peruse canvases by Jackson Pollock, Picasso and the giants of modern art. (www.guggenheim-venice.it)

Discover the Taste of Venice
Venice's version of tapas, bar snacks called *cicheti* are served in *osterie* across town at lunch and between 6pm and 8pm. Wash them down with a glass of local *prosecco*.

Live Like a Local
Many Venetians open their historical homes as B&Bs. Dorsoduro and San Polo are charming areas, near major museums and with plenty of bar action. Cannaregio is another good option, relatively untouristy and in parts picturesque.

Useful Websites
Turismo Venezia (www.turismovenezia.it) The city's official tourism site.

VeneziaUnica (www.veneziaunica.it) News, events and city passes for public transport, museums, churches and special events.

Venezia da Vivere (www.veneziadavivere.com) Music performances, art openings, nightlife and child-friendly events.

Trips Through Venice 1 2 8 14

ITALY
BY REGION

Driving in Italy is a thrilling way to experience the country in all its varied beauty. To help you on your way, we've divided the country into three areas and outlined what each has to offer.

Central Italy (p209)

Tour heavyweight destinations such as Rome, Florence and Assisi before branching off to explore frescoed Etruscan tombs, remote Tuscan monasteries and verdant valleys in Abruzzo, Umbria and Le Marche. Foodies can indulge their passions in the gourmet towns of Emilia-Romagna and Tuscany's historic vineyards.

Discover Etruscan treasures on Trip 20

Taste wine on Trip 24

Northern Italy (p63)

Revel in spectacular scenery as you drive epic Alpine roads, stunning coastlines and gorgeous lakesides. Our northern Italian trips take in everything from the wine-rich hills of Piedmont to the pink-hued Dolomites and Venetian villas, as well as the great cities of Genoa, Turin and Milan.

Tour art-rich cities on
Trip 8

Scale the Dolomites on
Trip 13

Southern Italy (p293)

In Italy's less-explored south, you can get off the beaten track in the wilds of Calabria and Basilicata and enjoy stunning seascapes in Puglia, Sardinia and on the Amalfi Coast. Sicily boasts artistic treasures and remnants of Greek civilisation, while near Naples Mt Vesuvius broods menacingly over ruined Pompeii.

Enjoy the Amalfi Coast on
Trip 29

Explore Greek ruins on
Trip 36

ITALY

Classic Trips

1

All the trips in this book show you the best of Italy, but we've chosen the eight below as our all-time favourites. These are our Classic Trips – the ones that lead you to the best of the iconic sights, the top activities and the unique Italian experiences.

Above: Boathouse at Lago di Braies, Dolomites
Left: St Peter's Basilica, Rome

Classic Trip

Grand Tour

The gap-year journey of its day, the Grand Tour is a search for art and enlightenment, adventure and debauchery.

TRIP HIGHLIGHTS

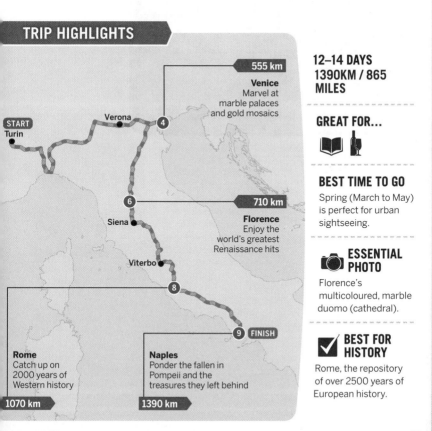

START
Turin

Verona

4

555 km

Venice
Marvel at marble palaces and gold mosaics

6

710 km

Siena

Florence
Enjoy the world's greatest Renaissance hits

Viterbo

8

9 **FINISH**

Rome
Catch up on 2000 years of Western history

1070 km

Naples
Ponder the fallen in Pompeii and the treasures they left behind

1390 km

12–14 DAYS
1390KM / 865 MILES

GREAT FOR...

BEST TIME TO GO
Spring (March to May) is perfect for urban sightseeing.

ESSENTIAL PHOTO
Florence's multicoloured, marble duomo (cathedral).

BEST FOR HISTORY
Rome, the repository of over 2500 years of European history.

1 Grand Tour

From the Savoy palaces of Turin and Leonardo's *Last Supper* to the dubious drinking dens of Genoa and the pleasure palaces of Rome, the Grand Tour is part scholar's pilgrimage and part rite of passage. Offering a chance to view some of the world's greatest masterpieces and hear Vivaldi played on 18th-century cellos, it is a rollicking trip filled with the sights, sounds and tastes that have shaped European society for centuries.

1 Turin

In his travel guide, *Voyage through Italy* (1670), travel writer and tutor Richard Lassels advocated a grand cultural tour of Europe, and in particular Italy, for young English aristocrats, during which the study of classical antiquity and the High Renaissance would ready them for future influential roles shaping the political, economic and social realities of the day.

First they travelled through France before crossing the Alps at Mt Cenis and heading to Turin (Torino), where letters of introduction admitted them to the city's agreeable Parisian-style social whirl. Turin's tree-lined boulevards still retain their elegant, French feel and many turn-of-the century cafes, such as **Caffè San Carlo** (Piazza San Carlo 156; ⏰8am-midnight Tue-Fri, to 1am Sat, to 9pm Mon), still serve Torinese hot chocolate beneath their gilded chandeliers.

Like the Medicis in Florence (Firenze) and the Borghese in Rome (Roma), Turin's Savoy princes had a penchant for extravagant architecture and interior decor. You suspect they also pined for their hunting lodges in Chambéry, France, from where they originated, as they

invited André le Nôtre, Versailles landscaper, to design the gardens of **Palazzo Reale** (www. ilpalazzorealeditorino.it; Piazza Castello; adult/reduced €12/6, 1st Sun of month free; ☻8.30am-7.30pm Tue-Sun) in 1697.

 📍 p46, p73, p81, p89

🔗 LINK YOUR TRIP

24 Tuscan Wine Tour

Linger in the bucolic hills around Florence and enjoy fine gourmet dining and world-renowned wine-tasting.

29 Amalfi Coast

Play truant from high-minded museums and head south from Naples for the Blue Ribbon drive on the Amalfi Coast.

The Drive » The two-hour (170km) drive to Genoa is all on autostrada, the final stretch twisting through the mountains. Leave Turin following signs for the A55 (towards Alessandria), which quickly merges with the A21 passing through the pretty Piedmontese countryside. Just before Alessandria turn south onto the A26 for Genoa/Livorno.

❷ Genoa

Some travellers, shy of crossing the Alps, might arrive by boat in Genoa (Genova). Despite its superb location, mild microclimate and lush flora, the city had a dubious reputation. Its historic centre was a warren of dark, insalubrious *caruggi* (alleys), stalked by prostitutes and beggars, while the excessive shrewdness of the Genovese banking families earned them a reputation, according to author Thomas Nugent, as 'a treacherous and over-reaching set of people'.

And yet with tourists and businessmen arriving from around the world, Genoa was, and still is, a cosmopolitan place. The **Rolli Palaces**, a collection of grand mansions originally meant to host visiting popes, dignitaries and royalty, made Via Balbi and Strada Nuova (now Via Giuseppe Garibaldi) two of the most famous streets in Europe. Visit the finest of them, the **Palazzo Spinola** (www. palazzospinola.beniculturali. it; Piazza Superiore di Pellicceria 1; adult/reduced €4/2; ⏰8.30am-7.30pm Tue-Sat, from 1.30pm Sun) and the **Palazzo Reale** (www. palazzorealegenova.benicul turali.it; Via Balbi 10; adult/ reduced €4/2; ⏰9am-7pm Tue-Sat, 1.30-7pm Sun). After stop for sweets at **Pietro Romanengo fu Stefano** (www.romanengo.com; Via Soziglia 74r; ⏰3.30-7.30pm Mon, 9am-1pm & 3.15-7.15pm Tue-Sat).

✕ p46, p97

The Drive » This 365km drive takes most of the day, so stop for lunch in Cremona (p46, p116). Although the drive is on autostrada, endless fields of corn line the route. Take the A7 north out of Genoa and at Tortona exit onto the A21 around industrial Piacenza to Brescia. At Brescia, change again onto the A4 direct to Padua.

❸ Padua

Bound for Venice (Venezia), Grand Tourists could hardly avoid visiting Padua (Padova), although by the 18th century international students no longer flocked to **Palazzo del Bò** (☏049 827 30 47; www.unipd. it/en/guidedtours; Via VIII Febbraio; adult/reduced €7/2;

DETOUR: MILAN

Start: ❶ Turin (p36)

No Grand Tour would be complete without a detour up the A4 to Milan (Milano) to eyeball Leonardo da Vinci's iconic mural **The Last Supper** (Il Cenacolo; ☏02 9280 0360; www.cenacolovinciano.net; Piazza Santa Maria delle Grazie 2; adult/reduced €6.50/3.25; ⏰8.15am-7pm Tue-Sun; Ⓜ Cadorna). Advance booking is essential (booking fee €1.50).

From his *Portrait of a Young Man* (c 1486) to portraits of Duke Ludovico Sforza's beautiful mistresses, *The Lady with the Ermine* (c 1489) and *La Belle Ferronière* (c 1490), Leonardo transformed the rigid conventions of portraiture to depict highly individual images imbued with naturalism. Then he evolved concepts of idealised proportions and the depiction of internal emotional states through physical dynamism *(St Jerome),* all of which cohere in the masterly *Il Cenacolo*.

While you're here, take some time to walk around other parts of the city, too (p116; p204).

see website for tour times), the Venetian Republic's radical university where Copernicus and Galileo taught classes.

You can visit the university's claustrophobic, wooden **anatomy theatre** (the first in the world), although it's no longer de rigueur to witness dissections on the average tourist itinerary. Afterwards don't forget to pay your respects to the skulls of noble professors who donated themselves for dissection because of the difficulty involved in acquiring fresh corpses. Their skulls are lined up in the graduation hall.

Beyond the university the melancholy air of the city did little to detain foreign visitors. Even Giotto's spectacular frescoes in the **Cappella degli Scrovegni** (Scrovegni Chapel; ✆049 201 00 20; www.cappelladegliscrovegni. it; Piazza Eremitani 8; adult/ reduced €13/6, night ticket €8/6; ☻9am-7pm), where advance reservations are essential, were of limited interest given medieval art was out of fashion, and only devout Catholics ventured to revere the strange relics of Saint Anthony in the **Basilica di Sant'Antonio** (Il Santo; ✆049 822 56 52; www.ba-silicadelsanto.org; Piazza del Santo; ☻6.20am-7.45pm Apr-Oct, to 6.45pm Nov-Mar).

✖ p117, p175

The Drive ❯❯ Barely 40km from Venice, the drive from Padua is through featureless areas of light industry along the A4 and then the A57.

- - - - - - - - - - - -

TRIP HIGHLIGHT

❹ Venice

Top of the itinerary, Venice at last! Then, as now, La Serenissima's watery landscape captured the imagination of travellers. At **Carnivale** (www.carnivale.venezia. it) in February numbers swelled to 30,000; now they number in the hundreds of thousands. You cannot take your car onto the lagoon islands so leave it in a secure garage in Mestre, such as **Garage Europa Mestre** (✆041 95 92 02; www. garageeuropamestre.com; Corso del Popolo 55, Mestre; per day €15; ☻8am-10pm), and hop on the train to Venice Santa Lucia where water taxis connect to all the islands.

Aside from the mind-improving art in the **Gallerie dell'Accademia** (✆041 520 03 45; www. gallerieaccademia.org; Campo della Carità 1050; adult/re-duced €10/8 plus supplement during special exhibitions, first Sun of the month free; ☻8.15am-2pm Mon, to 7.15pm Tue-Sun; ☻Accademia) and extraordinary architectural masterpieces such as the **Palazzo Ducale**, the **Campanile**, Long-hena's **Chiesa di Santa Maria della Salute** and the glittering domes of the **Basilica di San Marco** (St Mark's Basilica; ✆041 270

83 11; www.basilicasan marco.it; Piazza San Marco; ☻9.45am-5pm Mon-Sat, 2-5pm Sun summer, to 4pm Sun winter; ☻San Marco), Venice was considered an exciting den of debauchery. Venetian wives were notorious for keeping handsome escorts *(cicis-beo),* courtesans held powerful positions at court and much time was devoted to frequenting casinos and coffeehouses. **Caffè Florian** (✆041 520 56 41; www.caffeflorian.com; Piazza San Marco 56/59; drinks €10-25; ☻9am-midnight; ☻San Marco) still adheres to rules established in the 1700s.

So do as the Venetians would do: glide down the **Grand Canal** on the **No 1 Vaporetto** (ticket €7.50) for an architectural tour of 50 *palazzi* (mansions), gossip in the balconies of the **Teatro La Fenice** (✆041 78 66 72, tours 041 78 66 75; www.teatrolafenice. it; Campo San Fantin 1965; theatre visits adult/reduced €10/7, concert/opera tickets from €15/45; ☻Santa Maria dei Giglio), or listen for summer thunderstorms in Vivaldi's *Four Seasons,* played by **Interpreti Veneziani** (✆041 277 05 61; www.interpretiveneziani. com; Chiesa San Vidal, Campo di San Vidal 2862; adult/re-duced €28/23; ☻doors open 8.30pm; ☻Accademia).

For more earthly pleasures take a tour of Venice's centuries-old markets with a gourmet food walk (p202).

Classic Trip

DE AGOSTINI/A. DAGLI ORTI/GETTY IMAGES ©

DEA / G. CIGOLINI/GETTY IMAGES ©

WHY THIS IS A CLASSIC TRIP
PAULA HARDY,
WRITER

There's almost no need to explain why the Grand Tour is a classic trip. It is the template for all modern travel itineraries, where for the first time people travelled for curiosity, pleasure and learning. Covering Italy's show-stopping cities, it offers travellers a view of the country's very best art, architecture and antiquities, while transporting them from alpine peaks to sun-struck southern shores.

Top: Anatomy theatre, University of Padua
Left: Hall of Mirrors, Palazzo Reale, Genoa
Right: Teatro La Fenice, Venice

✕ 🛏 p46, p61, p117, p175

The Drive » Retrace your steps to Padua on the A57 and A4 and navigate around the ring road in the direction of Bologna to pick up the A13 southwest for this short two-hour drive. After Padua the dual carriageway dashes through wide-open farmland and crosses the Po river, which forms the southern border of the Veneto.

⑤ Bologna

Home to Europe's oldest university (established in 1088) and once the stomping ground of Dante, Boccaccio and Petrarch, Bologna had an enviable reputation for courtesy and culture. Its historic centre, complete with 20 soaring towers, is one of the best-preserved medieval cities in the world. In the **Basilica di San Petronio** (www.basilicadisanpetronio.it; Piazza Maggiore; ⊙7.45am-2pm & 3-6pm), originally intended to dwarf St Peter's in Rome, Giovanni Cassini's sundial (1655) proved the problems with the Julian calendar giving us the leap year, while Bolognesi students advanced human knowledge in obstetrics, natural science, zoology and anthropology. You can peer at their strange model waxworks and studiously labelled collections in the **Palazzo Poggi** (www.museopalazzopoggi.unibo.it; Via Zamboni 33; adult/reduced

€5/3; ⏰10am-1pm Tue-Sun mid-Jun–mid-Sep, 10am-4pm Tue-Fri, 10.30am-5.30pm Sat & Sun mid-Sep–mid-Jun).

In art as in science, the School of Bologna gave birth to the Carracci cousins Ludovico, Agostino and Annibale, who were among the founding fathers of Italian baroque and were deeply influenced by the Counter-Reformation. See their emotionally charged blockbusters in the **Pinacoteca Nazionale** (www.pinacotecabologna.beniculturali.it; Via delle Belle Arti 56; adult/reduced €4/2; ⏰9am-1.30pm Tue & Wed, 2-7pm Thu-Sun).

🍴 🛏 p47, p287

The Drive ≫ Bologna sits at the intersection of the A1, A13 and A14. Navigate west out of the city, across the river Reno, onto the A1. From here it's a straight shot into Florence for 100km, leaving the Po plains behind you and entering the low hills of Emilia-Romagna and the forested valleys of Tuscany.

TRIP HIGHLIGHT

⑥ Florence

From Filippo Brunelleschi's red-tiled dome atop Florence's **Duomo** (Cattedrale di Santa Maria del Fiore; www.operaduomo.firenze.it; Piazza del Duomo; ⏰10am-5pm Mon-Wed & Fri, to 4pm Thu, to 4.45pm Sat, 1.30-4.45pm Sun) to Michelangelo's and Botticelli's greatest hits, *David* and *The Birth of Venus,* in the **Galleria dell'Accademia** (📞055 29 48 83; www.firenzemusei.it; Via Ricasoli 60; adult/reduced €8/4, incl temporary exhibition €12.50/6.25; ⏰8.15am-6.50pm Tue-Sun) and the **Galleria degli Uffizi** (Uffizi Gallery; www.uffizi.beniculturali.it; Piazzale degli Uffizi 6; adult/reduced €8/4, incl temporary exhibition €12.50/6.25; ⏰8.15am-6.50pm Tue-Sun), Florence, according to Unesco, contains the highest number of artistic masterpieces in the world.

Whereas Rome and Milan have torn themselves down and been rebuilt many times, incorporating a multitude of architectural whims, central Florence looks much as it did in 1550, with stone towers and cypress-lined gardens.

🍴 🛏 p47, p60, p261, p271

The Drive ≫ The next 210km, continuing south along the A1, travels through some of Italy's most lovely scenery. Just southwest of Florence the vineyards of Greve in Chianti harbour some great farmstays, while Arezzo is to the east. At Orvieto exit onto the SS71 and skirt Lago di Bolsena for the final 45km into Viterbo.

---

⑦ Viterbo

From Florence the road to Rome crossed the dreaded and pestilential campagna (countryside), a swampy, mosquito-infested low-lying area. Unlike now, inns en route were uncomfortable and hazardous, so travellers hurried through Siena, stocking up on wine for the rough road ahead. They also stopped briefly in medieval Viterbo for a quick douse in the thermal springs at the **Terme dei Papi** (📞0761 35 03 90; www.termedeipapi.it; Strada Bagni 12; pool adult/child €12/8, Sun €18/8; ⏰9am-7pm Wed-Mon, plus 9pm-1am Sat), and a tour of the High Renaissance spectacle that is the **Villa Lante** (📞0761 28 80 08; Via Jacopo Barozzi 71; adult/reduced €5/2.50;

TOP TIP:
JUMP THE QUEUE IN FLORENCE

In July, August and other busy periods such as Easter, long queues are a fact of life at Florence's key museums. For a fee of €4 each, tickets to the Uffizi and Galleria dell'Accademia (where *David* lives) can be booked in advance. To organise your ticket, go to www.firenzemusei.it or call **Firenze Musei** (📞055 29 48 83; www.firenzemusei.it).

8.30am-1hr before sunset Tue-Sun).

The Drive » Rejoin the A1 after a 28km drive along the rural SS675. For the next 40km the A1 descends slowly into Lazio, criss-crossing the river Tevere and keeping the ridge of the Apennines to the left as it darts through tunnels. At Fiano Romano exit for Roma Nord onto the A1dir for the final 20km descent into the capital.

🗡 🛏 p235

TRIP HIGHLIGHT

8 Rome

In the 18th century Rome, even in ruins, was still thought of as the august capital of the world. Here more than anywhere the Grand Tourist was awakened to an interest in art and architecture, although the **Colosseum** (Colosseo; 📞06 3996 7700; www.coopculture.it; Piazza del Colosseo; adult/reduced incl Roman Forum & Palatino €12/7.50; 🕑8.30am-1hr before sunset; Ⓜ Colosseo) was still filled with debris and the Palatine Hill was covered in gardens, its excavated treasures slowly accumulating in the world's oldest national museum, the **Capitoline Museums** (Musei Capitolini; 📞06 06 08; www.museicapitolini.org; Piazza del Campidoglio 1; adult/reduced €12/10; 🕑9.30am-7.30pm, last admission 6.30pm; 🚌 Piazza Venezia).

Arriving through the Porta del Popolo, visitors first spied the dome of **St Peter's** (Basilica di San Pietro; www.vatican.va; St Peter's Sq;

TOP TIP:
ROME INFORMATION
LINE

The Comune di Roma (city council) runs a free multilingual **information line** (📞06 06 08; 🕑9am-9pm), providing information on culture, shows, hotels, transport etc. You can also book theatre, concert, exhibition and museum tickets on this number. The call centre, has staff who speak English, French, Arabic, German, Spanish, Italian and Chinese available from 4pm to 7pm.

🕑7am-7pm summer, to 6.30pm winter; Ⓜ Ottaviano-San Pietro) before clattering along the *corso* to the customs house. Once done, they headed to **Piazza di Spagna**, the city's principal meeting place where Keats penned his love poems and died of consumption.

Although the **Pantheon** (www.pantheonroma.com; Piazza della Rotonda; 🕑8.30am-7.30pm Mon-Sat, 9am-6pm Sun; 🚌 Largo di Torre Argentina) and **Vatican Museums** (Musei Vaticani; 📞06 6988 4676; http://mv.vatican.va; Viale Vaticano; adult/reduced €16/8, last Sun of month free; 🕑9am-4pm Mon-Sat, 9am-12.30pm last Sun of month; Ⓜ Ottaviano-San Pietro) were a must, most travellers preferred to socialise in the grounds of the **Borghese Palace** (📞06 3 28 10; www.galleriaborghese.it; Piazzale del Museo Borghese 5; adult/reduced €11/6.50; 🕑8.30am-7.30pm Tue-Sun; 🚌 Via Pinciana).

Follow their example and mix the choicest sights with more venal

pleasures such as fine dining at **Open Colonna** (📞06 4782 2641; www.antonellocolonna.it; Via Milano 9a; meals €20-80; 🕑12.30-3.30pm Tue-Sun, 7-11.30pm Tue-Sat; ✦; 🚌 Via Nazionale) and souvenir shopping at antique perfumery **Officina Profumo Farmaceutica di Santa Maria Novella** (www.smnovella.it; Corso del Rinascimento 47; 🕑10am-7.30pm Mon-Sat; 🚌 Corso del Rinascimento).

🗡 🛏 p47, p60

The Drive » Past Rome the landscape is hotter and drier, trees give way to Mediterranean shrubbery and the grass starts to yellow. Beyond the vineyards of Frascati, just 20km south of Rome, the A1 heads straight to Naples (Napoli) for 225km, a two-hour drive that often takes much longer due to heavy traffic.

TRIP HIGHLIGHT

9 Naples

Only the more adventurous Grand Tourists continued south to the salacious city of Naples. At the time Mt Vesuvius glowed menacingly,

JUSTIN FOULKES/LONELY PLANET ©

erupting six times during the 18th century and eight times in the 19th century. But Naples was the home of opera and *commedia dell'arte* (improvised comedic satire), and singing lessons and seats at **Teatro San Carlo** (☎081 797 23 31; www.teatrosancarlo. it; Via San Carlo 98; ⊙box office 10am-5.30pm Mon-Sat, to 2pm Sun; 🚇R2 to Via San Carlo) were obligatory.

Then there were the myths of Virgil and Dante to explore at Lago d'Averno and **Campi Flegrei** (the Phlegrean Fields). After the discovery of **Pompeii** (☎081 857 53 47; www.pompeiisites.org; entrances at Porta Marina, Piazza Esedra & Piazza Anfiteatro; adult/reduced €13/7.50, incl Herculaneum €22/12; ⊙9am-7.30pm summer, to 5pm winter) in 1748, the unfolding drama of a Roman town in its death throes drew throngs of visitors. Then, as now, it was the most popular tourist sight in Italy and its priceless mosaics, frescoes and colossal sculptures filled the **Museo Archeologico Nazionale** (☎081 442 21 49; http://cir.campania.beniculturali. it/museoarcheologiconazionale; Piazza Museo Nazionale 19; adult/reduced €8/4; ⊙9am-7.30pm Wed-Mon; Ⓜ Museo, Piazza Cavour).

 p47, p305

Florence View of the red-tiled dome of the Duomo

45

Eating & Sleeping

Turin ❶ see also p73, p81 and p89

🍷 Fiorio — Cafe

(Via Po 8; ⏰8.30am-1am Tue-Sun) Garner literary inspiration in Mark Twain's old window seat as you contemplate the gilded interior of a cafe where 19th-century students once plotted revolutions and the Count of Cavour deftly played whist. The bittersweet hot chocolate remains inspirational.

Genoa ❷ see also p97

🍴 Trattoria della Raibetta — Trattoria $$

(✒010 246 88 77; www.trattoriadellaraibetta. it; Vico Caprettari 10-12; meals €35; ⏰noon-2.30pm & 7.30-11pm Tue-Sun) Totally *typica* Genoese food can be found in the family-run joints hidden in the warren of streets near the cathedral. This, a snug trattoria with a low brick-vaulted ceiling, serves regional classics such as *trofiette al pesto* or octopus salad alongside excellent fresh fish.

Cremona ❷ see also p116

🍴 La Sosta — Osteria $$

(✒0372 45 66 56; www.osterialasosta.it; Via Sicardo 9; meals €35-40; ⏰12.15-2pm Tue-Sun, 7.15-10pm Tue-Sat) La Sosta is surrounded by violin-makers' workshops and is a suitably harmonious place to feast on regional delicacies such as *tortelli di zucca* (pumpkin pasta parcels) and baked snails. The entrance is plastered with so many approving restaurant-guide stickers that you can't see through the glass.

Venice ❹ see also p61, p117 and p175

🍴 Dalla Marisa — Venetian $$

(✒041 72 02 11; Fondamenta di San Giobbe 652b, Cannaregio; set menu lunch/dinner €15/35; ⏰noon-3pm daily, 7-11pm Thu-Sat; ⛴Crea) At this Cannaregio institution, you'll be seated where there's room and get no menu – you'll have whatever Marisa's cooking. And you'll like it. Lunches are a bargain at €15 for a first, main, side, wine, water and coffee – pace yourself through prawn risotto to finish with steak and grilled zucchini, or Marisa will jokingly scold you over coffee.

🍴 Ristoteca Oniga — Venetian $$

(✒041 522 44 10; www.oniga.it; Campo San Barnaba 2852; meals €19-35; ⏰noon-2.30pm & 7-10.30pm Wed-Mon; 🛜; ⛴Ca' Rezzonico) Its menu peppered with organic ingredients, Oniga serves exemplary *sarde in saor* (sardines in tangy onion marinade), seasonal pastas and the odd Hungarian classic like goulash (a nod to former chef Annika Major). Oenophiles will appreciate the selection of 100-plus wines, handy for toasting to the €19 set lunch menu. Grab a sunny spot in the *campo,* or get cosy in a wood-panelled corner.

🛏 Ca' Angeli — Boutique Hotel $$

(✒041 523 24 80; www.caangeli.it; Calle del Traghetto de la Madoneta 1434, San Polo; d €95-225, ste from €200; ❄🛜; ⛴San Silvestro) Murano glass chandeliers, a Louis XIV love-seat and namesake 16th-century angels set a refined tone at this restored, canalside *palazzo.* Guest rooms are a picture with beamed ceilings, antique carpets and big bathrooms, while the dining room looks out onto the Grand Canal. Breakfast includes organic products where possible.

Bologna 5 see also p287

✖ All'Osteria Bottega   Osteria $$

(☎051 58 51 11; Via Santa Caterina 51; meals €35-40; ⏱12.30-2.30pm & 8-10.30pm Tue-Sat) At this *osteria* truly worthy of the name, owners Daniele and Valeria lavish attention on every table between trips to the kitchen for plates of *culatello di Zibello* ham, tortellini in capon broth, pork shank in red wine reduction and other Slow Food delights. Desserts are homemade by Valeria, from the *ciambella* (Romagnola ring-shaped cake) to fresh fruit sorbets.

⏏ Bologna nel Cuore   B&B $$

(☎051 26 94 42; www.bolognanelcuore.it; Via Cesare Battisti 29; s €80-100, d €100-140, apt €125-130; P ❋ 🛜) This centrally located, immaculate and well-loved B&B features a pair of bright, high-ceilinged rooms with pretty tiled bathrooms and endless mod cons, plus two comfortable, spacious apartments with kitchen and laundry facilities. Owner and art historian Maria generously shares her knowledge of Bologna and serves breakfasts featuring jams made with fruit picked near her childhood home in the Dolomites.

Florence 6 see also p60, p261 and p271

✖ I Due Fratellini   Sandwiches $

(☎055 239 60 96; www.iduefratellini.com; Via dei Cimatori 38r; panini €3; ⏱10am-7pm) This hole-in-the-wall has been in business since 1875. Wash *panini* down with a beaker of wine and leave the empties on the wooden shelf outside.

⏏ Palazzo Guadagni Hotel   Hotel $$

(☎055 265 83 76; www.palazzoguadagni.com; Piazza Santo Spirito 9; d €130-230; ❋ 🛜) This romantic hotel overlooking Florence's liveliest summertime square is legendary – Zeffirelli shot scenes from *Tea with Mussolini* here. Housed in an artfully revamped Renaissance palace, it has 15 spacious if old-fashioned rooms and an impossibly romantic loggia terrace with wicker chairs and predictably dreamy views.

Rome 8 see also p60

✖ Necci   Cafe $$

(☎06 9760 1552; www.necci1924.com; Via Fanfulla da Lodi 68; dinner around €45, lunch mains around €8; ⏱8am-2am; 🛜; 🚌Via Prenestina) Iconic Necci opened as a gelateria in 1924 and later became a favourite of director Pier Paolo Pasolini. Good for a drink or a meal, it serves up sophisticated Italian cooking to an eclectic crowd of all ages, with a lovely, leafy garden terrace (ideal for families).

✖ Enoteca Regionale Palatium   Ristorante $$$

(☎06 6920 2132; Via Frattina 94; meals €55; ⏱11am-11pm Mon-Sat, closed Aug; 🚌Via del Corso) A rich showcase of regional bounty, run by the Lazio Regional Food Authority, this sleek wine bar serves excellent local specialities, such as *porchetta* (pork roasted with herbs) or *gnocchi alla Romana con crema da zucca* (potato dumplings Roman-style with cream of pumpkin), as well as an impressive array of Lazio wines (try lesser-known drops such as Aleatico).

⏏ Hotel Scalinata di Spagna   Hotel $$

(☎06 6994 0896; www.hotelscalinata.com; Piazza della Trinità dei Monti 17; d €130-260; ❋ @ 🛜; Ⓜ Spagna) Given its location – perched alongside the Spanish Steps – the Scalinata is surprisingly modestly priced. An informal and friendly place, it's something of a warren, with a great roof terrace and low corridors leading off to smallish, old-fashioned yet romantic rooms. Book early for a room with a view.

Naples 9 see also p305

⏏ Grand Hotel Vesuvio   Hotel $$$

(☎081 764 00 44; www.vesuvio.it; Via Partenope 45; s/d €280/310; ❋ @ 🛜; 🚌128 to Via Santa Lucia) Known for hosting legends – past guests include Rita Hayworth and Humphrey Bogart – this five-star heavyweight is a decadent melange of dripping chandeliers, period antiques and opulent rooms. Count your lucky stars while drinking a martini at the rooftop restaurant.

Classic Trip

World Heritage Wonders

2

From Rome to Venice, this tour of Unesco World Heritage Sites takes in some of Italy's greatest hits, including the Colosseum and the Leaning Tower of Pisa, and some lesser-known treasures.

TRIP HIGHLIGHTS

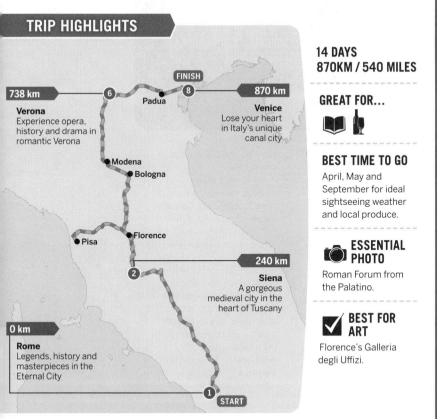

FINISH

738 km

Verona
Experience opera, history and drama in romantic Verona

Padua

870 km

Venice
Lose your heart in Italy's unique canal city

● Modena
● Bologna

● Florence

● Pisa

240 km

Siena
A gorgeous medieval city in the heart of Tuscany

0 km

Rome
Legends, history and masterpieces in the Eternal City

START

**14 DAYS
870KM / 540 MILES**

GREAT FOR...

BEST TIME TO GO
April, May and September for ideal sightseeing weather and local produce.

ESSENTIAL PHOTO
Roman Forum from the Palatino.

BEST FOR ART
Florence's Galleria degli Uffizi.

Classic Trip

2 World Heritage Wonders

Topping the Unesco charts with 51 World Heritage Sites, Italy offers the full gamut, ranging from historic city centres and man-made masterpieces to snow-capped mountains and areas of outstanding natural beauty. This trip through central and northern Italy touches on the country's unparalleled artistic and architectural legacy, taking in ancient Roman ruins, priceless Renaissance paintings, great cathedrals and, to cap it all off, Venice's unique canal-scape.

TRIP HIGHLIGHT

1 Rome

An epic, monumental metropolis, Italy's capital is a city of thrilling beauty and high drama. According to Unesco, its historic centre boasts some of aniquity's most important monuments and is well worth a stroll. Rome has been a World Heritage Site since 1980, and the **Vatican**, technically a separate state but in reality located within Rome's city limits, has

been on the Unesco list since 1984.

Of Rome's many ancient monuments, the most iconic is the **Colosseum** (Colosseo; ☎06 3996 7700; www.coopculture.it; Piazza del Colosseo; adult/reduced incl Roman Forum & Palatino €12/7.50; ⏰8.30am-1hr before sunset; MColosseo), the towering 1st-century-AD amphitheatre where gladiators met in mortal combat and condemned criminals fought off wild beasts. Nearby, the **Palatino** (Palatine Hill; ☎06 3996 7700; www.coopculture. it; Via di San Gregorio 30 &

Via Sacra; adult/reduced incl Colosseum & Roman Forum €12/7.50; 8.30am-1hr before sunset; MColosseo) was the ancient city's most exclusive neighbourhood, as well as its oldest – Romulus and Remus supposedly founded the city there in 753 BC. From the Palatino, you can descend to the skeletal ruins of the **Roman Forum** (Foro Romano; 06 3996 7700; www.coopculture.it; Largo della Salara Vecchia & Via Sacra; adult/reduced incl Colosseum & Palatino €12/7.50; 8.30am-1hr before sunset; Via dei Fori Imperiali), the once-beating heart of the ancient city. All three sights are covered by a single ticket.

To complete your tour of classical wonders search out the **Pantheon** (www.pantheonroma. com; Piazza della Rotonda; 8.30am-7.30pm Mon-Sat,

LINK YOUR TRIP

20 Etruscan Tuscany & Lazio

From Rome take the A12 autostrada up to Cerveteri and connect with this tour of ancient Etruscan treasures.

24 Tuscan Wine Tour

From Florence head south to Tuscany's Chianti wine country to indulge in some wine tasting at the area's historic vineyards.

9am-6pm Sun; 🚇Largo di Torre Argentina), the best preserved of Rome's ancient monuments. One of the most influential buildings in the world, this domed temple, now a church, is an extraordinary sight with its martial portico and soaring interior.

🍴 🛏 p47, p60

The Drive » The easiest route to Siena, about three hours away, is via the A1 autostrada. Join this from the Rome ring road, the GRA (Grande Raccordo Anulare), and head north, past Orvieto's dramatic cliff-top cathedral, to the Valdichiano exit. Take this and follow signs for Siena.

- - - - - - - - - -

`TRIP HIGHLIGHT`

2 Siena

Siena is one of Italy's most enchanting medieval towns. Its walled centre, a beautifully preserved warren of dark lanes, Gothic *palazzi* (mansions) and pretty piazzas, is centred on **Piazza del Campo** (known as Il Campo), the sloping shell-shaped square that stages the city's annual horse race,

DETOUR: SAN GIMIGNANO

Start: 2 Siena

Dubbed the medieval Manhattan thanks to its 15 11th-century towers, San Gimignano is a classic hilltop town and an easy detour from Siena. From the car park next to Porta San Giovanni, it's a short walk up to **Palazzo Comunale** (📞0577 28 63 00; Piazza del Duomo 2; adult/reduced €6/5; ⏰9.30am-7pm summer, 11am-5.30pm winter), which houses the town's art gallery, the **Pinacoteca**, and tallest tower, the **Torre Grossa**. Nearby, the Romanesque basilica, known as the **Collegiata** (Duomo or Basilica di Santa Maria Assunta; Piazza del Duomo; adult/reduced €4/2; ⏰10am-7pm Mon-Fri, to 5pm Sat, 12.30-7pm Sun summer, 10am-4.30pm Mon-Sat ,12.30-4.30pm Sun winter), boasts some remarkable Ghirlandaio frescoes.

Before leaving town, be sure to sample the local Vernaccia wine at the **Museo del Vino** (www. sangimignanomuseovernaccia.com; Via di Fugnano 19; ⏰11.30am-6.30pm Apr-Oct) next to the Rocca (fortress). San Gimignano is about 40km northwest of Siena. Head for Florence on the RA3 until Poggibonsi and then pick up the SS429.

Il Palio, on 2 July and 16 August.

On the piazza, the 102m-high **Torre del Mangia** (📞0577 29 26 15; Palazzo Comunale, Piazza del Campo 1; €10; ⏰10am-7pm summer, to 4pm winter) soars above the Gothic **Palazzo Pubblico** (Palazzo Comunale), home to the city's finest art museum, the **Museo Civico** (📞0577 29 26 15; Palazzo Comunale, Piazza del Campo 1; adult/ reduced €9/8; ⏰10am-7pm summer, to 6pm winter). Of Siena's churches, the one to see is the 13th-century **Duomo** (www.operaduomo. siena.it; Piazza del Duomo; summer/winter €4/free, when floor displayed €7; ⏰10.30am-7pm Mon-Sat,1.30-6pm Sun summer, 10.30am-5.30pm Mon-Sat, 1.30-5.30pm Sun winter), one of Italy's greatest Gothic churches. Highlights include the remarkable white, green and red facade, and, inside, the magnificent inlaid marble floor that illustrates historical and biblical stories.

🍴 🛏 p60, p279

The Drive » There are two alternatives to get to Florence. The quickest, which is via the fast RA3 Siena–Firenze Raccordo, takes about 1½ hours. But if you have the time, we recommend the scenic SR222, which snakes through the Chianti wine country, passing through quintessential hilltop towns and vine-laden slopes. Reckon on at least 2½ hours for this route.

❸ Florence

Cradle of the Renaissance and home of Michelangelo, Machiavelli and the Medici, Florence (Firenze) is magnetic, romantic, unique and busy. A couple of days is not long here but it's enough for a breathless introduction to the city's top sights, many of which can be enjoyed on foot (p290).

Towering above the medieval skyline, the **Duomo** (Cattedrale di Santa Maria del Fiore; www. operaduomo.firenze.it; Piazza del Duomo; ⏰10am-5pm Mon-Wed & Fri, to 4pm Thu, to 4.45pm Sat, 1.30-4.45pm Sun) dominates the city centre with its famous red-tiled dome and striking facade. A short hop away, **Piazza della Signoria** opens onto the sculpture-filled **Loggia dei Lanzi** and the **Torre d'Arnolfo** above **Palazzo Vecchio** (☎055 276 82 24; www.musefirenze.it; Piazza della Signoria; museum adult/reduced €10/8, tower €10/8, museum & tower €14/12, guided tour €4; ⏰museum 9am-11pm Fri-Wed, to 2pm Thu summer, 9am-7pm Fri-Wed, to 2pm Thu winter), Florence's lavish City Hall.

Next to the *palazzo,* the **Galleria degli Uffizi** (Uffizi Gallery; www.uffizi. beniculturali.it; Piazzale degli Uffizi 6; adult/reduced €8/4, incl temporary exhibition €12.50/6.25; ⏰8.15am-6.50pm Tue-Sun) houses one of the world's great art collections, including works by Botticelli, Leonardo da Vinci, Michelangelo, Raphael and many other Renaissance maestros.

✕ ▬ p47, p60, p261, p271

The Drive ⟫ From Florence it's about 1½ hours to Pisa along the A11 autostrada. At the end of the motorway, after the toll booth, head left onto Via Aurelia (SS1) and follow signs to Pisa *centro*.

WORLD HERITAGE SITES

With 51 World Heritage Sites, Italy has more than any other country. But what exactly is a World Heritage Site? Basically it's anywhere that Unesco's World Heritage Committee decides is of 'outstanding universal value' and inscribes on the World Heritage List. It could be a natural wonder such as the Great Barrier Reef in Australia or a man-made icon such as New York's Statue of Liberty, a historic city centre or a great work of art or architecture.

The list was set up in 1972 and has since grown to include 1031 sites from 163 countries. Italy first got in on the act in 1979 when it successfully nominated its first entry – the prehistoric rock drawings of the Valcamonica valley in northeastern Lombardy. The inscription process requires sites to be nominated by a country and then independently evaluated. If they pass scrutiny and meet at least one of 10 selection criteria, they get the green light at the World Heritage Committee's annual meeting. Once on the list, sites qualify for management support and access to the World Heritage Fund.

Italian nominations have generally fared well and since Rome's historic centre and the Chiesa di Santa Maria delle Grazie in Milan were inscribed in 1980, many of the nation's greatest attractions have made it onto the list – the historic centres of Florence, Naples, Siena and San Gimignano; the cities of Venice, Verona and Ferrara; the archaeological sites of Pompeii, Paestum and Agrigento; as well as natural beauties such as the Amalfi Coast, Aeolian Islands, Dolomites and Tuscany's Val d'Orcia.

---

❹ Pisa

Once a maritime republic to rival Genoa and Venice, Pisa now owes its fame to an architectural project gone horribly wrong. The **Leaning Tower** (Torre Pendente; www. opapisa.it; Piazza dei Miracoli; €18; ⏰9am-8pm summer, 10am-5pm winter) is an extraordinary sight and one of Italy's most photographed monuments. The

Classic Trip

PETE SEAWARD/LONELY PLANETS ©

BARRY WINIKER/GETTY IMAGES ©

WHY THIS IS A CLASSIC TRIP
DUNCAN GARWOOD, WRITER

Every one of the towns and cities on this drive is special. The great treasures of Rome, Florence and Venice are amazing but, for me, it's the lesser-known highlights that make this such an incredible trip – Modena's stunning Romanesque cathedral, the Cappella degli Scrovegni in Padua, and Verona's gorgeous medieval centre.

Top: Replica of Michelangelo's *David*, Piazza della Signoria, Florence
Left: The Duomo and the Leaning Tower, Pisa
Right: Looking towards Torre Ghirlandina, Modena

JULIAN ELLIOTT PHOTOGRAPHY/GETTY IMAGES ©

tower, originally erected as a *campanile* (bell tower) from the late 12th century, is one of three Romanesque buildings on the immaculate lawns of **Piazza dei Miracoli** (also known as Campo dei Miracoli or Piazza del Duomo).

The candy-striped **Duomo** (www.opapisa.it; Piazza dei Miracoli; ⊙10am-8pm summer, to 5pm winter), begun in 1063, has a graceful tiered facade and cavernous interior, while to its west, the cupcake-like **Battistero** (Baptistry; www.opapisa.it; Piazza dei . Miracoli; €5, with Camposanto & Museo delle Sinópie 2/3 sights €7/8; ⊙8am-8pm summer, 10am-5pm winter) is something of an architectural hybrid, with a Pisan-Romanesque lower section and a Gothic upper level and dome.

✕ p61

The Drive » It's a 2½-hour drive up to Modena from Pisa. Head back towards Florence on the A11 and then pick up the A1 to Bologna. Continue as the road twists and falls through the wooded Apennines before flattening out near Bologna. Exit at Modena Sud (Modena South) and follow for the *centro*.

- - - - - - - - - - - - -

⑤ Modena

One of Italy's top foodie towns, Modena boasts a stunning medieval centre and a trio of Unesco-listed sights. First up is the gorgeous **Duomo** (www.duomodimodena.it;

Corso Duomo; ⏱7am-7pm Tue-Sun, 7am-12.30pm & 3.30-7pm Mon), which is widely considered to be Italy's finest Romanesque church. Features to look out for include the Gothic rose window and a series of bas-reliefs depicting scenes from Genesis.

Nearby, the 13th-century **Torre Ghirlandina** (Corso Duomo; €3; ⏱9.30am-1pm & 3-7pm Tue-Fri, 9.30am-7pm Sat & Sun summer, 9.30am-1pm & 2.30-5.30pm Tue-Fri, 9.30am-5.30pm Sat & Sun winter), an 87m-high tower topped by a Gothic spire, was named after Seville's Giralda bell tower by exiled Spanish Jews in the early 16th century. The last of the Unesco threesome is **Piazza Grande**, just south of the cathedral. The city's focal square, this is flanked by the porticoed **Palazzo Comunale**, Modena's elegant town hall.

✖ 🛏 p61, p287

The Drive ›> From Modena reckon on about 1¼ hours to Verona, via the A1 and A22 autostradas. Follow the A22 as it traverses the flat Po valley plain, passing the medieval town of Mantua (Mantova; worth a quick break) before connecting with the A4. Turn off at Verona Sud and follow signs for the town centre.

TRIP HIGHLIGHT

❻ Verona

A World Heritage Site since 2000, Verona's historic centre is a beautiful compilation of architectural styles and inspiring buildings. Chief among these is its stunning Roman amphitheatre, the **Arena** (☎045 800 32 04; www.arena.it; Piazza Brà; adult/reduced €10/7.50; ⏱8.30am-7.30pm Tue-Sun, from 1.30pm Mon). Dating from the 1st century AD, this is Italy's third-largest amphitheatre after the Colosseum and Capua amphitheatre, and although it can no longer seat 30,000, it still draws sizeable crowds to its opera and concerts.

From the Arena, it's an easy walk to the river Adige and **Castelvecchio** (☎045 806 26 11; https://museodicastelvecchio. comune.verona.it; Corso Castelvecchio 2; adult/reduced €6/4.50; ⏱1.30-7.30pm Mon, 8.30am-7.30pm Tue-Sun; 🚻), a picturesque castle housing one of the city's top art museums. Like many of the city's outstanding monuments, this was built during the 14th-century reign of the tyrannical della Scala (Scaligeri) family, whose eye-catching Gothic tombs, the **Arche Scaligere** (Via Arche Scaligere), stand near elegant Piazza dei Signori.

✖ 🛏 p117, p183

The Drive ›> To Padua it's about an hour from Verona on the A4 Venice autostrada. Exit at Padova Ovest (Padua West) and join the SP47 after the toll booth. Follow this until you see, after a road bridge, a turn-off signposted to the *centro*.

❼ Padua

Travellers to Padua (Padova) usually make a beeline for the city's main attraction, the **Cappella degli Scrovegni** (Scrovegni Chapel; ☎049 201 00 20; www.cappelladegli scrovegni.it; Piazza Eremitani 8; adult/reduced €13/6, night ticket €8/6; ⏱9am-7pm), but there's more to Padua than Giotto frescoes and it's actually the **Orto Botanico** (☎049 827 39 39; www.ortobotanicopd.it; Via dell'Orto Botanico 15; adult/reduced €10/8; ⏱9am-7pm daily Apr & May, 9am-7pm Tue-Sun Jun-Sep, to 6pm Tue-Sun Oct, to 5pm Tue-Sun Nov-Mar; 🚻) that represents Padua on Unesco's list of World Heritage Sites. The oldest botanical garden in the world, this dates to 1545 when a group of medical students planted some rare plants in order to study their medicinal properties. A short walk from the garden, Padua's vast **Basilica di Sant'Antonio** (Il Santo; ☎049 822 56 52; www. basilicadelsanto.org; Piazza del Santo; ⏱6.20am-7.45pm Apr-Oct, to 6.45pm Nov-Mar) is a major pilgrimage destination, attracting thousands of visitors a year paying homage to St

ITALIAN ART & ARCHITECTURE

The Ancients
In pre-Roman times, the Greeks built theatres and proportionally perfect temples in their southern colonies at Agrigento, Syracuse and Paestum, whilst the Etruscans concentrated on funerary art, creating elaborate tombs at Tarquinia and Cerveteri. Coming in their wake, the Romans specialised in roads, aqueducts and monumental amphitheatres such as the Colosseum and Verona's Arena.

Romanesque
With the advent of Christianity in the 4th century, basilicas began to spring up, many with glittering Byzantine-style mosaics. The Romanesque period (c 1050–1200) saw the construction of fortified monasteries and robust, bulky churches such as Bari's Basilica di San Nicola and Modena's cathedral. Pisa's striking *duomo* (cathedral) displays a characteristic Tuscan variation on the style.

Gothic
Gothic architecture, epic in scale and typically embellished by gargoyles, pinnacles and statues, took on a more classical form in Italy. Assisi's Basilica di San Francesco is an outstanding early example, but for the full-blown Italian Gothic style check out the cathedrals in Florence, Venice, Siena and Orvieto.

Renaissance
From quiet beginnings in 14th-century Florence, the Renaissance erupted across Italy before spreading across Europe. In Italy, painters such as Giotto, Botticelli, Leonardo da Vinci and Raphael led the way, while architects Brunelleschi and Bramante rewrote the rule books with their beautifully proportioned basilicas. All-rounder Michelangelo worked his way into immortality, producing masterpieces such as *David* and the Sistine Chapel frescoes.

Baroque
Dominating the 17th century, the extravagant baroque style found fertile soil in Italy. Witness the Roman works of Gian Lorenzo Bernini and Francesco Borromini, Lecce's flamboyant *centro storico* (historic centre) and the magical baroque towns of southeastern Sicily.

Neoclassicism
Signalling a return to sober classical lines, neoclassicism majored in the late-18th and early-19th centuries. Signature works include Caserta's Palazzo Reale and La Scala opera house in Milan. In artistic terms, the most famous Italian exponent was Antonio Canova.

Anthony, the city's patron saint, who is buried here.

✂ p117, p175

The Drive » Traffic permitting, it's about 45 minutes from Padua to Venice, along the A4. Pass through industrial Mestre and over the Ponte della Libertà

lagoon bridge to the car park on Piazzale Roma.

- - - - - - - - - - - - -

TRIP HIGHLIGHT

⑧ Venice
The end of the road, quite literally, is Venice (Venezia). Of the city's many must-sees the most

famous are on Piazza San Marco, including the **Basilica di San Marco** (St Mark's Basilica; ☎041 270 83 11; www.basilicasanmarco.it; Piazza San Marco; ⏰9.45am-5pm Mon-Sat, 2-5pm Sun summer, to 4pm Sun winter; ⛴San Marco), **Venice's**

great showpiece church. Built originally to house the bones of St Mark, it's a truly awe-inspiring vision with its spangled spires, Byzantine domes, luminous mosaics and lavish marble work. For a bird's-eye view, head to the nearby **campanile** (Bell Tower; www.basilicasan marco.it; Piazza San Marco; €8; ☺9am-9pm summer, to 7pm spring & autumn, 9.30am-3.45pm winter; ☺San Marco).

Adjacent to the basilica, the **Palazzo Ducale** (Ducal Palace; ☎041 271 59 11; www.palazzoducale. visitmuve.it; Piazzetta San Marco 52; adult/reduced incl Museo Correr €19/12; ☺8.30am-7pm summer, to 5.30pm winter; ☺San Zaccaria) was the official residence of Venice's doges (ruling dukes) from the 9th century. Inside, its lavishly decorated chambers harbour some seriously heavyweight art, including Tintoretto's gigantic *Paradiso* (Paradise) in the Sala del Maggiore Consiglio. Joining the palace to the city dungeons, the **Ponte dei Sospiri** (Bridge of Sighs) was named after the sighs that prisoners – including Casanova – emitted en route from court to cell. If you're hungry, hit the streets on foot for a real taste of the city (p202).

✕ ⊨ p46, p61, p117, p175

Venice Ponte dei Sospiri (Bridge of Sighs)

Classic Trip

Eating & Sleeping

Rome ➊ see also p47

✗ Trattoria Monti   Ristorante $$

(☎06 446 65 73; Via di San Vito 13a; meals €40-45; ⏱1-3pm Tue-Sun, 8-11pm Tue-Sat, closed Aug; Ⓜ Vittorio Emanuele) The Camerucci family runs this elegant brick-arched place, proffering top-notch traditional cooking from Le Marche region. There are wonderful *fritti* (fried things), delicate pastas and ingredients such as *pecorino di fossa* (sheep's cheese aged in caves), goose, swordfish and truffles. Try the egg-yolk *tortelli* pasta. Desserts are delectable, including apple pie with *zabaglione*. Word has spread, so book ahead.

✗ Casa Coppelle   Ristorante $$

(☎06 6889 1707; www.casacoppelle.it; Piazza delle Coppelle 49; meals €45; ⏱noon-3.30pm & 6.30-11.30pm; ❑Corso del Rinascimento) Exposed brick walls, flowers and subdued lighting set the stage for creative Italian- and French-inspired food at this intimate, romantic restaurant. There's a full range of starters and pastas, but the real tour de force are the rich, decadent meat dishes. Service is attentive and the setting, on a small piazza near the Pantheon, memorable. Book ahead.

🛏 La Piccola Maison   B&B $$

(☎06 4201 6331; www.lapiccolamaison.com; Via dei Cappuccini 30; s €50-180, d €70-200, tr €110-270; ❄❂; Ⓜ Barberini) The excellent Piccola Maison is housed in a 19th-century building in a great location close to Piazza Barberini, and has pleasingly plain, neutrally decorated rooms and thoughtful staff. It's a great deal.

Siena ➋ see also p279

✗ Enoteca I Terzi   Tuscan $$

(☎0577 4 43 29; www.enotecaiterzi.it; Via dei Termini 7; meals €35-40; ⏱11am-1am summer, 11am-4pm & 6.30pm-midnight winter, closed Sun) A favourite for many locals who head to this historic *enoteca* to linger over lunches, *aperitivi* and casual dinners featuring top-notch Tuscan *salumi* (cured meats), delicate handmade pasta and wonderful wines.

Florence ➌ see also p47, p262 and p271

✗ Trattoria Cibrèo   Tuscan $$

(www.edizioniteatrodelsalecibreofirenze.it; Via dei Macci 122r; meals €30; ⏱12.50-2.30pm & 6.50-11pm Tue-Sat, closed Aug) Dine here and you'll instantly understand why a queue gathers outside before it opens. Once inside, revel in top-notch Tuscan cuisine: perhaps *pappa al pomodoro* (a thick soupy mash of tomato, bread and basil) followed by *polpettine di pollo e ricotta* (chicken and ricotta meatballs). No reservations, no credit cards, no coffee, no pasta and arrive early to snag a table.

✗ L'Osteria di Giovanni   Tuscan $$$

(☎055 28 48 97; www.osteriadigiovanni.it; Via del Moro 22; meals €50; ⏱7-10pm Mon-Fri, 12.30-3pm & 7-10pm Sat & Sun) Cuisine at this smart neighbourhood eatery is sumptuously Tuscan. Imagine truffles, tender steaks and pastas such as *pici al sugo di salsiccia e cavolo nero* (thick spaghetti with a sauce of sausage and black cabbage). Throw in a complimentary glass of *prosecco* and you'll want to return time and again.

Hotel L'O
Design Hotel $$$

(☎055 27 73 80; www.hotelorologioflorence.
com; Piazza di Santa Maria Novella 24; d from
€150; P ✷ @ 🛜) The type of seductive
address James Bond would feel right at home
in, this super-stylish hotel oozes panache.
Designed as a showcase for the (very wealthy)
owner's (exceedingly expensive) luxury
wristwatch collection, L'O (the hip take on its full
name, Hotel L'Orologio) has four stars, rooms
named after watches and clocks pretty much
everywhere. Don't be late...

Pisa ❹

Sottobosco
Cafe $

(www.sottoboscocafe.it; Piazza San Paolo
all'Orto; lunches €15; ⊙3pm-midnight Tue-Fri,
6pm-1am Sat, 6pm-midnight Sun winter, noon-
3pm & 6pm-midnight Tue-Fri, 6pm-1am Sat, 6pm-
midnight Sun summer, closed Jul & Aug) What
a tourist-free breath of fresh air this creative
cafe is! Tuck into a sugary ring doughnut and
cappuccino at a glass-topped table filled with
artists' crayons perhaps, or a collection of
buttons. Lunch dishes (salads, pies and pasta)
are simple and homemade, and come dusk, jazz
bands play or DJs spin tunes.

Modena ❺ see also p287

Hosteria Giusti
Gastronomy $$$

(☎059 22 25 33; www.hosteriagiusti.it; Vicolo
Squallore 46; meals €50, with half portions €35;
⊙12.30-2pm Tue-Sat) With only four tables,
a narrow back-alley location, no real signage
and a 90-minute daily opening window, this
perplexingly unassuming *osteria* isn't really
setting itself up for legendary status. But
tentative whispers turn to exuberant shouts
when regional specialities like *cotechino fritto
con zabaglione al lambrusco* (fried Modena
sausage with wine-flavoured egg custard) arrive
at your table. Booking essential.

Hotel Cervetta 5
Hotel $$

(☎059 23 84 47; www.hotelcervetta5.com;
Via Cervetta 5; s €90-115, d €128-215; ✷ 🛜)

Cervetta is about as posh as Modena gets
without pampering to the convention crowd.
A location adjacent to intimate Piazza Grande
is complemented by quasi-boutique facilities,
clean, modern bathrooms and the latest in
TV technology. Fruity breakfasts and wi-fi are
included; garage parking (€15) isn't.

Venice ❽ see also p46, p117 and p175

All'Arco
Venetian $

(☎041 520 56 66; Calle dell'Ochialer 436, San
Polo; cicheti from €1.50; ⊙8am-8pm Wed-Fri, to
3pm Mon, Tue & Sat; 🚤Rialto-Mercato) Search
out this authentic neighbourhood *osteria*
(casual tavern) for some of the best *cicheti*
(bar snacks) in town. Armed with ingredients
from the nearby Rialto market, father-son
team Francesco and Matteo serve miniature
masterpieces such as *cannocchia* (mantis
shrimp) with pumpkin and roe, and *otrega
crudo* (raw butterfish) with mint-and-olive-oil
marinade.

Anice Stellato
Venetian $$$

(☎041 72 07 44; www.osterianicestellato.
com; Fondamenta de la Sensa 3272; bar snacks
€13.50, meals €45-50; ⊙10.30am-3.30pm
& 6.30pm-midnight Wed-Sun; 🚤Madonna
dell'Orto) Tin lamps, unadorned rustic tables
and a small wooden bar set the scene for quality
seafood at this excellent canal-side *bacaro*
(bar). You can munch on bar-side *cicheti* or go
for the full à la carte menu and swoon over juicy
scampi in *saor* (vinegar marinade) and grilled
tuna. Reservations recommended.

Novecento
Boutique Hotel $$$

(☎041 241 37 65; www.novecento.biz; Calle del
Dose 2683/84; d €140-350; ✷ 🛜; 🚤Santa
Maria del Giglio) Sporting a boho-chic look, the
Novecento is a real charmer. Its nine individually
designed rooms ooze style with Turkish kilim
pillows, Fortuny draperies and 19th-century
carved bedsteads. Outside, its garden is a lovely
spot to linger over breakfast.

Northern Italy

FROM THE SNOWY SLOPES OF THE MILKY WAY to villas framed by gazebos and mould-breaking art and architecture, northern Italy is as action packed as it is artful. Its mountains, lakes and coastal villages have been luring artists, celebrities and moneyed Mitteleuropeans since the days of the Grand Tour, and it's easy to see what drew them here: world-class art, an embarrassment of culinary riches, cult wines and a slew of sophisticated cities.

While Venice's city of palaces dazzles and Milan's Golden Quad rapidly helps to relieve you of your hard-earned cash, you're never far from a rural hinterland that still moves with the rhythm of the seasons and that seems largely untouched by modern tourism.

Lago di Como Bellagio village
IZZET KERIBAR/GETTY IMAGES ©

Northern Italy

Cappella degli Scrovegni

See the Renaissance blossoming through the tears in Giotto's moving frescoes for the Cappella degli Scrovegni on Trips **1** **8** **14**

Portofino Peninsula

Steal a march on Cinque Terre hikers and walk the quiet pathways on the Portofino peninsula, ending with a harbourside meal at Ristorante Puny on Trip **7**

Truffles

Strike gastronomic gold in Alba, and dine on prized white truffles on Trip **4**

Terme Merano

Dip in and out of hot and cold pools amid stunning mountain scenery, just as Austrian royals, and Kafka, have done before you on Trip **11**

Walking the Alta Vie

Walk on the roof of the Dolomites through Alpine meadows strewn with wildflowers on Trip **13**

Grande Strada delle Dolomiti 7–10 Days
Admire the rocky amphitheatre of the rose-coloured Dolomites. (p155)

A Venetian Sojourn 4–5 Days
Glide along the Brenta Canal to splendid frescoed villas. (p167)

Valpolicella Wine Country 4 Days
Stop by historic wineries en route from Verona to Lake Garda. (p177)

The Venetian Dolomites 7 Days
Medieval towns, elegant country villas, sparkling *prosecco* and majestic mountain scenery. (p185)

Trieste to Tarvisio 7 Days
From Italo-Austrian Trieste, zigzag through vineyards to Alpine Tarvisio. (p195)

Savoy Palace Circuit

3

Bisected by the Po and overshadowed by the Alps, Turin has an air of importance, adorned as it is with sumptuous Savoy palaces, grand hunting lodges and Napoleonic boulevards.

TRIP HIGHLIGHTS

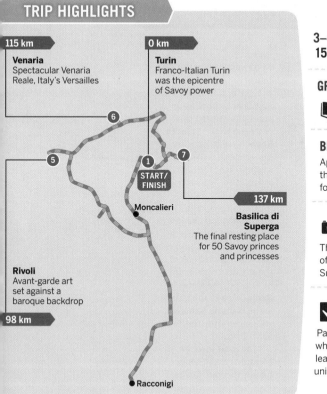

115 km

Venaria
Spectacular Venaria Reale, Italy's Versailles

0 km

Turin
Franco-Italian Turin was the epicentre of Savoy power

6

5

1
START/ FINISH

7

Moncalieri

137 km

Basilica di Superga
The final resting place for 50 Savoy princes and princesses

Rivoli
Avant-garde art set against a baroque backdrop

98 km

Racconigi

3–4 DAYS
152KM / 94 MILES

GREAT FOR...

BEST TIME TO GO
April to October, when the castles are open for viewing.

 ESSENTIAL PHOTO

The classical facade of the Basilica di Superga.

 BEST FOR HISTORY

Palazzo Carignano, where key events leading to Italian unification took place.

Savoy Palace Circuit

The Savoys abandoned their old capital of Chambéry in France in 1563 and set up home in Turin (Torino). To make themselves comfortable they spent the next 300 years building an array of princely palaces (many of them designed by Sicilian architect and stage-set designer Filippo Juvarra), country retreats and a grand mausoleum. They encircle Turin like an extravagant baroque garland and make for fascinating day trips or an easy long-weekend tour.

TRIP HIGHLIGHT

❶ Turin

Piazza Castello served as the seat of dynastic power for the House of Savoy. It is dominated by **Palazzo Madama** (☎011 443 35 01; www.palazzo madamatorino.it; Piazza Castello; adult/reduced €10/8; ⏰10am-7pm Wed-Mon), a part-medieval, part-baroque castle built in the 13th century on the site of the old Roman gate and named after Madama Reale Maria Cristina (widow of Vittorio Amedeo I, also known as the Lion of Susa and nominally King of Cyprus and Jerusalem),

who lived here in the 17th century.

Nearby statues of mythical twins Castor and Pollux guard the entrance to the **Palazzo Reale** (www.ilpalazzoreale ditorino.it; Piazza Castello; adult/reduced €12/6, 1st Sun of month free; ⏰8.30am-7.30pm Tue-Sun). Built for Carlo Emanuele II around 1646, its lavishly decorated rooms house an assortment of gilded furnishings and one of the greatest armouries in Europe, the **Armeria Reale**. Also in the palace is the **Galleria Sabauda**, which contains the Savoy art collection.

'The road through Memphis and Thebes passes through Turin',

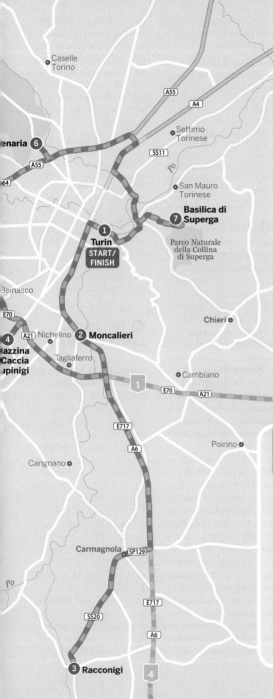

trumpeted French hieroglyphic decoder Jean-François Champollion in the 19th century, and he wasn't far wrong. The **Palazzo dell'Accademia delle Scienze** houses the most important collection of Egyptian treasure outside Cairo in the **Museo Egizio** (Egyptian Museum; ☎011 561 77 76; www. museoegizio.it; Via Accademia delle Scienze 6; adult/reduced €15/11; ⏱8.30am-7.30pm Tue-Sun, 9am-2pm Mon).

Opposite, **Palazzo Carignano** is where Carlo Alberto (1798–1849) and the first King of Italy, Vittorio Emanuele II (1820–78), were born, and it provided the seat for Italy's first parliament. Now it houses the unmissable **Museo Nazionale del Risorgimento Italiano** (☎011 562 11 47; www.museorisorgimento torino.it; Via Accademia delle

LINK YOUR TRIP

1 Grand Tour

From Italy's first capital to a Grand Tour of the peninsula, continue from Turin to Genoa (Genova) on the A21 and A7.

4 Gourmet Piedmont

Head south of Turin on the A6 to tour the rich culinary hinterland of the Langhe, Piedmont's jealously guarded larder.

Scienze 5; adult/reduced €10/8; ⊙10am-6pm Tue-Sun), which charts the course of the modern nation state.

✕ ⊨ p46, p73, p81, p89

The Drive » Drive south along Corso Unitá d'Italia. This busy dual carriageway turns into Corso Trieste and then Via Custoza. Take a right for Moncalieri, beneath the A6 and across the river Po on Via Martiri della Libertá. Turn right on Via Arduino and you'll arrive at the castle after about 9km.

- - - - - - - - - - - - - -

❷ Moncalieri

The 12th-century **Castello di Moncalieri** (Piazza Baden Baden 4; adult/reduced gardens only €5/3) **was** the first fortress built by Thomas I of Savoy just south of the centre of Turin, commanding the southern access to the city. The family then upped sticks and moved to more splendid accommodation in the city centre.

Since 1921 it has been the HQ for the *carabinieri* (military police), the police corps created by Victor Emanuele I of Savoy in 1726 as a police force for the island of Sardinia (briefly within Savoy dominion) and which later became Italy's first police force following unification in 1861. While the royal apartments can only be visited on a pre-booked guided tour you can

wander round the garden and enjoy the view from the belvedere.

The Drive » Leave Moncalieri heading southwest, following signs saying *tutte le direzioni* (all directions) and then pick up the A6 southbound towards Savona/Piacenza. Drive 15km on the autostrada, then exit for Carmagnola, which will put you first on the SP129 (as you skirt Carmagnola) and then on the SS20 towards Racconigi, a further 12km southwest.

- - - - - - - - - - - - - -

❸ Racconigi

South of Moncalieri, the enormous **Castello di Racconigi** (www.ilcastello diracconigi.it; Via Morosini 3; adult/reduced €5/2.50; ⊙9am-7pm Tue-Sun Apr-Oct, 9am-7pm Wed, Fri, Sat & Sun Nov-Mar) **was** another 12th-century fortress, guarding the contested borderlands around Turin. Originally the domain of the Marquis of Saluzzo, the castle came into Savoy possession through marriage and inheritance.

Inhabited by various branches of the family up until WWII, the castle was a favourite for summering royals, hosting Tsar Nicholas II of Russia in 1918. In 1904 the last king of Italy, Umberto II, was born in the castle and in 1925 the grand wedding of Philip of Hesse and Mafalda of Savoy was hosted here. Tragically, Mafalda later died in the death camp of Buchenwald. Now you

can wander the strangely intimate apartments of kings and queens – full of elegant furnishings, family photos and personal objects – and enjoy the grand portrait gallery with its 1875 dynastic portraits.

The Drive » The 38km drive north to Palazzina di Caccia Stupinigi retraces much of the previous journey, first on the SS20 and then the A6. However, after 14km on the autostrada, before you reach Moncalieri, take the exit for the E70 (Tangenziale) towards Aosta. Now heading northwest, drive a further 8.5km and then take the exit for Stupinigi. The Viale Torino runs right up to the *palazzina* (hunting lodge).

- - - - - - - - - - - - - -

❹ Palazzina di Caccia Stupinigi

The Savoy's finest hunting park, the **Palazzina di Caccia Stupinigi** (☎011 620 06 34; www.ordinemau riziano.it; Piazza Principe Amedeo 7; adult/reduced €12/8; ⊙10am-5.30pm Tue-Fri, to 6.30pm Sat & Sun) was cleverly acquired by the almost landless Emanuele Filiberto, Duke of Savoy from 1553 to 1580. Known as *Testa di Ferro* ('Ironhead') due to his military prowess, Emanuele was the only child of Charles III, Duke of Savoy, and Beatrice of Portugal, who left him little more than his title when they died. However, through diligent service in the armies of the Austro-Hungarian

Turin Piazza Carignano

empire he slowly and surely reclaimed Savoyard lands, including the Stupinigi park and Turin, where he moved the family seat in 1563.

The fabulous *palazzina* came later, thanks to Vittorio Amadeo II, who set Filippo Juvarra to work in 1729. He enlisted decorators from Venice to attend to the interiors covering the 137 rooms and 17 galleries in *trompe l'œil* hunting scenes such as the *Triumph of Diana* in the main salon. Now the rooms accommodate the **Museo di Arte e Ammobiliamento**, a fabulous museum of arts and furnishings, many of them original to the lodge.

The Drive » Continue on the Turin periphery (E70) heading further northwest towards Fréjus for the 21km drive to Rivoli. You'll be on the E70 for 11km before exiting at Rosta/Avigliana. From here it's a short 4km drive before exiting on the SS25 towards Rivoli. Brown signs direct you to the castle.

TRIP HIGHLIGHT

⑤ Rivoli

Works by Franz Ackermann, Gilbert and George, and Sophie Calle would have been beyond the wildest imagination of the Savoy family, who used the 17th-century **Castello di Rivoli** as one of their country retreats.

Since 1984, the cutting edge of Turin's contemporary art scene has been housed here in the **Museo d'Arte Contemporanea** (www.castellodirivoli. org; Piazza Mafalda di Savoia; adult/reduced €6.50/4.50; ⊙10am-5pm Tue-Fri, to 7pm Sat & Sun), **creating shocking juxtapositions between the classical architecture and the art, such as the 1997 exhibition that showcased Mau-** rizio Cattelan's taxidermy horse suspended from the rococo ceiling.

As well as its permanent collection, the castle also hosts bold temporary exhibits such as Paloma Varga Weisz' solo exhibition, Root of a Dream, in 2015.

✖ p73

The Drive » Return to the Tangenziale via the SS25 and continue northeast in the direction of Aosta/Mont Blanc/Milano. This puts you on the A55/E64 for 9km. Then take the exit for Venaria and at the traffic lights turn left onto Corso Giuseppe Garibaldi, from where you'll see the palace signposted.

TRIP HIGHLIGHT

⑥ Venaria

The **Reggia di Venaria Reale** (☎011 499 23 33; www. lavenaria.it; Piazza della Repubblica; €25, Reggia & gardens only €16, gardens only €5; ⊙9am-5pm Tue-Fri, to 6.30pm

MAFALDA OF SAVOY (1902–44)

Mafalda of Savoy was the second of four daughters of King Victor Emmanuel III of Italy and Elena of Montenegro. Known for her cultured, pious character, she made a grand marriage to Prince Philip, Landgrave of Hesse, grandson of German Emperor Frederick III and great-grandson of Queen Victoria of England. Affiliated with the German National Socialist (Nazi) movement, Philip, with his international connections, rose rapidly in the Nazi hierarchy, becoming a trusted member of the Reichstag and acting as an intermediary between Hitler and Mussolini. But Hitler distrusted the outspoken Mafalda and suspected her of working against the German war effort. When her father, Victor Emmanuel, ordered the arrest of Mussolini in July 1943 and signed the armistice with the Allies, the Gestapo reacted by arresting Mafalda for subversive activities and transferring her to Buchenwald concentration camp. There she was wounded during an Allied attack on the camp's munitions factory in 1944, and she later died of her wounds, beseeching fellow prisoners to remember her not as an Italian princess, but an Italian sister.

Sat & Sun) is a Unesco-listed palace complex built by Amadeo di Castellamonte for Carlo Emanuele II between 1667 and 1690. It's one of the biggest royal residences in the world and lengthy restoration works were concluded in late 2010. The full trajectory of the buildings stretches 2km. Highlights include the **Galleria Grande**, the **Cappella di Sant'Uberto** and the **Juvarra stables**.

Outside, there are more: 17th-century grottoes, the **Fontana del Cervo** (Stag Fountain), the **Rose Garden** and the 17th-century **Potager Garden**, all of which took eight years to restore and required the replanting of 50,000 plants. It's all set against the 3000-hectare La Mandria park.

✗ p73

The Drive » First return to the A55/E64 and continue northeast for 6km, then take the Falchera exit for Torino Nord. Follow the signs for Torino Centro and merge southwards onto the A4 for 2.5km. Before you hit the river Po, turn left onto Lungo Stura Lazio, which skirts the river before crossing over it. The next 5km are through a natural park until you reach the suburb of Sassi where you turn left onto the Strada Comunale Superga.

- - - - - - - - - -

TRIP HIGHLIGHT

❼ Basilica di Superga

In 1706 Vittorio Amedeo II promised to build a basilica to honour the Virgin Mary if Turin was saved from besieging French and Spanish armies. Like a religious epiphany, the city was saved, so Duke Amadeo once again commissioned

Juvarra to build the **Basilica di Superga** (www.basilicadisuperga.com; Strada della Basilica di Superga 75; adult/reduced €5/4; ⊘10am-1.30pm & 2.30-6pm Thu-Tue Mar-Oct, Sat & Sun only Nov-Feb) on a hill across the Po river in 1717.

Magnificently sited as it is, with a crowning dome 65m high, it is visible for miles around and in due course it became the final resting place for 50 members of the Savoy family. Their lavish tombs make for interesting viewing. In their company, at the rear of the church, lies a tomb commemorating the Gran Torino football team, all of whom died in 1949 when their plane crashed into the basilica in thick fog.

Eating & Sleeping

Turin ❶ see also p46, p81 and p89

✖ Gofri Piemontéisa Fast Food €

(www.gofriemiassepiemontesi.it; Via San Tommaso 4a; gofri €4.40-5; ⏰11.30am-7.30pm Mon-Sat) *Gofri*, thin waffles snap cooked in hot irons, are a traditional dish from the mountainous regions of northern Piedmont and have been reinvented here by a local chef as tasty fast food. Try the house *gofre* with ham, *toma* (alpine cheese) and artichokes or one of the equally delicious *miasse*, a corn-based variation, also adapted from ancient recipes.

✖ Porto di Savona Trattoria €€

(☎011 817 35 00; www.foodandcompany.com; Piazza Vittorio Veneto 2; meals €28; ⏰12.30-2.30pm & 7.30-10.30pm) An unpretentious trattoria that dates to Turin's capital days (ie the 1860s), it has a deserved reputation for superb *agnolotti al sugo arrosto* (Piedmontese ravioli in a meat gravy), and *gnocchi di patate al gorgonzola*. The mains – including *bollito misto alla piemontese* (boiled meat and vegetable stew) – are equally memorable.

✖ Scannabue Piedmont €€

(☎011 669 66 93; www.scannabue.it; Largo Saluzzo 25h; meals €35; ⏰12.30-2.30pm & 7.30pm-midnight) Scannabue, housed in a former corner garage, is a retro-fitted bistro that has a touch of Paris in its cast iron doors and tiled floors. There's a casual feel, but the cooking is some of Turin's most lauded.

⛏ Via Stampatori B&B €

(☎339 2581330; www.viastampatori.com; Via Stampatori 4; s/d €70/110; 📶) This utterly lovely B&B occupies the top floor of a frescoed Renaissance building. Six bright, stylish and uniquely furnished rooms overlook either a sunny terrace or a leafy inner courtyard. The owner's personal collection of 20th-century design is used throughout the rooms and several serene common areas. It's central but blissfully quiet.

⛏ NH Piazza Carlina Design Hotel €€€

(☎848 390230; www.nh-hotels.com; Piazza Carlo Emanuele II; s/d €180/220) Situated on one of Turin's most beautiful squares, this sprawling property occupies a 17th-century building, once the Albergo di Virtù, a Savoy charitable institution; it also once housed the political theorist Antonio Gramsci. The decor is cutting edge, highly atmospheric and deeply luxurious. Guests have access to roof-top terraces, and breakfast is served in a stately courtyard.

Rivoli ❺

✖ Combal Zero Gastronomy €€€

(☎011 956 52 25; www.combal.org; Piazza Mafalda di Savoia; 5-course tasting menu from €130; ⏰8-11pm Tue-Sat) Davide Scabin's tasting menus are theatrical, visual, visceral and mischievous, but despite such experimentation are still deeply rooted in Piedmontese culinary traditions.

Venaria ❻

✖ Caffè degli Argenti Cafe €

(Reggia di Venaria Reale, Piazza della Repubblica 4; panini €5; ⏰10am-4.30pm Tue-Fri, to 7.15pm Sat & Sun) Sip cups of molten coffee in the glorious, gold-on-black Sala Cinese of the Venaria Reale palace. Also on order are top-quality *panini*, pastries and ice cream, which can be enjoyed on the terrace overlooking the Grand Parterre garden.

✖ Chiosco delle Rose Gelateria €

(Piazza della Repubblica; ice cream €3-5; ⏰noon-4.30pm Sat, to 6.30pm Sun Apr-Oct) The Reggia di Venaria Reale's (p71) ice-cream parlour is located in the Rose Garden in the 19th-century summerhouse. Choose from artisanal flavours and enjoy a picnic beneath the pergolas.

Gourmet Piedmont

4

Immersed in tradition as old as the towns that fostered it, Piedmont's cuisine is the toast of Italy. It is also home to the Slow Food movement, Alba truffles and big-hitting Barolo wines.

TRIP HIGHLIGHTS

0 km

Turin
Sample 'Sweet Moments in Turin' in Italy's chocolate capital

220 km

Asti
Raise a glass of Asti's signature fizz, Asti Spumante

1 START

7 FINISH

170 km

Alba
Sniff precious white truffles at Alba's truffle fair

● Bra
5
● Cherasco
4

● Fossano

Barolo
Home town of the Ferrari of Italian red wines

155 km

● Cuneo

---

6 DAYS
220KM / 137 MILES

GREAT FOR...

BEST TIME TO GO
September to November for autumn food festivals.

ESSENTIAL PHOTO
Endless vistas of vines in Barolo or Barbaresco.

BEST FOR OENOPHILES
Sampling glasses of Barolo for only €3 at Castello Falletti.

---

ba White truffles and a truffle slicer

4 Gourmet Piedmont

The rolling hills, valleys and towns of Piedmont are northern Italy's specialist pantry, weighed down with sweet hazelnuts, rare white truffles, Arborio rice and Nebbiolo grapes that metamorphose into Barolo and Barbaresco wines. Out here they give out Michelin stars like overzealous schoolteachers give out house points, and with good reason. Trace a gourmet route, and counter the calorific overload with rural walks and bike rides.

TRIP HIGHLIGHT

❶ Turin

The innovative Torinese gave the world its first saleable hard chocolate, perpetuated one of its greatest mysteries (the Holy Shroud) and played a key role in the creation of the Italian state. You can follow the epic story in the **Museo Nazionale del Risorgimento Italiano** (☎011 562 11 47; www.museorisorgimento torino.it; Via Accademia delle Scienze 5; adult/reduced €10/8; ☉10am-6pm Tue-Sun).

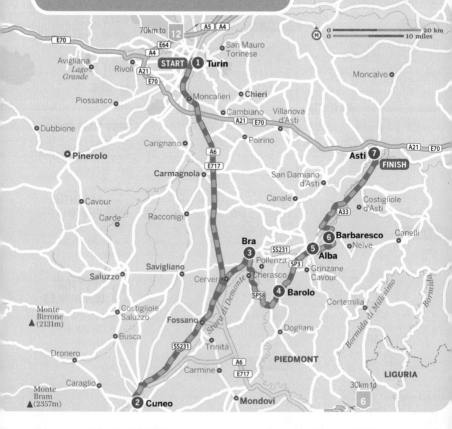

Aside from the national narrative and the intriguing Shroud of Turin, on display in the **Duomo** (www.duomoditorino.it; Piazza San Giovanni; ⏱8am-7pm Mon-Sat), you've come to Turin for chocolate.

Planning your trip for November, when the **Cioccolatò** (www.cioccolato.it) festival is in full swing, is a good start. Otherwise visit **Al Bicerin** (www.bicerin.it; Piazza della Consolata 5; ⏱8.30am-7.30pm Thu-Tue, closed Aug), named from *bicerin,* a caffeine-charged hot drink of chocolate, coffee and cream. Then there's **Peyrano** (www.peyrano.com; Corso Vittorio Emanuele 76; ⏱9am-12.30pm & 1.30-6pm Mon-Sat), specialist chocolatiers since 1914 and creators of *Dolci Momenti a Torino* (Sweet Moments in Turin).

LINK YOUR TRIP

6 **Italian Riviera**
From Bra continue south along the A6 to enjoy a tour of the olive groves and gardens along the Italian Riviera.

12 **Valle d'Aosta**
Cheese-lovers beware: the A5 from Turin takes you into the heart of the Valle d'Aosta, where days of hiking end with fontina fondues.

Beyond the chocolate, Turin is home to Slow Food's groundbreaking 'supermarket', **Eataly** (www.eataly.net; Via Nizza 230; ⏱10am-10.30pm). Housed in a converted factory, it showcases a staggering array of sustainable food and beverages and hosts regular tastings and cookery workshops.

🍴 p46, p73, p81, p89

The Drive » Cuneo lies 100km south of Turin, virtually a straight shot down the A6 autostrada. Head out of Turin on Corso Unità d'Italia and across the river Po. Then join the autostrada for 70km. Exit at Fossano and join the SS231 for the final 20km.

❷ Cuneo

A condensed version of Turin, Cuneo is a genteel town with an impressive Renaissance square, the grand arcaded **Piazza Galimberti**, where market stalls set up every Tuesday. It's a good place for festivals, too, such as the music festival in June, the Tour de France in July and the impressive Chestnut Fair in October, which fills the town. The city's signature rum-filled chocolates though, can be sampled year-round.

The deconsecrated San Francisco convent and church today house the **Museo Civico di Cuneo** (Via Santa María 10; adult/reduced €3/2; ⏱3.30-6.30pm Tue-Sun), which tells the

history of the town and province.

🍴 🛏 p81, p89

The Drive » The 44km journey to Bra retraces much of the previous drive along the SS231. Head back to Fossano, but instead of reconnecting with the A6, take the periphery north and continue northeast through Cervere, where the countryside opens out into green fields.

❸ Bra

Up on the 1st floor of a recessed courtyard, the little **Osteria del Boccondivino** (☎0172 42 56 74; www.boccondivinoslow.it; Via Mendicità Istruita 14, Bra; meals €25-32; ⏱noon-2.30pm & 7-10pm Tue-Sat), lined with wine bottles, was the first restaurant to be opened by Slow Food in the 1980s. The food is predictably excellent, and the local Langhe menu changes daily. In the same courtyard you'll find the **Slow Food headquarters** (www.slowfood.it), which includes a small bookshop selling guides to all of Italy's Slow Food–accredited restaurants and heritage producers.

Just outside Bra, in the village of Pollenza, 4km southeast, is the Slow Food **Università di Scienze Gastronomiche** (University of Gastronomic Sciences; www.unisg.it; Piazza Vittorio Emanuele 9). It offers three-year courses in gastronomy and food management.

Next door is the **Banca del Vino** ($\square$0172 45 80 45; www.bancadelvino.it; Piazza Vittorio Emanuele II 13; tour & tastings €3-20), and a wine-cellar 'library' of Italian wines. Reserve for guided tastings. Also nearby is the acclaimed **Guido Ristorante** ($\square$0173 62 61 62; www.guidoristorante.it; Via Alba 15, Serralunga d'Alba; set menus €110; $\bigcirc$7.30-10.30pm Tue-Sat, 12.30-2.30pm Sat & Sun, closed Jan & Aug) that people have been known to cross borders to visit, especially for the veal.

The Drive » From Bra to Barolo is a lovely 20km drive through the gentle Langhe Hills. Head east along the SS231 for 3km before turning southeast onto the SP7, then the SP58. The latter passes through orchards and vineyards and offers up photogenic views of old stone farmhouses.

SNAILS, GLORIOUS SNAILS

Set within the Langhe's lush wine country, Cherasco, just south of Bra, is best known for *lumache* (snails). Snails in this neck of the woods are dished up *nudo* (shell-free). They can be pan-fried, roasted, dressed in an artichoke sauce or minced inside ravioli. Piedmontese specialities include *lumache al barbera* (snails simmered in Barbera wine and ground nuts) and *lumache alla Piemontese* (snails stewed with onions, nuts, anchovies and parsley in a tomato sauce).

Traditional trattorias serving such dishes include **Osteria della Rosa Rossa** ($\square$0172 48 81 33; Via San Pietro 31; set menus €30-35; $\bigcirc$noon-2pm & 7-11pm Wed-Mon) in Alba.

Langhe Hills Vineyards around Treiso village

TRIP HIGHLIGHT

④ Barolo

Wine-lovers rejoice! This tiny 1800-hectare parcel of undulating land immediately southwest of Alba knocks out the Ferrari of Italian reds, Barolo. Many argue it is Italy's finest wine.

The eponymous village is dominated by the **Castello Falletti**, once owned by the powerful Falletti banking family. Today it houses the **Museo del Vino a Barolo** (www.wimubarolo.it; Castello Comunale Falletti di Barolo; adult/reduced €8/6; ⏰10.30am-

7pm, closed Jan & Feb), where multimedia displays tell the story of wine through history, art, music, films and literature.

Also, in the cellars, the **Enoteca Regionale del Barolo** (Piazza Falletti; ⏰10am-12.30pm & 3-6.30pm Fri-Wed) is run by the region's 11 wine-growing communities. It offers three Barolo wines for tasting each day, costing from €3 each.

🛏 p81

The Drive » The short 15km hop from Barolo to Alba is another pleasant drive through Barolo's vineyards as you head northeast along the SP3. The

SP3 takes you all the way into the centre of Alba.

TRIP HIGHLIGHT

⑤ Alba

Alba's fertile hinterland, the vine-striped Langhe Hills, radiates out from the town, an undulating vegetable garden replete with grapes, hazelnut groves and vineyards. Exploring them on foot or with two wheels is a rare pleasure. Alba's **tourist office** (☎0173 3 58 33; www.langheroero.it; Piazza Risorgimento 2; ⏰9am-6pm Mon-Fri, from 9.30am Sat & Sun) can organise an astounding

SLOW FOOD

Slow Food (www.slowfood.it) was the 1980s brainchild of a group of disenchanted Italian journalists from the Piedmontese town of Bra who, united by their taste buds, successfully ignited a global crusade against the fast-food juggernaut whose tentacles were threatening to engulf Italy's gastronomic heritage. Their mantra was pleasure over speed and taste over convenience in a manifesto that promoted sustainability, local production and the protection of longstanding epicurean traditions. Today, Slow Food has over 100,000 members in 160 countries.

number of Langhe/Roero valley excursions, including a variety of cross-country walks through chestnut groves and vineyards, winery tours, cycling tours and truffle-hunting excursions (price depends on the group).

In October and November the town hosts its renowned **truffle fair** (every weekend), and the equally ecstatic *vendemia* (grape harvest).

✗ ⌂ p81

The Drive » Barbaresco sits in the hills just 10km northeast of Alba. Exit Alba along Viale Cherasca and then pick up the narrow, winding SP3 as it loops through the pretty residential suburb of Altavilla and out into the countryside.

⑥ Barbaresco

Only a few kilometres separate Barolo from Barbaresco, but a rainier microclimate and fewer ageing requirements have made the latter into a softer, more delicate red.

Sample it at the atmospheric **Enoteca Regionale del Barbaresco** (www.enotecadelbarbaresco.it; Piazza del Municipio 7; ⊙10am-7pm Mon-Sat, 10am-1pm & 2-7pm Sun), housed inside a deconsecrated church. The *enoteca* (wine bar) also has information on walking trails in the vicinity.

If you haven't had your fill of wine yet, head a further 4km east to the pin-drop-quiet village of Neive, where you'll find the **Bottega dei Quattro Vini** (www.bottegadei4vini.com; Piazza Italia 2; ⊙10am-6pm). This two-room shop was set up by the local community to showcase the four 'DOC' wines (Dolcetto d'Alba, Barbaresco, Moscato and Barbera d'Alba) produced on Neive's hills.

✗ p81

The Drive » The final 30km stretch to Asti leaves Barbaresco's vineyards behind on the SP3 and rejoins the A33 for an uninterrupted drive to Asti. Although it's a two-lane highway, it slices through more unspoilt farmland.

 TRIP HIGHLIGHT

⑦ Asti

Asti and Alba were fierce medieval rivals ruled over by feuding royal families, who built Asti's legendary 150 towers. Of these only 12 remain, and only the **Torre Troyana o Dell'Orologio** (✆0141 39 94 89; Piazza Medici; adult/reduced €2.60/1.10; ⊙10am-1pm & 4-7pm Sat & Sun Apr-Sep) can be climbed if you make a reservation. Asti's rivalry with Alba is still recalled in the annual **Palio d'Asti**, a bareback horse race on the third Sunday of September that commemorates a victorious battle.

The 10-day **Douja d'Or** (a *douja* being a terracotta wine jug unique to Asti), in the first or second week in September, is complemented by the **Delle Sagre** food festival on the second Sunday of September. Otherwise you can sample the city's eponymous wine, Asti Spumante, at the **Enoteca Boero di Boero Mario** (Piazza Astesano 17; ⊙9am-noon & 3-8pm Tue-Sun, 3-8pm Mon).

Like Alba, the countryside around Asti contains precious black and white truffles. Asti's **truffle fair** is in November.

✗ p81

Eating & Sleeping

Turin ❶ see also p46, p73 and p89

✗ Perino Vesco — Bakery €

(📞011 068 60 56; www.perinovesco.it; Via Cavour 10; snacks from €5; ⏰7.30am-7.30pm Mon-Sat) Cult Slow Food baker Andrea Perino turns out the city's best *grissini* (bread sticks) along with dense, fragrant *torta langarola* (hazelnut cake), naturally yeasted *panettone* and focaccia that draws sighs from homesick Ligurians. Join the queues for takeaway pizza and focaccia or head out the back for sandwiches, pizza, savoury tarts and coffee.

Cuneo ❷ see also p89

✗ Osteria della Chiocciola — Gastronomy €€

(📞0171 6 62 77; www.osteriadellachiocciola.it; Via Fossano 1; meals €30, degustation €38; ⏰12.30-11pm Mon-Sat) Slow Food–affiliated Chiocciola's upstairs dining room is the colour of buttercups and makes for a soothing setting to linger over expertly crafted local, seasonal dishes. Its lunch menu (meals €15 to €23) is a fabulous deal, or if on the fly, you can still stop by for a glass of wine with cheese.

⌂ Hotel Royal Superga — Hotel €

(📞0171 69 32 23; www.hotelroyalsuperga.com; Via Pascal 3; s/d €70/95; P ❄ @ 🛜) This appealing old-fashioned hotel hidden off a corner of Piazza Galimberti mixes some regal touches with friendly, professional staff who go way beyond the call of duty. Breakfast is a delicious spread of organic produce.

Barolo ❹

⌂ Hotel Barolo — Hotel €€

(📞0173 5 63 54; www.hotelbarolo.it; Via Lomondo 2; s/d €80/120; P @ 🛜) Hotel Barolo is a fabulously old-school place; sit back on the terrace with a glass of you know what, contemplating the 18th-century Piedmontese architecture that guards its shimmering swimming pool. Follow up with a meal at the in-house restaurant (it's been serving up truffles and the like for four generations).

Alba ❺

✗ Piazza Duomo — Gastronomy €€€

(📞0173 44 28 00; www.piazzaduomoalba.it; Piazza Risorgimento 4; meals €150, set menus €200-240; ⏰12.30-2pm & 7.30-10pm Tue-Sat) Enrico Crippa's Michelin-starred restaurant is now in its second decade and considered one of Italy's best. Dreamlike frescoes by Francesco Clemente fill the dining room, which is otherwise a bastion of restraint. On the plate, expect spectacular produce (this *is* truffle country), including vegetables from the restaurant's own garden.

⌂ Casa Dellatorre — B&B €€

(📞0173 44 12 04; www.casadellatorre.net; Via Elvio Pertinace 20; s/d €115/140; ❄) Three sisters run this central, upmarket B&B, once their family home. Three classically decorated, antique-filled rooms share an internal courtyard. Breakfast is served in the courtyard in summer, and in the pretty cafe in winter.

Barbaresco ❻

✗ Ristorante Rabayà — Italian €€

(📞0173 63 52 23; Via Rabayà 9; set menus €30-45; ⏰noon-2pm & 7-10pm Tue-Sun) Rabayà, on the fringe of the village, has the ambience of dining at a private home. Try the signature rabbit in Barbaresco in the antique-furnished dining room in front of a roaring fire; the terrace set high above the vineyards is perfect for a summer evening plate of cheese. Snails also make the occasional appearance on the menu.

Asti ❼

✗ Osteria La Vecchia Carrozza — Osteria €

(📞0141 53 86 57; www.lavecchiacarrozza.com; Via Caducci 41; meals €18-25; ⏰noon-2.30pm & 7-11pm Tue-Sat) You could be sharing this *osteria*, bedecked with white tablecloths, with a quartet of nuns or a birthday party of celebrating college graduates. At this local spot, your truffle-scented pasta comes with much down-to-earth Piedmontese cheer.

Meandering the Maritime Alps

5

In the Susa Valley and Maritime Alps you'll encounter a rich diversity of marmots, ibex and grouse. That's when you're not skiing the Milky Way or hiking old salt routes.

TRIP HIGHLIGHTS

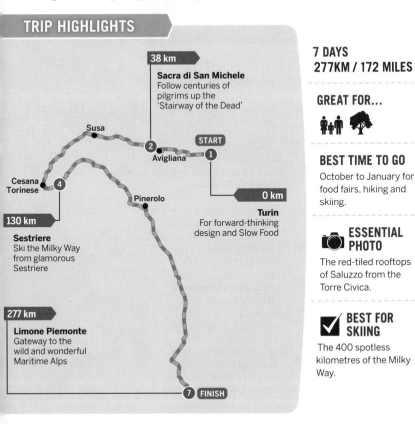

38 km

Sacra di San Michele
Follow centuries of pilgrims up the 'Stairway of the Dead'

Susa

START

2

Avigliana

1

Cesana Torinese

4

Pinerolo

0 km

Turin
For forward-thinking design and Slow Food

130 km

Sestriere
Ski the Milky Way from glamorous Sestriere

277 km

Limone Piemonte
Gateway to the wild and wonderful Maritime Alps

7 **FINISH**

7 DAYS
277KM / 172 MILES

GREAT FOR...

BEST TIME TO GO
October to January for food fairs, hiking and skiing.

ESSENTIAL PHOTO
The red-tiled rooftops of Saluzzo from the Torre Civica.

BEST FOR SKIING
The 400 spotless kilometres of the Milky Way.

Susa Valley View from Sacra di San Michele

Meandering the Maritime Alps

5

Shoehorned between the rice-growing plains of Piedmont and the sparkling coastline of Liguria lie the brooding Maritime Alps – a unique pocket of dramatically sculpted mountains that rise like a stony-faced border guard along the frontier of Italy and France. Traverse their valleys and peaks to gaze in mirror-like lakes, ski the spotless Milky Way and hike amid forests rich with chestnuts.

TRIP HIGHLIGHT

❶ Turin

In 2008 Turin (Torino) held the title of European Capital of Design, and no wonder; the city's architecture mirrors its trajectory from the baroque elegance of the **Palazzo Reale** (www.ilpalazzoreale ditorino.it; Piazza Castello; adult/reduced €12/6, 1st Sun of month free; ⏰8.30am-7.30pm Tue-Sun), seat of the monarchic House of Savoy, to the futuristic steel-and-glass **Mole Antonelliana**, symbol of the city's industrial rebirth and now the repository for the **Museo Nazionale del Cinema** (www.museo cinema.it; Via Montebello 20;

adult/reduced €10/8, incl panoramic lift €14/11; ⏰9am-8pm Tue-Fri & Sun, to 11pm Sat). Take the panoramic lift to the roof terrace for 360-degree views.

From the Mole you may just be able to spy **Lingotto Fiere** (www. lingottofiere.it; Via Nizza 294; Ⓜ Lingotto), Turin's former Fiat factory, redesigned by Renzo Piano into an exhibition centre. It also houses the 'treasure chest' rooftop gallery **Pinacoteca Giovanni e Marella Agnelli** (Lingotto; www.pinacoteca-agnelli.it; Via Nizza 230; adult/reduced €8/3.50; ⏰10am-7pm Tue-Sun; Ⓜ Lingotto), with masterpieces by Canaletto, Manet, Matisse and Picasso. Equally dazzling

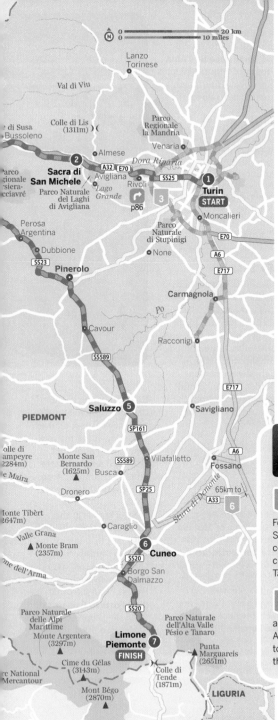

are the stalls in the famous Slow Food supermarket, **Eataly** (www.eataly.net; Via Nizza 230; ⏰10am-10.30pm) next door.

🛏 p46, p73, p81, p89

The Drive » Leave Turin westwards along Corso Vittorio Emanuele II following signs for the A32/E70 to Bardonecchia/Fréjus. Join the autostrada for 11km and then take exit 2, Avigliana Est. Follow the road for 4km. At the roundabout turn right up the Via Sacra (SP188) to San Michele.

TRIP HIGHLIGHT

② Sacra di San Michele

Brooding above the A32, once a key stretch of the Via Francigena pilgrim path from Canterbury through Rome to Monte Sant'Angelo in Puglia, is the **Sacra di San Michele** (www.sacradisanmichele.com;

LINK YOUR TRIP

3 **Savoy Palace Circuit**

For more bombastic Savoy palaces and castles continue from Rivoli on a circuit around Turin on the Tangenziale.

6 **Italian Riviera**

From Cuneo cut across eastwards along the A33 and then down the A6 to Savona for a cruise along the Italian Riviera.

Via alla Sacra 14; adult/reduced €8/6; ⊘9.30am-12.30pm & 2.30-6pm, closed Mon Oct-May, reduced hours winter). This Gothic-Romanesque abbey has kept sentry atop Monte Pirchiriano (962m) since the 10th century and exerted enormous power over abbeys throughout Italy, France and Spain, including Mont Saint Michel in France. It looks familiar, because Umberto Eco used it as the basis for the abbey in *The Name of the Rose*.

Approach as pilgrims would up the **Scalone dei Morti** (Stairway of the Dead), flanked by arches that would once have held the skeletons of dead monks. At the top enter through the whimsical, 12th-century Zodiac Door. Within the walls, the complex houses a frescoed church

and the remnants of the monastery, crowned by the **Torre della Bell'Alda** (Tower of Beautiful Alda). More beautiful though are the views down the Susa Valley.

The Drive ≫ Return to the A32 down the Via Sacra (SP188) for the 40km drive to Susa. Although you're on the autostrada the entire way, the journey passes through dense forests with snow-capped peaks slowly rising ahead of you. Just after Bussoleno, exit for Susa Est.

- - - - - - - - - - - -

❸ Susa

The Romans marched up the **Valle di Susa** and crossed the Alps to secure a passage to the French ports of Nice and Marseille. They enjoyed the thermal baths in Belvédère across the border in France, and grabbed Susa from the Gauls, thus securing

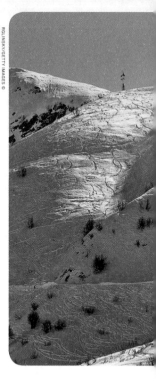

the high passes of the Cottian Alps. You'll find evidence of them all over town, including the remnants of an **aqueduct**, a still-used **amphitheatre** and the triumphal **Arco d'Augusto**, dating from 9 BC.

Susa stands at the gateway to the Valle di Susa, cut through by the Dora di Bardonecchia river and littered with stone towns such as Exilles, with its forbidding **Forte di Exilles**, said to be the keep of the Man in the Iron Mask between 1681 and 1687.

🛏 p89

DETOUR: RIVOLI

Start: ❶ Turin (p84)

Works by Franz Ackermann, Gilbert and George, and Frank Gehry now sit amid the splendour of **Castello di Rivoli**, once the home of Savoy princes and now the venue for the **Museo d'Arte Contemporanea** (Museo d'Arte Contemporanea; www.castellodirivoli.org; Piazza Mafalda di Savoia; adult/reduced €6.50/4.50; ⊘10am-5pm Tue-Fri, to 7pm Sat & Sun). The startling contrasts between the historic house and the avant-garde art are worth the trip. You can mix contemporary art with contemporary food at **Combal Zero** (✆011 956 52 25; www.combal.org; Piazza Mafalda di Savoia; 5-course tasting menu from €130; ⊘8-11pm Tue-Sat).

Limone Piemonte Ski runs and chairlifts for winter sports

The Drive » The 46km drive from Susa to Sestriere is a scenic mountain drive. Rejoin the A32, heading for Fréjus, for 20km (you'll pass the exit for Exilles after 12km). Exit at Oulx Est onto the SS24 and follow the gushing torrent of Dora-Riparia to Cesana Torinese (p89). Alternatively you can head uphill and base yourself in Sauze d'Oulx. When the road forks, veer left onto the SS23 for the final winding ascent to Sestriere.

- - - - - - - - - - -

TRIP HIGHLIGHT

❹ Sestriere

Developed in the 1930s by the Agnelli clan of Fiat, Sestriere ranks among Europe's most glamorous ski resorts due to its enviable location in the eastern realms of the **Via Lattea** (www. vialattea.it) ski area. Neither chocolate bar nor a galaxy of stars, the Via Lattea, or Milky Way, incorporates some 400km of piste and five interlinked ski resorts: Sestriere (2035m), Sauze d'Oulx (1509m), Sansicario (1700m), Cesana Torinese (1350m) and Claviere (1760m) in Italy; and Montgenèvre (1850m) in neighbouring France.

Outside of ski season the **tourist office** (☎0122 75 54 44; Via Louset, Sestriere; ◷9am-1pm & 2-6pm) has information on every conceivable summer activity, including golfing on Europe's highest golf course, walking, free climbing and mountain biking.

The Drive » The longest journey on this tour is the 86km out of the mountains to Saluzzo. Continue on the winding SS23 through mountain towns for 33km and descend southeast to Pinerolo. Then take the ramp to the SS589 (towards Cuneo), which brings you to Saluzzo after 29km.

❺ Saluzzo

Situated at the foot of Monte Viso, Saluzzo was once a powerful marquisate that lasted four centuries until the Savoys won it in a 1601 treaty with France. Its historic significance – although diminished – has left a stirring legacy in its old centre.

The imposing castle, known locally as **La Castiglia** (Piazza Castello; adult/reduced €7/3.50; ⊘10am-1pm & 3-6pm Wed, Fri, Sat & Sun, 3-6pm Thu), overlooks the cobbled alleys and Gothic and Renaissance mansions of the old town, which cluster around the **Salita al Castello**, literally 'the ascent to the castle'. Nearby are the town hall and the **Torre Civica** (Via San Giovanni; adult/reduced €3/1.50; ⊘10.30am-12.30pm Fri, 10.30am-12.30pm & 3-6.30pm Sat & Sun), which you can climb for views over the burnt-red-tiled rooftops.

✕ p89

The Drive ❯❯ It's a scenic 54km drive from Saluzzo to Cuneo, first on the SP161 and then on the SP25 after Villafalletto. Dropping from mountains into low-lying plains and up again, the road passes through vineyards and orchards and across mountain torrents.

❻ Cuneo

Sitting on a promontory between the Gesso and Stura di Demonte rivers, Cuneo enjoys excellent Alpine views framed by the high pyramid-shaped peak of Monte Viso (3841m). To the southwest lie the Maritime Alps, a rugged outdoor-adventure playground. After a hard day out hiking, you'll be thankful for the heart-warming buzz of a *cuneesi al rhum* – a large, rum-laced praline, which you can lay your hands on at 1920s-vintage chocolatier **Arione** (www.arione-cuneo.com; Piazza Galimberti 14; ⊘8am-8pm Tue-Sat, 8am-1pm & 3.30-8pm Sun), located in magnificent **Piazza Galimberti**.

The deconsecrated San Francisco convent today houses the **Museo Civico di Cuneo** (Via Santa María 10; adult/reduced €3/2; ⊘3.30-6.30pm Tue-Sun), tracking the history of the town.

✕ 🛏 p81, p89

The Drive ❯❯ The final 28km to Limone Piemonte provide another picturesque mountain road. Leave Cuneo heading southwest on the SS20 to Borgo San Dalmazzo, where you veer left (keeping on the SS20) across the Torrente Gesso and up into the mountains.

TRIP HIGHLIGHT

❼ Limone Piemonte

To the southwest of Cuneo lies the **Parco Naturale delle Alpi Marittime** (www.parcoalpi marittime.it). Despite their diminutive size, there's a palpable wilderness feel to be found among these Maritime peaks. The park is a walker's paradise, stocked with ibex, chamois and whistling marmots, which scurry around rocky crags covered in mist above a well-marked network of mountain trails, some of them old salt routes, others supply lines left over from two world wars.

The best-equipped town for access to the park is picturesque **Limone Piemonte** (www.limonepiemonte.it). One of the oldest Alpine ski stations, Limone has been in operation since 1907 and maintains 15 lifts and 80km of runs.

🛏 p89

MARGUAREIS CIRCUIT

The Marguareis Circuit is a 35km, two-day hike that starts in Limone Piemonte and tracks up across the mountain passes and ridges to the **Rifugio Garelli** (🕿0171 73 80 78; dm €17, with half-board €40; ⊘mid-Jun–mid-Sep). The peaks of the Argentera and Cime du Gélas massifs are clearly visible from the summit of Punta Marguareis (2651m), the highest point in the park. On day two, 4km of the trek passes through a mountainous nodule of France before swinging back round into Italy.

Eating & Sleeping

Turin ① see also p46, p73 and p81

🛏 NH Lingotto Tech   Business Hotel €€

(☎011 664 20 00; www.nh-hotels.com; Via Nizza 262; d €130-200; P ❄ 🛜) This old Fiat factory hotel comes with a unique perk: the 1km running track on the roof is Fiat's former testing track and featured in the film *The Italian Job*. Twentieth-century industrial bones also mean rooms are huge and bright; the fit-out is slick, industrial too. As a corporate favourite, its facilities are comprehensive and include a 24-hour gym.

Susa ③

🛏 Hotel Susa Stazione   Hotel €

(☎0122 62 22 26; www.hotelsusa.it; Corso Stati Uniti 4/6, Susa; s/d €55/86; P) A handy all-round base for the area and located directly opposite Susa's train station, this cycle-friendly hotel has 12 pleasantly old-school rooms, plus a restaurant with a good local menu (meals €20 to €28). Staff hand out maps and itinerary proposals. Free ski shuttle bus stop outside the door.

Cesana Torinese ③

🛏 Casa Cesana   Hotel €

(☎0122 8 94 62; www.hotelcasacesana.com; Viale Bouvier, Cesana Torinese; s/d €60/90, weekly only in high season; P ❄) Right across from Cesana Torinese's ski lift, this timber chalet was built for the 2006 Olympics. Its rooms are light-filled and spotless, there's a bustling restaurant open to nonguests (set menus from €20) and its bar is one of the area's liveliest.

Saluzzo ⑤

🍴 Terra Gemella   Piedmont €€

(☎347 642 72 61; Via Seminario 28; meals €20-35; ☺noon-3pm & 6-11.30pm Tue-Sat, noon-3pm Sun) Terra Gemella is a wonderful '50s throwback, with pistachio-green walls, chandeliers and traditional tiled floors. Owners Omar and Romina take care of everything personally, and the small menu, featuring classics like gnocchi with gorgonzola, changes frequently.

Cuneo ⑥ see also p81

🍴 4 Ciance   Piedmont €

(☎0171 48 90 27; www.4cianceristorante.it; Via Dronero 8c; meals €25, degustation €32; ☺7.45-10pm Mon, noon-2pm & 7.45-10pm Tue-Sat) A warm, unpretentious place that makes everything from scratch, including the bread. Local specialities (beef cheek in Nebbiolo wine) are requisitely earthy but plated with an unexpected elegance for such a well-priced restaurant.

Limone Piemonte ⑦

🛏 Hotel Marguareis   Hotel €

(☎0171 92 75 67; www.hotelmarguareis.com; Via Genova 30; d €75-95) A small, family run hotel in the centre of Limone, well located for an early morning start on the Marguareis Circuit. Rooms are small, neat and retro-Alpine in style.

Italian Riviera

Curving west in a broad arc, backed by the Maritime Alps, the Italian Riviera sweeps down from Genoa through ancient hamlets and terraced olive groves to the French border at Ventimiglia.

TRIP HIGHLIGHTS

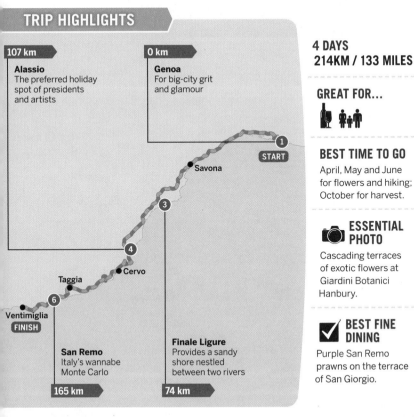

107 km

Alassio
The preferred holiday spot of presidents and artists

0 km

Genoa
For big-city grit and glamour

Savona

START 1

3

4

Cervo

Taggia

6

Ventimiglia
FINISH

San Remo
Italy's wannabe Monte Carlo

165 km

Finale Ligure
Provides a sandy shore nestled between two rivers

74 km

4 DAYS
214KM / 133 MILES

GREAT FOR...

BEST TIME TO GO
April, May and June for flowers and hiking; October for harvest.

ESSENTIAL PHOTO
Cascading terraces of exotic flowers at Giardini Botanici Hanbury.

BEST FINE DINING
Purple San Remo prawns on the terrace of San Giorgio.

6 Italian Riviera

The contrast between sun-washed, sophisticated coastal towns and a deeply rural, mountainous hinterland, full of heritage farms, olive oil producers and wineries, gave rise to the Riviera's 19th-century fame, when European expatriates outnumbered locals. They amused themselves in lavish botanical gardens, gambled in the casino of San Remo and dined in style in fine art-nouveau villas, much as you will on this tour.

TRIP HIGHLIGHT

❶ Genoa

Like Dr Jekyll and Mr Hyde, Genoa (Genova) is a city with a split personality. At its centre, medieval *caruggi* (alleyways) untangle outwards to the **Porto Antico** and teem with hawkers, merchants and office workers. Along Via Garibaldi and Via XXV Aprile is another Genoa, one of Unesco-sponsored palaces, smart shops and grand architectural gestures like **Piazza de Ferrari** with its

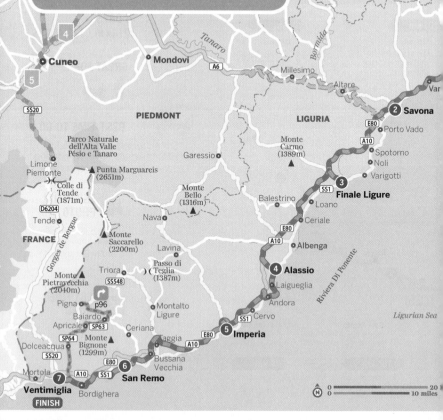

monumental fountain, art nouveau **Palazzo Borsa** (once the city's stock exchange) and the neoclassical **Teatro Carlo Felice** (☎010 538 12 24; www.carlofelice.it; Passo Eugenio Montale 4).

Join the well-dressed *haute bourgeoisie* enjoying high-profile art exhibits in the grand Mannerist halls of the **Palazzo Ducale** (www.palazzoducale.genova.it; Piazza Giacomo Matteotti 9; price varies by exhibition; ⏲hours vary), then retire to sip *spritz* amid Bernardo Strozzi's 17th-

century frescoes at **Cambi Cafe** (www.cambicafe.com; Via Falamonica 9; ⏲10am-11pm).

✖ p46, p97

The Drive ≫ Exit Genoa westward, through a tangle of flyovers and tunnels to access the A10 for the first 56km drive to Savona. Once out of the suburbs the forested slopes of the Maritime Alps rise to your right and sea views peep out from the left as you duck through tunnels.

- - - - - - - - - - - - - -

❷ Savona

Don't be put off by Savona's horrifying industrial sprawl; the Savonesi were a powerful maritime people and the town centre is unexpectedly graceful. Standing near the port are three of the many medieval towers that once studded the cityscape. As Genoa's greatest rival the town was savagely sacked in 1528, the castle dismantled and most of the population slaughtered, but somehow the **Fortezza del Priamàr**

(Piazza Priamar) and the **Cattedrale di Nostra Signora Assunta** (Piazza Cattedrale; ⏲7.30am-7.30pm) survived.

But you're not here for the architecture – you're here for the food. The covered **market** (Via Pietro Giuria; ⏲7am-1.30pm Mon-Sat) is crammed with fruit-and-veg stalls and fish stands stacked with salt cod. **Grigiomar** (Via Pietro Giuria 42r; ⏲9am-6pm Mon-Fri, 9am-1pm Sat) salts its own local anchovies. Then there are the local *amaretti* biscuits, made with bitter and sweet almonds, available at **Pasticceria Besio** (www.amarettibesio.com; Via Sormano 16r; ⏲2.30-7pm Mon, 9am-7pm Tue-Sat), and the *farinata di grano* (wheat-flour pancakes) at **Vino e Farinata** (Via Pia 15; meals €20; ⏲11am-10pm Tue-Sat).

The Drive ≫ Rejoin the A10 and leave the industrial chimneys of Savona behind you. For the first 13km the A10 continues with views of the sea, then at Spotorno it ducks inland for the final 15km to the Finale Ligure

A26
A10 SS1
Itri
Pegli
nzano
Genoa
START ❶

Golfo di Genova

🔗 LINK YOUR TRIP

4 **Gourmet Piedmont**
Up the A6 from foodtown Savona is Slow Food HQ Bra and the start of a gourmet tour of the Langhe.

5 **Meandering the Maritime Alps**
From Ventimiglia slice through France on the D6204 to Limone Piemonte to start an adventure in the Maritime Alps.

exit. Descend steeply for 3km to the Finale hamlets on the coast.

– – – – – – – – – – – – –

TRIP HIGHLIGHT

❸ Finale Ligure

Finale Ligure comprises several seaside districts. The marina is narrow and charming, spreading along the sandy shore between two small rivers, the Porra and the Sciusa. East of the Sciusa is Finale Ligure Pia, where you'll find **Alimentari Magnone** (Via Moletti 17), which stocks excellent extra virgin olive oils from local growers. Nearby the Benedictine abbey houses the **Azienda Agricola Apiario Benedettino** (Via Santuario 59; ◷9am-12.30pm Mon-Sat), where you can buy honey, grappa and organic beauty products.

At the other end of town, **Finalborgo** is the old medieval centre. Each year in March, Finalborgo's cloisters are home to the **Salone**

dell'Agroalimentare Ligure**, where local farmers hawk seasonal delicacies and vintages.

On Thursday it's worth driving 9km up the coast to picturesque **Noli** for the weekly outdoor market on Corso d'Italia.

🍴 🛏 p97

The Drive » Once again take the high road away from the coast and follow the A10 for a further 35km to Alassio. Near Albenga you'll cross the river Centa and the broad valley where dozens of hothouses dot the landscape.

– – – – – – – – – – – – –

TRIP HIGHLIGHT

❹ Alassio

Less than 100km from the French border, Alassio's popularity among the 18th- and 19th-century jet set has left it with an elegant colonial character. Its pastel-hued villas range around a broad, sandy beach, which stretches all the way to **Laigueglia** (4km to the south). American

ROLINSKY/GETTY IMAGES ©

president Thomas Jefferson holidayed here in 1787 and Edward Elgar composed *In the South* inspired by his stay in 1904. **Il Muretto**, a ceramic-covered wall, records the names of 550 celebrities who've passed through.

Follow the local lead and promenade along Via XX Settembre or the unspoilt waterfront. Take coffee at **Antico Caffè Pasticceria Balzola** (www.balzola1902.com; Piazza Matteotti 26; ◷9am-midnight Tue-Sun) and enjoy gelato on the beach beneath a stripy umbrella.

🛏 p97

SAN GIORGIO

Cult restaurant **San Giorgio** (☎0183 40 01 75; www.ristorantesangiorgio.net; Via A Volta 19, Cervo; meals €40-60; ◷12.30-2pm & 7.30-10pm Wed-Mon, closed Jan) has been quietly wowing gourmets with its authentic Ligurian cooking since the 1950s when mother-and-son team Caterina and Alessandro opened the doors of their home in the *borgo* (medieval town) of **Cervo Alta**. Dine out on the bougainvillea-draped terrace in summer, or in intimate dining rooms cluttered with family silverware and antiques in winter. Below the restaurant, in an old oil mill, is the less formal wine bar and deli **San Giorgino**.

Genoa Fountain in the Piazza de Ferrari

The Drive » If you have time take the scenic coast road, SS1 (Via Roma), from Alassio through Laigueglia and Marina di Andora to Imperia. It is a shorter and more scenic jaunt when traffic is light. The alternative, when traffic is heavy, is to head back to the A10.

❺ Imperia

Imperia consists of two small seaside towns, Oneglia and Porto Maurizio, on either side of the Impero river.

Oneglia, birthplace of Admiral Doria, the Genoese Republic's greatest naval hero, is the less attractive of the two, although **Piazza Dante**, with its arcaded walkways, is a pleasant place to grab a coffee. This is also where the great olive-oil dynasties made their name. Visit the **Museo dell'Olio** (www. museodellolivo.com; Via Garessio 13; adult/reduced €5/2.50; ⏰9am-12.30pm & 3-6.30pm Mon-Sat), housed in a lovely art-nouveau mansion belonging to the heritage Fratelli Carli factory. The museum is surprisingly extensive and details the history of the Ligurian industry from the 2nd century BC. Buy quality oil here or anywhere in town.

West of Oneglia is pirate haven **Porto Maurizio**, perched on a rocky spur that overlooks a yacht-filled harbour.

The Drive » Rejoining the A10 at Imperia, the landscape begins to change. The olive terraces are dense, spear-like cypresses and umbrella pines shade the hillsides, and the fragrant *maquis* (Mediterranean scrub) is prolific. Loop inland around Taggia and then descend slowly into San Remo.

TRIP HIGHLIGHT

❻ San Remo

San Remo, Italy's wannabe Monte Carlo, is a sun-dappled Mediterranean resort with a grand

DETOUR: L'ENTROTERRA

Start: ❼ Ventimiglia

The designation 'Riviera' omits the pleated, mountainous interior – *l'entroterra* – that makes up nine-tenths of Liguria. Harried by invasions, coast-dwellers took to these vertical landscapes over a thousand years ago, hewing their perched villages from the rock face of the Maritime Alps. You'll want to set aside two extra days to drive the coiling roads that rise up from Ventimiglia to **Dolceacqua**, **Apricale** and **Pigna**. If you do make the effort, book into gorgeous boutique hotel **Apricus Locanda** (📞 339 6008622; www.apricuslocanda.com; Via IV Novembre 5, Apricale; s/d €95/105; 🅿🐕); it's worth it for the breakfast and see-forever panoramas.

belle-époque **casino** (www.casinosanremo.it; Corso degli Inglesi) and lashings of Riviera-style grandeur.

During the mid-19th century the city became a magnet for European exiles such as Czar Nicolas of Russia, who favoured the town's balmy winters. They built an onion-domed **Russian Orthodox church** (Via Nuvoloni 2; €1; 🕐9.30am-noon & 3-6pm) reminiscent of Moscow's St Basil's Cathedral, which still turns heads down by the seafront. Swedish inventor Alfred Nobel also maintained a villa here, the **Villa Nobel** (Corso Felice Cavallotti 112; adult/reduced €5.50/4; 🕐10am-12.30pm Tue-Thu, 10am-12.30pm & 5-8pm Fri-Sun Jun-Sep), **which**

now houses a museum dedicated to him.

Beyond the waterfront, San Remo hides a little-visited old town, a labyrinth of twisting lanes that cascade down the Ligurian hillside. Curling around the base is the **Italian Cycling Riviera**, a path that tracks the coast as far as Imperia. For bike hire, enquire at the **tourist office** (www.visitrivieradeifiori.it; Largo Nuvoloni 1; 🕐9am-7pm Mon-Sat, 9am-1pm Sun; 🛈).

🍴 🛏 p97

The Drive ⟩⟩ For the final 17km stretch to Ventimiglia take the SS1 coastal road, which hugs the base of the mountains and offers uninterrupted sea views. In summer and at Easter, however, when traffic is heavy, your best bet is the A10.

❼ Ventimiglia

Despite its enviable position between the glitter of San Remo and the Côte d'Azur, Ventimiglia is a soulful but disorderly border town, its Roman past still evident in its bridges, amphitheatre and ruined baths. Now it's the huge **Friday market** (🕐8am-3pm Fri) that draws the crowds.

If you can't find a souvenir here then consider one of the prized artisanal honeys produced by **Marco Ballestra** (📞0184 35 16 72; www.ilmieledelbrichetto.it; Via Girolamo Rossi 5), which has hives in the hills above the Valle Roya. There are over a dozen different types.

To end the tour head over to the pretty western suburb of Ponte San Ludovico to the **Giardini Botanici Hanbury** (www.giardinihanbury.com; Corso Montecarlo 43; adult/reduced €9/7.50; 🕐9.30am-6pm), the 18-hectare estate of English businessman Sir Thomas Hanbury; he planted it with an extravagant 5800 botanical species from five continents.

🍴 p97

Eating & Sleeping

Genoa ❶ see also p46

✖ Il Marin   Seafood €€€

(Eataly Genova; ☎010 869 87 22; www.eataly.
net; Porto Antico; meals €50; ◷ noon-3pm &
7-10.30pm) **Eating by the water often means a
compromise in quality, but Eataly's 3rd-floor
fine-dining space delivers both panoramic port
views and Genoa's most innovative seafood
menu.** Rustic wooden tables, Renzo Piano–
blessed furniture and an open kitchen make
for an easy, relaxed glamour, while dishes use
unusual Mediterranean-sourced produce and
look gorgeous on the plate.

Finale Ligure ❸

✖ Osteria ai Cuattru Canti   Osteria €

(Via Torcelli 22; set menus €20; ◷ noon-2pm
& 8-10pm Tue-Sun) **Simple and good Ligurian
specialities are cooked up at this rustic place in
Finalborgo's historic centre.**

🛏 Val Ponce   Agriturismo €

(☎329 3154169; www.valleponci.it; Val Ponci
22, Localita Verzi; d/apt €85/165) **Only 4km
from the beach, Val Ponce feels deliciously wild,
tucked away in a rugged Ligurian valley.** Horses
graze, grapevines bud and the restaurant turns
out fresh Ligurian dishes, with vegetables
and herbs from a kitchen garden. On weekend
evenings and Sunday lunch, there's live music
or classic vinyl. Rooms are simple but show the
keen eye of the Milanese escapee owners.

🛏 Hotel Florenz   Hotel €€

(☎019 69 56 67; www.hotelflorenz.it; Via Celesia
1; s/d €86/132; ◷ closed Nov & Feb; P @ 🐾)
**This rambling 18th-century former convent just
outside Finalborgo's village walls (800m from
the sea) is simple and homey but one of the
area's most atmospheric spots to sleep.**

Alassio ❹

🛏 Villa della Pergola   Boutique Hotel €€€

(☎0182 64 61 30; www.villadellapergola.com;
Via Privata Montagu 9/1; d from €315; P 🐾)
**Sitting in a tropical garden that rivals the
famous Villa Hanbury, Villa della Pergola was the
home of eminent Victorian, General McMurdo.**
He bought the plot in 1875 and designed the
villa in Anglo-Indian style with large airy rooms,
broad verandahs and cascading terraces with
peerless sea views.

San Remo ❻

✖ Ristorante Urbicia Vivas   Ligurian €€

(☎0184 57 55 66; Piazza Dolori 5; meals €30;
◷10.30am-midnight) **Basking in a quiet
medieval square in San Remo's remarkable old
town, Urbicia is slavishly faithful to old Ligurian
recipes with a strong bias towards seafood.**
There's a €12 lunch deal and Friday night is
risotto night.

🛏 Hotel Liberty   Hotel €

(☎0184 50 99 52; www.hotellibertysanremo.
com; Rondò Garibaldi 2; s €55, d €85-100;
P ❄) **A 10-room hotel is set in a Liberty-style
villa off a small traffic circle about 100m from
the train station. It's quiet, clean and run by
helpful young owners.**

Ventimiglia ❼

✖ Pasta & Basta   Ligurian €

(☎0184 23 08 78; www.pastaebastaventimiglia.
com; Via Marconi 20; meals €20; ◷ noon-3pm
& 7-10pm Tue-Sun, lunch only Mon) **Duck into
the underpass near the seafront on the border
side of town to the perpetually redeveloping
port area.** Various house-made fresh pasta can
be mixed and matched with a large menu of
sauces, including a good pesto or *salsa di noci*
(walnut purée), and washed down with a carafe
of pale and refreshing Pigato, a local white.

Cinematic Cinque Terre

7

From the Portofino peninsula, via the Cinque Terre's cliff-side villages to Portovenere, this trip exudes Riviera glamour. But amid billionaire motor yachts you'll find a hard-working community.

TRIP HIGHLIGHTS

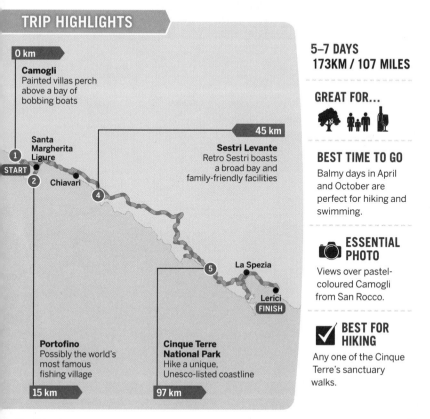

0 km

Camogli
Painted villas perch above a bay of bobbing boats

Santa Margherita Ligure
1
START
2
Chiavari
4

45 km

Sestri Levante
Retro Sestri boasts a broad bay and family-friendly facilities

5
La Spezia

Lerici
FINISH

Portofino
Possibly the world's most famous fishing village

15 km

Cinque Terre National Park
Hike a unique, Unesco-listed coastline

97 km

5–7 DAYS
173KM / 107 MILES

GREAT FOR...

BEST TIME TO GO

Balmy days in April and October are perfect for hiking and swimming.

ESSENTIAL PHOTO

Views over pastel-coloured Camogli from San Rocco.

BEST FOR HIKING

Any one of the Cinque Terre's sanctuary walks.

que Terre Manarola

7

Cinematic Cinque Terre

Challenged by a landscape of soaring mountains, Ligurian farmers have been reclaiming the Levante's wild slopes with neatly banded stone terraces for over 2000 years. The work that went into them took centuries and is comparable, it is said, to the building of the Great Wall of China. Planted with olives, grapes, basil and garlic, they snake from sea level to crest gravity-defying precipices and are now protected as a Unesco World Heritage Site.

TRIP HIGHLIGHT

❶ Camogli

Still an authentic fishing village with tall, *trompe l'œil* painted villas and a broad curving beach, Camogli's name is said to derive from *case delle mogli* (the wives' houses) for the women left behind when their husbands went fishing. In the 19th century it had the largest merchant fleet in the Mediterranean, but now it's a charming holiday spot for week-ending Milanese who

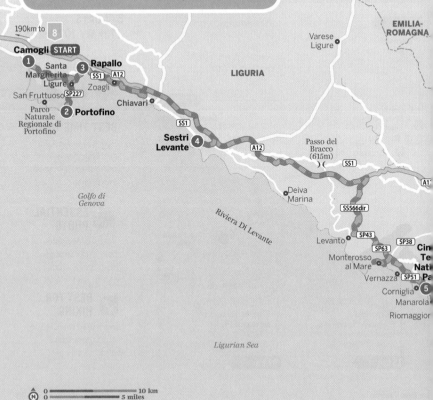

shop for supplies in the Wednesday **market** (Via 20 Settembre; ⊘8am-1pm).

Fishing traditions also continue here, such as the *tonnara di Punta Chiappa,* a large, complex fishing net between Camogli and San Fruttuoso, which is used for the trapping of tuna between April and September. It's been here since the 1600s and during the season it's pulled up by hand once or twice a day. Boats leave from Via Garibaldi to the **Punta Chiappa** where you can swim and sunbathe in

summer. In May the village celebrates the **Sagra del Pesce** (Fish Festival) with a huge fry-up – hundreds of fish are cooked in 3m-wide pans along the busy waterfront.

For the best views in town, take a short drive up to **San Rocco di Camogli**, a small hamlet wrapped in olive groves with panoramic views. Trailheads crossing **Monte di Portofino** start here.

✕ ⊫ p106

The Drive ≫ Climb out of Camogli and pick up the SS1 in the direction of Santa Margherita Ligure. The cypress-lined road sweeps around the headland past gloriously grand villas. Just past San Lorenzo della Costa, exit right and descend steeply into Santa Margherita. When you hit the waterfront turn right on Corso Marconi (SP227), past Villa Durazzo, and follow the waterfront 5km to Portofino.

- - - - - - - - - - -

TRIP HIGHLIGHT

➋ Portofino

With its striking setting and pastel-hued villas framed by the dense pine-covered slopes of the peninsula, Portofino ranks among the world's most famous fishing villages. A favourite destination of billionaires and celebrities, it has long been exclusive and expensive. In the late 16th century, aristocratic traveller Giambattista Confalonieri complained, 'You were charged not only for the room, but for the very air you breathed'.

Surprisingly, though, the best experience in Portofino is free: a hike along one of the 60km of trails that criss-cross the natural **park** (www. parks.it/parco.portofino). Enquire at the tourist office for maps. You can walk the full 18km from Portofino to Camogli, via San Fruttuoso. Otherwise take the Salita San Giorgio stairs from the harbour, past the **Chiesa di San Giorgio**, to Portofino's unusual **Castello Brown** (www.castellobrown. com; Via alla Penisola 13a; €5; ⊘10am-7pm summer, 10am-5pm Sat & Sun winter). In 1867 it became the

75km to
26
● Pontremoli
A15

TUSCANY

A15

Varo

.a Spezia
A15   A12
SS1
SP331
70
SS530   **Lerici** ➐
6   **FINISH**
tovenere   Tellaro ●
Isola   Parco di
Palmaria   Montemarcello-
Magra
Isola
del Tino

 LINK YOUR TRIP

 Northern Cities
Swap the coastal scenery for the cultural cities of the Po plain by driving north to Milan (Milano) on the A7.

26 **Foodie Emilia-Romagna**
From Lerici, head up the A15 to Parma to sample the gourmet hams, cheese and pasta of Emilia-Romagna.

private home of British diplomat Montague Yeats Brown, who no doubt derived endless pleasure from the spectacular views from its garden.

✕ ⤸ p106

The Drive » This short 9km seafront drive is fantastically scenic. Taking the only road out of town (SP227), follow its path back to Santa Margherita, where you can take a quick stroll in the gorgeous gardens of Villa Durazzo. The rest of the journey wends its way through Santa Margherita, which merges almost seamlessly with Rapallo.

③ Rapallo

WB Yeats, Max Beer-bohm and Ezra Pound all garnered inspiration in Rapallo and it's not difficult to see why. Set on a curving bay lined with striped umbrellas and palm trees, and backed by the 1900m Montal-legro, Rapallo is the picture of Riviera living.

On Thursday the historic centre comes alive when weekly market stalls fill **Piazza Cile**. Otherwise stroll the gorgeous **Lungomare Vittorio Veneto**, explore temporary exhibitions in the castle and take the 1934-vintage **cable car** (Piazzale Solari 2; one way/return €5.50/8; ☺9am-12.30pm & 2-5pm) up to the **Santuario Basilico di Montallegro** (612m), built on the spot where the Virgin Mary was reportedly sighted in 1557. Given the

heavenly view, it's hardly surprising.

✕ ⤸ p106

The Drive » You can do the 25km drive from Rapallo to Sestri Levante all along the autostrada if you're pressed for time. Otherwise, it's worth taking the more scenic route out of Rapallo along the coast road (SS1) through Zoagli and rejoining the autostrada just before Chiavari (famous for its *farinata* flat bread). From here

it's a further 13km to Sestri Levante.

TRIP HIGHLIGHT

④ Sestri Levante

Set in a broad flat valley with a long sandy beach and two sheltered bays, Sestri, as the locals call it, has something of a 1950s feel. This might have something to do with the striped umbrel-

Sestri Levante Baia del Silenzio (Bay of Silence)

las that dot the beach, the old-style refreshment kiosks, play areas and amusements along the waterfront and the meandering cycle paths where well-dressed ladies pedal with brightly coloured towels in their baskets. Many of the beachfront apartments are owned by Milanese and Genovese families, so you can be sure of a high standard of restaurants, cafes and ice-cream shops in the densely packed historic centre, which sits squeezed between the **Baia del Silenzio** (Bay of Silence) and the **Baia della Favola** (Bay of Fairy Tales), the latter named after fairy-tale author Hans Christian Andersen, who lived in Sestri in the early 19th century.

Aside from the fabulous beachfront, Sestri is surrounded by olive trees, and family owned **Frantoio Bo** (www.frantoio-bo.it; Via della Chiusa 70; ⊘8.30am-6pm Mon-Sat) makes some of the finest oil on the Riviera. The top of the line is called Le Due Baie (The Two Bays) and is composed of handpicked Lavagnina, Razzola and Pignola olives.

🛏 p107

The Drive ›› From Sestri head southeast onto the A12 autostrada for the 42km drive to the Monterosso al Mare. The first 13km are uneventful, but once you exit onto the SS566dir to Monterosso you descend steeply through the forested mountains along an improbable mountain road. The views, across deep valleys to the sea, are superb. There are two car parks on either side of the village: Fegina (€12 per day) and Loreto (€15 per day).

TRIP HIGHLIGHT

❺ Cinque Terre National Park

Five dramatically perched seaside villages – **Corniglia, Monterosso al Mare, Vernazza**, , **Manarola** and **Riomaggiore** – make up the five communities of the Unesco-protected **Parco Nazionale delle Cinque Terre** (http://parconazionale5terre.it). A site of genuine and marvellous beauty, it may not be the undiscovered Eden it was 100 years ago, but frankly – who cares? Sinuous paths traverse seemingly impregnable cliffs, while a 19th-century railway line cuts through coastal tunnels linking village to village. Cars are banned, so park in Monterosso or Riomaggiore, and take to the hills on foot or skirt the spectacular cliffs by boat.

Rooted in antiquity, the Cinque Terre's five towns date from the early medieval period, and include several castles and a quintet of illustrious parish churches. Buildings aside, the Cinque Terre's most unique feature is the steeply terraced cliffs banded by a complicated system of fields and gardens that have been chiselled, shaped and layered over the course of two millennia. Since the 2011 floods, many of the Cinque Terre's walking paths have been in a delicate state. While most of the spectacular network of trails is open and you can plan some excellent village-to-village hikes along 30 numbered paths, only part of the iconic **Sentiero Azzurro** (Blue Path; No 2 on maps) is open. To hike any of the trails you must purchase a Cinque Terre card.

From late March to October, the **Consorzio Marittimo Turistico Cinque Terre Golfo dei Poeti** (www.navigazione golfodeipoeti.it) runs daily shuttle boats between the villages.

🍴 🛏 p107

The Drive ›› If the roads are busy take the longer, 67km autostrada route via the A12 and A15. However, if you have more time you can take the more scenic, but winding SP51 and SS370 through the mountains of the Cinque Terre National Park until you hit the coast just south of La Spezia. From here turn southwards on the SS530 for the final 12km coastal drive into Portovenere.

TOP TIP: CINQUE TERRE CARD

The best way to get around the Cinque Terre is with the Cinque Terre card (one/two days €7.50/14, four-person family card €19.60), which gives you unlimited use of walking paths and electric village buses, as well as the elevator in Riomaggiore and cultural exhibitions. With the addition of train travel, a one-/two-day card is €12/23, while a four-person family card costs €31.50.

Cards are sold at all Cinque Terre park **information offices** (www.parconazionale5terre.it; ⏱7am-8pm), located in the village train stations.

❻ Portovenere

If the Cinque Terre had to pick an honorary sixth member, Portovenere would surely be it. Perched on the western promontory of the Gulf of Poets (Shelley and Byron were regulars here), the village's seven-storey houses form a citadel around **Castello Doria** (adult/reduced

€5/3; ⏲10.30am-6.30pm summer, 10.30am-5pm Sat & Sun winter). No one knows the origins of the castle, although Portus Veneris was a Roman base en route from Gaul to Spain. The current structure dates from the 16th century and offers wonderful views from its terraced gardens. Just off the promontory you'll spy the tiny islands of Palmaria, Tino and Tinetto.

The wave-lashed **Chiesa di San Pietro** sits atop a Roman temple dedicated to the goddess Venus (born from the foam of the sea) from whom Portovenere takes its name. At the end of the quay a Cinque Terre panorama unfolds from the **Grotta Arpaia**, a former haunt of Lord Byron, who once swam across the gulf to Lerici to visit his fellow romantic, Shelley.

✗ p107

The Drive ›› Head north to La Spezia via the SS530 and cross through town to exit eastwards on the SP331. Driving along waterfront boulevards lined with umbrella pines you'll pass La Spezia's marina, then go through suburbs such as San Terenzo, until at Pugliola you turn right onto the SP28 and climb up the villa-lined road into Lerici.

SANCTUARY WALKS

Each of Cinque Terre's villages is associated with a sanctuary perched high on the cliff sides. Reaching these religious retreats used to be an act of penance, but these days the walks are for pure pleasure.

» **Monterosso to Santuario della Madonna di Soviore** Follow trail No 9 up through forest to Liguria's oldest sanctuary.

» **Vernazza to Santuario della Madonna di Reggio** Follow trail No 8 past 14 sculpted Stations of the Cross to this 11th-century chapel with a Romanesque facade.

» **Corniglia to Santuario della Madonna delle Grazie** Ascend the spectacular Sella di Comeneco on trail No 7 to this church with its adored image of the Madonna and Child.

» **Manarola to Santuario della Madonna delle Salute** The pick of all the sanctuary walks is this breathtaking traverse (trail No 6) through Cinque Terre's finest vineyards.

» **Riomaggiore to Santuario della Madonna di Montenero** Trail No 3 ascends to this frescoed 18th-century chapel that sits atop an astounding viewpoint.

- - - - - - - - - - - -

7 **Lerici**

Magnolia, yew and cedar trees grow in the 1930s public gardens at Lerici, an exclusive retreat of handsome villas that cling to the cliffs along its beach. In another age Byron and Shelley sought inspiration here and gave the Gulf of Poets its name. The Shelleys stayed at the waterfront **Villa Magni** (closed to visitors) in the early 1820s but sadly Percy drowned here when his boat sank off the coast in 1822.

From Lerici a scenic 4km stroll takes you south past the magnificent bay of Fiascherino to **Tellaro**, a fishing hamlet with pink-and-orange houses cluttered about narrow lanes and tiny squares. Sit on the rocks at the **Chiesa San Giorgio** and imagine an octopus ringing the church bells – which, according to legend, it did to warn the villagers of a Saracen attack.

🛏 p107

Eating & Sleeping

Camogli ❶

✕ La Bossa di Mario — Seafood €€

(📞0185 77 25 05; www.labossa.it; Via della Repubblica 124; meals €25-35; ☺6pm-midnight Thu-Tue) You'll drink your fill of over 130 fine local and Italian wines in this elegant bar. To accompany them, choose something off the seasonal menu, such as Camogli tuna on a bed of the sweetest vine tomatoes, or the raw fish of the day with a squeeze of citrus and fragrant coriander.

✕ La Cucina di Nonna Nina — Trattoria €€

(📞0185 77 38 55; www.nonnanina.it; Viale Franco Molfino 126, San Rocco di Camogli; meals €35-50; ☺12.30-2.30pm & 7.30-10pm Thu-Tue) In the leafy heights of San Rocco di Camogli you'll find the only Slow Food–recommended restaurant along the coast, named for grandmother Nina, whose heirloom recipes have been adapted with love by Paolo Delphin. Your culinary odyssey will include fabulous traditional dishes such as air-dried cod stewed with pine nuts, potatoes and local Taggiasca olives, and *rossetti* (minnow) and artichoke soup.

🛏 Villa Rosmarino — B&B €€

(📞0185 77 15 80; www.villarosmarino.com; Via Figari 38; d €140-280; 🅿 ❄ 🛜 🏊) Villa Rosmarino's motto is 'you don't stay, you live' and it's apt. Simply taking in the views here is life affirming. This elegant pink 1907 villa is a typical Ligurian beauty on the outside, a calming oasis of modernity on the inside.

🛏 Hotel Cenobio dei Dogi — Hotel €€€

(📞0185 72 41; www.cenobio.com; Via Cuneo 34; s/d €130/220; 🅿 ❄ 🛜 🏊) The Cenobio's name means 'gathering place of the doges', and yes, the Genovese dukes used to holiday here aeons ago. A private beach and saltwater swimming pool signal you're in the Riviera, as do the 105 refined, if old-fashioned, rooms.

Portofino ❷

✕ Ristorante Puny — Ligurian €€

(📞0185 26 90 37; Piazza Martiri dell'Olivetta; meals €40; ☺ noon-3pm & 7-11pm Wed-Fri) Puny's harbourside location is the one you've come to Portofino for and the owners treat everyone like they're a visiting celeb. The food sticks loyally to Ligurian specialities, especially seafood.

🛏 Eden — Boutique Hotel €€€

(📞0185 26 90 91; www.hoteledenportofino. com; Vico Dritto 18; s €80-160, d €140-290; 🅿 ❄) Pretty and unpretentious Eden feels like it slipped out of an EM Forster novel. Its floral wallpaper and residence-hotel appeal is coupled with a great location, 100m up a quiet cobbled side street from the harbour.

Rapallo ❸

✕ Vecchia Rapallo — Seafood €€

(📞0185 5 00 53; www.vecchiarapallo.com; Via Cairoli 20/24; meals €30; ☺ noon-2.30pm & 6-11pm daily summer, shorter hours winter) Seafood is the star here, and it's done well with the occasional creative touch. House-made stuffed pastas have particular appeal – snapper ravioli comes with beetroot and prawn sauce, while a chard-filled variety is shaved with truffles. There's a cocktail and wine bar if you're just after a drink too.

🛏 Europa Hotel Design Spa 1877 — Hotel €€

(📞0185 66 95 21; www.gruppoplinio.it/ europahotel; Via Milite Ignoto 2; s €80-170, d €135-225; 🅿 ❄ 🛜) Close to the beach and with its own spa facilities – a thermal bath and steam room – this recently refurbished place is super relaxing. Whitewashed rooms are pretty but modern while public areas do the shiny Italian glam thing.

Sestri Levante ④

🛏 Hotel Helvetia · Hotel €€€

(📞0185 4 11 75; www.hotelhelvetia.it; Via Cappuccini 43; d €170-350; 🅿 @ ✺) Leaning over the invisible edge of the swimming pool and gazing down on the Baia del Silenzio and the broad curve of the beach, you have to agree that few hotels can rival Helvetia's views. Then there's the private beach, the terrace restaurant and cool white rooms with balconies or garden views.

Cinque Terre National Park ⑤

🍷 La Scuna · Bar

(📞347 7997527; Via Fieschi 185, Corniglia; 🕒9am-1am late-March–Nov) Vinyl, beer and a panoramic terrace? This bastion of hipsterdom comes as a surprise in this most traditional of regions but Andrea's welcome is warm and the beers on tap are both cold and a cut way above bottled Peroni.

✕ Miky · Seafood €€€

(📞0187 81 76 08; www.ristorantemiky.it; Lungomare Fegina 104, Monterosso; meals €45-60; 🕒noon-2.30pm & 7-10pm Wed-Mon summer) If you're looking for something a little more elegant than a seafront fry-up, Miky does a seasonal fish menu in a moody, modern dining room. Booking ahead is advised. If you miss out on a table, casual beach-side tables are available at its cantina (wine bar); ask for directions.

🛏 Gianni Franzi Rooms · B&B €€

(📞0187 82 10 03; www.giannifranzi.it; Via San Giovanni Battista 41, Vernazza; d €130; 🛜) Spread over two locations, one above the attached restaurant, the other up the hill, rooms here are an atmospheric mix of antique furniture and super simple traditional architecture, all kept with care. Breakfast on their deck delivers not just cornetti and cappucino, but sublime sea-drenched views; there's a small garden under the Doria castle for guest use.

🛏 Hotel Pasquale · Hotel €€

(📞0187 81 74 77; www.hotelpasquale.it; Via Fegina 4, Monterosso; s €80-160, d €140-220, tr €170-300; 🕒Mar–mid-Nov; ❄ 🛜) Offering soothing views and 15 unusually stylish, modern guest rooms, this friendly seafront hotel is built into Monterosso's medieval sea walls. To find it, exit the train station and go left through the tunnel towards the centro storico.

Portovenere ⑥

✕ Anciua · Street Food €

(📞331 7719605; Via Cappellini 40; snacks from €5; 🕒10am-7pm) A perfect spot to pick up something to snack on while dangling your feet in the nearby water, this is Ligurian street food made with love. Grab a panini stuffed with anchovies or cod and olive paste, or pick up a whole spinach pie for a picnic. The sweet, fragrant rice-pudding cake is also highly recommended.

Lerici ⑦

🛏 Locanda Miranda · Inn €€

(📞0187 96 40 12; www.locandamiranda.com; Via Fiascherina 92; d €100, set menus €40-60; 🅿) Tellaro, a few kilometres around the bay from Lerici proper, is home to this gourmet hideaway, a traditional seven-room inn with art- and antiques-decorated rooms, and a Michelin-starred restaurant specialising exclusively in seafood. Half-board packages can be arranged.

Northern Cities

The Po valley, with its waving fields of corn and rice paddies, hosts some of Italy's most handsome and prosperous towns, from Milan and Bergamo in the west to Verona and Venice in the east.

TRIP HIGHLIGHTS

395 km

Venice
Explore the drama and intrigue of the Palazzo Ducale

257 km

Verona
Shout 'Brava!' for opera diva encores at the Arena

Bergamo

Vicenza

Mestre

Milan
START

6

Soave

7

8
FINISH

5

219 km

Mantua
Renown for Mantegna's frescoes and fine dining

334 km

Padua
See the Renaissance dawning in Giotto's moving frescoes

7–10 DAYS
395KM / 245 MILES

GREAT FOR...

BEST TIME TO GO
September to May to avoid the crowds.

ESSENTIAL PHOTO
The golden domes and precious mosaics of San Marco in Venice.

BEST FOR SURPRISES
The little-known treasures in Bergamo's Accademia Carrara.

8 Northern Cities

Ever since Julius Caesar granted Roman citizenship to the people of the plains, the Po valley has prospered. Wend your way through the cornfields from the Lombard powerhouse of Milan to Roman Brixia (Brescia), the Gonzaga stronghold of Mantua and the serene Republic of Venice. This is a land of legends spun by Virgil, Dante and Shakespeare, where grand dynasties fought for power and patronised some of the finest works of art in the world.

① Milan

From Charlemagne to Napoleon, and even Silvio Berlusconi, mercantile Milan (Milano) has always attracted the moneyed and the Machiavellian. Follow the city's changing fortunes through the frescoed halls of the **Castello Sforzesco** (☎02 8846 3703; www.milanocastello.it; Piazza Castello; adult/reduced €5/3; ☺9am-7.30pm Tue-Sun, to 10.30pm Thu; Ⓜ Cairoli), some of them decorated by Leonardo da Vinci, where exquisite

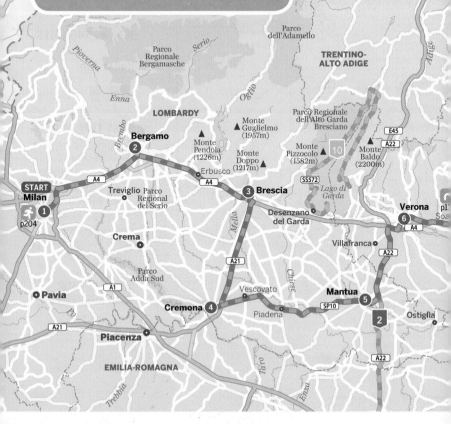

sculptures, paintings and weapons tell the turbulent tale of the city. From its ramparts, look out over the **Parco Sempione** and spy the pearly pinnacles of the **Duomo** (www.duomomilano. it; Piazza del Duomo; roof terraces adult/reduced via stairs €11/6, lift €15/8, Battistero di San Giovanni €4/2; ☉ duomo 8am-7pm, roof terraces 9am-7pm, battistero 9am-6pm Tue-Sun; M Duomo). Begun in 1387 the Duomo took six centuries to build, rushed to completion in the 19th century so that Napoleon could crown

himself King of Italy in its cavernous interior.

True to Milan's spirit of free enterprise, one of the city's finest art collections is the private collection of **Museo Poldi Pezzoli** (☎02 79 48 89; www.museopol-dipezzoli.it; Via Alessandro Manzoni 12; adult/reduced €10/7; ☉10am-6pm Wed-Mon; M Montenapoleone), where priceless Bellinis and Botticellis hang in Pezzoli's 19th-century *palazzo* (mansion). From here walk around the city's nearby 'Golden

Quadrangle' of designer shops (p204).

✕ p116

The Drive » Make your way northeast out of town along Corso Venezia, or via the ring road, depending on where you're staying in town. Merge with the A4 Milan–Brescia autostrada for an uneventful 56km drive to Bergamo.

----

② Bergamo

Beautiful Bergamo, its domes and towers piled on a promontory at the foot of the Alps, is one of the most arresting urban views in Italy. Le Corbusier admired the incredible beauty of **Piazza Vecchia**, its magnificent ensemble of medieval and Renaissance buildings much influenced by Venetian fashions, with the lion

LINK YOUR TRIP

10 **A Weekend at Lake Garda**

Got an urge for the outdoors? Jump off the A4 before Verona to Desenzano del Garda and mess around Lake Garda for a weekend.

2 **World Heritage Wonders**

Further the tour of artistic and architectural blockbusters by continuing on the A22 from Mantua to Modena.

FRIULI VENEZIA-GIULIA

Livenza

VENETO

A31

Brenta

Castelfranco Veneto

Treviso

A27

A4

p206

Vicenza

A4

Mestre

A4

A57

8 Venice

Padua 7

E55

FINISH

p202

Monteforte d'Alpone

Adriatic Sea

Este

Legnago

A13

Valle Berluzzi

Po

EMILIA-ROMAGNA

Po Delta

Panaro

N 0   50 km
   0   25 miles

Reno

of St Mark's emblazoned on the **Palazzo della Ragione**.

Through the arches of the Palazzo della Ragione you'll glimpse a second square, the **Piazza Duomo**, fronted by the extraordinary polychromatic marble facade of the **Cappella Colleoni** (Piazza Duomo; ⊗9am-12.30pm & 2-6.30pm Mar-Oct, 9am-12.30pm & 2-4.30pm Tue-Sun Nov-Feb), the mausoleum-cum-chapel of Venice's most famous mercenary commander, Bartolomeo Colleoni (1696–1770).

Just east of the old city walls, the **Accademia Carrara** (☑035 23 43 96; www.lacarrara.it; Piazza Carrara 82; adult/reduced €10/8; ⊗10am-7pm) is one of Italy's great art repositories. Founded in 1780, it contains an exceptional range of Italian masters.

⚔ 🛏 p116, p129

The Drive ≫ Leave Bergamo via the *citta bassa* (lower town) southwards and rejoin the A4 in the direction of Brescia. Surprisingly this 55km stretch is relatively scenic, especially as you drive through the wine region of Franciacorta.

- - - - - - - - - - - - - -

❸ Brescia

Despite its seedy urban periphery, Brescia's old town contains some of the most important Roman ruins in Lombardy and an extraordinary, circular Roman church, the **Duomo Vecchio** (Old Cathedral;

Piazza Paolo VI; ⊗9am-noon & 3-7pm Tue-Sat, 9-10.45am & 3-7pm Sun), built over the ancient Roman baths.

From here the Via dei Musei, the ancient *decumanus maximus* (east–west main street), leads to the heart of Roman Brixia, **Piazza del Foro**, which sits beneath the columns of the **Tempio Capitolino**, erected by Vespasian in AD 73 and preserved for posterity by a medieval mudslide. Next to the ruined temple is the unexcavated *cavea* (semicircular, tiered auditorium) of the **Teatro Romano**, and beside that the **Santa Giulia** (Museo della Città; ☑030 297 78 34; www.bresciamusei.com; Via dei Musei 81; adult/reduced €10/5.50; ⊗10.30am-7pm Tue-Sun mid-Jun–Sep, shorter hours winter), a vast monastery complex and museum that charts the layers of Brescian history. Best of all are the two Roman houses, which were absorbed wholesale into the monastery. Their mosaic floors and frescoes are real highlights.

⚔ p116

The Drive ≫ Wend your way southwards out of Brescia's complicated suburbs following signs for the A21. Smaller and less heavily trafficked than the A4, the 53km drive to Cremona takes you through some unspoilt farmland dotted with the occasional farmhouse.

❹ Cremona

Famous for violins, nougat and the tallest bell tower in Italy (111m), Cremona is a charming stopover. The stout-hearted can climb the 502 steps to the top of the *campanile* for scenic views. The **cathedral** (Piazza del Comune; ⊗8am-noon & 2.30-6pm Mon-Sat, noon-12.30pm & 3.30-6pm Sun) next door is one of the most exuberant expressions of Lombard Romanesque architecture.

Aside from the views, Cremona made a name for itself as the violin capital of Europe, after Andrea Amati discovered in 1566 that with a bit of adjustment his old medieval fiddle could be made to sing the sweetest tunes. By the 18th century Andrea's son, Nicolò Amati, his pupil Antonio Stradivarius and Giuseppe Guarneri were crafting the best violins ever. See the originals in Cremona's state-of-the-art **Museo del Violino** (☑0372 08 08 09; www.museodelviolino. org; Piazza Marconi 5; adult/reduced €10/7; ⊗10am-6pm Tue-Sun). To hear them, head to the **Teatro Amilcare Ponchielli** (☑0372 02 20 01; www.teatroponchielli. it; Corso Vittorio Emanuele II 52); its season runs from October to June.

⚔ p116

Verona Roman Arena

The Drive >> You're off the main roads between Cremona and Mantua. Take Via Mantova east out of town and join the SP10. The tree-lined single carriageway passes through cornfields and the small towns of Vescovato and Piadena before reaching the watery outskirts of Mantua.

TRIP HIGHLIGHT

❺ Mantua

The Latin poet Virgil was born just outside Mantua (Mantova) in 70 BC, and the modern town preserves its antique timeline in its art and architecture. Ruled by the Gonzaga dynasty for three centuries, the court attracted artists of the highest calibre, including Pisanello, Rubens and, more famously, Andrea Mantegna, who was court painter from 1460 until his death in 1506. It's their dazzling frescoes that decorate the

Palazzo Ducale (☏041 241 18 97; www.ducalemantova. org; Piazza Sordello 40; adult/reduced €13/8; ⊙8.15am-7.15pm Tue-Sun). During busy periods you may have to book to see the biggest draw – Mantegna's 15th-century frescoes in the **Camera degli Sposi** (Bridal Chamber).

Hardly more modest in scale is the Gonzaga's suburban villa, the **Palazzo Te** (☏0376 32 32 66; www.palazzote. it; Viale Te 13; adult/reduced €12/9; ⊙1-6pm Mon, 9am-6pm Tue-Sun; P). Mainly used by Duke Federico II to rendezvous with his mistress, Isabella Boschetti, it is decorated in playboy style with playful motifs and encoded love symbols.

✕ ⊨ p116

The Drive >> From Mantua head almost directly north for Verona. Leave town on Via Legnago, crossing the causeway that separates Lago di Mezzo from Lago Inferiore, then pick up the A22 autostrada for an easy 40km drive to Verona.

TRIP HIGHLIGHT

❻ Verona

Shakespeare placed star-crossed Romeo Montague and Juliet Capulet in Verona for good reason: romance, drama and fatal family feuds have been the city's hallmark for centuries.

From the 3rd century BC, Verona was a Roman trade centre, with ancient gates, a forum (now Piazza delle Erbe) and a grand **Roman Arena** (☏045 800 32 04; www.arena.it; Piazza Brà; adult/reduced €10/7.50; ⊙8.30am-7.30pm Tue-Sun, from 1.30pm Mon), which still hosts live summer opera performances.

After Mastino della Scala (aka Scaligeri) lost

DETOUR: SOAVE

Start: ⑥ Verona (p113)

East of Verona, Soave serves its namesake DOC white wine in a storybook setting. Built by Verona's fratricidal Scaligeri family, the **Castello di Soave** (☎045 768 00 36; www.castellodisoave.it; adult/reduced €7/4; ⏰9am-noon & 3-6.30pm Tue-Sun Apr-Oct, 9am-noon & 2-4pm Nov-Mar) encompasses an early Renaissance villa, grassy courtyards and the Mastio – a defensive tower apparently used as a dungeon. More inviting is the **Azienda Agricola Coffele** (☎045 768 00 07; www.coffele.it; Via Roma 5; wine tasting €9-12; ⏰10am-1pm & 2-7pm Mon-Sat, by appointment Sun), a family-run winery across from the church in the old town, where you can taste the lemon-zesty DOC Soave Classico and the bubbly DOCG Recioto di Soave, both bearing the regional quality-control standard of the Denominazione di Origine Controllata (DOC). Or try **Locanda Lo Scudo** (p117).

re-election to Verona's *comune* in 1262, he claimed absolute control, until murdered by his rivals. On the north side of **Piazza dei Signori** stands the early Renaissance **Loggia del Consiglio**, the 15th-century city council. Through the archway you'll find the **Arche Scaligere** – elaborate tombs of the Scaligeri family, where murderers are interred next to the relatives they killed.

Paranoid for good reason, the fratricidal Cangrande II (1351–59) built the **Castelvecchio** (☎045 806 26 11; https://museodicastelvecchio.comune.verona.it; Corso Castelvecchio 2; adult/reduced €6/4.50; ⏰1.30-7.30pm Mon, 8.30am-7.30pm Tue-Sun) to guard the river Adige, which snakes through town. Now it houses Verona's main museum with works by Tiepolo, Carpaccio and Veronese.

For discounted entry to all of Verona's major monuments, museums and churches, plus unlimited travel on city buses, consider purchasing a Verona Card (24/48 hours €18/22), on sale at most major tourist sights as well as tobacconists.

✕ ⏢ p117, p183

The Drive » The 95km drive from Verona to Padua is once again along the A4. This stretch of road is heavily trafficked by heavy-goods vehicles. The only rewards are glimpses of Soave's crenellated castle to your left and the tall church spire of Monteforte d'Alpone. You could extend your trip with a stop to take in the World Heritage architecture of Vicenza.

TRIP HIGHLIGHT

⑦ Padua

Dante, da Vinci, Boccaccio and Vasari all honour Giotto as the artist who ended the Dark Ages. Giotto's startlingly humanist approach not only changed how people saw the heavenly company, it changed how they saw themselves; not as lowly vassals but as vessels for the divine, however flawed. This humanising approach was especially well suited to the **Cappella degli Scrovegni** (Scrovegni Chapel; ☎049 201 00 20; www.cappelladeglis-crovegni.it; Piazza Eremitani 8; adult/reduced €13/6, night ticket €8/6; ⏰9am-7pm), the chapel in Padua (Padova) that Enrico Scrovegni commissioned in memory of his father, who as a moneylender was denied a Christian burial. Think how radical the scenes must have been for medieval churchgoers witnessing exhausted new dad Joseph asleep in the manger or onlookers gossiping as Anne tenderly kisses Joachim.

Afterwards, tour the **Musei Civici agli Eremitani** (☎049 820 45 51; Piazza Eremitani 8; adult/reduced €10/8; ⏰9am-7pm Tue-Sun) for pre-Roman Padua downstairs and a pantheon of Veneto artists upstairs.

✖ p117, p175

The Drive ›› The 40km drive from Padua to Venice is through a tangle of suburban neighbourhoods and featureless areas of light industry along the A4 and then the A57.

- - - - - - - - - - - - - - - -

TRIP HIGHLIGHT

8 Venice

Like its signature landmark, the **Basilica di San Marco** (St Mark's Basilica; ☎041 270 83 11; www.basilicasanmarco.it; Piazza San Marco; ⏱9.45am-5pm Mon-Sat, 2-5pm Sun summer, to 4pm Sun winter; 🚤San Marco), the Venetian empire was dazzlingly cosmopolitan. Armenians, Turks, Greeks and Germans were neighbours along the **Grand Canal**, and Jewish communities persecuted elsewhere in Europe founded publishing houses and banks. By the mid-15th century, Venice (Venezia) was swathed in golden mosaics, imported silks and clouds of incense.

Don't be fooled though by the Gothic elegance: underneath the lacy pink cladding the **Palazzo Ducale** (Ducal Palace; ☎041 271 59 11; www.palazzoducale.visitmuve.it; Piazzetta San Marco 52; adult/reduced incl Museo Correr €19/12; ⏱8.30am-7pm summer, to 5.30pm winter; 🚤San Zaccaria) ran an uncompromising dictatorship. Discover state secrets on the **Itinerari Segreti** (Secret Passages; ☎041 4273 0892; adult/reduced €20.50/14.50; ⏱tours in English 9.55am, 10.45am & 11.35am, in Italian 9.30am & 11.10am, in French 10.20am & noon), a tour that takes you to the sinister Trial Chamber and Interrogation Room.

Centuries later, Napoleon took some of Venice's finest heirlooms to France. But the biggest treasure in the **Museo Correr** (☎041 4273 0892; http://correr.visitmuve.it/; Piazza San Marco 52; adult/reduced incl Palazzo Ducale €19/12; ⏱10am-7pm summer, to 5pm winter; 🚤San Marco) couldn't be lifted: Jacopo Sansovino's **Libreria Nazionale Marciana**, covered with larger-than-life philosophers by Veronese, Titian and Tintoretto.

Head for the **Gallerie dell'Accademia** (☎041 520 03 45; www.gallerieaccademia.org; Campo della Carità 1050; adult/reduced €10/8 plus supplement during special exhibitions, first Sun of the month free; ⏱8.15am-2pm Mon, to 7.15pm Tue-Sun; 🚤Accademia), whose hallowed halls contain more murderous intrigue and forbidden romance than most Venetian parties. Alternatively, immerse yourself in the lagoon larder by walking around the city's markets and bars (p202).

You cannot take your car onto the lagoon islands so leave it in a secure garage in Mestre, such as **Garage Europa** (☎041 95 92 02; www.garageeuropamestre.com; Corso del Popolo 55, Mestre; per day €15; ⏱8am-10pm), and hop on the train to Venice Santa Lucia, where water taxis connect to all the islands.

✖ 🛏 p46, p61, p117, p175

THE ORIGINAL GHETTO

In medieval times, the Cannaregio island of **Ghetto Nuovo** housed a *getto* (foundry) – but its role as Venice's designated Jewish quarter from the 16th to 18th centuries gave the word its current meaning. In accordance with the Venetian Republic's 1516 decree, Jewish lenders, doctors and clothing merchants were allowed to attend to Venice's commercial interests by day, while at night and on Christian holidays, most were restricted to the gated island of Ghetto Nuovo.

When Jewish merchants fled the Spanish Inquisition for Venice in 1541, there was no place to go in the Ghetto but up: around **Campo del Ghetto Nuovo**, upper storeys housed new arrivals, synagogues and publishing houses. Despite a 10-year censorship order issued by the church in Rome in 1553, Jewish Venetian publishers contributed hundreds of titles popularising new Renaissance ideas on religion, humanist philosophy and medicine.

Eating & Sleeping

Milan ❶

🍴 Trattoria da Pino   Milanese €

(📞02 7600 0532; Via Cerva 14; meals €20-25; 🕐noon-3pm Mon-Sat; Ⓜ San Babila) In a city full of models in Michelin-starred restaurants, working-class da Pino offers the perfect antidote. Sit elbow-to-elbow at long cafeteria-style tables and order up bowls of *bollito misto* (mixed boiled meats), handmade pasta and curried veal nuggets.

🍴 Giacomo Arengario   Bistro €€€

(📞02 7209 3814; www.giacomoarengario. com; Via Guglielmo Marconi 1; meals €50-60; 🕐noon-midnight; ❄ ; Ⓜ Duomo) The 3rd-floor bistro of the Museo del Novecento offers extraordinary views over the *duomo*. The artful decor combines beaux-arts brasswork, velvet sofas and lacquer finishes for a luxurious but understated atmosphere. Top-notch bistro fare, including fish platters, truffles and game are served by jacketed waiters. If you can, get a table on the glass-covered terrace.

Bergamo ❷   see also p129

🍴 Osteria della Birra   Osteria €€

(📞035 24 24 40; www.elavbrewery.com; Piazza Mascheroni 1; 🕐noon-3pm & 6pm-2am Mon-Fri, noon-2am Sat & Sun) Being the official *osteria* of craft brewers this convivial eatery ensures there's a top selection on tap; the tangy Indie Ale tastes particularly fine. So squeeze in at a tiny table or lounge in the courtyard and chow down on platters piled high with local meats, or polenta with beef simmered in Elav's own-brewed beer.

Brescia ❸

🍴 Osteria al Bianchi   Osteria €€

(📞030 29 23 28; www.osteriaalbianchi.it; Via Gasparo da Salò 32; meals €25; 🕐9am-2.30pm & 4.30pm-midnight Thu-Mon) Squeeze inside this classic bar, in business since 1880, or grab a pavement table and be tempted by the *pappardelle al taleggio e zucca* (broad ribbon pasta with Taleggio cheese and pumpkin), followed by anything from *brasato d'asino* (braised donkey) to *pestöm* (minced pork served with polenta).

Cremona ❹   see also p46

🍴 Hosteria '700   Cremonese €€

(📞0372 3 61 75; Piazza Gallina 1; meals €30-35; 🕐noon-3pm Wed-Mon, 7.30-10pm Wed-Sun) Behind the dilapidated facade lurks a sparkling gem. Some of the vaulted rooms come with ceiling frescoes, dark timber tables come with ancient wooden chairs, and the hearty Lombard cuisine comes at a refreshingly competitive cost.

Mantua ❺

🍴 Il Cigno   Modern Italian €€€

(📞0376 32 71 01; www. ristoranteilcignomantova.com; Piazza d'Arco 1; meals €55-65; 🕐12.30-2.30pm & 7-11pm Wed-Sun, closed part of Aug) The building is as beautiful as the food: a lemon-yellow facade dotted with faded olive-green shutters. Inside, Mantua's gourmets graze on delicately steamed risotto with spring greens, poached cod with polenta or gamey guinea fowl with spicy Mantuan *mostarda*.

🛏 C'a delle Erbe   B&B €€

(📞0376 22 61 61; www.cadelleerbe.it; Via Broletto 24; d €120-140; ❄ 🛰) In this exquisite 16th-century townhouse historic features have had a minimalist makeover: exposed stone walls surround paired-down furniture; white-painted beams coexist with lavish bathrooms and modern art. The pick of the bedrooms? The one with the balcony overlooking the iconic Piazza delle Erbe.

Verona 6 see also p183

✕ Pescheria I Masenini   Seafood €€€

(☎045 929 80 15; www.imasenini.com; Piazzetta Pescheria 9; meals €50; ☺7.30-10pm Tue, 12.30-2pm & 7.30-10pm Wed-Sun; 🛜) Located on the piazza where Verona's Roman fish market once held sway, softly lit Masenini quietly serves up Verona's most imaginative, modern fish dishes. Inspired flavour combinations might see fresh sea bass carpaccio paired with zesty green apple and pink pepper, black-ink gnocchi schmoozing with lobster *ragù*, or sliced amberjack delightfully matched with crumbed almonds, honey, spinach and raspberries.

🛏 Corte delle Pigne   B&B €€

(☎333 7584141; www.cortedellepigne.it; Via Pigna 6a; s €60-90, d €90-130, tr & q €110-150; P ❄ 🛜) In the heart of the historic centre, this three-room B&B is set around a quiet internal courtyard. It offers tasteful rooms and plenty of personal touches: sweet jars, luxury toiletries and even a jacuzzi for one lucky couple.

Soave 6

✕ Locanda Lo Scudo   Modern Italian €€

(☎045 768 07 66; www.loscudo.vr.it; Via Covergnino 9; meals €35, s/d €65/80; ☺ noon-2.30pm & 7.30-10.30pm Tue-Sat, noon-2.30pm Sun; 🛜) Just outside the medieval walls of Soave, Lo Scudo is half country inn and half high-powered gastronomy. Cult classics include a risotto of scallops and porcini mushrooms, though – if it's on the menu – only a fool would resist the extraordinary dish of tortelloni stuffed with local pumpkin, Grana Padano, cinnamon, mustard and Amaretto, and topped with crispy fried sage.

Padua 7 see also p175

☕ Caffè Pedrocchi   Cafe

(☎049 878 12 31; www.caffepedrocchi.it; Via VIII Febbraio 15; ☺9am-10pm Sun-Wed, 9am-1am Thu-Sat) Since 1831, this neoclassical landmark has been a favourite of Stendhal and other pillars of Padua's cafe society for heart-poundingly powerful coffee and *caffè correto* (coffee cocktails). The grand 1st floor is decorated in styles ranging from ancient Egyptian to Imperial, and during the day you can visit the Museo del Risorgimento e dell'Età Contemporanea.

✕ Osteria Dal Capo   Osteria €€

(☎049 66 31 05; www.osteriadalcapo.it; Via degli Obizzi 2; meals €25-35; ☺7-10.30pm Mon, 12.30-2.30pm & 7-10.30pm Tue-Sat) Rub elbows with locals – literally – at tiny tables precariously piled with traditional Venetian seafood and a few inspired novelties, such as *caviale di melanzane con bufala* (eggplant caviar with buffalo mozzarella atop crispy wafer bread). Reservations and a sociable nature advised.

Venice 8 see also p46, p61 and p175

✕ Osteria Trefanti   Venetian €€

(☎041 520 17 89; www.osteriatrefanti.it; Fondamenta Garzotti 888, Santa Croce; meals €40; ☺ noon-2.30pm & 7-10.30pm Tue-Sat, noon-2.45pm Sun; 🛜; 🚤Riva de Biasio) La Serenissima's spice trade lives on at simple, elegant Trefanti, where a dish of marinated prawns, hazelnuts, berries and caramel might get an intriguing kick from garam masala. Furnished with old pews and recycled copper lamps, it's the domain of the competent Sam Metcalfe and Umberto Slongo, whose passion for quality extends to a small, beautifully curated selection of local and organic wines.

✕ Osteria L'Orto dei Mori   Modern Italian €€

(☎041 524 36 77; www.osteriaortodeimori.com; Campo dei Mori 3386; meals €25-45; ☺12.30-3.30pm & 7.30pm-midnight Wed-Mon; 🚤Madonna dell'Orto) Not since Tintoretto lived next door has this neighbourhood seen so much action, thanks to this bustling *osteria*. Sicilian chef Lorenzo makes fresh surf-and-turf pasta daily, including squid atop spinach *tagliolini* and pasta with zucchini blossoms and scampi. Upbeat staff and fish-shaped lamps set a playful mood, and you'll be handed *prosecco* to help you endure waits for tables.

🛏 Hotel Flora   Hotel €€

(☎041 520 58 44; www.hotelflora.it; Calle Bergamaschi 2283a; d €105-365; ❄ 🛜; 🚤Santa Maria del Giglio) Down a lane from glitzy Calle Larga XXII Marzo, this ivy-covered retreat quietly outclasses brash designer neighbours with its delightful tearoom, breakfasts around the garden fountain and gym offering shiatsu massage. Guest rooms feature antique mirrors, fluffy duvets atop hand-carved beds, and tiled en-suite baths with apothecary-style amenities. Damask-clad superior rooms overlook the garden. Strollers and kids' teatime are complimentary; babysitting available.

The Graceful Italian Lakes

9

Writers from Goethe to Hemingway have lavished praise on the Italian lakes, dramatically ringed by snow-powdered mountains and garlanded by grand villas and exotic, tropical flora.

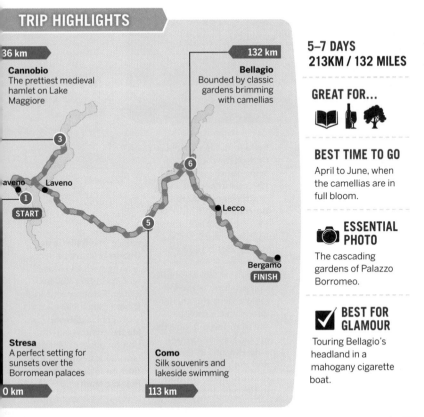

TRIP HIGHLIGHTS

36 km

Cannobio
The prettiest medieval hamlet on Lake Maggiore

132 km

Bellagio
Bounded by classic gardens brimming with camellias

Laveno · Laveno
START

Lecco

Bergamo
FINISH

Stresa
A perfect setting for sunsets over the Borromean palaces

0 km

Como
Silk souvenirs and lakeside swimming

113 km

5–7 DAYS
213KM / 132 MILES

GREAT FOR...

BEST TIME TO GO
April to June, when the camellias are in full bloom.

ESSENTIAL PHOTO
The cascading gardens of Palazzo Borromeo.

BEST FOR GLAMOUR
Touring Bellagio's headland in a mahogany cigarette boat.

agio The gardens of Villa Melzi d'Eril on the banks of Lago di Como

9 The Graceful Italian Lakes

Formed at the end of the last ice age, and a popular holiday spot since Roman times, the Italian lakes have an enduring natural beauty. At Lago Maggiore (Lake Maggiore) the palaces of the Borromean Islands lie like a fleet of fine vessels in the gulf, their grand ballrooms and shell-encrusted grottoes once host to Napoleon and Princess Diana, while the siren call of Lago di Como (Lake Como) draws Arabian sheikhs and Hollywood movie stars to its discreet forested slopes.

1 Stresa

More than Como and Garda, Lago Maggiore has retained the belle époque air of its early tourist heyday. Attracted by the mild climate and the easy access the new 1855 railway provided, the European *haute bourgeoisie* flocked to buy and build grand lakeside villas.

The star attractions are the Borromean Islands (Isole Borromee) and their palaces. **Isola Bella** took the name of Carlo III's wife, the *bella* Isabella, in the 17th century, when its centrepiece, **Palazzo Borromeo** (☎0323 3 05 56; www.isoleborromee.it; Isola Bella; adult/child €15/8.50, incl Palazzo Madre adult/child €20.50/10; ☻9am-5.30pm mid-Mar–mid-Oct) was built. Construction of the villa and gardens was thought out in such a way that the island would have the appearance of a vessel, with the villa at the prow and the gardens dripping down 10 tiered terraces at the rear. Inside the palace, the **Galleria dei Quadri** (Picture Gallery) is hung with Old Masters, including Rubens, Titian, Veronese and José Ribera (Spagnoletto).

By contrast, **Isola Madre** eschews ostentation for a more romantic, familial atmosphere. The 16th- to 18th-century **Palazzo Madre** (☎0323

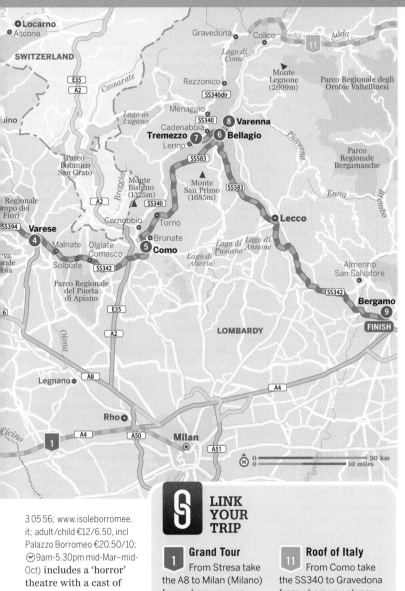

3 05 56; www.isoleborromee.
it; adult/child €12/6.50, incl
Palazzo Borromeo €20.50/10;
⊙9am-5.30pm mid-Mar–mid-
Oct) includes a 'horror'
theatre with a cast of
devilish marionettes,
while Chinese pheas-
ants stalk the English
gardens.

✕ p129

LINK YOUR TRIP

1 Grand Tour
From Stresa take
the A8 to Milan (Milano)
from where you can
commence your own
Grand Tour of Italy.

11 Roof of Italy
From Como take
the SS340 to Gravedona
from where you plunge
eastwards into the
Valtellina vineyards and
over the Alps to Merano.

Classic Trip

The Drive » Leave Stresa westwards on the Via Sempione (SS33) skirting the edge of the lake for this short, 14km drive. Pass through Baveno and round the western edge of the gulf through the greenery of the Fondo Toce natural reserve. When you reach the junction with the SS34, turn right for Verbania.

② Verbania

The late-19th-century **Villa Taranto** (📞 0323 55 66 67; www.villataranto.it; Via Vittorio Veneto 111, Verbania Pallanza; adult/reduced €10/5.50; ⏰ 8.30am-6.30pm mid-Mar–Sep, 9am-4pm Oct; 🅿) sits just outside Verbania. In 1931, royal archer and Scottish captain Neil McEacharn

bought the villa from the Savoy family and started to plant some 20,000 species. With its rolling hillsides of purple rhododendrons and camellias, acres of tulip flowers and hothouses full of equatorial lilies it is considered one of Europe's finest botanical gardens. During the last week in April, **Settimana del Tulipano** takes place, when tens of thousands of tulips erupt in magnificent multicoloured bloom.

✕ p129

The Drive » Pick up the SS34 again, continuing in a northeasterly direction out of Verbania, through the suburbs of Intra and Pallanza. Once you've cleared the town the 20km to Cannobio are the prettiest on the tour, shadowing the lake shore the entire way with views across the water.

> **DETOUR:**
> **LAGO D'ORTA**
>
> **Start: ① Stresa (p120)**
>
> Separated from Lake Maggiore by Monte Mottarone (1492m) and enveloped by thick, dark-green woodlands, Lago d'Orta would make a perfect elopers' getaway. At 13.4km long by 2.5km wide you can drive around the lake in a day. The focal point is the captivating medieval village of **Orta San Giulio**, which sits across from Isola San Giulio, where you'll spy the frescoed, 12th-century **Basilica di San Giulio** (⏰ 9.30am-6pm Tue-Sun, 2-5pm Mon Apr-Sep, 9.30am-noon & 2-5pm Tue-Sun, 2-5pm Mon Oct-Mar). Come during the week and you'll have the place largely to yourself.

TRIP HIGHLIGHT

③ Cannobio

Sheltered by a high mountain and sitting at the foot of the Cannobino valley, the medieval hamlet of Cannobio is located 5km from the Swiss border. It is a dreamy place. **Piazza di Vittorio Emanuele III**, lined with pastel-hued houses, is the location of a huge **Sunday market** that attracts visitors from Switzerland. Right in the heart of the historic centre, in a 15th-century monastery that later became the home of the Pironi family, is the atmospheric **Hotel Pironi** (📞 0323 7 06 24; www.pironihotel. it; Via Marconi 35; s €120, d €150-195, tr €185-230; 🅿🛜). Behind its thickset walls are rooms with frescoed vaults, exposed timber beams and an assortment of tastefully decorated bedrooms.

You can hire small **sailing boats** (€35/55 per one/two hours) and make an excursion to the ruined **Castelli della Malpaga**, located on two rocky islets to the south of Cannobio. In summer it is a favourite picnic spot.

Alternatively, explore the wild beauty of the Valle Cannobina up the SS631, following the surging Torrente Cannobino stream into the heavily wooded hillsides to Malesco. Just 2.5km along the valley, in Sant'Anna, the torrent forces its way powerfully through a narrow gorge known as the **Orrido di Sant'Anna**, crossed at its narrowest part by a Romanesque bridge.

The Drive » The next part of the journey involves retracing the previous 22km drive to Verbania-Intra to board the cross-lake ferry to Laveno. Ferries run every 20 minutes (one-way tickets cost €8 to €13 for car and driver). Once in Laveno pick up the SP394dir and then the SP1var and SS394 for the 23km drive to Varese.

----

④ Varese

Spread out to the south of the Campo dei Fiori hills, Varese is a prosperous provincial capital. From the 17th century onwards, Milanese nobles began to build second residences here, the most sumptuous being the **Palazzo Estense**, completed in 1771 for Francesco III d'Este, the governor of the Duchy of Milan. Although you cannot visit the palace you are free to wander the vast Italianate **gardens** (open 8am to dusk).

To the north of the city sits another great villa, **Villa Panza** (☏0332 28 39 60; www.fondoambiente. it; Piazza Litta 1; adult/reduced €10/5; ⊙10am-6pm Tue-Sun), donated to the state in 1996. Part of the donation were 150 contemporary canvases collected by Giuseppe

LAGO MAGGIORE EXPRESS

The **Lago Maggiore Express** (☏091 756 04 00; www. lagomaggioreexpress.com; adult/child 1-day tour €34/17, 2-day tour €44/22) is a picturesque day trip you can do without the car. It includes train travel from Arona or Stresa to Domodossola, from where you get the charming *Centovalli* train, crossing 100 valleys, to Locarno in Switzerland and a ferry back to Stresa. The two-day version is perhaps better value if you have the time.

Panza di Biumo, mostly by post-WWII American artists. One of the finest rooms is the 1830 **Salone Impero** (Empire Hall), with heavy chandeliers and four canvases by David Simpson (born in 1928).

The Drive » The 28km drive from Varese to Como isn't terribly scenic, passing through a string of small towns and suburbs nestled in the wooded hills. The single-lane SS342 passes through Malnate, Solbiate and Olgiate Comasco before reaching Como.

TRIP HIGHLIGHT

⑤ Como

Built on the wealth of its silk industry, Como is an elegant town and remains Europe's most important producer of silk products. The **Museo della Seta** (Silk Museum; ☏031 30 31 80; www.museosetacomo.com; Via Castelnuovo 9; adult/reduced €10/7; ⊙10am-6pm Tue-Fri, to 1pm Sat) unravels the town's industrial history, with early dyeing and printing equipment on display. At **A Picci** (☏031 26 13 69; Via Vittorio Emanuele II 54; ⊙3-7.30pm Mon, 9am-12.30pm & 3-7.30pm Tue-Sat) you can buy top-quality scarves, ties and fabrics for a fraction of the cost you'd pay elsewhere.

After wandering the medieval alleys of the historic centre take a stroll along **Passeggiata Lino Gelpi**, where you pass a series of waterfront mansions, finally arriving at **Villa Olmo** (☏031 25 23 52; Via Cantoni 1; gardens free, villa entry varies by exhibition; ⊙villa during exhibitions 9am-12.30pm & 2-5pm Mon-Sat, gardens 7.30am-11pm summer, to 7pm winter). Set grandly facing the lake, this Como landmark was built in 1728 by the Odescalchi family, related to Pope Innocent XI, and now hosts blockbuster art shows. During the summer the **Lido di Villa Olmo** (☏031 57 08 71; www.lidovillaolmo.it; Via Cernobbio 2; adult/reduced €8/4; ⊙9am-7pm mid-May–Sep), an open-air swimming pool and lakeside bar, is open to the public.

Classic Trip

WHY THIS IS A CLASSIC TRIP
PAULA HARDY, WRITER

Despite centuries of fame as a tourist destination, there's a timeless glamour to the Italian lakes, especially Lago di Como with its mountainous amphitheatre of snow-capped Alps. One of the best ways to see it is to walk the old mule tracks. There are some easy walks with fabulous views around Brunate. Pick up a map showing the trails from the Como tourist office.

Top: Villa Serbelloni, Bellagio, Lago di Como
Left: Market stalls in Cannobio, Lago Maggiore
Right: The gardens of Villa Monastero, Varenna, Lago di Como

FRANCESCO IACOBELLI/GETTY IMAGES ©

On the other side of Como's marina, the **Funicolare Como-Brunate** (☎031 30 36 08; www.funicolarecomo.it; Piazza de Gasperi 4; adult one way/return €3/5.50, reduced €2/3.20; ☉half-hourly departures 6am-midnight summer, to 10.30pm winter) whisks you uphill to the quiet village of **Brunate** for splendid views across the lake.

✗ ▨ 🛏 p129

The Drive » The 32km drive from Como to Bellagio along the SS583 is spectacular. The narrow road swoops and twists around the lake shore the entire way and rises up out of Como giving panoramic views over the lake. There are plenty of spots en route where you can pull over for photographs.

TRIP HIGHLIGHT

6 Bellagio

It's impossible not to be charmed by Bellagio's waterfront of bobbing boats, its maze of stone staircases, cypress groves and showy gardens. **Villa Serbelloni** (☎031 95 15 55; Piazza della Chiesa 14; adult/child €9/5; ☉tours 11.30am & 2.30pm Tue-Sun mid-Mar–Oct) covers much of the promontory on which Bellagio sits. Although owned by the Rockefeller Foundation, you can still tour the gardens on a guided tour. Otherwise stroll the grounds of neoclassical **Villa Melzi d'Eril** (☎339 4573838; www.giardinidivillamelzi.it; Lungo Lario Manzoni; adult/reduced

€6.50/4; ⊘9.30am-6.30pm
Apr-Oct), which run right
down to the lake and are
adorned with classical
statues couched in blush-
ing azaleas.

Barindelli's (☏338
2110337; www.barindellitaxi
boats.it; Piazza Mazzini; tours
per hour €140) operates
slick, mahogany cigarette
boats in which you can
tool around the headland
in for a sunset tour
(boats seat 10 people).

🛏 p129

The Drive » The best way to
reach Tremezzo, without driving
all the way around the bottom of
the lake, is to take the ferry from
Piazza Mazzini. One-way fares
cost €4.60, but for sightseeing
you may want to consider the
one-day central lake ticket,
covering Bellagio, Varenna,
Tremezzo and Cadenabbia,
for €15.

7 Tremezzo

Tremezzo is high on
everyone's list for a
visit to the 17th-century
Villa Carlotta (☏034 44
04 05; www.villacarlotta.it; Via
Regina 2; adult/reduced €9/7;
⊘9am-7.30pm Apr–mid-Oct),
whose botanic gardens
are filled with orange
trees knitted into pergo-
las and some of Europe's
finest rhododendrons,
azaleas and camellias.
The villa, which is
strung with paintings

Tremezzo Villa Carlotta on the shore of Lago di Como

Classic Trip

and fine alabaster-white sculptures (especially lovely are those by Antonio Canova), takes its name from the Prussian princess who was given the palace in 1847 as a wedding present from her mother.

The Drive » As with the trip to Tremezzo, the best way to travel to Varenna is by passenger ferry either from Tremezzo or Bellagio.

- - - - - - - - - - - - - - - -

⑧ Varenna

Wander the flower-laden pathway from Piazzale Martiri della Libertà to the gardens of **Villa Cipressi** (📞 0341 83 01 13; www.hotelvillacipressi.it; Via IV Novembre 22; adult/child €4/2; ⏰ 10am-6pm Mar-Oct), now a luxury hotel (singles €140 to €160, doubles €170 to €230), and, 100m further south, **Villa Monastero** (📞 0341 29 54 50; www.villamonastero. eu; Via IV Novembre; villa & gardens adult/reduced €8/4,

gardens only €5/2; ⏰ gardens 9.30am-7pm year-round, villa 10am-6pm Fri-Sun Mar-May & Oct, 2-6pm Wed, 9.30am-7pm Thu-Sun Jun, Jul & Sep, 9.30am-7pm Aug, 11am-5pm Nov), a former convent turned into a vast residence by the Mornico family in the 17th century. In both cases, you can stroll through the verdant gardens admiring magnolias, camellias and exotic yuccas.

The Drive » Departing Bellagio, pick up the SS583, but this time head southeast towards Lecco down the other 'leg' of Lago di Como. As with the stretch from Como to Bellagio, the road hugs the lake, offering spectacular views the whole 20km to Lecco. Once you reach Lecco head south out of town down Via Industriale and pick up the SS342 for the final 40km to Bergamo.

- - - - - - - - - - - - - - - -

⑨ Bergamo

Although Milan's skyscrapers are visible on a clear day, historically Bergamo was more closely associated with Venice (Venezia). Hence the elegant Venetian-style architecture of **Piazza Vecchia**, appreciated

by Le Corbusier for its beautiful and harmonious arrangement.

Behind this secular core sits the **Piazza del Duomo** with its modest baroque cathedral. A great deal more interesting is the **Basilica di Santa Maria Maggiore** (Piazza Duomo; ⏰ 9am-12.30pm & 2.30-6pm Apr-Oct, shorter hours Nov-Mar) next door. To its whirl of frescoed, Romanesque apses, begun in 1137, Gothic touches were added as was the Renaissance **Cappella Colleoni** (Piazza Duomo; ⏰ 9am-12.30pm & 2-6.30pm Mar-Oct, 9am-12.30pm & 2-4.30pm Tue-Sun Nov-Feb), the mausoleum-cum-chapel of the famous mercenary commander, Bartolomeo Colleoni (1696–1770). Demolishing an entire apse of the basilica, he commissioned Giovanni Antonio Amadeo to create a tomb that is now considered a masterpiece of Lombard art with its exuberant rococo frescoes by Giambattista Tiepolo.

Also like Venice, Bergamo has a grand art academy. Recently reopened after a seven year renovation, the **Accademia Carrara** (📞 035 23 43 96; www. lacarrara.it; Piazza Carrara 82; adult/reduced €10/8; ⏰ 10am-7pm) is both school and museum, its stunning collection of 1800 Renaissance paintings amassed by local scholar Count Giacomo Carrara.

✕ 🛏 p116, p129

SEAPLANES ON THE LAKE

For a touch of Hollywood glamour, check out **Aero Club Como** (📞 031 57 44 95; www.aeroclubcomo.com; Viale Masia 44; 30min flight from €140), which has been sending seaplanes out over the lakes since 1930. The 30-minute flight to Bellagio from Como costs €140 for two people. Longer excursions over Lake Maggiore are also possible. In summer you need to reserve at least three days in advance.

Eating & Sleeping

Stresa ❶

✘ Ristorante Il Vicoletto   Ristorante €€

(📞0323 93 21 02; www.ristorantevicoletto.com; Vicolo del Pocivo 3; meals €30-45; 🕐noon-2pm & 6.30-10pm Fri-Wed) Located a short, uphill walk from the centre of Stresa, Il Vicoletto has a commendable regional menu including lake trout, wild asparagus, and traditional risotto with radicchio and Taleggio cheese. The dining room is modestly elegant with bottle-lined dressers and linen-covered tables, while the local clientele speaks volumes in this tourist town.

Verbania ❷

✘ Ristorante Milano   Modern Italian €€€

(📞0323 55 68 16; www.ristorantemilano lagomaggiore.it; Corso Zanitello 2, Verbania Pallanza; meals €50-70; 🕐noon-2pm & 7-9pm Wed-Sun, noon-2pm Mon; ✳) The setting really is hard to beat: Milano directly overlooks Pallanza's minuscule horseshoe-shaped harbour (200m south of the ferry jetty); a scattering of tables sits on lakeside lawns amid the trees. It's an idyllic spot to enjoy lake fish, local lamb and innovative Italian cuisine, such as *risotto ai petali di rosa* (risotto with rose petals).

Como ❺

✘ Osteria del Gallo   Italian €€

(📞031 27 25 91; www.osteriadelgallo-como.it; Via Vitani 16; meals €25-30; 🕐12.30-3pm Mon, to 10pm Tue-Sat) An ageless *osteria* that looks exactly the part. In the wood-lined dining room, wine bottles and other goodies fill the shelves, and diners tuck into traditional local food. The menu is chalked up daily and might include a first course of *zuppa di ceci* (chickpea soup), followed by lightly fried lake fish.

✘ Ristorante Sociale   Italian €€

(📞031 26 40 42; www.ristorantesociale.it; Via Rodari 6; meals €20-30; 🕐noon-2pm & 7-10.30pm Wed-Mon) A workaday street round the back of the *duomo* is an unlikely spot for such a bewitching restaurant. The menu is packed with local meat and lake produce, and might feature perch and porcini mushrooms. Tuck in under the red-brick barrel ceiling, or in the charming courtyard.

🛏 Avenue Hotel   Boutique Hotel €€

(📞031 27 21 86; www.avenuehotel.it; Piazzolo Terragni 6; d €170-240, ste from €340; 🅿✳🛜) An assured sense of style at this delightful hotel sees ultramodern rooms team crisp white walls with shots of purple or fuchsia-pink. Breakfast is served in a chic courtyard, service is warm but discreet, and you can borrow a bike for free.

Bellagio ❻

🛏 Hotel Silvio   Hotel €€

(📞031 95 03 22; www.bellagiosilvio.com; Via Carcano 10; d from €115-185, meals €30-40; 🅿✳🛜🍽) Located above the fishing hamlet of Loppia a short walk from the village, this family-run hotel is one of Bellagio's best. Here you can wake up in a contemporary Zen-like room and gaze over the gardens of some of Lago di Como's most prestigious villas. Then spend the morning at Bellagio's *lido*; it's free for hotel guests.

Bergamo ❾   see also p116

✘ Colleoni & Dell'Angelo   Italian €€€

(📞035 23 25 96; www.colleonidellangelo.com; Piazza Vecchia 7; meals €50-60; 🕐noon-2.30pm & 7-10.30pm Tue-Sun) Grand Piazza Vecchia provides the ideal backdrop to savour truly top-class creative cuisine. Sit at an outside table in summer or opt for the noble 15th-century interior; either way expect to encounter dishes such as black risotto with ricotta and grilled cuttlefish, or venison medallions with chestnut purée and redcurrant jam.

🛏 Hotel Piazza Vecchia   Hotel €€

(📞035 25 31 79; www.hotelpiazzavecchia.it; Via Colleoni 3; d €130-300; ✳@🛜) The perfect Città Alta bolt-hole, this 13th-century townhouse oozes atmosphere, from the honey-coloured beams and exposed stone to the tasteful art on the walls. Rooms have parquet floors and bathrooms that gleam with chrome; the deluxe rooms have a lounge and a balcony with mountain views.

A Weekend at Lake Garda

10

Poets, politicians, divas and dictators: they've all been drawn to glorious Lake Garda with mountains to the north, vine-clad hills to the south and a string of medieval towns encircling its shores.

TRIP HIGHLIGHTS

29 km

Salò
Refined Salò was capital of Mussolini's last republic

72 km

Riva del Garda
A landscaped lakefront backed by soaring mountains

Limone sul Garda

Malcesine

Toscolano-Maderno

108 km

Torri del Benaco
A pint-sized harbour overlooked by a Scaligero castle

Padenghe sul Garda

Bardolino
FINISH

START

Sirmione
Roman ruins cascade down Sirmione's promontory

0 km

4 DAYS
135KM / 84 MILES

GREAT FOR...

BEST TIME TO GO
July for lake swimming and October for Bardolino's wine festival.

ESSENTIAL PHOTO
Lakeside towns backed by mountains from aboard a boat.

BEST FOR FAMILIES
Night swimming off pontoons floating along Riva's waterfront.

10 | A Weekend at Lake Garda

At 370 sq km Lago di Garda (Lake Garda) is the largest of the Italian lakes, straddling the border between Lombardy and the Veneto. Vineyards, olive groves and citrus orchards range up the slopes and ensure the tables of Garda's trattorias are stocked with fine wines and oils. Boats buzz across the water and songbirds fill the crumbling terraces of Sirmione's Roman ruins. All you need now is a vintage Alfa Romeo to tool around the lakeside admiring the views.

TRIP HIGHLIGHT

1 Sirmione

Over the centuries impossibly pretty Sirmione has drawn the likes of Catullus and Maria Callas to its banks. The village sits astride a slender peninsula that juts out into the lake and is occupied in large part by the **Grotte di Catullo** (☎030 91 61 57; www.grottedi catullo.beniculturali.it; Piazzale Orti Manara 4; adult/reduced €6/3; ◷8.30am-7.30pm Tue-Sat, 9.30am-6.30pm Sun Apr-Oct, 8.30am-2pm Tue-Sun Nov-Mar), a misnomer for the ruins of an extensive Roman villa now comprising teetering stone arches

and tumbledown walls. There's no evidence that Catullus actually lived here, but who cares? The wraparound lake views from its terraced hillside are legendary.

In true Roman style, there's even an offshore thermal spring that pumps out water at a natural 37°C. Wallow lakeside in the outdoor pool at **Aquaria** (☎030 91 60 44; www.termedisirmione. com; Piazza Piatti; pools per hour/day €15/53, treatments from €30; ◷ pools 9am-10pm Sun-Wed, to midnight Thu-Sat Mar-Jun & Sep-Dec, 9am-midnight Jul & Aug, hours vary Jan & Feb).

✕ 🛏 p137

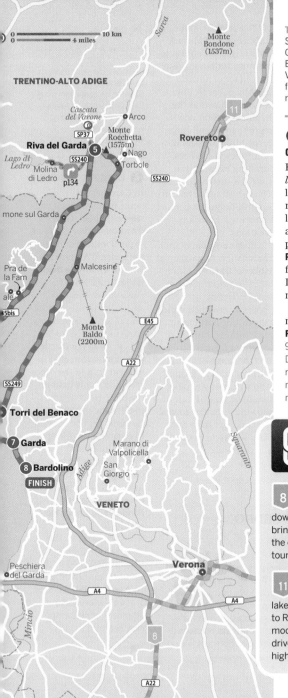

The Drive » The first 7km from Sirmione to Desenzano del Garda is on the SS572 lake road. Exit Sirmione past the Garda Village campground and at the first major roundabout turn right towards Desenzano.

- - - - - - - - - - - - - - - - - - -

❷ Desenzano del Garda

Known as the *porta del lago* (gateway to the lake), Desenzano may not be as pretty as other lakeside towns, but its ancient harbour, broad promenades and vibrant **Piazza Matteotti** make for pleasant wanderings. It is also a hub for summer nightlife.

Best of all are the mosaics in Desenzano's **Roman Villa** (✆030 914 35 47; Via Crocifisso 2, Desenzano del Garda; adult/ reduced €2/1; ⏰8.30am-7pm mid-Mar–mid-Oct, to 4.30pm mid-Oct–mid-Mar, closed Mon).

🔗 LINK YOUR TRIP

8 **Northern Cities**
A 30-minute drive down the A22 and A4 brings you to Verona and the cultural Northern Cities tour.

11 **Roof of Italy**
Climb out of the lake basin on the SS240 to Rovereto for a dose of modern art and an epic drive across Europe's highest pass.

Wooden walkways lead directly over vivid scenes of chariot-riding, grape-gathering cherubs.

Stretching north of Desenzano, the rolling hills of the Valtenesi are etched with vine trellises and olive groves, Garda's Mediterranean micro-climate ensuring ideal olive-growing conditions. **Frantoio Montecroce** (☎030 991 15 04; www.frantoiomontecroce.it; Viale Ettore Andreis 84; ☺by appointment) offers tutored oil tastings.

The Drive » From Desenzano return to the SS572 and start to meander north right by the lake shore. The first 6km to Padenghe sul Garda are some of the most scenic on the lake, lined with cypresses and umbrella pines with clear views over the water.

TRIP HIGHLIGHT

❸ Salò

Sedate and refined as Salò is today, in 1943 it was named the capital of the Social Republic of Italy as part of Mussolini's last-ditch efforts to organise Italian fascism in the face of advancing Allied forces. This episode, known as the Republic of Salò, saw more than 16 buildings turned into Mussolini's ministries and offices. Strolling between the sites is a surreal tour. The tourist office has an English-language booklet featuring significant locations.

Offshore you may spot the small, comma-shaped **Isola del Garda** (☎328 6126943; www.isoladelgarda.com; tour incl boat ride €27-32; ☺Apr-Oct) crowned with neo-Gothic battlements and frothing with a luxuriant formal garden. It is the home of Contessa Cavazza and her family, who will host you on a two-hour guided tour of the villa's opulent rooms. Boats depart from Salò, Gardone Riviera, Garda and Sirmione.

DETOUR: LAGO DI LEDRO

Start: ❺ Riva del Garda

From Riva take the SP37 and then the SS240 west into the mountains, past olive groves and vine-lined terraces. After 11km the road flattens and **Lago di Ledro** (www.vallediledro.com) comes into view. Only 2.5km long and 2km wide, this diminutive lake sits at an altitude of 650m and is set in a gorgeous valley beneath tree-covered mountains. **Molina di Ledro** is at the lake's eastern end, where thatched huts line up beside beaches and boat-hire pontoons.

✕ ⊨ p137

The Drive » Exit the medieval centre of Salò uphill on Via Umberto I and pick up the SS45bis heading north to Gardone. It's barely 7km along the narrow single carriageway, past old stone walls hiding lemon-coloured villas surrounded by luxuriant flora.

---

❹ Gardone Riviera

In Gardone tour the home of Italy's most controversial poet, Gabriele d'Annunzio. Poet, soldier, hypochondriac and proto-fascist, d'Annunzio's home **Il Vittoriale degli Italiani** (☎0365 29 65 11; www.vittoriale.it; Piazza Vittoriale; gardens & museums adult/reduced €16/12; ☺9am-8pm Apr-Oct, to 5pm Tue-Sun Nov-Mar; ℗) is as bombastic and extravagant as it is unsettling, and the decor certainly sheds light on the man. He retreated to Gardone in 1922, claiming that he wanted to escape the world that made him sick.

For something less oppressive visit the flower-filled oasis of **Giardino Botanico Fondazione André Heller** (☎336 410877; www.hellergarden.com; Via Roma 2; adult/child €11/5; ☺9am-7pm Mar-Oct), designed in the 1990s by multimedia artist André Heller. Hidden among the greenery are 30 pieces of contemporary sculpture.

⊨ p137

Sirmione Ruins of a Roman villa at Grotte di Catullo

The Drive » Exit Gardone northeast on Corso Zanardelli for a long, scenic 43km drive north. At Tignale and Limone sul Garda you'll pass the stone pillars of Garda's lemon-houses. The final 12km from Limone to Riva del Garda are extraordinary, passing through dynamite-blasted tunnels dramatic enough to make this the location for the opening chase scene in *Casino Royale*.

- - - - - - - - - -

TRIP HIGHLIGHT

⑤ Riva del Garda

Even on a lake blessed by dramatic scenery, Riva del Garda still comes out on top. Encircled by towering rock faces and a looping landscaped waterfront, its appeal- ing centre is a medley of grand architecture and wide squares. The town's strategic position was fought over for centuries and exhibits in the **Museo Alto Garda** (La Rocca; ☎0464 57 38 69; www.museoaltogarda.it; Piazza Cesare Battisti 3; adult/ reduced €5/2; ◷10am-6pm Tue-Sun mid-Mar–May & Oct, daily Jun-Sep) **reflect this turbulent past.**

Riva makes a natural starting point for walks and bike rides, includ- ing trails around **Monte Rocchetta** (1575m), which looms over the northern end of the lake. Immediately south of the town is the shingle beach and landscaped park, cut throughout with a cycle path that extends 3km to neighbouring **Torbole**.

The other natural spectacle worth a trip is the **Cascata del Varone** (☎0464 52 14 21; www. cascata-varone.com; Via Cascata 12; adult/reduced €5.50/2.50; ◷9am-7pm May-Aug, to 6pm Apr & Sep, to 5pm Mar & Oct), **a 100m water- fall that thunders down the sheer limestone cliffs into a dripping gorge.**

✕ 🛏 p137

The Drive » From Riva pick up the SS240 around Torbole and then turn south on the SS249. Lake views abound through columned 'windows' as you pass through mountain tunnels, and

✓ TOP TIP: LAKE CRUISING

Fleets of ferries link many Lake Garda communities, providing a series of scenic mini-cruises. They're run by **Navigazione sul Lago di Garda** (www.navigazionelaghi.it), which publishes English-language timetables online. A one-day, unlimited travel ticket costs €34.30/17.60 per adult/child. A return fare for a single trip is €6.

Car ferries cross year-round from Toscolano-Maderno on the west bank to Torri del Benaco on the east bank.

to the left Monte Baldo rises above the lake. A cable car runs to the summit from Malcesine, from where it's 22km to Torri del Benaco.

TRIP HIGHLIGHT

❻ Torri del Benaco

Picturesque Torri del Benaco is one of the most appealing stops on the eastern bank. The 14th-century **Castello Scaligero** (☏045 629 61 11; Viale Frateli Lavanda 2; adult/child €3/1; ☉9.30am-12.30pm & 2.30-6pm Apr–mid-Jun & mid-Sep–Oct, 9.30am-1pm & 4.30-7.30pm mid-Jun–mid-Sep) overlooks a pint-sized harbour and packs a wealth of history into dozens of rooms, including exhibits on the lake's traditional industries of fishing, olive-oil production and lemon growing.

The Drive ❯❯ From the waterfront at Torri del Benaco it's a short 7km drive to Garda, around the headland. En route low stone walls or railings are all that stand between you and the water, while cypresses line front lawns to your left.

❼ Garda

The bustling town of Garda lacks obvious charms, but it does boast the leafy headland of **Punta San Vigilio**, a gorgeous crescent bay backed by olive trees 3km to the north. The privately owned **Parco Baia delle Sirene** (☏045 725 58 84; www.parcobaiadellesirene.it; Punta San Vigilio; adult/child €12/6, reduced admission after 4.30pm; ☉10am-7pm Apr & May, 9.30am-8pm Jun-Aug; ℗) has sun loungers and picnic tables beneath the trees; there's also a children's play area. Prices are seasonal and range from €5 to €12 per adult (€2 to €5 per child) per day.

The tiny headland is also the location of **Locanda San Vigilio** (☏045 725 66 88; www.punta-sanvigilio.it; Punta San Vigilio; d €270-375, ste €440-900; ℗❋@❊), with its excellent harbourside taverna. Book for one of the truly memorable candlelight buffets on Friday and Saturday.

The Drive ❯❯ The final 4km drive to Bardolino, continuing on the SS249, gives you your last fill of big views. Over the short distance the road rises up, giving you lofty views over the water before dropping down amid olive groves into Bardolino.

❽ Bardolino

More than 70 vineyards and wine cellars grace the gentle hills that roll east from Bardolino's shores, many within DOC and the even stricter DOCG regional quality-control classifications. They produce an impressive array of pink Chiaretto, ruby Classico, dry Superiore and young Novello.

One of the most atmospheric ways to savour their flavours is a tutored tasting (€5 per person) at the **Museo del Vino** (☏045 622 83 31; www.museodelvino.it; Via Costabella 9; ☉9am-1pm & 2.30-7pm mid-Mar–Sep, hours vary Oct–mid-Mar), which is housed within the **Zeni Winery**. Zeni has been crafting quality wines from Bardolino's morainic hills since 1870.

Bardolino is at its most Bacchic during the **Festa dell'Uva e del Vino** in early October, when the town's waterfront fills with food and wine stands.

 p183

Eating & Sleeping

Sirmione ❶

🍴 La Fiasca — Trattoria €€

(📞030 990 61 11; www.trattorialafiasca.it; Via Santa Maria Maggiore; meals €30; ⏰noon-2.30pm & 7-10.30pm Thu-Tue) In this authentic trattoria, tucked away in a backstreet just off the main square, the atmosphere is warm and bustling, and the dishes are packed with traditional Lago di Garda produce. Prepare for some gutsy flavours: *bigoli* (thick spaghetti) with sardines, fillets of perch with asparagus, and duck with cognac and juniper.

🛏 Grifone — Hotel €

(📞030 91 60 14; www.gardalakegrifonehotel. eu; Via Gaetano Bocchio 4; s €65-80, d €80-120, tr €125-145) The location is superb: set right beside the shore, Grifone's many bedrooms directly overlook the lake and Sirmione's castle. With this family-run hotel you get five-star views for two-star prices. Inside it's all old-school simplicity, but very spick and span.

Salò ❸

🍴 Osteria di Mezzo — Osteria €€

(📞036 529 09 66; Via di Mezzo 10; meals €35; ⏰noon-11pm Wed-Mon) At this intimate *osteria* a constant stream of hearty meals heads into a dining room lined with antique mirrors and weathered stone. Pumpkin gnocchi, grilled perch, and rabbit with smoked ham and prunes are just some of the delights to choose from.

🛏 Villa Arcadio — Villa €€€

(📞0365 4 22 81; www.hotelvillaarcadio.it; Via Palazzina 2, Salò; d €150-270, ste €300-450; P ❄ @ 🤶 🧖 👶) Perched above Salò on the wooded hillside, this converted convent is the essence of lakeside glamour. Enjoy the vista of glassy lake and misty mountains from the panoramic pool or retreat inside to frescoed rooms and ancient wood-beamed halls.

Gardone Riviera ❹

🛏 Locanda Agli Angeli — B&B €€

(📞0365 2 09 91; www.agliangeli.biz; Via Dosso 7; s €70, d €135-180; P ❄ 🧖 👶) It's a perfect hillside Lago di Garda bolt-hole: a beautifully restored, rustic-chic *locanda* (inn) with a pint-sized pool and a terrace dotted with armchairs. Ask for room 29 for a balcony with grandstand lake and hill views, but even the smaller bedrooms are full of charm.

Riva del Garda ❺

🍴 Osteria Le Servite — Osteria €€

(📞0464 55 74 11; www.leservite.com; Via Passirone 68, Arco; meals €30-45; ⏰7-10.30pm Tue-Sun Apr-Sep, 7-10.30pm Wed-Sat Oct-Mar; P 🤶) Tucked away in Arco's wine-growing region, this elegant little *osteria* serves dishes that are so seasonal the menu changes weekly. You might be eating mimosa gnocchi, tender *salmerino* (Arctic char) or organic ravioli with *stracchino* cheese.

🛏 Hotel Garni Villa Maria — Hotel €

(📞0464 55 22 88; www.garnimaria.com; Viale dei Tigli; s €40-75, d €70-115, apt €100-340; P ❄ 🤶) Beautifully designed, ubermodern rooms make this small family run hotel a superb deal. Pristine bedrooms have a Scandinavian vibe, with all-white linens, sleek modern bathrooms and accents of orange and lime green. There's a tiny roof garden, and bedrooms with balconies offer soaring mountain views.

Roof of Italy

11

Traversing the Alps, from Lago di Como (Lake Como) through the Valtellina's vine-covered slopes and across the hair-raising Passo dello Stelvio to Merano, this is one of the north's most spectacular roads.

TRIP HIGHLIGHTS

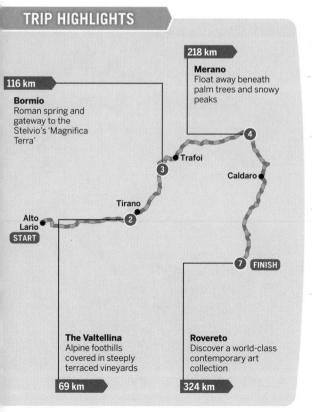

116 km

Bormio
Roman spring and gateway to the Stelvio's 'Magnifica Terra'

218 km

Merano
Float away beneath palm trees and snowy peaks

● Trafoi

Caldaro ●

Tirano

Alto Lario
START

7 **FINISH**

The Valtellina
Alpine foothills covered in steeply terraced vineyards

69 km

Rovereto
Discover a world-class contemporary art collection

324 km

6 DAYS
324KM / 201 MILES

GREAT FOR...

BEST TIME TO GO
June to September, when the Passo dello Stelvio is open.

ESSENTIAL PHOTO
Cloud-busting views on the Passo dello Stelvio.

BEST FOR WELL-BEING
Dipping in Merano's hot and cold spa pools amid mountain peaks.

11 Roof of Italy

Tracing the foothills of the Orobie Alps and the high passes of Parco Nazionale dello Stelvio, the borderlands of northern Italy offer up stunning wildernesses, stupendous scenery and warm welcomes in wooden farmhouses. Vineyards and orchards cloak the valleys of the Valtellina and Adige, while the region's historic cities – Merano, Trento and Rovereto – combine Austrian and Italian influences, creating a unique cultural and culinary melange.

① Alto Lario

The towns of **Dongo**, **Gravedona** and **Sorico** once formed the independent republic of the Tre Pievi (Three Parishes) and were a hotbed of Cathar heresy. Now they're more popular with watersports enthusiasts than Inquisitors. Lake Lario is another name for Lago di Como (Lake Como), so the area takes its name from being at the top *(alto)* of the lake. Gravedona, the largest of the three towns, sits on

Parco Nazionale dello Stelvio

Malles
Venosta

Tubre

SWITZERLAND

Gomag

Passo dello Stelvio
(2757m)

Livigno

*Lago di
Cancano*

St Moritz

③ **Bormio**

Valdisotto

Bernina Pass
(2253m)

*Lago
Bianco*

Cima
Lago Spalmo
(3291m)

Punta di
Pietra Rossa
(3212m)

SS38

Lago N

*Lago di
Poschiavo*

Grosio

Sondalo

Chiuri

Tirano

*Lag
d'Av*

The Valtellina

Teglio

Bianzone

*Lago
Aviolo*

START
Alto Lario ①

Sorico

② **Sondrio**

Teglio

Adda

Passo
d'Aprica
(1176m)

Aprica

Parco
dell'Adamel

Gravedona ①

SS38

Dongo

SS340dir

Monte
Legnone
(2700m)

LOMBARDY

*Lago di
Piano*

*Lago di
Como*

Lake
Barbellino

Oglio

*Lago di
Legnano*

Tremezzo

Pioverna

Parco
Regionale
Bergamasche

9

Enna

Brembo

Serio

*Lago
d'Iseo*

*L
d'*

a gently curved bay with views across to Monte Legnone.

Up on the plateau at Peglio, **Chiesa di Sant'Eusebio** (⊙3-6pm Tue, Thu & Sun Jul, 3-6pm Tue-Thu & Sun Aug) offers lake views and masterly frescoes by Como painter Giovan Mauro della Rovere, better known as Il Fiammenghino (Little Fleming). He sought refuge here after murdering a man and did penance painting the vivid *Last Judgement*.

Sorico, the most northerly of the three towns, guards the mouth of the river Mera, which flows into shallow **Lago di Mezzola**, once part of Lake Como and now a bird-breeding nature reserve.

The Drive » From Sorico take the SS340dir north. Cross over the waterway that connects Lake Como and Lago di Mezzola and continue until you hit a T-junction. Turn right, and at the roundabout turn left onto the SS38 towards Morbegno. Continue for a further 36km, chasing the Adda river all the way to Sondrio.

TRIP HIGHLIGHT

❷ The Valtellina

The Valtellina cuts a broad swath down the Adda valley, where villages and vineyards hang precariously on the slopes of the Orobie Alps. The steep northern flank is carpeted by Nebbiolo grapes, which yield a light-red wine. Both body and alcohol content improve with altitude, so generations of Valtenesi built upwards, carrying the soil in woven baskets to high mountain terraces. Their rewards: a DOC regional quality-standard classification for Valtellina Superiore since 1968. In **Sondrio**, it's possible, by appointment, to visit the cellars of **Pellizzatti Perego**

LINK YOUR TRIP

9 The Graceful Italian Lakes

Take the scenic SS340dir to Tremezzo to tour Como's luxuriant gardens and Maggiore's Borromean palaces.

13 Grande Strada delle Dolomiti

Descend into Bolzano from Castello Firmiano on the SS42 and head east into the Dolomites for mountain hikes and gourmet dinners.

(📞0342 21 41 20; www.
arpepe.com; Via Buon Con-
siglio, Sondrio), and in **Chiuri, Nino Negri** (📞0342
48 52 11; www.ninonegri.it; Via
Ghibellini 3, Chiuri).

The prettiest town
in the valley is **Tirano**,
where mule trains once
came from Venice and
Brescia, and which is
now the departure point
for the **Trenino Rosso
del Bernina** (📞0342 70
62 63; www.treninorosso.it;
adult/child return €58/15),
a gravity-defying rail
track that traverses 196
bridges, crests the Bernina Pass (2253m) and
crosses the Morteratsch
glacier on the way to St
Moritz in Switzerland.

✗ p145

The Drive » From Tirano it is 37
scenic kilometres to the heady
heights of Bormio. Continue
northeast on the SS38, still
tracking the Adda river and
rising up through the terraces,
past small hamlets such as
Grosio and Sondalo and into the
snow-capped mountains.

TRIP HIGHLIGHT

❸ Bormio

Splendidly sited in
a mountain basin at
1225m, Bormio was once
the heart of a region
dubbed Magnifica Terra.
Most of the region's mag-
nificent territory now lies
within northern Italy's
largest national park, the
**Parco Nazionale dello
Stelvio** (www.parks.it/
parco.nazionale.stelvio),
an icy land of 100 gla-
ciers that includes one
of Europe's largest, the
Ghiacciaio dei Forni.

The Stelvio is largely
the preserve of walk-
ers, who come for the
extensive network of
well-organised mountain
huts and marked trails –
but there are a couple of
well-serviced ski runs
at **Solda** and the **Passo
dello Stelvio** (2757m),
both of which offer year-
round skiing.

DETOUR: MALLES VENOSTA

Start: ❸ Bormio

Just north of Bormio on the scenic SS40 sits the
old customs point of Malles Venosta. Aside from its
handsome Gothic churches and historic centre, it
sits just beneath the vast **Abbazia di Monte Maria**
(📞0473 84 39 80; www.marienberg.it; Schlinig 1, Malles;
adult/reduced €5/2.50; ⏰10am-5pm Mon-Sat), the highest
Benedictine monastery in Europe. In the crypt are a
series of superb Byzantine-Romanesque frescoes,
which were only discovered in 1980. Their almost
pristine condition makes them quite unique.

Back in Bormio's
medieval centre, the
Bagni di Bormio (📞0342
91 01 31; www.bagnidibormio.
it; Via Statale Stelvio; d €248-
450, spa admission €42-50;
⏰Bagni Vecchi 10am-8pm,
Bagni Nuovi 11am-8pm, to 11pm
Fri & Sat) was much loved
by the likes of Pliny the
Elder and Leonardo da
Vinci. Hotel stays include
unlimited spa access,
but day passes are also
available.

The Drive » The most difficult,
and awe-inspiring, 96km is the
road from Bormio to Merano,
which crosses the cloud-covered
Stelvio pass, 25km from Bormio.
Approaching along the SS38,
the road rises through a series
of switchbacks, some with very
steep gradients, and descends
via alarming hairpin bends to
quaint Trafoi on the other side.
One of the highest roads in
Europe, it is not for the fainthearted. From Trafoi continue on
the SS38 to Merano. When the
pass is closed, take the 140km
route around via the SS301 and
SS41.

TRIP HIGHLIGHT

❹ Merano

Merano is where 19th-
century Mitteleuropeans
came to soothe their
weary bones, do a 'grape'
cure, and, perhaps,
embark on a dalliance or
two. The Hapsburg-era
spa was the hot destina-
tion of its day and the
city's therapeutic tradi-
tions have served it well
in the new millennium,
with the striking modern
redevelopment of the
Terme Merano (📞0473 25

Trenino Rosso del Bernina The train runs from Tirano in Italy to St Moritz in Switzerland

20 00; www.thermemeran.it; Piazza Terme 1; bathing pass 2hr/all day €13/19; ⊙9am-10pm). Swim through the sluice towards 12 outdoor pools in summer to see palm-studded gardens and snow-topped mountains beyond.

You could also give over an entire day to the botanical gardens at **Castel Trauttmansdorff** (www.trauttmansdorff.it; Via San Valentino 51a; garden & museum adult/reduced €12/10; ⊙9am-7pm Apr-Nov, to 11pm Fri Jun-Aug), where exotic cacti and palms, beds of lilies, irises and tulips all cascade down the hillside surrounding a castle where Sissi (Empress Elisabeth) spent the summer.

✖ ⊨ p145

The Drive » From Merano to Bolzano and the Castello Firmiano, the SS38 becomes a dual-lane autostrada, so the next 30km are easy motorway driving as you leave the high mountains behind you.

- - - - - - - - - - -

⑤ Castello Firmiano

Known as the 'Crown of Sigismund', the expansive walls and battlements of Castello Firmiano encircle the hilltop overlooking Bolzano and Appiano just like a princely coronet.

Fought over for 1000 years, it has long been a symbol of Tyrolean independence and now houses the **Messner Mountain Museum** (MMM Firmian; ☎0471 63 31 45; www.messner-mountain-museum.it; Via Castel Firmiano 53; adult/reduced €10/8; ⊙10am-6pm Fri-Wed Apr–mid-Nov), named after celebrated mountaineer Reinhold Messner. Exhibits explore humanity's relationship with the mountains while the inspiring design, involving hundreds of stairs, suggests shifting altitudes and uneven mountain terrain.

South of the castle stretches the **Weinstrasse**

TOP TIP: PASSO DELLO STELVIO

The high and hair-raising Passo dello Stelvio (www.stelvio.net) is only open from June to October, and is always subject to closures dependent on early or late snow falls. For the rest of the year, you'll need to skirt around the pass to get to Merano by taking the SS301 to Livigno and then route 28 through Switzerland to Tubre and then on to Merano via the SS38.

(www.suedtiroler-weinstrasse.it), a wine road winding through the Adige valley along the SP14 all the way to Trento. Producers line the route, although the hub of the region is **Caldaro**.

The Drive >> South of Bolzano the autostrada carves a straight line through the midst of the Adige valley. It's a fast, scenic route with the mountains overlapping in descending order in front of you. If you have more time, however, the preferred route is to pick up the SP14 from the castle to Caldaro and follow the wine route all the way to Magrè, where you can stop and taste some of the prized Adige wines (p145).

6 Trento

During the tumultuous years of the Counter-Reformation, the Council of Trent convened here, dishing out far-reaching condemnations to uppity Protestants. Modern Trento is less preachy: quietly confident and easy to like. Frescoed streets fan out from the **Duomo** (Cattedrale di San Vigilio;

⊙6.30am-6pm), which sits above a 6th-century temple and a **Paleo-Christian archaeological area** (adult/reduced €1.50/1; ⊙10am-noon & 2-5.30pm Mon-Sat).

On the opposite side of the square is the former bishop's residence, **Palazzo Pretoria** (Palazzo Pretorio; ☑0461 23 44 19; Piazza del Duomo 18; adult/reduced incl archaeological area €5/3; ⊙10am-1pm & 2-6pm Wed-Mon, to 5.30pm winter), where illuminated manuscripts and paintings depict the Council of Trent.

Above it all, the mighty **Castello del Buonconsiglio** (☑0461 23 37 70; www.buonconsiglio.it; Via Clesio 5; adult/reduced €10/8; ⊙9.30am-5pm Tue-Sun) is a reminder of the bloody history of these borderlands. During WWI, Italian patriot Cesare Battisti was held in the castle dungeon before being hanged by the Austrians as a traitor.

✗ ⨝ p145

The Drive >> The final 30km drive south on the A22 leaves

most of the majestic scenery behind, and the broad valley tapers out towards Rovereto.

TRIP HIGHLIGHT

7 Rovereto

In the winter of 1769, Leopold Mozart and his soon-to-be-famous musical son visited Rovereto. Musical pilgrims come to visit the **Church of San Marco** (Piazza San Marco; ⊙8.30am-noon & 2-7pm), where the 13-year-old Wolfgang wowed the Roveretini, and for the annual **Mozart Festival** (www.wamrovereto.com) in August.

The town that Mozart knew still has its tightly coiled streets, but it's the shock of the new that lures most to the **Museo di Arte Moderna e Contemporanea** (MART; ☑0464 43 88 87; http://english.mart.trento.it; Corso Bettini 43; adult/reduced €11/7, incl Casa del Depero €13/9; ⊙10am-6pm Tue-Thu, Sat & Sun, to 9pm Fri), one of Italy's best 20th-century art museums. Designed by Ticinese architect Mario Botta, it is a fitting home for some huge 20th-century works, including Warhol's *Four Marilyns* (1962), several Picassos and a clutch of contemporary art stars. Italian work is, naturally, well represented, with excellent pieces from Balla, Morandi, de Chirico, Fontana and Manzoni.

✗ p145

Eating & Sleeping

The Valtellina ②

✗ Altavilla   Gastronomy €€

(📞0342 72 03 55; www.altavilla.info; Via ai Monti
46, Bianzone; meals €35; ⏱noon-2.30pm &
7-10pm Tue-Sun, daily Aug; P🖥🎣) In this
charming Alpine chalet try traditional mountain
dishes such as *sciàtt* (buckwheat pancakes
stuffed with Bitto cheese) and *pizzocheri*
buckwheat pasta. The salami, mountain venison
and aged Bitto cheese are particular highlights.

✗ Osteria del Crotto   Osteria €€

(📞0342 61 48 00; www.osteriadelcrotto.it; Via
Pedemontana 22; meals €25-40; ⏱noon-3pm
& 7.30-11pm Mon-Sat, noon-3pm Sun) Osteria
del Crotto serves a whole slew of Slow Food
Movement–authenticated products such as
violino di capra della Valchiavenna (literally
'violin goat of the Valchiavenna'), a traditional
salami which is sliced by resting it on the
shoulder and shaving it as a violin player would
move their bow.

Merano ④

✗ Pur Südtirol   Deli €

(www.pursuedtirol.com; Corso della Libertà
35; plates from €9; ⏱9am-7.30pm Mon-Fri, to
2pm Sat) This stylish regional showcase has
an amazing selection of farm produce: wine,
cider, some 80 varieties of cheese, speck and
sausage, pastries and breads and tisanes.

🛏 Ottmanngut   Boutique Hotel €€

(📞0473 44 96 56; www.ottmanngut.it; Via Verdi
18; s €130, d €160-240; 🎣) This boutique hotel
encapsulates Merano's beguiling mix of stately
sophistication with nine antique-strewn rooms
scattered over three floors. It's set among
terraced vineyards a scant five-minute walk
from the centre.

🛏 Hotel Aurora   Hotel €€

(📞0473 21 18 00; www.hotelaurora.bz;
Passeggiata lungo Passirio 38; s €120, d €150-
190; P❄🎣) A traditional family hotel, just
across the river from the Terme, is working
some fresh ideas. 'New' rooms are Italian
designed, bright and slick, but the parquetry-
floored '60s originals have their own vintage
charm, along with river-facing balconies.

Magrè ⑤

🍷 Paradeis   Wine Bar

(Alois Lageder; 📞0471 80 95 80; www.
aloislageder.eu/paradeis; Piazza Geltrude 5,
Magrè; meals €40-65; ⏱10am-8pm, dining room
noon-4pm Mon-Sat, to 11pm Thu) Take a seat
at the long communal table at this biodynamic
weinschenke/vineria (winery), and start tasting.
Book for lunch in the stunning dining room or
linger over a bottle and plate of cheese in the
pretty courtyard.

Trento ⑥

✗ Scrigno del Duomo   Gastronomy €€

(📞0461 22 00 30; www.scrignodelduomo.com;
Piazza del Duomo 29; meals €35, degustation
from €55; ⏱wine bar 11am-2.30pm & 6-11pm,
dining room 12.30-2.30pm & 7.30-10pm Tue-Sun,
dinner only Sat) Trento's culinary and social
epicentre is discreetly housed in a building
dating back to the 1200s. For degustation
dining take the stairs down to the formal
restaurant, with its glassed-in Roman-era cellar.
Or stay upstairs where there's simple, stylishly
done local specialities.

🛏 Elisa B&B   B&B €

(📞0461 92 21 33; www.bbelisa.com; Viale
Rovereto 17; s/d €65/90; ❄🎣) This is a true
B&B in an architect's beautiful family home,
with two private, stylish rooms and breakfasts
that are a feast of home-baked cakes, freshly
squeezed juice and artisanal cheese. It's
located in a smart residential neighbourhood, a
pleasant stroll from the city centre.

Rovereto ⑦

🍷 Osteria del Pettirosso   Wine Bar

(www.osteriadelpettirosso.com; Corso Bettini 24;
⏱10am-11pm Mon-Sat) Most people come here
for the blackboard menu of wines by the glass,
many from small producers, a plate of cheese
(€8) or a couple of *crostone all lardo* (toasts
with cured pork fat).

Valle d'Aosta

12

The Valle d'Aosta carves a deep and scenic path through the Alps to Mont Blanc (Monte Bianco). Explore a hybrid culture, sample Franco-Provençal food and eyeball epic peaks from cable cars.

TRIP HIGHLIGHTS

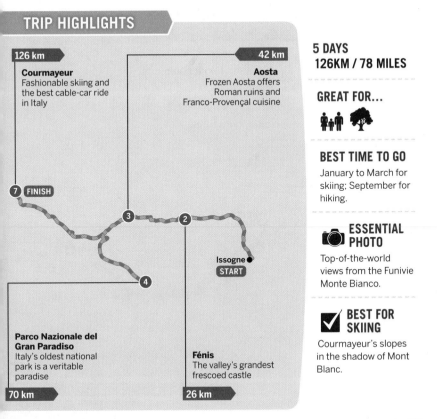

126 km

Courmayeur
Fashionable skiing and the best cable-car ride in Italy

42 km

Aosta
Frozen Aosta offers Roman ruins and Franco-Provençal cuisine

7 FINISH

3

2

Issogne
START

4

Parco Nazionale del Gran Paradiso
Italy's oldest national park is a veritable paradise

70 km

Fénis
The valley's grandest frescoed castle

26 km

5 DAYS
126KM / 78 MILES

GREAT FOR...

BEST TIME TO GO
January to March for skiing; September for hiking.

📷 **ESSENTIAL PHOTO**
Top-of-the-world views from the Funivie Monte Bianco.

✓ **BEST FOR SKIING**
Courmayeur's slopes in the shadow of Mont Blanc.

arco Nazionale del Gran Paradiso Lago Agnel and Lago Serrù

12 Valle d'Aosta

Touring the Valle d'Aosta's castle-tipped peaks and glacial valley makes for one of Italy's most scenic drives. Courmayeur's fashion-parade of skiers hits the high slopes of Mont Blanc, while Valdostan farmers cultivate Alpine wines and ferment famous fontina cheeses in the pastures below. When the snow melts, the hiking in the Gran Paradiso park and along Aosta's high-altitude trails is even more sublime.

① Issogne

The Valle d'Aosta's peaks are crowned with castles, each within view of the next, so messages could be transferred up and down the valley via flag signals. Although many were little more than fortified barracks, as time progressed so their lordly inhabitants became more mindful of appearances. The **Castello d'Issogne** (☎0125 92 93 73; adult/reduced €5/3; ☉9am-7pm Mar-Sep, 10am-1pm & 2-5pm Oct-Dec), for example, sitting on the right bank

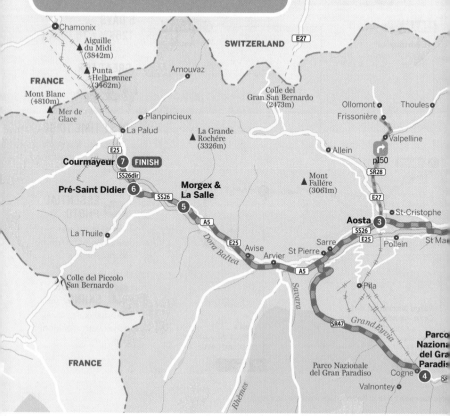

of the Dora Baltea river and located on one of the only navigable routes over the Alps, is more of a seignorial Renaissance residence, the interior decorated with rare Alpine frescoes. It looks quite different to the dour **Castello di Verrès** (☎0125 92 90 67; adult/reduced €3/2; ⊙9am-7pm Mar-Sep, 10am-1pm & 2-5pm Oct-Dec), located on the opposite bank, with which it was in constant conflict.

The Drive » From Issogne it's a 26km drive along the A5 autostrada to Fénis. The peaks

of the lower Alps are already visible and frame your route. After Montjovet duck through a series of tunnels as you sweep westwards into the valley. Take the exit for Nus and follow signs for the castle.

TRIP HIGHLIGHT

❷ Fénis

The finest castle in the Valle d'Aosta is without a doubt the magnificently restored **Castello di Fénis** (adult/reduced €5/3.50; ⊙9am-7pm Mar-Sep, 10am-1pm & 2-5pm Oct-Dec), owned by the powerful Challant clan from 1242 onwards. It features rich

frescoes, including an impressive etching of St George slaying a fiery dragon. The castle is laid out in a pentagonal shape with square and cylindrical turrets lording it over the lush chestnut forests. It was never really used as a defensive post, but served as a plush residence for the Challants until 1716. The on-site **museum** allows access to a weaponry display, the kitchens, the battlements, the former residential quarters and the frescoed chapel.

The Drive » Aosta is just 16km from the Castello di Fénis. Rejoin the A5/E25 for 8km through pretty mountainous forests. Then exit towards Aosta Est onto the E27 for 1.2km, and after you pass through the toll booths follow signs for Aosta Centro, which is a further 4km.

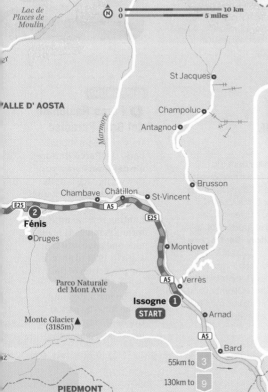

⑤ LINK YOUR TRIP

3 Savoy Palace Circuit

The Gran Paradiso was the hunting preserve of the Dukes of Savoy; pick up their trail in Turin, down the A5 from Issogne.

9 The Graceful Italian Lakes

From Alpine peaks to a Mediterranean microclimate, take the A5 and A4 from Issogne to Lago d'Orta.

149

TRIP HIGHLIGHT

❸ Aosta

Jagged Alpine peaks rise like marble cathedrals above the town of Aosta, a once-important Roman settlement that has sprawled rather untidily across the valley floor since the opening of the Mont Blanc tunnel in the 1960s. But its 2000-year-old centre still harbours Roman relics, such as the **Arco di Augusto** (Piazza Arco di Augusto), the **Roman bridge**, spanning the Buthier river since the 1st century, and the **Porta Praetoria**, the main gate to the Roman city. Even the **Roman Theatre** (Via Porta Praetoria; ⊘9am-7pm Sep-Jun, to 8pm Jul & Aug) remains in use as a venue for summer concerts.

Otherwise, more Challant-commissioned artworks can be seen in the **Chiesa di Sant'Orso** (Via Sant'Orso; ⊘9am-5.30pm), which dates back to the 10th century.

For skiing and hiking on the slopes above, ascend the **Aosta-Pila cable car** (one way/return €3/5; ⊘8am-12.45pm & 2.15-5.30pm mid-Jun–early Sep) to the 1800m-high resort of **Pila**.

✗ 🛏 p153

The Drive ≫ Leave Aosta heading westwards for the next scenic 26km to Cogne. You'll pick up the Viale Piccolo San Bernardino first for a couple of kilometres and then merge with the SS26. After about 3km turn left onto the SR47 and start the beautiful, mountain-hugging ascent into the Gran Paradiso.

DETOUR: VALPELLINE

Start: ❸ Aosta

Aosta's signature cheese is made from the full-cream, unpasteurised milk of Valdostan cows that have grazed on pastures up to 2700m above sea level, before being matured for three months in underground rock tunnels. You can learn more about the history, 'terroir' and production of Aostan cheeses at the **Valpelline Visitors' Centre** (www.fontinacoop.it; Frissonière; ⊘8.30am-12.30pm & 2.30-6.30pm Mon-Fri, 9am-noon & 3-6pm Sat & Sun, closed Sat & Sun winter). Follow the SR28 for 7km north to the Valpelline valley, turn east towards Ollomont and after 1.5km turn west along a mountain road to Frissonière, where the centre is located.

TRIP HIGHLIGHT

❹ Parco Nazionale del Gran Paradiso

Italy's oldest national park, the **Parco Nazionale del Gran Paradiso** (www.pngp.it), is aptly named. Originally it was the Savoy's own private hunting reserve until Vittorio Emanuele II made nice and gave it to the state in 1922 to ensure the protection of the endangered ibex.

The main stepping stone into the park is **Cogne** (1534m), famous for its lace-making,

Aosta Roman Theatre

samples of which you can buy at **Le Marché Aux Puces** (Rue Grand Paradis 4; ⊙closed Wed). Easy walks in the park are possible, such as the 3km stroll to the village of **Lillaz** on trail 23, where there is a geological park and a waterfall that drops 150m. Trails 22 and 23 will get you to the village of **Valnontey**, where you can visit the **Giardino Alpino Paradisia** (☎0165 7 53 01; www.pngp.it; adult/reduced €3/1.50; ⊙10am-5.30pm mid-Jun–mid-Sep, to 6.30pm Jul & Aug), an Alpine garden displaying mountain flora and rare butterflies.

✕ 🛏 p153

The Drive ⟩⟩ The longest drive on the tour is 42km to Morgex and La Salle. The first 20km involve retracing your route down the SR47 out of the mountains. When you reach the bottom follow signs to rejoin the A5/E25 autostrada in the direction of Mont Blanc. From here it's 18km to Morgex through the forested valley.

- - - - - - - - - - -

5 Morgex & La Salle

The ruined towers of **Châtelard**, which guard the road over the Piccolo San Bernardo pass, also cast a shadow over Europe's highest vine-yards strung out between the two communes of Morgex and La Salle. The wines from these Alpine vines, produced almost exclusively from the Prié Blanc grape grown be-tween 900m and 1200m, is light and fruity with overtones of mountain herbs and freshly cut hay.

Given the extremes of temperature at this altitude (some vines run almost to the snow line), vintners employ a unique system of cultivation called *pergola bassa* (low-level arbours), where vines are planted low to the ground to protect them. Since 1983 the

SKIING MONT BLANC

Courmayeur offers some extraordinary skiing in the shadow of Mont Blanc. The two main ski areas – the **Plan Checrouit** and **Pre de Pascal** – are interlinked by 100km of runs. Three lifts leave from the valley floor: one from Courmayeur itself, one from the village of **Dolonne** and one from nearby **Val Veny**. They are run by **Funivie Courmayeur Mont Blanc** (www.courmayeur-montblanc.com).

Aostan government has sought to preserve these ancient traditions by setting up the cooperative **Cave Mont Blanc de Morgex et La Salle** (www.cavemontblanc.com; Chemin des Iles 31; ☺10am-noon & 3.30-6.30pm Mon-Sat), which processes the grapes from the 90 or so local small-holdings. Aosta's **tourist office** (www.lovevda.it; Piazza Porta Praetoria 3; ☺9am-7pm; 🛈) has an English-language booklet with information on individual cellars and the cooperative.

The Drive ›› From either La Salle or Morgex descend through the vineyards and rejoin the SS26 for the short 7km drive to Pré-Saint Didier. The road passes under the A5 and then wriggles alongside the river Thuile all the way to Pré.

- - - - - - - - - - - - -

❻ Pré-Saint Didier

Bubbling at a natural 37°C from the mountains' depths, where the river Thuile forces its way through a narrow gorge into the Dora valley, the thermal waters at **Terme di Pré-Saint-Didier** (☎0165 86 72 72; www.termedipre.it; Allée des Thermes; admission €35-50; ☺9.30am-9pm Mon-Thu, 8.30am-11pm Fri & Sat, to 9pm Sun) have been a source of therapeutic treatment since the bath-loving Romans were in town. In addition to saunas, whirlpools and toning waterfalls there's an indoor-outdoor thermal pool. It's lit by candles and torches on Saturday nights, when it is spectacular amid the snow and stars.

The Drive ›› The scenic drive to Courmayeur is on the SS26dir. Cross over the river Thuile in Pré and head westwards with the towering snow-capped peaks of the high passes in front of you. They're an awesome sight, especially in spring when they're framed by the deepest green conifers.

- - - - - - - - - - - - -

`TRIP HIGHLIGHT`

❼ Courmayeur

Flush up against France and linked by a dra-matic cable-car ride to its cross-border cousin in Chamonix, Courmayeur has grafted upmarket ski facilities onto an ancient Roman base. Its pièce de résistance is lofty **Mont Blanc**, western Europe's highest mountain, 4810m of solid rock and ice that rises like an impregnable wall above the Valle d'Aosta. Ride the **Funivie Monte Bianco** (Skyway; www.montebianco.com; return €45, Pavillon du Mt Fréty return €25; ☺8.30am-4pm) for transglacial views that will take your breath away.

First stop is the 2173m-high midstation **Pavillon du Mt Fréty**, where there's a restaurant and the **Mt Fréty Nature Oasis**. At the top of the ridge is **Punta Helbronner** (3462m). From Punta Helbronner another cable car (late May to late September) takes you on a spectacular 5km ride across the Italian border to the **Aiguille du Midi** (3842m) in France, from where the world's highest cable car transports you into Chamonix. The journey from Courmayeur to Chamonix costs €77 and the journey back to Courmayeur by bus is €15. It's worth every penny.

 p153

Eating & Sleeping

Aosta ③

✗ Vecchia Aosta   Italian €€

(☎0165 36 11 86; Piazza Porta Praetoria 4; set menus €30-35; ☺ noon-2.30pm & 7.30-10.30pm; ✳) Grafted onto a section of the old Roman wall, the Vecchia's setting is highly atmospheric. No post-piste boozer, this is a formal place with knowledgeable, sometimes capricious, staff and a traditional menu that includes *crespella alla Valdostana* (*fontina*-and-ham-filled crêpes) and beef braised in red wine.

✗ Trattoria degli Artisti   Trattoria €€

(Via Maillet 5-7; meals €22-30; ☺12.30-2.30pm & 7-10pm Tue-Sat) Fabulous Valdostan cuisine is dished up at this dark and cosy trattoria, tucked down an alleyway off Via E Aubert. Antipasti such as puff pastry filled with Valdostan fondue, cured ham and regional salami are followed by dishes such as roe venison with polenta, and beef braised in Morgex et de La Salle white wine.

⌂ Hotel Milleluci   Hotel €€€

(☎0165 4 42 74; www.hotelmilleluci.com; Loc Porossan 15; d €180-270; P ✳ @ ⧆) Old wooden skis, traditionally carved wooden shoes, claw-foot baths, indoor and outdoor pools, a jacuzzi, sauna and gym, and sumptuous skiers' breakfasts make this large, family-run converted farmhouse seem more like a luxury resort. Set on a hillside above town, its balconied rooms look out to the eponymous 'thousand lights' twinkling from Aosta below.

Parco Nazionale del Gran Paradiso ④

✗ Hotel Ristorante Petit Dahu   Italian €€

(☎0165 7 41 46; www.hotelpetitdahu.com; Frazone Valnontey 27; meals €35; ☺ closed May & Oct; P) Straddling two traditional stone-and-wood buildings, this friendly, family-run spot has a wonderful restaurant (also open to nonguests) preparing rustic mountain cooking using wild Alpine herbs. It also has pretty rooms to stay in (single/double half-board €80/140).

⌂ Hotel Sant'Orso   Hotel €€

(☎0165 7 48 21; www.hotelsantorso.com; Via Bourgeois 2; d €140-180; ☺ spring & autumn closures vary; P ⧆) Tranquil, courteous and understated, the Sant'Orso is nonetheless equipped with plenty of hidden extras, including a wellness area and huge gardens. Further kudos that you can start your cross-country skiing pretty much from the front door.

⌂ Hotel Bellevue   Heritage Hotel €€€

(☎0165 7 48 25; www.hotelbellevue.it; Rue Grand Paradis 22; s €220, d €190-290, 2-person chalets €270-330; ☺ mid-Dec–mid-Oct; P ⧆) This green-shuttered mountain hideaway evokes its 1920s origins with romantic canopied timber 'cabin beds', cowbells strung from old beams, claw-foot baths and the occasional open fire (it's definitely not for minimalists). Afternoon tea is included in the price, as is use of the health spa, and you can rent mountain bikes and snowshoes.

Courmayeur ⑦

✗ La Terraza   International, Pizza €€

(www.ristorantelaterrazza.com; Via Circonvalazione 73; meals €40; ☺ noon-2.30pm & 7-10.30pm) This lively, central bar-restaurant-pizzeria has the full gamut of pizzas, steaks and the usual over-ambitious international-style après-ski nosh. There are also plenty of Valdostan dishes, including venison with mushrooms.

✗ La Chaumière   Italian €€

(Località Planchecrouit 15; meals €25-40; ☺9am-5pm) Set on the slopes above Courmayeur, within walking distance of the cable car, is the fabulous sun-kissed terrace of La Chaumière. Views straight down the Aosta valley are accompanied by superlative polenta and 38 carefully sourced wines.

⌂ Hotel Bouton d'Or   Hotel €€

(☎0165 84 67 29; www.hotelboutondor.com; Strada Statale 26/10; s €95, d €180; P ✳ @ ⧆) Charmingly folksy Bouton d'Or is in the centre of Courmayeur and not only has incredible views of the imposing hulk of Mont Blanc, but also a sauna, a lounge full of interesting Alpine paraphernalia and, in summer, a peaceful garden.

Grande Strada delle Dolomiti

13

The Dolomites are one of the most beautiful mountain ranges in the world. Devotees come for skiing in winter, hiking and rock climbing in spring and summer, and harvest festivals in autumn.

TRIP HIGHLIGHTS

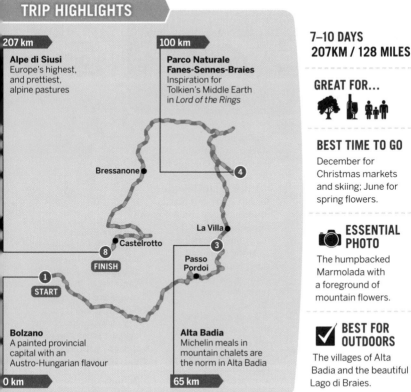

207 km

Alpe di Siusi
Europe's highest, and prettiest, alpine pastures

100 km

Parco Naturale Fanes-Sennes-Braies
Inspiration for Tolkien's Middle Earth in *Lord of the Rings*

Bressanone

④

La Villa

③

Castelrotto

⑧

FINISH

Passo Pordoi

①

START

Bolzano
A painted provincial capital with an Austro-Hungarian flavour

0 km

Alta Badia
Michelin meals in mountain chalets are the norm in Alta Badia

65 km

**7–10 DAYS
207KM / 128 MILES**

GREAT FOR...

BEST TIME TO GO

December for Christmas markets and skiing; June for spring flowers.

ESSENTIAL PHOTO

The humpbacked Marmolada with a foreground of mountain flowers.

BEST FOR OUTDOORS

The villages of Alta Badia and the beautiful Lago di Braies.

Classic Trip

13 Grande Strada delle Dolomiti

Ranging across the South Tyrol, Alto Adige and Veneto, the Dolomites (Dolomiti) combine Austrian and Italian influences with the local Ladin culture. On this grand road trip (*grande strada*) your hosts may wear lederhosen, cure ham in their chimneys and use sleighs to travel from village to village. More recently a new generation of eco-chic hotels, cutting-edge spas and Michelin-starred restaurants have started grabbing the headlines, but overall these mountain peaks remain very low key.

TRIP HIGHLIGHT

❶ Bolzano

Once a stop on the coach route between Italy and the flourishing Austro-Hungarian Empire, Bolzano has been a long-time conduit between cultures. The city's fine museums include the **Museo Archeologico dell'Alto Adige** (☏0471 32 01 00; www.iceman.it; Via Museo 43; adult/reduced €9/7; ⏱10am-6pm Tue-Sun), where the mummified remains of the 5300-year-old iceman, Ötzi, are on display. He was found 3200m up the melting glacier on Hauslabjoch Pass in 1991, but how he got there, 52 centuries before alpinism became a serious sport, is a matter of some debate and the museum explores the many mooted scenarios.

At the other end of the spectrum, the city's contemporary art museum, **Museion** (☏0471 22 34 13; www.museion.it; Via Dante 2; adult/reduced €7/3.50, from 6pm Fri free; ⏱10am-6pm Tue-Sun, to 10pm Fri), is housed in a huge multifaceted glass cube, a surprising architec-tural assertion that beautifully vignettes the old-town rooftops and surrounding mountains from within. There's an impressive permanent collection, and temporary shows highlight the local art scene's ongoing dialogue with Austria and Germany.

✕ p165

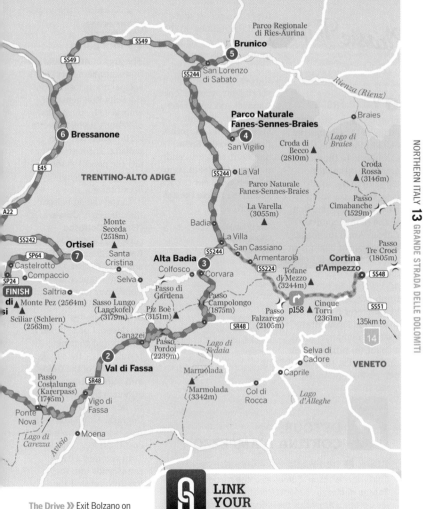

The Drive » Exit Bolzano on the SS241 to the Val di Fassa. The road is the start of a long ascent, the first section through a steep-sided canyon. At Ponte Nova the first peaks of the Dolomites come into view, and after 26km Lago di Carezza is visible on your right.

LINK YOUR TRIP

10 A Weekend at Lake Garda

Tool down the A22 to Lake Garda and visit the vineyards and olive groves around its shores.

14 A Venetian Sojourn

Drop down from Cortina d'Ampezzo on the SS51 and A27 for a tour of Venetian palaces and frescoes.

Classic Trip

② Val di Fassa

Framed by the stirring peaks of the Gruppo del Sella to the north, the Catinaccio to the west and the Marmolada (3342m) to the south-east, the Fassa Valley is a beautiful introduction to the rising mountain ranges. Amid the forests, the iridescent blue-green **Lago di Carezza** is known locally as *de lec ergobando* ('the lake of the rainbow'), as legend tells of a sorcerer who, trying to win the favour of the resident nymph, created a beautiful rainbow over the lake. Alas, the fearful nymph fled and in his fury the sorcerer shattered the rainbow in the lake, forever giving it its luminous colour.

The hub of the valley is the beautifully sited, but verging on overdeveloped, **Canazei** and, to a lesser extent, the riverside village of **Moena**. To access the **Gruppo del Sella** mountain range ascend to **Passo Pordoi** (2239m), where a cable car carries you to the **Sasso Pordoi** (2950m).

The Drive » From Lago di Carezza it's 38km up a series of rapid switchbacks to Passo Pordoi. From the lofty summit, you'll have a view over the 33 hairpin bends that you'll be descending on the SR48. It's only 7km, but it's slow going and the views over meadows and villages are superb. At Arabba bear left on the SS244 for Corvara.

↱ DETOUR: CORTINA D'AMPEZZO

Start: ③ Alta Badia

Thirty-four winding kilometres in the shadow of **Tofane di Mezzo** (3244m) from La Villa lies pricey, icy Cortina d'Ampezzo, the Italian supermodel of ski resorts. Sitting in a crescent-shaped glacial valley surrounded by wooded slopes, Cortina is undeniably beautiful, gaining international fame in the '60s and '70s when Elizabeth Taylor and Henry Fonda came to town to film *Ash Wednesday*. Unapologetically Italian in feel, ladies in fur coats *passeggiata* (stroll) along the Corso with their pampered pooches.

Book a table on the terrace at **Da'Aurelio** (☎0437 72 01 18; www.da-aurelio.it; Passo Giau 5, Colle Santa Lucia; tasting menu €48, meals €45; ☺noon-2pm & 6.30-10pm; **P**) for local specialities as exquisite as the Alpine views. See also p192 and p193.

TRIP HIGHLIGHT

③ Alta Badia

The area of **Alta Badia** (www.altabadia.org) is spectacularly located on the Sella Ronda massif, embraced by the peaks of Pelmo (3168m), Civetta (3218m) and the Marmolada. Throughout the day the play of shadow and light on them is breathtaking.

In the valleys below, the villages of **Corvara** (1568m), **Colfosco** (1645m), **La Villa** (1433m), **Badia** (1324m), **San Cassiano** (1537m) and **La Val** (1348m) connect 130km of slopes over four mountain passes. Undoubtedly one of the Dolomites' premier ski destinations – luxury chalets and gourmet restaurants – the villages are all part of the **Dolomiti Superski network**, although the best access to the slopes is from Corvara. Alta Badia–only passes for one/three days cost €47/136.

In summer a cable car ascends into the Parco Naturale Fanes-Sennes-Braies from the **Passo Falzarego** (2105m). Alternatively, pick up trail No 12, near La Villa, or trail No 11, which joins the Alta Via pathway No 1 at the Capanna Alpina. Either will take you up to the Alpe di Fanes.

Horse-riding, mountain biking and hang-gliding are other popular valley activities. Tourist offices can advise on bike hire, although hotels often provide them gratis.

✕ 🛏 p165

The Drive » From Corvara the 27km to San Vigilio, the unofficial HQ of the Fanes-Sennes-Braies park, is a pleasant, easy drive down the SS244. Chalets dot the hillsides and Alpine cows graze in the valleys, making for an idyllic scene. After 23km turn right on Via Longega for San Vigilio.

TRIP HIGHLIGHT

❹ Parco Naturale Fanes-Sennes-Braies

Hidden behind a wall of rocks northeast of Corvara is the Parco Naturale Fanes-Sennes-Braies, a 25,680 hectare windswept plain, potent with Ladin legends that inspired JRR Tolkien's Middle Earth in *Lord of the Rings*. Not surprisingly, the valley and the high Fanes plateau, with its sculpted ridges and buttress towers of rock, are considered among the most evocative places in the Dolomites and have transfixed artists and poets for centuries. Wordsworth considered it a heavenly environment and architect Le Corbusier envisioned the rocky pinnacles as a form of spectacular natural architecture.

East down the Val Pusteria is the mystical **Lago di Braies**, a glassy lake set within an amphitheatre of stone. Crouched at its southern edge is 'Gate

Mountain', **Sas dla Porta**, once thought to hide a gateway to the underworld. A wooden platform stretches out into the lake for those brave enough to swim in its chilling waters; otherwise stroll the banks and ponder legends of lost worlds.

The Drive » Head back down the hill from San Vigilio to the SS244 and take a right for Brunico, 17km north. As you descend the valley the scenery, while still bucolic, is less dramatic. At picturesque San Lorenzo di Sabato you'll cross the milky Rio di Pusteria as you enter Brunico.

---

❺ Brunico

The Val Pusteria's big smoke, Brunico, gets a bad rap from those who've only driven through its unremarkable main drag. The Tyrolean historic centre, is, however, delightful.

Right by the town gate is **Acherer Patisserie & Blumen** (☎0474 41 00 30; www.acherer.com; Via Centrale; ◷8am-12.30pm & 2.30-7pm Mon-Fri, 8am-1pm & 2-6pm Sat), creator of the region's best apple strudel and Sachertorte. The

young owner reopened his grandfather's former bakery after apprenticing in Vienna. His inventive chocolates and seasonal preserves have won accolades from gourmet bible *Gambero Rosso*.

On the outskirts of town, visit local wool manufacturer **Moessmer** (www.moessmer.it; Via Vogelweide; ◷9am-12.30pm & 2.30-6pm Mon-Fri, 9am-2.30pm Sat) for top-quality cashmere and Tyrolean tweeds from its outlet shop.

The Drive » Exit Brunico onto the main SS49/E66 autostrada and follow the winding Rio di Pusteria river up the valley to Bressanone. After 21km you'll pass the frescoed Castello di Rodengo high up on your left, before dropping down through the vineyards of Varna into Bressanone.

---

❻ Bressanone

Beautiful Bressanone (Brixen), with its palace of the prince-bishops and illustrious history, is the artistic and cultural capital of the Val Pusteria.

The first **cathedral** (Piazza del Duomo; ◷6am-6pm Apr-Oct & Dec, 6am-noon & 3-6pm Nov, Jan-Mar) was

WHY THIS IS A CLASSIC TRIP
PAULA HARDY, WRITER

It's hard to overstate the incredible natural beauty of the Dolomites, whose shapes, colours and contours are endlessly varied. Walking the *alta vie* (high ways) you honestly feel like Heidi. I'll never forget sitting down at Gostner Schwaige, a mountain hut near Castelrotto, and being presented with a creamy soup served in a bowl made of bread that was sitting on a hay base sprinkled with still-fragrant wildflowers.

Top: Christmas market stalls in front of the cathedral, Bressanone
Left: Wood carver at work, Val Gardena
Right: Boathouse, Lago di Braies
Overleaf: Gruppo del Sella, Dolomites

built here in the 10th century by the Bishop of Säben. Though rebuilt in the 18th century along baroque lines, it retains its fabulous 12th-century cloister, the cross-vaults decorated with superb 15th-century frescoes. Bressanone's prince-bishops obviously had an eye for art, and their Renaissance palace, the Hofburg – which now houses the **Museo Diocesano** (📞0472 83 05 05; www.hofburg.it; Piazza Palazzo Vescovile 2; €7; 🕐10am-5pm Tue-Sun Mar-Oct, 10am-5pm daily Dec-early Jan) – was similarly decorated in lavish style.

✕ p165

The Drive ≫ From Bressanone you'll rejoin the main A22 autostrada south towards Modena. It winds through forested valleys for 20km, past Castello di Velturno on your right and above the river Isarco. Exit for the Val Gardena onto the SS242 for the scenic 15km climb to Ortisei at 1236m.

- - - - - - - - - -

❼ Ortisei

Ortisei is the main hub of the Val Gardena and the Alpe di Siusi mountain region. The valley's historical isolation has ensured the survival of many traditions. Like the Alta Badia and Val di Fassa, this is one of only five valleys where Ladin is a majority tongue, while the villages of **Ortisei** (1236m), **Santa Cristina** (1428m) and **Selva**

Classic Trip

(1563m) are characterised by folksy architecture and a profusion of wood-carving shops. Ortisei's **Museum de Gherdëina** (☎0471 79 75 54; www.museumgherdeina.it; Via Rezia 83, Ortisei; adult/reduced €7/5.50; ⏰10am-12.30pm & 2-6pm Mon-Fri, closed Mon winter) has a particularly beautiful collection of wooden toys and sculptures, as does the church, **St Ulrich**.

From the centre of Ortisei a high-speed cable car ascends the slopes of Alpe di Siusi, Europe's largest high-altitude Alpine meadow. To the northeast, another cable car ascends to **Monte Seceda** (2518m) with

unforgettable views of the **Gruppo di Odle**, a cathedral-like series of mountain spires. From Seceda, trail No 2A passes through sloping pastures dotted with wooden *malghe* (shepherds' huts).

Afterwards descend for traditional après-ski at the five-star **Hotel Adler** (www.adler-dolomiti.com), which has been serving up cocktails since 1810.

🛏 p165

The Drive » The 15km drive to Siusi is staggeringly beautiful. Take the SS242 back towards the autostrada but after 1.2km veer left onto the SP64. Views of the rocky peaks surround you as you pass quaint shepherds' huts. At 1060m you'll pass through Castelrotto with its onion-domed church, from where you take the SP24 for the final 10km.

TRIP HIGHLIGHT

❽ Alpe di Siusi

There are few more beautiful juxtapositions than the undulating green pastures of the Alpe di Siusi ending dramatically at the base of the Sciliar Mountains. To the southeast lies the Catinaccio range, its German name 'Rosengarten' is an apt description of the eerie pink hue given off by the dolomite rock at sunset. Signposted by their onion-domed churches, the villages that dot the valleys – including **Castelrotto** (Kastelruth), **Fié allo Sciliar** (Völs am Schlern) and **Siusi** – are unexpectedly sophisticated.

The gentle slopes of the Alpe di Siusi are great hiking terrain, and average stamina will get you to the **Rifugio Bolzano** (☎0471 61 20 24; www.schlernhaus.it; ⏰Jun-Oct), one of the Alps' oldest mountain huts, which rests just under **Monte Pez** (2564m). Take the **Panorama chairlift** (one way/return €3.50/5) from Compaccio to the Alpenhotel, from where it's a three-hour walk to the *rifugio* along paths S, No 5 and No 1.

Horses are also a big part of local life and culture. **Gstatschhof Ponyhof** (☎0471 72 78 14; www.gstatschhof.com; Via Alpe di Siusi 39) offers accommodation and summer programs.

🍴 p165

LOCAL KNOWLEDGE: WALK THE HIGH PASSES

The Dolomites' *alta vie* – literally high ways – are high-altitude paths designed for experienced walkers, although most do not require mountaineering skills or equipment. From mid-June to mid-September a network of mountain huts offering food and accommodation line the route. In high season (July and August) it's advisable to book in advance. Information on hikes can be found on the park's website (www.dolomitipark.it).

Alta Via No 1 Lago di Braies to Belluno, north to south

Alta Via No 2 Bressanone to Feltre, passing through Odle, the mythical Ladin kingdom

Alta Via No 3 Villabassa to Longarone

Alta Via No 4 San Candido to Pieve di Cadore

Eating & Sleeping

Bolzano ①

🍴 Zur Kaiserkron   Südtirolean €€

(📞0471 98 02 14; www.kaiserkron.bz; Piazza della Mostra 2; meals €45; ⊘ noon-2.30pm & 7-9.30pm Mon-Sat) Refined but unfussy takes on regional favourites fill the menu at this calm and elegant dining room, and excellent produce is allowed to shine. It's tempting to just choose a selection from the interesting starters – say, spelt ravioli with fresh curd cheese or mountain lentil soup with speck chips – but meaty mains are particularly well executed.

Alta Badia ③

🍴 Restaurant Ladinia   Südtirolean €€

(📞0471 83 60 10; www.berghotelladinia.it; Pedecorvara 10, Corvara; meals €28, 4-course menu €40; ⊘ noon-2pm & 7-9pm) The Berghotel Ladinia's dining room is appealingly cosy, or you can soak up the sun on a protected terrace on warmer days. Mountain-style food is done in a fresh but unpretentious way: trout carpaccio with chicory, *paccheri* (pasta) with freshwater crayfish, salmon with mashed purple carrots and artichokes, and a yoghurt mousse dessert will wake up stew-and-dumpling-dulled palettes.

🛏 Berghotel Ladinia   Boutique Hotel €€

(📞0471 83 60 10; www.berghotelladinia.it; Pedecorvara 10, Corvara; d €160-235; P ❄ 🛜) Hotel La Perla's family owners have taken over this traditional small hotel just above their luxurious place. Rooms are exquisitely simple and the location is sublime. Room rates usually include a food credit (€40 per person per day) to be used at either the hotel restaurant or at one of La Perla's. Four-day minimum stay.

🛏 Lagacio Mountain Residence   Apartment, Hotel €€€

(📞0471 84 95 03; www.lagacio.com; Strada Micurá de Rü 48, San Cassiano; apt €210-350; P ❄ 🛜) A stylish residence hotel with young, happy staff and a casual vibe. Pared-back apartments are decorated with wood, wool and leather; all have heated floors, big baths and balconies. Attention to detail is keen: kitchens come with top-of-the-line equipment, Nespresso machines and filtered mountain water. There are good spa facilities as well as a guest-only bar.

Bressanone ⑥

🍴 Oste Scuro   Südtirolean €€

(Restaurant Finsterwirt; 📞0472 83 53 43; www.ostescuro.com; Vicolo del Duomo 3; meals €45; ⊘11.45am-2.15pm & 6.45-9.15pm Tue-Sat, noon-3pm Sun) This place would be worth a visit for the decor alone – a wonderful series of dark-wooded rooms strewn with moody mountain paintings and Alpine curios – but the food here is very good if seriously rich. Tips: lunch menus are a steal at €16 to €20, and don't pass up the postprandial nut-infused digestives.

Ortisei ⑦

🛏 Saslong Smart Hotel   Hotel €€

(📞0471 77 44 44; www.saslong.eu; Strada Palua, Santa Christina; d €100-130; 🛜) Rooms are small but comfortable and slick (Antonio Citterio had a hand in the design), staff are friendly and the restaurant is great. The 'smart' concept keeps rates low by making daily cleaning and breakfast optional, plus the longer you stay the cheaper the rate.

🛏 Chalet Gerard   Hotel €€€

(📞0471 79 52 74; www.chalet-gerard.com; Plan de Gralba; half-board s €180, d €240-320; 🛜) Stunning modern chalet with panoramic views, 10 minutes' drive from Selva proper. There are lots of cosy lolling by the fire, a steam room and the option to ski in, plus super cute rooms. The restaurant is relaxingly homey and romantic – all pine, felt and candlelight – and highly regarded.

Alpe di Siusi ⑧

🍴 Gostner Schwaige   Südtirolean €€

(📞347 836 81 54; footpath No 3 from Compaccio; meals €35-50; ⊘Jun-Oct & Dec-Apr) Chef Franz Mulser gives new meaning to the tag 'locally sourced' at his mountain refuge (elevation 1930m). The butter and cheese come from the barn next door, and herbs from the garden outside. Boards of salami, steaming broth and slow-cooked stews are the order of the day.

Classic Trip

A Venetian Sojourn

14

Pinch yourself, and you might expect to wake from this dream of pink palaces, teal waters and golden domes. Instead, you're in the Veneto, where gondoliers call Ooeee! and water laps at your feet.

TRIP HIGHLIGHTS

135 km

Asolo
Get your camera ready for the 'town of 100 vistas'

0 km

Venice
Cruise the Grand Canal for scene-stealing backdrops

7

Bassano del Grappa

Riese Pio X

Treviso
FINISH

5

Mestre

3 **Dolo**

1 **START**

Vicenza
See European architecture change course in Vicenza

80 km

Brenta Riviera
Visit the country retreats of fashionable Venetians

35 km

4–5 DAYS
186KM / 115 MILES

GREAT FOR...

BEST TIME TO GO
January to June for snow-covered gondolas, Carnival and the Biennale.

ESSENTIAL PHOTO
The Ponte di Rialto from a Grand Canal perspective.

BEST FOR ART
From the avant-garde in Venice to Tiepolo frescoes in Palladian villas.

14 A Venetian Sojourn

Scan the Veneto coastline and you might spot signs of modern life – beach resorts, malls, traffic. But look closer and you'll catch the waft of fresh espresso from Piazza San Marco's 250-year-old cafes, faded villas on the Brenta Riviera and masterpieces everywhere: Titians in Venice (Venezia), Palladios in Vicenza and Giottos in Padua (Padova). This calls for a toast with bubbly local *prosecco* – so raise your glass to *la bea vita* (the good life).

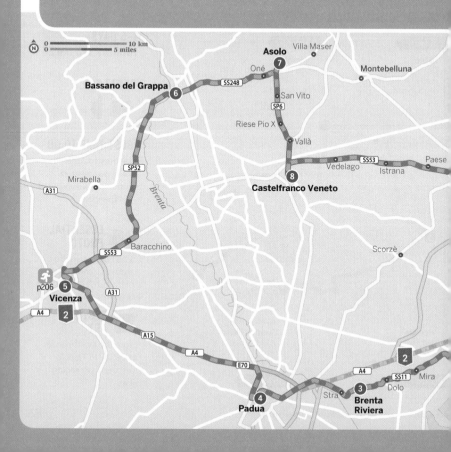

TRIP HIGHLIGHT

❶ Venice

Take the No 1 *vaporetto* (passenger ferry; €7.50) down the **Grand Canal** for scene-stealing backdrops featured in four James Bond films. It starts with controversy at the **Ponte di Calatrava**, a luminous glass-and-steel bridge that cost triple the original €4-million estimate. Ahead are castle-like **Fondaco dei Turchi**, the historic Turkish trading house, and **Ca d'Oro**, a 1430 filigree Gothic marvel.

Points of Venetian pride include the **Pescaria** (Fish Market; Rialto; ⏰7am-2pm Tue-Sun; 🚤Rialto), where fishmongers have been slinging lagoon crab for 700 years, before the marble marvel of the **Ponte di Rialto**. If you're feeling peckish, jump ashore for a gourmet food tour (p202).

The next two canal bends could cause architectural whiplash, with Renaissance **Palazzo Grimani**, followed by **Palazzo Grassi** (📞041 523 16 80, box office 199 13 91 39; www.palazzograssi.it; Campo San Samuele 3231; adult/reduced €15/10, 72hr ticket incl Punta della Dogana €20/15; ⏰10am-7pm Wed-Mon mid-Apr–Nov; 🚤San Samuele), site of contemporary-art sensations between Biennales, and Baldassare Longhena's baroque jewel box **Ca' Rezzonico** (Museum of the 18th Century; 📞041 241 01 00; www.visitmuve.it; Fondamenta Rezzonico 3136; adult/reduced €10.50/8, or Museum Pass; ⏰10am-6pm Wed-Mon summer, to 5pm winter; 🚤Ca' Rezzonico).

Finally, stone lions flank the **Peggy Guggenheim Collection** (📞041 240 54 11; www.guggenheim-venice.it; Palazzo Venier dei Leoni 704; adult/reduced €15/9; ⏰10am-6pm Wed-Mon; 🚤Accademia), where the American heiress collected ideas, lovers and art. It's situated just before the dramatic dome of Longhena's **Chiesa di Santa Maria della Salute** comes into view.

🛏 p46, p61, p117, p175

The Drive ≫ The first leg of this journey is by boat rather than car. Take *vaporetto* No 4.1, the Circular line, to Murano. Nos 4.2 and 13 also head here.

❷ Murano

Woe betide the glassblower with wanderlust: Murano's trade secrets were so jealously guarded that any glass-worker who left the city was accused of treason and

LINK YOUR TRIP

2 **World Heritage Wonders**

Start with the wonders of Venice then for more of Unesco's list of World Heritage Sites, continue down the A4 from Vicenza to Verona.

17 **Trieste to Tarvisio**

Look eastwards down the A4 to Trieste and the borderlands with Slovenia, as many Venetians have done before you.

A27

Piave

viso
FINISH

A27

85km to
17

A4

Mestre

Murano
❷

Venice ❶
START
p202

Lido di
Venezia

Adriatic Sea

subject to assassination. Today, glass artisans ply their trade at workshops along Murano's **Fondamenta dei Vetrai**, marked by 'Fornace' (Furnace) signs.

If you're not in the market for an enormous chandelier shaped like an escaping lagoon monster, then make your way to the **Museo del Vetro** (Glass Museum; ☎041 527 47 18; www.museovetro.visitmuve. it; Fondamenta Giustinian 8; adult/reduced €10.50/8; ⏰10am-6pm summer, to 5pm winter; 🚊Museo), which has been showcasing Murano's glass-making prowess since 1861.

The Drive » Ironically the first 15km of the drive, from Venice to the Brenta Canal's most romantic villa, is the least attractive part of this route, which takes you through the industrial wastelands of Mestre along the SS11. For

Villa Pisani and Villa Foscarini Rossi continue a further 19km on the gradually more scenic Via Nazionale through Mira and Dolo.

TRIP HIGHLIGHT

❸ Brenta Riviera

Every 13 June for 300 years, summer officially kicked off with a traffic jam along the Grand Canal, as a flotilla of fashionable Venetians headed to their villas along the Brenta Riviera. Eighty villas still strike elegant poses, although private ownership and privacy hedges leave much to the imagination. Just four of them are open to the public as museums.

The most romantic of the four is the Palladio-designed, 1555–60 **Villa Foscari** (☎041 520 39 66; www.lamalcontenta.com; Via dei Turisti 9, Malcontenta; admission €10; ⏰9am-noon Tue & Sat May-Oct), also known as 'La Malcontenta' for the grand dame of the Foscari clan allegedly exiled here for

adultery. Further downriver, at Stra, **Villa Pisani Nazionale** (☎049 50 20 74; www.villapisani.beniculturali.it; Via Doge Pisani 7, Stra; adult/reduced €10/7.50, park only €7.50/5; ⏰9am-7pm Tue-Sun Apr-Sep, to 5pm Oct, to 4pm Nov-Mar) provides a Versailles-like reminder with its 114 rooms, vast gardens and reflecting pools.

Well-heeled Venetians wouldn't dream of decamping to the Brenta without their favourite cobblers, sparking a local tradition of high-end shoemaking. Their art is commemorated with a Shoemakers' Museum in **Villa Foscarini Rossi** (☎049 980 10 91; www. villafoscarini.it; Via Doge Pisani 1/2, Stra; adult/reduced €7/5; ⏰9am-1pm & 2-6pm Mon-Fri, 2.30-6pm Sat & Sun Apr-Oct, 9am-1pm Mon-Fri Nov-Mar).

✗ p175

The Drive » From Stra it's a short 13km drive through the Padovan periphery into Padua. Leave Stra northwest on Via Venezia, cross beneath the A4 autostrada and follow the road round to merge with the Tangenziale Nord into Padua.

---

❹ Padua

The Brenta Canal once ran right through Padua, 40km west of Venice. It made things a lot more convenient for Padua-bound Venetians when the city came under Venetian dominion in 1405. Venetian governors

---

✓ **TOP TIP:**
CRUISING THE VENETIAN RIVIERA

You can travel the entire length of the Brenta Canal on **Il Burchiello** (☎049 876 02 33; www.ilburchiello. it; adult/reduced half-day cruise from €55/45, full day €99/55), a luxury barge that lets you watch 50 villas drift by from velvet couches. Full-day cruises leave from Venice's Pontile della Pietà pier on Riva degli Schiavoni (Tuesday, Thursday and Saturday) or from Padua's Pontile del Portello pier (Wednesday, Friday and Sunday).

set up house in the triple-decker, Gothic **Palazzo della Ragione** (☑049 820 50 06; Piazza delle Erbe; adult/reduced €6/4; ⏱9am-7pm Tue-Sun, to 6pm Nov-Jan), its vast main hall frescoed by Giotto acolytes Giusto de' Menabuoi and Nicolò Mireto.

One illustrious Venetian, general Erasmo da Narni (aka Gattamelata or 'Honeyed Cat'), is commemorated with a bronze equestrian statue in front of the epic **Basilica di Sant'Antonio** (Il Santo; ☑049 822 56 52; www.basilicadelsanto.org; Piazza del Santo; ⏱6.20am-7.45pm Apr-Oct, to 6.45pm Nov-Mar). It was cast in 1453, and was the first life-size casting since antiquity. Not far from Gattamelata is the **Oratorio di San Giorgio** (☑049 822 56 52; Piazza del Santo; adult/reduced €5/4; ⏱9am-12.30pm & 2.30-7pm Apr-Sep, to 5pm Oct-Mar), where Titian's 1511 portrait of St Anthony shows him calmly reattaching his own foot.

By now it will be clear that Padua's place in the history of art is a distinguished one. The presence of the university at **Palazzo Bo** attracted big names such as Giotto, Fra Filippo Lippi, Donatello and even Mantegna. Padua was also the birthplace of Palladio, and Antonio Canova sculpted his first marble here for the **Prato della Valle**. See the original in the **Musei Civici agli Eremitani**

(☑049 820 45 51; Piazza Eremitani 8; adult/reduced €10/8; ⏱9am-7pm Tue-Sun) along with Giotto's heavenly vision in the **Cappella degli Scrovegni** (Scrovegni Chapel; ☑049 201 00 20; www.cappelladegliscrovegni.it; Piazza Eremitani 8; adult/reduced €13/6, night ticket €8/6; ⏱9am-7pm).

✗ p117, p175

The Drive ❯❯ Leave Padua following signs for Verona and the A4 autostrada for the 42km drive northwest to Vicenza. Although the A4 is heavily trafficked, as you leave Padua behind the road becomes more scenic and you'll spy the Euganean hills to the south.

- - - - - - - - - - - -

TRIP HIGHLIGHT

❺ Vicenza

When Andrea Palladio moved from Padua to Vicenza he began to produce some extraordinary buildings, marrying sophistication and rustic simplicity, reverent classicism and bold innovation. Go for a walk while you're here to see some of his finest works (p206). His showstopper, **La Rotonda** (☑049 879 13 80; www.villalarotonda.it; Via della Rotonda 45; villa/gardens €10/5; ⏱villa 10am-noon & 3-6pm Wed & Sat mid-Mar–Oct, 10am-noon & 2.30-5pm Wed & Sat Nov–mid-Mar, gardens 10am-noon & 3-6pm Tue-Sun mid-Mar–Oct, 10am-noon & 2.30-5pm Tue-Sun Nov–mid-Mar), sits on a hill overlooking the city, its namesake dome and identical colon-

naded facades giving it the ultimate classical proportions.

Walk up the narrow path opposite to **Villa Valmarana 'ai Nani'** (☑0444 32 18 03; www.villavalmarana.com; Stradella dei Nani 8; adult/reduced €10/7; ⏱10am-12.30pm & 3-6pm Tue-Fri, 10am-6pm Sat & Sun early Mar-early Nov, by appointment rest of year), which is nicknamed for the 17 dwarfs ('ai Nani') who guard the garden walls. In 1757 the entire interior was redecorated with frescoes by Giambattista Tiepolo and his son Giandomenico.

📖 p175

The Drive ❯❯ Pushing away from the autostrada, northwards towards Bassano del Grappa, the scenery becomes decidedly rural, passing through vineyards, cornfields and small towns. Drive 7km northeast on the SS53 and just past Baracchino turn left onto the SP52 for the final 20km to Bassano del Grappa.

- - - - - - - - - - - -

❻ Bassano del Grappa

Bassano del Grappa sits with charming simplicity on the banks of the river Brenta as it winds its way free from Alpine foothills. It is broached by the **Ponte degli Alpini**, Palladio's 1569 covered bridge. Fragile as it seems it is cleverly designed to withstand the rush of spring meltwaters from Monte Grappa. It's

SLOW IMAGES/GETTY IMAGES ©

ROBERTO SONCIN GEROMETTA/GETTY IMAGES ©

WHY THIS IS A CLASSIC TRIP
PAULA HARDY, WRITER

This trip is a fantastic combination of grand-slam sites and delightful out-of-the-way surprises. Venice's marble palaces and Giotto's ground-breaking frescoes in the Cappella degli Scrovegni are understandably world famous, but who knows about the 1500 pairs of historic shoes in Villa Foscarini Rossi or the floor-to-ceiling frescoes at Villa Valmarana and Villa Maser? These places are quite wonderful, and what's more you'll often have them all to yourself.

Top: Gardens of Villa Pisani Nazionale, Brenta Riviera
Left: Villa Foscari, Brenta Riviera
Right: Ponte degli Alpini, Bassano del Grappa

always been critical in times of war: Napoleon bivouacked here for many months and in the Great War hundreds of soldiers died on the slopes of Monte Grappa, where Ernest Hemingway drove his ambulance and came to town after the conflict to write *A Farewell to Arms*.

The town is also famous for its after-dinner firewater, grappa, which was invented here. At the **Poli Museo della Grappa** (📞0424 52 44 26; www.poligrappa.com; Via Gamba 6; admission free, distillery guided tour €5; ⊙museum 9am-7pm Mon-Sat, distillery guided tours 8.30am-1pm & 2-6pm Mon-Fri) you can explore four centuries of production and enjoy a free tasting.

The Drive » The 18km drive along the SS248 from Bassano to Asolo passes through small towns and large, flat fields. Just past Oné you'll enter the lower reaches of Asolo; turn left at the sign and climb the cypress-clad hillside to the historic centre. For Villa Maser continue a further 5km on the SS248.

- - - - - - - - - - -

TRIP HIGHLIGHT

❼ Asolo

East of Bassano rises Asolo, known as the 'town of 100 vistas' for its panoramic hillside location. It was once the haunt of the Romans and a personal gift from Venice to Caterina, 15th-century queen of Cyprus, in exchange for her

abdication. A historic hit with writers, poet Robert Browning bought a house here and named his last work *Asolando* (1889). Try to catch the **antiques market**, held every second Sunday of the month.

Beneath Asolo's forested hilltop, Palladio and Veronese conspired to create the Veneto's finest monument to *la bea vita* at **Villa di Maser** (Villa Barbaro; ☎0423 92 30 04; www.villadimaser. it; Via Barbaro 4; adult/reduced €9/7; ☺10.30am-6pm Tue-Sat, from 11am Sun Mar-Oct, 11am-5pm Sat & Sun Nov-Feb; P). Palladio set the arcaded villa into a verdant hillside, while inside Veronese imagined an Arcadian idyll in his floor-to-ceiling *trompe l'œil* frescoes.

✘ p175

The Drive ›› Descend from Asolo's sylvan heights and zigzag across the SS248 onto the SP6 towards Castelfranco Veneto for a 15km drive south through the small towns of San Vito, Riese Pio X and Vallà.

❽ Castelfranco Veneto

Giorgio Barbarelli da Castelfranco (aka Giorgione) was one of the great masters of the High Renaissance, and one of its most mysterious. Born in Castelfranco he was a contemporary of Titian but an early death from the plague in 1510 left an adoring public with just six acclaimed canvases. Like Titian, with whom he worked on the frescoes of Fondaco dei Tedeschi in Venice, he is credited with revolutionising Renaissance painting, freeing it from its linear constraints and using a refined chiaroscuro technique called *sfumato* ('smokey') to blur hard lines and enhance the emotional quality of the colour, light and perspective.

Luckily for Castelfranco, one of his few surviving works, an altarpiece known as *Castelfranco Madonna,* still hangs in the Cappella Costanza in the **Duomo** (http://duomocastelfranco.it; Vicolo del Christo 10; ☺9am-noon & 3.30-6.30pm Mon-Sat, 3.30-6.30pm Sun). More of the Giorgione school of work can be viewed in the **Casa di Giorgione** (www.museocasagiorgione.it; Piazza San Liberale; adult/reduced €5/3; ☺9.30am-12.30pm & 2.30-6.30pm Fri-Sun, 9.30am-12.30pm Tue-Thu).

The Drive ›› At Castelfranco Veneto you're back on the SS53 again, this time heading 27km further east towards Treviso. Pass through Vedelago and on through flat, flat fields of corn to Istrana, Paese and then Treviso.

❾ Treviso

Totally outdone by supermodel La Serenissima (Venice), Treviso seems becalmed beyond the tourist mayhem, its quiet canals, weeping willows and frescoed facades the backdrop to another midsized Italian town. So why drop in? Well, Treviso has made a handsome contribution to human happiness, giving us DēLonghi appliances, Pinarello bicycles, *radicchio Trevisano* (red radicchio, in season from December through February) and Italy's favourite dessert, tiramisu. You can trace its provenance back to **Antico Ristorante Alle Beccherie** (☎0422 54 08 71; www.lebeccherie.it; Piazza Ancilotto 9; meals €35-40; ☺12.30-2.30pm & 7.30-10pm Wed-Mon, 7.30-10pm Tue), where the coffee-soaked dessert was allegedly designed as a pick-me-up for city prostitutes.

You can also cycle along the river Sile and gaze on Titian's *Annunciation* in the **Duomo** (Piazza del Duomo; ☺8am-noon & 3.30-6.30pm), but the best reason to come to Treviso is to shop and eat. What better way to end a tour of the Veneto?

✘ 🛏 p175

Eating & Sleeping

Venice ❶ see also p46, p61 and p117

🛏 Venissa   Inn €€

(☎041 527 22 81; www.venissa.it; Fondamenta di Santa Caterina 3, Mazzorbo; d €125-225; ⏰Feb-Dec; 🏵🛰; 🚤Mazzorbo) Gourmet getaways are made in the shade of the vineyards at Venissa, which offers some of the lagoon's finest, freshest dining as well as six Scandinavian-chic rooms under the farmhouse rafters. Breakfast – if that's what you can call the lavish gourmet affair – is extra, either prix fixe (€15) or à la carte.

🛏 Oltre il Giardino   Boutique Hotel €€€

(☎041 275 00 15; www.oltreilgiardino-venezia.com; Fondamenta Contarini, San Polo 2542; d €180-250, ste €200-500; 🏵🛰; 🚤San Tomà) Live the dream in this garden villa, the 1920s home of Alma Mahler, the composer's widow. Hidden behind a lush walled garden, its six high-ceilinged guest rooms marry historic charm with modern comfort: marquetry composer's desks, candelabras and 19th-century poker chairs sit alongside flat-screen TVs and designer bathrooms, while outside, pomegranate trees flower in the garden.

Brenta Riviera ❸

🍴 Da Conte   Modern Italian €

(☎041 47 95 71; Via Caltana 133, Mira; meals €10-15; ⏰dinner Tue-Sat) An unlikely bastion of sophistication lodged practically underneath an overpass, Da Conte has one of the best wine lists in the region, and offers creative takes on classic lagoon cuisine, such as roasted quail.

Padua ❹ see also p117

🍴 Osteria dei Fabbri   Osteria €€

(☎049 65 03 36; Via dei Fabbri 13; meals €30; ⏰noon-3pm & 7-10.30pm Mon-Sat) Rustic wooden tables, wine-filled tumblers and a single-sheet menu packed with hearty dishes keep things real at dei Fabbri. Slurp on superlative *zuppe* (soups) like sweet red-onion soup, or tuck into comforting meat dishes such as oven-roasted pork shank with Marsala, sultanas and polenta.

Vicenza ❺

🛏 Hotel Palladio   Hotel €€

(☎0444 32 53 47; www.hotel-palladio.it; Contrà Oratorio dei Servi 25; s/d €110/170; 🏵🛰) The top choice in central Vicenza, this friendly four-star hotel delivers crisp, whitewashed rooms with earthy accents and contemporary bathrooms, many of which feature generously sized showers. The lobby's stone column and rustic ceiling beams attest to the *palazzo's* Renaissance pedigree.

Asolo ❼

🍴 Villa Cipriani   Modern Italian €€€

(☎0423 52 34 11; www.villaciprianiasolo.com; Via Canova 298, Asolo; meals €60; ⏰12.30-2.30pm & 8-10.30pm-; 🅿) The Ciprianis behind this Renaissance villa are the same as those in Venice, and they are just the latest in a long line of illustrious owners including the Guinnesses, Galantis and poet Robert Browning. Now you, too, can enjoy the perfumed rose garden, not to mention the kitchen's seasonal, market-driven menus; the pasta dishes are particularly seductive.

Treviso ❾

🍴 Antico Morer   Seafood €€

(☎0422 59 03 45; www.ristorante anticomorertreviso.com; Via Riccati 28; meals €40-45; ⏰noon-2.30pm & 7.30-10.30pm Tue-Sun) Named after an old mulberry tree, this classy restaurant serves some of Treviso's finest seafood. Chef Gaetano selects the finest ingredients from the fish market each day for his grand platters.

🛏 Maison Matilda   B&B €€€

(☎0422 58 22 12; www.maisonmatilda.com; Via Riccati 44; d €180-350; 🅿🛰) This darkly beautiful townhouse is the perfect display of contemporary Italian design, from its Carrara marble bathrooms and deco bedrooms to its sleek modernist furniture.

Valpolicella Wine Country

15

The vineyards of Valpolicella are within easy reach of Lake Garda and Verona. The Romans started the region's wine production and today Valpolicella produces some of Italy's best reds.

TRIP HIGHLIGHTS

54 km

Lasize
Bathe in thermal lakes equipped with hydromassage

27 km

Fumane
Admire the strange architecture of Villa della Torre

FINISH

Bardolino

Sant'Ambrogio di Valpolicella

Negrar

6

4

START

1

33 km

San Pietro in Cariano
Meet pioneering vintners breaking with tradition

Verona
Watch opera beneath the stars in Verona's Roman Arena

0 km

4 DAYS
60KM / 37 MILES

GREAT FOR...

BEST TIME TO GO
April and May for walking; autumn for harvest.

ESSENTIAL PHOTO
Views over the vineyards from Castelrotto.

BEST FOR FOODIES
A glass of Quintarelli's rich, red Amarone.

policella vineyards The region is known for its Amarone and Recioto wines

177

15 Valpolicella Wine Country

The 'valley of many cellars', from which Valpolicella gets its name, has been in the business of wine production since the ancient Greeks introduced their *passito* technique (using partially dried grapes) to create the blockbuster flavours still enjoyed in the region's Amarone and Recioto wines. Spread across 240 sq km, the vine-clad valleys are dotted with villas and ancient hamlets and harbour as much heritage and culture as they do wine.

TRIP HIGHLIGHT

❶ Verona

Strategically situated at the foot of the Italian-Austrian Alps, Verona has been a successful trade centre since Roman times. Its ancient gates and busy forum (now **Piazza delle Erbe**) are testament to its prosperity, as is the grand **Roman Arena** (☏045 800 32 04; www.arena.it; Piazza Brà; adult/reduced €10/7.50; ⏰8.30am-7.30pm Tue-Sun, from 1.30pm Mon), which still serves as one of the

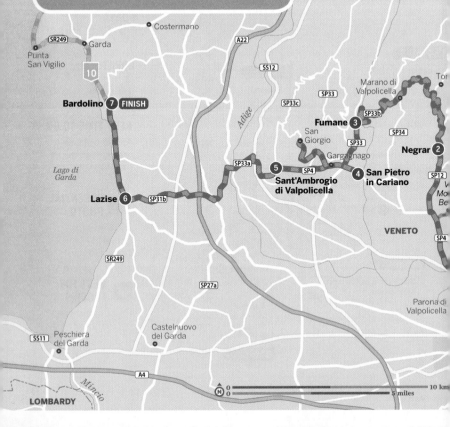

world's great opera venues. The city's handsome profile combines Renaissance gardens with the grand Gothic architecture of showcase churches, such as the **Basilica di Sant'Anastasia** (www.chieseverona.it; Piazza di Sant'Anastasia; admission €2.50; ⊗9am-6pm Mon-Sat, 1-6pm Sun Mar-Oct, 10am-1pm & 1.30-5pm Mon-Sat, 1-5pm Sun Nov-Feb).

In summer people flock here to listen to opera beneath the stars, but in spring, food and wine professionals descend on the city for Italy's most important national wine fair, **Vinitaly** (www.vinitaly.com). Unsurprisingly, Verona is also big on *aperitivo* culture.

Antica Bottega del Vino (☏045 800 45 35; www.bottegavini.it; Vicolo Scudo di Francia 3; cicheti €2, meals €40; ⊗noon-11pm) is an oenophile institution, its 19th-century cellars filled with over 4000 labels.

✗ ⛴ p117, p183

The Drive » Head northwest out of Verona on the SS12 crossing the Rio Adige before turning left onto the SP1. After 2.5km take the Arbizzano exit right onto the SP4, gradually leaving the suburbs behind and heading into the hills. At Arbizzano continue straight onto the SP12 towards Negrar.

- - - - - - - - - - - - - - -

② Negrar

Five communities make up the DOC quality-controlled heart of Valpolicella: Negrar, Marano di Valpolicella, San Pietro in Cariano, Fumane and Sant'Ambrogio di Valpolicella. Tiny Negrar, so-called 'city of wine', is the largest and is set amid a patchwork of pergola vineyards, criss-crossed by lines of *marogne* (drystone walls) typical of the region. Amarone acolytes flock here to the iconic **Giuseppe Quintarelli** (☏045 750 00 16; giuseppe.quintarelli@tin.it; Via Cerè 1, Negrar; wine tastings €20; ⊗by appointment) estate, which, despite its modest appearance, produces one of the biggest, deepest, richest red wines this side of Porto.

Younger innovators, such as the brothers at **Fratelli Vogadori** (☏328 941 72 28; www.vogadorivini.it; Via Vigolo 16, Negrar; ⊗8am-noon & 1-6pm Mon-Sat, 8am-noon Sun), are meticulous in producing organic wines using unusual native varieties such as Oseleta and Negrara. The result: the full-bodied Amarone Riserva Forlago (2004) and the deservedly famous 2007 Recioto della Valpolicella, which pairs wickedly with dark chocolate cake.

✗ p183

LINK YOUR TRIP

10 A Weekend at Lake Garda
From Bardolino continue on the SS249 and circumnavigate Lake Garda for a spot of boating and wild swimming.

14 A Venetian Sojourn
From Verona head down the A4 to Vicenza for a dose of high-octane culture in the Venetian countryside.

SP6

Grezzana

SP34b

SP6

46km to 14

START
① Verona

Adige

The Drive » Follow the SP12 north out of Negrar and after 3km turn left onto Via Ca'Righetto, climbing into the terraced hills before dropping down to Marano with its Romanesque church. From here take the SP33b to Fumane.

TRIP HIGHLIGHT

❸ Fumane

In Fumane you'll find **Allegrini** (☎045 683 20 11; http://allegrini.it; Via Giare 9/11, Fumane; wine tasting & cellar tour €20, tour of villa €10, tour of villa with wine tasting & snack €30-40; ⊙ cellar tour & wine tasting 10.30am & 3.30pm Mon-Fri by appointment, villa tours 11am & 4pm Mon-Sat by appointment; **P**), one of the leading wineries of the region, where wine tastings are held in the fabulous 16th-century **Villa della Torre**. Built for humanist scholar and law professor Giulio della Torre (1480–1563), the villa has one of the earliest mannerist gardens in Italy. Mannerism was a rebellious strand of the Renaissance that produced some of the most intriguing interiors and garden landscapes of the period. The Italian word *maniera* means 'style' and mannerist art and architecture is highly stylised and fantastical.

On its surface the Villa della Torre and its garden appear to present a regular Renaissance scene, but look closer and you'll find grotesque masks spitting water at promenaders, fireplaces that look like roaring monsters and a grotto that resembles a snarling hell's mouth. All of it together wittily suggests the veneer of civilisation is fragile and despite men's best efforts the primitive forces of nature are always lurking just beneath the surface.

✗ 🛏 p183

The Drive » Drive south on the SP33 from Fumane for the short 6km drive to San Pietro in Cariano. Otherwise known as the 'Via della Valle', the route is lined with lush pergola vines. When you eventually hit a roundabout, take the third exit left into San Pietro.

TRIP HIGHLIGHT

❹ San Pietro in Cariano

At the heart of Valpolicella is San Pietro in Cariano, an ancient hamlet surrounded by elegant Palladian villas such as **San Giona** dating back to the period of Venetian domination. Traces of the town's Roman heritage are also visible in the 12th-century parish church of **Pieve di San Floriano** (Via della Pieve, Località San Floriano; ⊙7.30am-noon & 3.30-6pm), with its spare tripartite, tufa facade and serene, arcaded cloister.

But despite its impressive heritage San Pietro hasn't stayed stuck in the past. Take the strikingly contemporary, award-winning winery **Zýmē** (☎045 770 11 08; www.zyme.it; Via Cà del Pipa 1, San Pietro in Cariano; wine tastings €15; ⊙ shop 9am-5pm Mon-Sat, tastings by appointment 9am-noon & 2-6pm Mon-Fri, 10.30am, 2pm & 4pm Sat), which is headed up by Moreno Zurlo. It has a reputation for bold, big-blend wines, the most famous of which is Harlequin, a thrilling IGP wine made using 15 local grape varieties. In town, you can sample award-winning Amarone at **Montecariano Cellars** (☎045 683 83 35; www.montecariano.it; Via Valena 3, San Pietro in Cariano; ⊙ by

Fumane Villa della Torre

appointment Mon-Fri), just off central Piazza San Giuseppe.

The Drive » A short 10km hop gets you from San Pietro in Cariano to Sant'Ambrogio via San Giorgio, a fraction (subdivision) of Sant'Ambrogio. Pick up the SP4 and head west out of San Pietro. After 2km turn right on Via Case Sparse Conca d'Oro, which leads uphill to San Giorgio. Then retrace your steps to the SP4 and continue west to Sant'Ambrogio.

- - - - - - - - - - - -

⑤ Sant'Ambrogio di Valpolicella

Part of the wealth of Valpolicella comes from the marble quarries at Sant'Ambrogio. The town was already quarrying Rosso Broccato and Bronzetto marble in the Roman period. Much of it went to build Verona's Arena and grand city gates, and even today the **Marble School** is the only one of its kind in Italy.

Perched 375m up on a hill, in the fraction of San Giorgio di Valpolicella, the **Pieve di San Giorgio** (⏱7am-6pm) is the area's oldest Christian church, dating back to 712. Built in Romanesque style from local limestone, the interior displays some beautiful frescoed fragments. Behind the church you can pick up the **Sentiero della Salute**, a 2.5km (one hour) walk through the woods.

The Drive » The next drive takes you out of the bucolic Valpolicella hills and across a tangle of autostradas running down the eastern shore of Lake Garda. Exit Sant'Ambrogio west on the SP4 and then dog-leg across the SS12 onto the SP33a. Wend your way along here, merging with the SP27a and SP31b to Lazise, 11km away.

- - - - - - - - - - - -

TRIP HIGHLIGHT

⑥ Lazise

Sitting at the foot of the gentle hills of Valpolicella on the shores of Lake Garda is Lazise.

DETOUR: VILLA MOSCONI BERTANI

Start: ❶ Verona (p178)

Before you reach Negrar take a quick 1.5km detour off the SP4 down Via Novare to the **Villa Mosconi Bertani** (☎045 602 07 44; www.mosconibertani.it; Via Novare, Arbizzano; tours €9, tastings €20-72; ⊙by appointment Mon-Fri) in Arbizzano. Arguably one of the most beautifully sited villas in Valpolicella, this winery is one of the oldest continuously operating wine businesses in Italy. What's more, the lovely neoclassical residence, completed in 1769, with a phalanx of Greek gods perched on the facade and a grand, frescoed **Chamber of the Muses** designed for small operatic performances, is a listed historic landmark and is well worth a tour. Beyond the house are 8 hectares of English-style Romantic gardens, lakes, orchards and Guyot vineyards to explore. Tours and tastings run regularly between April and October, but require pre-booking.

Dominated for centuries by the powerful and murderous Scaligeri clan from Verona, the town retains its impressive, turreted castle (privately owned) and encircling walls. Look out for the huge hole in the north wall of the main tower, made by a cannon during the 15th-century wars between Venice and Milan.

As an important medieval customs point, Lazise is surrounded by numerous grand villas such as **Villa dei Cedri**, set back from the waterfront in Colà. These days it is home to the fabulous **Parco Thermale del Garda** (☎045 759 09 88; www.villadeicedri.it; Piazza di Sopra 4, Colà; adult/reduced €24/15; ⊙9am-10pm Mon-Thu, to 11pm Fri & Sun, to 1am Sat), a 13-acre natural spa with a couple of enormous thermal lakes fed by underground hot springs pumping out water at a balmy 33°C.

The Drive » A short, lovely 6km lakeside drive takes you north up the SR249 from Lazise to Bardolino. To your left the large, blue expanse of the lake stretches out lazily while to your right ranks of olives and cypresses line the hillsides.

❼ Bardolino

Prosperous Bardolino is a town in love with the grape. More than 70 vineyards grace the surrounding morainic hills interspersed with silvery olive groves, dark cypresses and cheerful pink oleanders. The tourist office has a map of local producers on the **Strada del Vino** (www.stradadelbardolino.com).

The **Museo del Vino** (☎045 622 83 31; www.museodelvino.it; Via Costabella 9; ⊙9am-1pm & 2.30-7pm mid-Mar–Sep, hours vary Oct–mid-Mar) is set within the **Zeni Winery** (☎045 721 00 22; www.zeni.it; Via Costabella 9; tours €5) and offers a good insight into local production methods and grape varieties, coupled with a mini-tasting in the *cantina*. Wines to sample are the local Chiaretto and the young Novello, which rarely make it out of Italy. If you happen to be visiting in May, October or November you can likely catch one of the town's numerous **wine festivals**, when the waterfront fills up with food and wine stands, as well as musicians and dancers. Otherwise, plan your visit on a Thursday in order to catch the weekly market.

✕ 🛏 p183

Eating & Sleeping

Verona ❶ see also p117

✖ Locanda 4 Cuochi   Modern Italian €€

(☎045 803 03 11; www.locanda4cuochi.it; Via Alberto Mario 12; meals €35, 3-course set menu €24; ⏱7.30-10.30pm Tue, 12.30-2.30pm & 7.30-10.30pm Wed-Sun; 🤚) With its open kitchen, urbane vibe and hotshot chefs, you're right to expect great things. Culinary acrobatics play second fiddle to prime produce cooked with skill and subtle twists. Whether it's perfectly crisp suckling pig with lemon and sage, or an epilogue of whipped ricotta cut with raspberry salsa and pistachio crumble, expect to swoon.

🛏 Agriturismo San Mattia   Agriturismo €€

(☎045 91 37 97; www.agriturismosanmattia.it; Via Santa Giuliana 2a, Verona; s €60-100, d €80-120, apt from €150; 🅿) Make friends with the chickens, ducks and horses as you wander through San Mattia's olive groves, orchards and vineyards, then sit back on the patio and soak up the stunning views of Verona. Host Giovanni Ederle is the tour de force behind this 14-room farm, its popular Slow-Food–focused restaurant and Valpolicella vintages (€8.50 to €40).

Negrar ❷

✖ Trattoria Caprini   Trattoria €€

(☎045 750 05 11; www.trattoriacaprini.it; Via Zanotti 9, Torbe; meals €30; ⏱noon-2.30pm & 7-10pm Thu-Tue) A little north of Negrar in the hamlet of Torbe, family-run Caprini serves heart-warming grub you wish your mamma could make. Many menu items are homemade, including the delicious *lasagnetta* with hand-rolled pasta, and a *ragù* of beef, tomato, porcini and finferli mushrooms. Downstairs, beside the fire of the old *pistoria* (bakery), you can sample some 200 Valpolicella labels.

Fumane ❸

✖ Enoteca della Valpolicella   Venetian €€

(☎045 683 91 46; www.enotecadellavalpolicella.it; Via Osan 47, Fumane; meals €25; ⏱noon-2.30pm Sun, noon-2.30pm & 7.30-10pm Tue-Sat) Gastronomes flock to Fumane where an ancient farmhouse has found renewed vigour as a rustically elegant restaurant. Put your trust in gracious owners Ada and Carlotta, who will eagerly guide you through the day's menu, a showcase for fresh, local produce.

🛏 La Meridiana   B&B €

(☎045 683 91 46; www.lameridiana-valpolicella.it; Via Osan 16c; s/d €70/90; 🅿🤚🎫) This delightful B&B is set in a 1600s stable, with beautifully renovated guest rooms – ask for the garden room with the barrel-vaulted stone ceiling – and bountiful breakfasts at the Enoteca della Valpolicella, run by the same owners. You can also swim at a pool 1km away.

Bardolino ❼

✖ Il Giardino delle Esperidi   Osteria €€

(☎045 621 04 77; Via Goffredo Mameli 1; meals €35-50; ⏱7-10pm Mon & Wed-Fri, noon-2.30pm & 7-10pm Sat & Sun) Bardolino's gourmets head for this intimate little *osteria*, where sourcing local delicacies is a labour of love. The intensely flavoured baked truffles with *parmigiano reggiano* (Parmesan) are legendary, and the highly seasonal menu may feature rarities such as goose salami or guinea fowl salad.

🛏 Corte San Luca   Apartment €

(☎345 8212906; www.cortesanluca.com; Piazza Porta San Giovanni 15; d €90, 4-person apt from €200; 🅿❄🤚🎫) A flair for design stamps these 11 smart central apartments – expect suspended furniture, moulded chairs and glass-topped tables. With their fully kitted-out kitchens, laundries and 32-inch TVs, the apartments are a particularly smart home away from home. There's a minimum week stay in July and August.

The Venetian Dolomites

16

It's hard to believe that in a few hours you can go from canals to the crisp Alpine clarity of Cortina d'Ampezzo – land of idyllic hikes, razor-sharp peaks and Italy's most fashion-conscious skiing.

TRIP HIGHLIGHTS

FINISH
Cortina d'Ampezzo
7

165 km
Belluno
Majestically sited town on the edge of the Dolomiti Bellunesi

Cinque Torri
Stunning mountain panoramas and rocky pinnacles

246 km

6

4

3
Conegliano

48 km
Maser
Enjoy one of the Veneto's finest country houses

Castelfranco Veneto
Treviso
START

Valdobbiadene
Hop between wineries on the Strada di Prosecco

70 km

7 DAYS
263KM / 163 MILES

GREAT FOR...

BEST TIME TO GO
December to March for snow sports; July for mountain hikes.

ESSENTIAL PHOTO
The five mythical peaks of the Cinque Torri at sunset.

BEST FOR FOODIES
Refuelling after skiing on delicious, deep-fried Schiz cheese.

rtina d'Ampezzo A chic winter ski venue and summer base for hiking, cycling and rock climbing

16 The Venetian Dolomites

A road trip through the Venetian Dolomites takes you through one of Italy's most sophisticated and least visited stretches of countryside. Some of the Veneto's finest country villas and medieval walled towns are to be found here, while a little further north *prosecco* vines dip and crest across the undulating foothills of the Alps. Crowning it all is the Italian supermodel of ski resorts, Cortina d'Ampezzo – fashionable, pricey and undeniably beautiful.

❶ Treviso

Treviso has everything you could want from a mid-sized Veneto city: medieval walls, pretty canals, narrow cobbled streets and frescoed churches. Despite this it receives few visitors, eclipsed by its more impressive neighbour – Venice. However, if you want to experience authentic Veneto life away from the tourist crowds, this is a great place to come.

Like its neighbour, Treviso is encircled by water. Its defensive walls are surrounded by a moat fed by the River Sile, which runs to the south of town. Grassy parks, weeping willows and waterwheels lend it a charming air, as does the island-bound fish market. Pick up a map from the tourist office and follow one of the easy walking itineraries, then pop into the **Duomo** (Piazza del Duomo; ☺8am-noon & 3.30-6.30pm) to see the local Titian, and fresco-filled **Chiesa di Santa Lucia** (Piazza San Vito; ☺8am-noon Mon-Fri, 8am-noon & 4-6.30pm Sat, 9am-12.30pm & 4-6.30pm Sun), painted by local talent Tommaso da Modena.

For an authentic experience, visit a traditional *osteria* around Piazza dei Signori, such as **Osteria Dalla Gigia** (Via Barberia 20; snacks €1.50-3; ☺9.30am-2pm & 4-8.30pm Mon-Sat) or

Dai Naneti (Vicolo Broli 2; sandwiches €3-4; ☺9am-2.30pm & 5.30-8.30pm Mon-Fri, 9.30am-2pm & 5.30-9pm Sat, 11am-2pm & 4.30-8pm Sun).

✕ ⊨ p175

The Drive » Head west out of Treviso on the regional road SR53 towards Castelfranco Veneto. It's a pleasant 27km drive through flat cornfields and the small provincial towns of Paese, Istrana and Vedelago.

❷ Castelfranco Veneto

The main reason to visit Castelfranco is its charmingly tiny old town, complete with medieval walls, towers and moat. The church in the pretty central square is home to the *Castelfranco Madonna,* one of Renaissance master Giorgione's few surviving works. Born in Castelfranco Veneto as Giorgio Barbarelli da Castelfranco, Giorgione revolutionised Renaissance painting before dying aged 30 of the plague.

The masterpiece hangs in the **Cappella Costanza** in the **Duomo** (http://duomocastelfranco.it; Vicolo del Christo 10; ☺9am-noon & 3.30-6.30pm Mon-Sat, 3.30-6.30pm Sun), and demonstrates Giorgione's subtle new style, which freed Renaissance painting from its linear constraints by using a chiaroscuro technique called *sfumato* ('smokey') to blur hard lines and enhance the emotional quality. As you

look at the painting note how it is suffused with light that has no clear source. Is the sun rising, or setting? Or, is the scene illuminated from another unseen source as the figures of St Francis and the armoured saint suggest? What's more, all three figures appear withdrawn and mysteriously preoccupied with events or emotions beyond their physical setting. It is an intriguing composition, and profoundly moving.

The Drive >> From Castelfranco strike out northwards on the SS667. Ahead you'll see the rising foothills of the Dolomites while you pass through increasingly rural countryside. At Marturo take a left onto the SS248 and then the first right onto Via Caldretta (SP1), which takes you into the centre of Maser. Take a right down Via Cornuda to the Villa di Maser.

LINK YOUR TRIP

13 **Grande Strada delle Dolomiti**

From Cortina head up the SS224 to the Alta Badia. From here you can pick up an epic mountain road trip.

14 **A Venetian Sojourn**
Continue west from Maser on the SS248 to Bassano del Grappa and then loop around for more countryside culture.

AGUSTAVOP/GETTY IMAGES ©

TRIP HIGHLIGHT

③ Maser

Andrea Palladio managed to synthesise the classical past without doggedly copying it, creating buildings that were at once inviting, useful and incomparably elegant.

A prime example of this domestic perfection is Palladio's butter-yellow **Villa di Maser** (Villa Barbaro; ☏0423 92 30 04; www.villadimaser.it; Via Barbaro 4; adult/reduced €9/7; ☉10.30am-6pm Tue-Sat, from 11am Sun Mar-Oct, 11am-5pm Sat & Sun Nov-Feb; **P**) set amid a *prosecco* vineyard in Maser. Inside, Paolo Veronese nearly upstages his collaborator with wildly imaginative *trompe l'œil* architecture of his own. Vines climb the walls of the **Stanza di Baccho**; an alert watchdog keeps one eye on the painted door of the **Stanza di Canuccio** (Little Dog Room); and in a corner of the frescoed grand salon, the painter has apparently forgotten his spattered shoes and broom. At the **wine-tasting room** by the villa's parking lot, you can raise a toast to Palladio and Veronese with the estate's own *prosecco*.

Just east of the villa's gates, you can admire Palladio's **Tempietto**. The domed, centrally planned church is a graceful,

Cinque Torri Aerial view from Lagazuoi

189

DETOUR: POSSAGNO

Start: ❸ Maser (p188)

On the slopes of Monte Grappa, the dazzling, white neoclassical **Tempio** peeps above the treetops as if some part of ancient Rome had come to holiday in the Veneto. It's the parish church of Possagno, where Italy's master-neoclassical sculptor, Antonio Canova, was born in 1757. Canova laid the first stone in 1819, and came to final rest here in 1822.

More interesting is his home and **Gipsoteca**, a light-filled gallery designed by Scarpa to showcase Canova's working models and plaster casts; you'll find it at the **Museo Canova** (☑0423 54 43 23; www. museocanova.it; Via Canova 74; adult/reduced €10/6; ⏱9.30am-6pm Tue-Sun). The plaster casts reveal the laborious process through which Canova arrived at his glossy, seemingly effortless marbles. Fascinating rough clay models give way to plaster figures cast in gesso, which were then used to map out the final marble in minute detail with small nails. It's the most complete display of an artist's working models in Europe.

miniature version of the Pantheon in Rome.

The Drive » The next 22km from Maser to Valdobbiadene are delightful. Rejoin Via Cornuda and continue northeast past the Maser vineyards and into Cornuda. Pass through the tiny centre and then take a left onto the SP84, which will take you across the broad Piave river and up into the vine-striped hills of *prosecco* country.

TRIP HIGHLIGHT

❹ Valdobbiadene

Prosecco can be traced back to the Romans. It was then known as 'Pucino' and was shipped direct to the court of Empress Livia from Aquileia, where it was produced with grapes from the Carso. During the Venetian Republic the vines were transferred to the Prosecco DOCG (quality-controlled) area, a small triangle of land between the towns of Valdobbiadene, Conegliano and Vittorio Veneto.

Valdobbiadene sits at the heart of *prosecco* country, vines dipping and cresting across its hillsides. Take the **Strada di Prosecco** (www.con eglianovaldobbiadene. it) to discover some of the area's best wineries, such as **Azienda Agricola Frozza** (☑0423 98 70 69; www.frozza.it; Via Martiri 31, Colbertaldo di Vidor), where

six generations of the Frozza family have been tending Galera vines on a sun-struck Colbertaldo hillside since 1870. Their 2011 Brut is a particularly good vintage with a fruity fragrance and a well-structured, mineral-rich body. Prices range from €4 to €9 per bottle.

✕ 🛏 p193

The Drive » Take the next 35km on the SP34 and SP38 at a leisurely pace. The views across the vineyards are timeless and very pretty when set against the blue, blue sky. At Parè turn left onto the slightly more busy SS13 for the final 7.5km into Conegliano.

❺ Conegliano

At the foothills of the Alps, Conegliano is the toast of the Veneto. Its hillsides produce *prosecco* in *spumante* (bubbly), *frizzante* (sparkling) or still varieties. Conegliano's *prosecco* was promoted to DOCG status in 2009, Italy's highest oenological distinction.

At the heart of the old town, Via XX Settembre is lined with frescoed buildings and elegant *palazzi*, beneath which a long arcade keeps window shoppers sheltered. Among the palaces is **Palazzo Sarcinelli**, which is often used for art exhibitions. Even more impressive is the eye-catching **Scuola dei Battuti** (☑0422 184 89 04;

rotaryconegliano2060@gmail.com; ☺Sala dei Battuti 10am-noon & 3-5pm Sun or by appointment), covered inside and out with 16th-century frescoes by Ludovico Pozzoserrato. This building was once home to a religious lay group known as *battuti* (beaters) for their enthusiastic self-flagellation. Enter the **Duomo** through the *scuola* to enjoy the 1492–93 altarpiece by local master Cima da Conegliano. Before you leave, be sure to pop into one of the bars around central **Piazza Cima** and enjoy a glass of fizz with the locals.

The Drive ❯❯ The 53km drive to Belluno is less scenic. Most of the way you'll be on the fast A27 autostrada (tolls apply). After 45km, take the exit for Belluno, which will put you on the SP1 for the final 11km climb into town.

TRIP HIGHLIGHT

⑥ Belluno

Perched on high bluffs above the Piave river and backed majestically by the snowcapped Dolomites, Belluno makes a scenic and strategic base to explore the 31,500-hectare **Parco Nazionale delle Dolomiti Bellunesi** (www.dolomitipark.it). And you'll be happy to fuel up for ski trails and hikes on the city's hearty cuisine, including Italy's most remarkable cheeses: Schiz (semisoft cow's-milk cheese, usually fried in butter) and the flaky, butter-yellow Malga Bellunense.

When yoou're not out on the slopes, the historical old town is its own attraction, mixing stunning views with Renaissance-era buildings. **Piazza dei Martiri** (Martyrs' Square), Belluno's main pedestrian square, is named after four partisans hanged here during WWII. On sunny days and warm nights, its cafes overflow with young and old alike. Nearby, the Piazza del Duomo is framed by the early-16th-century Renaissance **Cattedrale di San Martino**, the 16th-century **Palazzo Rosso** and the **Palazzo dei Vescovi**, with a striking 12th-century tower.

✗ 🛏 p193

The Drive ❯❯ The two-hour (81km) drive from Belluno to the Cinque Torri is one of this trip's highlights. Cutting right through Parco Nazionale delle Dolomiti Bellunesi on the SR203, it offers stunning mountain panoramas and a nerve-tingling traverse of the Falzarego pass. Note: in winter, weather conditions may close the high passes. If so, take the A27 and SS51 direct to Cortina d'Ampezzo.

TRIP HIGHLIGHT

⑦ Cinque Torri

At the heart of the Dolomites, just 16km west of Cortina at the confluence of the Ampezzo, Badia and Cordevole valleys, is the gorgeous area of **Cinque Torri** (www.5torri.it). It is accessible from Cortina by buses – ski shuttles in winter (free to ski-pass holders) and a Dolomiti Bus service in summer – which connect with the lifts at Passo Falzarego.

Hard though it is to believe, some of the fiercest fighting of WWI

LOCAL KNOWLEDGE: PROSECCO LOW-DOWN

Prosecco is Italy's most famous sparkling wine and in the Veneto it is a firm favourite, costing less than bottled water in many places. It is made predominantly from the Glera grape and it comes in three forms: *spumante* (sparkling), *frizzante* (semi-sparkling) and *tranquillo* (still). You can tell a good *prosecco* by its straw-like colour and greenish reflections. When it is *spumante*, the bubbles should be tiny, numerous and long-lasting, tickling your nose with the smell of white fruit or freshly cut grass. It's meant to be drunk young (and often!) and pairs best with local salami, creamy Asiago cheese and roasted chestnuts in autumn.

TOP TIP: PRIMAVERA DEL PROSECCO

Every May the 30 *prosecco*-producing villages in the DOC quality-controlled area participate in the **Primavera del Prosecco** (Prosecco Spring; www. primaveradelprosecco.it), putting on a weekend party with food stalls and all-day *prosecco* tasting.

took place in these idyllic mountains between Italian and Austro-Hungarian troops. Now you can wander over 5km of restored trenches in an enormous open-air museum between Lagazuoi and the Tre Sassi fort. Guided tours are offered by the Gruppo Guide Alpine, and in winter you can ski the 80km **Great War Ski Tour** with the Dolomiti Superski ski pass. En route, mountain refuges provide standout lunches with spectacular views.

✖ p193

The Drive ≫ Another super, swooping drive along mountain roads lined with conifers. At Cinque Torri, pick up the SS48 (Passo Falzarego) and wind your way slowly down the twisting route into Cortina d'Ampezzo, 16km away.

❽ Cortina d'Ampezzo

The spiked peaks and emerald-green valleys of the Dolomites are so beautiful, and their ecosystem so unique, they've won Unesco protection. In winter, Cortina d'Ampezzo is the place to be, with fashion-conscious snow bunnies crowding its excellent slopes. In summer, it doubles as a slightly less glamorous but still stunning base for hiking, cycling and rock climbing.

Two cable cars whisk skiers and walkers from Cortina's town centre to a central departure point for chairlifts, cable cars and trails. They usually run from 9am to 5pm daily mid-December to April and resume June to

October. Dolomiti Super-ski passes provide access to 12 runs in the area, and are sold at Cortina's **ski pass office** (☏0436 86 21 71; www.skipasscortina. com; Via Marconi 15; 1-/3-/7-day Valley pass €40/117/218; ⊙8.30am-12.30pm & 3.30-7pm Mon-Sat, 8.30am-12.30pm & 5-7pm Sun winter only). Other winter adventures include dog sledding, ice climbing and skating at the **Olympic Ice Stadium** (☏0436 88 18 11; Via dello Stadio 1; adult/reduced incl skate rental €10/9; ⊙10.30am-12.30pm & 3.30-5.30pm Dec-Apr), built for the 1956 Winter Olympics. **Guide Alpine Cortina d'Ampezzo** (☏0436 86 85 05; www.guidecortina. com; Corso Italia 69a) runs rock-climbing courses and guided nature hikes, off-trail skiing and snow-shoeing.

✖ 🛏 p193

Eating & Sleeping

Valdobbiadene ④

✘ Agriturismo Da Ottavio   Venetian €

(☎0423 98 11 13; Via Campion 2, San Giovanni di Valdobbiadene; meals €15-20; ☺noon-3pm Sat, Sun & holidays, closed Sep) *Prosecco* is typically drunk with *sopressa*, a fresh local salami, as the sparkling *spumante* cleans the palate and refreshes the mouth. There's no better way to test this than at Da Ottavio, where everything on the table, *sopressa* and *prosecco* included, is homemade by the Spada family.

⌂ Azienda Agricola Campion   Farmstay €

(☎0423 98 04 32; www.campionspumanti.it; Via Campion 2, San Giovanni di Valdobbiadene; s €45-55, d €65-80; ☺tasting room 9am-noon & 2-6pm; P✱🛜🐾) Why not quit worrying about the challenges of *prosecco* tasting and driving and instead bed down at this farmstay amid 14 hectares of vines in the heart of Valdobbiadene? The four rooms occupy converted farm buildings, with warm, rustic styling and the added perk of a kitchenette in each.

Belluno ⑥

✘ Al Borgo   Italian €€

(☎0437 92 67 55; www.alborgo.to; Via Anconetta 8; meals €30-40; ☺noon-2.30pm Mon, noon-2.30pm & 7.30-10.30pm Wed-Sun) Seek out this delightful restaurant in an 18th-century villa in the hills about 3km south of Belluno. Considered the area's best, the kitchen produces everything from homemade salami and roast lamb to artisanal gelato. Wines are also skilfully chosen and grappa locally sourced.

⌂ Alla Casetta   B&B €

(☎0439 4 28 91; www.allacasetta.com; Via Strada delle Negre 10, Cesiomaggiore; d/tr/q €65/80/100; P@) It might take the navigation skills of an alpinist to find this patch of paradise on the Caorame river, but persevere. Hosts Christian and Amy hand-draw hiking and biking maps (the Alta Via 2 and Via Claudia Augusta bike trail are nearby), steer you towards the nearest *malga* (cheese-making hut) and point out choice fishing and kayaking spots.

Cinque Torri ⑦

✘ Rifugio Scoiattoli   Veneto €€

(☎333 8146960; www.5torri.it/rifugio-scoiattoli; Località Potor, 2255m; meals €25-30, dm/d €58/126; ☺9am-9pm) In 1969 Alpine guide Lorenzo Lorenzi built this refuge and it is still managed by his family today. Accessible by foot from the Cinque Torri chairlift, the terrace offers gorgeous panoramic views to accompany the typical Ampezzo dishes the refuge serves, such as pasta with wild blueberries. Rooms are also available as is an outdoor hot tub.

Cortina d'Ampezzo ⑧

✘ Agriturismo El Brite de Larieto   Veneto €

(☎368 7008083; www.elbritedelarieto.it; Passo Tre Croci, Località Larieto; meals €22-30; ☺noon-3pm & 7-10pm, closed Thu out of season; P) Located 5km northwest of Cortina off the SS48 towards Passo Tre Croci, this idyllic farm enjoys a sunny situation amid thick larch forest. It produces all its own dairy products, vegetables and much of the meat on the menu, and its *canederli* (dumplings) are a highlight.

✘ El Camineto   Italian €€€

(☎0436 44 32; www.ilmeloncino.it; Locale Rumerlo 1, Cortina d'Ampezzo; meals €45-60; ☺noon-2.30pm & 7-10pm, closed Tue summer; P) With a rustically elegant dining room and spectacular terrace, Il Meloncino is one of the few finer restaurants that stays open almost year-round (though it does close for part of May and June). The roasted boar and venison-stuffed ravioli in a hazelnut sauce are as jaw-dropping as the Alpine views.

⌂ Hotel Montana   Hotel €

(☎0436 86 21 26; www.cortina-hotel.com; Corso Italia 94, Cortina d'Ampezzo; s €52-78, d €85-175; @) Right in the heart of Cortina, this friendly, vintage 1920s Alpine hotel offers simple but well-maintained rooms. In winter, there's a seven-night minimum (€320 to €560 per person), but call for last-minute cancellations. Reception areas double as gallery space for local artists.

Trieste to Tarvisio

17

Meander the borderlands from Trieste to Tarvisio and you'll find an amazing reserve of historical sights amid the Alpine hillsides. So kick back with the locals and toast this curious corner of Italy.

TRIP HIGHLIGHTS

225 km

7 FINISH

Tarvisio
Wander lakeside and ski cross-border into Slovenia

● Osoppo

Como di Rozzano ●

4

100 km

Gradisca d'Isonzo ●

Collio
Sip Friulano amid the rolling hills of Collio

2 Sistiana ●

1 START

50 km

Aquileia
Once one of the largest and richest cities in the Roman Empire

0 km

Trieste
Commune with literary ghosts in Trieste's grand cafes

7 DAYS
225KM / 140 MILES

GREAT FOR...

BEST TIME TO GO
May to October for fine weather and the grape harvest.

ESSENTIAL PHOTO
Mosaic sea monsters and songbirds at Aquileia.

BEST FOR CULTURE
A true borderland: multilingual, multicultural and historically fascinating.

17 Trieste to Tarvisio

With its triple-barrelled moniker, Friuli Venezia Giulia's multicultural nature should come as no surprise on this tour of the region. Starting in the capital Trieste, the home of Habsburg princes and for centuries Austria's seaside salon, climb the steep plateau to Cividale, the city of Julius Caesar, eavesdrop on multilingual gossip in Gorizia, drink Hungarian-style Tocai in Collio and end in the Giulie Alps where you can ski into Slovenia.

TRIP HIGHLIGHT

1 Trieste

From as long ago as the 1300s, Trieste has faced east. It flourished under Habsburg patronage between 1382 and 1918, attracting writers and philosophers such as Thomas Mann and James Joyce to the busy cafes on **Piazza dell'Unità d'Italia**. There they enjoyed the city's fluid character where Latin, Slavic, Jewish and Germanic culture intermingled.

The neighbourhood of **Borgo Teresiano** reflects this cultural melange and on Via San Francesco d'Assisi you can tour Trieste's nationally important **Synagogue**

(☎040 37 14 66; www.triestebraica.it; Via San Francesco d'Assisi 19; adult/reduced €3.50/2.50; ⏰guided tours 3.45pm, 4.45pm & 5.45pm Mon & Wed, 9.30am, 10.30am & 11.30am Tue).

Seven kilometres from the city centre, **Castello di Miramare** (☎040 22 41 43; www.castello-miramare.it; Viale Miramare; adult/reduced €8/5; ⏰9am-7pm) is Trieste's bookend to Austrian rule, the fanciful neo-Gothic home of Archduke Maximilian, commander in chief of Austria's Imperial Navy, who came to Trieste as an ambitious young aristocrat in the 1850s and was shot by firing squad in Mexico in 1867. The

house is a reflection of his eccentric wanderlust.

✗ ⊨ p201

The Drive » Head northwest out of Trieste along Viale Miramare (SS14), where you'll keep sea views to your left for almost 20km. At Sistiana join the A4 (towards Venice) for 18km to Redipuglia. Then exit southwest towards Papariano and Aquileia for the final 16km through rural farmland.

- - - - - - - - - - - - - -

TRIP HIGHLIGHT

② Aquileia

Colonised by Rome in 181 BC, Aquileia was one of the largest and richest cities of the empire. Levelled by Attila's Huns in AD 452, the city's inhabitants fled south and west where they founded Grado and then Venice. A smaller town rose in its place in the early Middle Ages with the construction of the

LINK YOUR TRIP

13 Grande Strada delle Dolomiti

Just after Osoppo exit the A23 for Tolmezzo and weave your way along the SS52 to Cortina d'Ampezzo and the Dolomites beyond.

14 A Venetian Sojourn

From Aquileia hop onto the A4 for a fast ride down to the Venetian lagoon, where golden domes and frescoed palaces await.

present **basilica** (www. basilicadiaquileia.it; Piazza Capitolo; crypts adult/reduced €4/3, bell tower €2; ☺9am-7pm Apr-Sep, shorter hours winter, bell tower summer only), which is carpeted with one of the largest and most spectacular Roman-era mosaics in the world.

Beyond the basilica explore the scattered ruins of the **Porto Fluviale**, the old port, and the standing columns of the ancient **Forum** on Via Giulia Augusta. Then visit the **Museo Archeologico Nazionale** (✆0431 9 10 16; www.museoarcheo-aquileia.it; Via Roma 1; adult/reduced €4/2; ☺8.30am-7.30pm Tue-Sun) for one of Italy's most important collections of Roman artefacts.

The Drive ❯❯ Exit Aquileia north on the SS352 and after 3km veer off northeast onto the SS351 through open farmland towards Gradisca d'Isonzo. Then cross the broad Isonzo river before merging with Via Raccordo Villese-Gorizia after 10km. Drive a further 15km before exiting on the SR56 into Gorizia.

❸ Gorizia

An often-contested border zone and the scene of some of the most bitter fighting of WWI's eastern front, Gorizia was, most recently, an Iron Curtain checkpoint. Its crumbling fences and watchtowers can still be seen on **Piazza Transalpina**, which since 2007 has marked the Slovenian border.

For a salutary lesson in its bloody past visit the imposing **Borgo Castello** (✆0481 53 51 46; Borgo Castello 36; adult/reduced €6/3; ☺10am-7pm Tue-Sun, 9.30-11.30am Mon) and the **Museo della Grande Guerra** (✆0481 53 39 26; Borgo Castello 13-15; admission with Borgo Castello; ☺9am-7pm Tue-Sun), which charts the tragic story of WWI, when Gorizia sat on the Italian-Austrian frontline.

✕ 🍴 p201

The Drive ❯❯ The short 14km trip to Cormòns is a very pretty rural drive. Exit Gorizia westwards on Via Udine and then turn off northwards on the SR56 at San Lorenzo Isontino. From here it's a 7km drive through vineyards to Cormòns.

TRIP HIGHLIGHT

❹ Collio

Famed for its wine-makers and country restaurants, the Collio produces some of the finest, mineral-rich white wines in Italy from local varietals such as Friulano, Malvasia Istriana and Ribolla Gialla. The area's vineyards are arranged like a quilt around the town of **Cormòns**, where the local wine shop, **Enoteca di Cormòns** (✆0481 63 03 71; www.enoteca-cormons.it; Piazza XXIV Maggio 21; ☺11am-10pm Wed-Mon), offers tastings with platters of Montasio cheese.

Even in high season, it is easy to drop in to dozens of family run wineries and taste rare vintages with vintners such as **Renato Keber** (✆0481 63 98 44; www.renato keber.com; Località Zegla 15). Larger vineyards, offering international export, are **Venica & Venica** (✆0481 6 12 64; www.venica.it; Località Cerò 8, Dolegna del Collio).

If you feel peckish, drop into **La Subida** (✆0481 6 05 31; www.la subida.it; Via Subida, Cormons; meals €50; ☺noon-2.30pm & 7-11pm Sat & Sun, 7-11pm Mon, Thu & Fri), where

---

✔ **TOP TIP: SKI PASSES**

Multiday passes (two/four/six days from €61/113/158) enable you to ski in Italy, Slovenia and Austria, on the slopes of Sella Nevea, Tarvisio, Zoncolan, Bovec, Krajnska Gora and Arnoldstein. The Monte Canin ski lift is free to Friuli Venezia Giulia Card holders; this regional discount card entitles card holders to discounts on multiday passes and equipment hire. **Promotur** (✆0428 65 39 15; www. promotur.org) sells passes at each of the resorts.

Trieste Balcony at the Castello di Miramare

border-crossing dishes and ingredients bring the landscape to the plate.

✖️ p201

The Drive ❯❯ The next 18km to Cividale del Friuli are the most scenic on the trip. Rolling northwards from Cormòns on a country lane through the vineyards on the SS356, you'll pass through small villages such as Como di Rozzano, where Perusini offers tastings.

- - - - - - - - - - - -

❺ Cividale del Friuli

Founded by Julius Caesar in 50 BC as Forum de Lulii (ultimately 'Friuli'), Cividale's picturesque stone streets are worth a morning's quiet con-templation. Splitting the town in two is the **Ponte del Diavolo** (Devil's Bridge), its central arch supported by a huge rock said to have been thrown into the river by the devil.

Cividale's most important sight is the **Tempietto Longobardo** (Oratorio di Santa Maria in Valle; ☎0432 70 08 67; www. tempiettolongobardo.it; Borgo Brossano; adult/reduced €4/3; ⏰10am-1pm & 3-5pm Mon-Fri, 10am-6pm Sat & Sun). Dating from the 8th century AD, its frescoes and ancient Lombard woodwork are both unusual and extremely moving. After-wards head to the **Museo Cristiano** (Piazza del Duomo; museo adult/reduced €4/3; ⏰museo 10am-1pm & 3-6pm Wed-Sun) in the cathedral, where you can see the 8th-century, stone Altar of Ratchis.

The Drive ❯❯ Wend your way out of Cividale across the Natisone river on Via Fiore dei Liberti. To your right you'll get a great view of the Ponte del Diavolo. Then take a hard left onto Viale Udine, which becomes the SS54 and carries you 18km to Udine.

- - - - - - - - - - - -

❻ Udine

While reluctantly ceding its premier status to Tri-este in the 1950s, Udine

DETOUR: SAN DANIELE DEL FRIULI

Start: ⑥ Udine (p199)

Just northwest of Udine, on the SR464, San Daniele del Friuli sits in an undulating landscape. Its 8000 inhabitants prepare Friuli's greatest gastronomic export, the dark, exquisitely sweet Prosciutto di San Daniele. Salt is the only method of preservation allowed and the 27 *prosciuttifici* (ham-curing plants) in the town are safeguarded by EU regulations. Try the ham at **Bottega di Prosciutto** (☏0432 957 043; www.bottegadelprosciutto.com; 2 Via Umberto I; ⊘9am-noon Mon-Sat, 3.30-7pm Tue & Thu-Sat).

In August, the town holds the **Aria di Festa**, a four-day festival of open-house tours and tastings. For a list of *prosciuttifici* that are open year-round, see the **tourist office** (☏0432 94 07 65; Via Roma 3; ⊘9.30am-noon Mon-Fri, 4-6pm Tue, Wed & Fri, 10.30am-12.30pm & 4-6pm Sat & Sun).

---

remains the spiritual, and gastronomic, capital of Friuli. At the heart of its walled medieval centre sits the **Piazza della Libertà**, dubbed the most beautiful Venetian square on the mainland.

Other Venetian echoes can be seen in the shimmering Tiepolo frescoes in the **cathedral** (www.cattedraleudine.it; Piazza del Duomo; ⊘8am-noon & 4-6pm Mon-Sat, 4-6pm Sun) and the **Oratorio della Purità** (Piazza del Duomo; ⊘10am-noon, ask for key at the cathedral if closed), open for guided tours only. The *Assumption* on the ceiling was one of Giambattista's very first commissions, while the eight biblical scenes in chiaroscuro are by his son Giandomenico. For more Tiepolos and rare views of the city framed by the Alps beyond, walk up the hill to the **castle**.

Local legend has it that when Attila the Hun plundered Aquileia in AD 452, he ordered his soldiers to build the hill from where he could witness its destruction. Now it houses the **Galleria d'Arte Antica** (☏0432 27 15 91; Colle del Castello; adult/reduced €8/5; ⊘10.30am-5pm Tue-Sun, to 7pm summer).

✕ ⇤ p201

The Drive » From Udine join the A23 all the way to Tarvisio. The first 30km continue through the same low-lying rural landscape, with the forested slopes of the Carnic Alps coming into sharp perspective at Osoppo. Here you'll cross the Tagliamento river and sweep eastwards into the Giulie Alps for the remaining 70km to Tarvisio.

TRIP HIGHLIGHT

⑦ Tarvisio

Wedged into the Val Canale between the Giulie and eastern Carnic Alps, Tarvisio is just 7km short of the Austrian border and 11km from Slovenia.

Despite its modest elevations, this is the snowiest (and coldest) pocket in the whole Alpine region, with heavy snowfalls not uncommon into May. The main ski centres are at Tarvisio, with a good open 4km run that promises breathtaking views, and 60km of cross-country tracks; and at **Sella Nevea** (www.sellanevea.net). Sella Nevea is linked to Bovec in Slovenia. In summer the hiking, caving, canoeing and windsurfing are all good, especially around the **Laghi di Fusine** (Fusine Lakes).

⇤ p201

Eating & Sleeping

Trieste ❶

🍷 Caffè Tommaseo   Bar

(☎040 36 26 66; www.caffetommaseo.com;
Riva III Novembre; meals €30; ◷9am-10pm)
Virtually unchanged since its 1830 opening, the
rich ceiling reliefs, primrose-yellow walls and
Viennese mirrors here couldn't be any more
evocative. Take coffee at the bar or sit down for
some *fritto misto* (fried seafood).

🛏 L'Albero Nascosto   Boutique Hotel €€

(☎040 30 01 88; www.alberonascosto.it; Via
Felice Venezian 18; s €85, d €125-170; ❀🛜) A
delightful little hotel in the middle of the old town,
Nascosto is a model of discreet style. Rooms are
spacious and tastefully decked out with parquet
floors, original artworks, books and a vintage
piece or two; most also have a small kitchen
corner. Breakfasts are simple with local cheeses,
top-quality preserves and Illy coffee.

Gorizia ❸

🍴 Majda   Gorizian €

(☎0481 3 08 71; Via Duca D'Aosta 71; meals
€25; ◷noon-3pm & 7.30-11pm Mon-Sat) With
a courtyard bar, friendly staff and enthusiastic
decor, Majda is a happy place to sample local
specialities such as ravioli filled with potato
(Slovenian-style) or beetroot and local herbs,
wild boar on polenta and interesting sides like
steamed wild dandelion.

🛏 Palazzo Lantieri   B&B €€

(☎0481 53 32 84; www.palazzo-lantieri.com;
Piazza Sant'Antonio 6; s/d €80/140; P🛜) This
palazzo-stay offers light, spacious rooms in the
main house or self-catering apartments in former
farm buildings, all overlooking a glorious Persian-
styled garden. Goethe, Kant and Empress Maria
Theresa were repeat guests back in the day.

Collio ❹

🍴 Terre e Vini   Friulian €€€

(☎0481 6 00 28; www.terrevini.it; Via XXIV
Maggio, Brazzano di Cormons; meals €52;
◷noon-2.30pm Tue-Sun, 7-10pm Tue-Sat) The

Felluga family are Friulian wine royalty and their
cosy 19th-century *osteria* looks out over the
plantings. Feast on tripe on Thursdays, salt cod
on Fridays and goose stew or herbed frittata any
day of the week. Book ahead for Sunday lunch.

Udine ❻

🍴 Trattoria ai Frati   Friulian €€

(☎0432 50 69 26; Piazzetta Antonini 5; meals
€25-30; ◷10am-11pm Mon-Sat) A popular old-
style eatery on a cobbled cul-de-sac where you
can expect local specialities such as *frico* (fried
cheese), pumpkin gnocchi with smoked ricotta.
It's loved by locals for its whopper steaks and its
raucous front bar.

🛏 Hotel Clocchiatti
Next   Design Hotel €€

(☎0432 50 50 47; www.hotelclocchiatti.it; Via
Cividale 29; s/d villa €90/130, annexe €150/190;
P❀🛜🏊) Two properties, one location: older-
style (cheaper) rooms are in the original villa,
while the contemporary steel-and-glass 'Next'
rooms line up around a pool and outdoor bar in
the garden. It's a pleasant walk from the centre,
with easy access out of the city if you're driving.

San Daniele del Friuli

🍴 Ai Bintars   Italian €

(☎0432 95 73 22; www.aibintars.com; Via Trento
Trieste 67; mains €15-25; ◷noon-2.30pm &
7-10pm Fri-Tue, 7-10pm Wed; P) No menu, no
fuss, no kerbside appeal, Ai Bintars simply serves
the best prosciutto and salami alongside small
plates of marinated vegetables, local cheeses
and generous hunks of bread.

Tarvisio ❼

🛏 Hotel Edelhof   Hotel €€

(☎0428 4 00 81; www.hoteledelhof.com; Via
Armando Diaz 13; s/d €75/140; P🛜) Situated
right by the lifts with large, airy rooms furnished
with hand-painted wooden furniture and a
basement spa. Seven-night minimum in high
season.

Start/Finish: Rialto Market

Distance: 3.5km

Duration: 3 hours

Venice's cosmopolitan outlook has kept the city ahead of the locavore curve and makes local cuisine anything but predictable. Take this tour of the city's famous markets and backstreet bacarie (bars) to sample the unique fusion of flavours in Venice (Venezia).

Take this walk on Trips

Rialto Market & Pescaria

Any tour through Venice's gourmet history starts at the 600-year-old **Rialto Market** (☎041 296 06 58; ⏰7am-2pm; 🚤Rialto-Mercato). Hear grocers singing the praises of island-grown produce. Nearby fishmongers call out the day's catch at the **Pescaria** (Fish Market; ⏰7am-2pm Tue-Sun). You cannot take your car onto the lagoon islands so leave it in a secure garage in Mestre, such as **Garage Europa** (☎041 95 92 02; www.garageeuropa mestre.com; Corso del Popolo 55, Mestre; per day €15; ⏰8am-10pm), and hop on the train to Venice Santa Lucia where you can pick up a *vaporetto* (water taxi) to Rialto-Mercato.

The Walk >> Around the corner from the Pescaria, at Ruga degli Spezieri 381, Drogheria Mascari displays the trade-route spices that made Venice's fortune. Down the road, duck into Calle dell'Arco.

All'Arco

At **All'Arco** (☎041 520 56 66; Calle dell'Ochialer 436, San Polo; cicheti from €1.50; ⏰8am-8pm Wed-Fri, to 3pm Mon, Tue & Sat; 🚤Rialto-Mercato) father and son chefs Francesco and Matteo invent Venice's best *cicheti,* the dainty bar snacks that are Venice's version of tapas. If you wait patiently, they'll invent a seasonal speciality for you.

The Walk >> Pick up Calle Raspi and weave your way northwest over the Rio di San Cassiano, past Veneziastampa on Campo Santa Maria Mater Domini, and on to Palazzo Mocenigo.

Palazzo Mocenigo

Costume dramas unfold in the **Palazzo Mocenigo** (☎041 72 17 98; http://mocenigo. visitmuve.it; Salizada di San Stae 1992, Santa Croce; adult/reduced €8/5.50; ⏰10am-5pm Tue-Sun summer, to 4pm winter; 🚤San Stae), once the Mocenigo's swanky pad and now a showcase for the fashions of Venice's elite. Necklines plunge in the Red Living Room, lethal corsets come undone in the Contessa's bedroom and men's paisley knee-breeches show some leg in the dining room.

The Walk >> Continue up Calle del Tintor and across the Ponte del Megio. AS soon as you cross

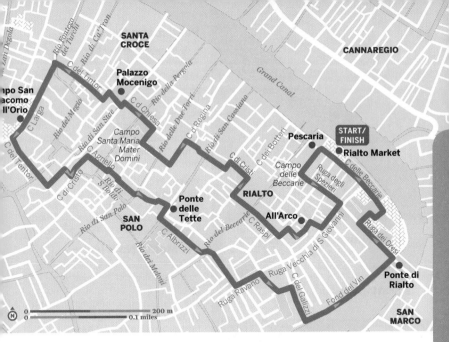

the bridge turn left and then take the first right into the Campo San Giacomo dell'Orio.

Campo San Giacomo dell'Orio

You can pop your head into the church, but the real attraction of this *campo* is **Al Prosecco** (📞041 524 02 22; www.al prosecco.com; Campo San Giacomo dell'Orio, Santa Croce 1503; ⏰10am-8pm; 🚤San Stae), where from 10am they're popping corks and raising glasses of *vini naturi* (natural process wines) and *ombre* (wine by the glass).

The Walk >> Head southeast from Campo San Giacomo, quickly crossing a small canal and turn left on Calle di Cristo and then right down Calle Agnello, which will bring you to the high-arched Ponte delle Tette.

Ponte delle Tette

No one remembers the original name of the Ponte delle Tette, known since the 15th century as 'Tits Bridge'. Back in those days, the shadowy porticos flanking this bridge were a designated red-light zone where prostitutes displayed their wares. For educated conversation,

cortigione (courtesans) might charge 60 times more than the basic rate: fees were set by the state and posted in Rialto brothels.

The Walk >> Continue down Calle Albrizzi across the Rio del Beccarie at Ponte Storte and dog-leg down Ruga Ravano and Calle del Galizzi towards the waterfront; then turn left along the Fond del Vin. In front of you, you'll be greeted by the splendid sight of the Ponte di Rialto.

Ponte di Rialto

An amazing feat of engineering in its day (1592), Antonio da Ponte's marble Ponte di Rialto was for centuries the only land link across the Grand Canal. The construction cost 250,000 gold ducats, a staggering sum that puts cost overruns for the contemporary Calatrava bridge into perspective. The southern side faces San Marco, and when shutterbugs clear out around sunset it offers a romantic long view of gondolas pulling up to Grand Canal *palazzi* (mansions).

The Walk >> To return to the Rialto Market head northwest up Ruga dei Oresi, past the Hotel San Salvadore and right down Sestiere San Polo.

STRETCH YOUR LEGS
MILAN

Start/Finish: Pasticceria Cova

Distance: 2.5km

Duration: 2 hours

For anyone interested in the fall of a frock or the cut of a jacket, a stroll around the Quadrilatero d'Oro, the world's most famous shopping district, is a must. Even if you don't have the slightest urge to sling a swag of glossy carrier bags over your arm, the people-watching is priceless.

Take this walk on Trips

Pasticceria Cova

Coffee and pastries at **Pasticceria Cova** (☎02 7600 5599; www.pasticceriacova.com; Via Monte Napoleone 8; ⏰7.30am-8.30pm Mon-Sat; Ⓜ Montenapoleone) provide a glimpse into the world of the Quad: aggressively accessorised matrons crowd the neoclassical bar, barking pastry orders at the aproned staff. This is the oldest cafe in Milan (Milano), opened in 1817 by Antonio Cova, a soldier of Napoleon.

The Walk ›› Cova sits on the corner of Via Monte Napoleone and Via Sant'Andrea. Walk northwest up Monte Nap past lavish designer window displays in old aristocratic mansions, such as the Palazzo Melzi di Cusano at number 18.

Via Monte Napoleone

Via Monte Napoleone is the most important street of the Quad, lined with global marques such as Etro, Armani and Prada. Among the designer giants, heritage names persist, such as classic Milanese fashion brand **Aspesi** (☎02 7602 2478; www.aspesi.com; Via Monte Napoleone 13; ⏰10am-7pm Mon-Sat; Ⓜ San Babila, Montenapoleone).

The Walk ›› Halfway up Via Monte Napoleone, beside the glowing windows of Acqua di Parma, you'll see the narrow opening of Via Gesù. Head down there, past the hallowed doors of the Brioni atelier and in front of the Four Seasons you'll find the entrance to the Bagatti Valsecchi mansion.

Four Seasons

The Quad's most discreet and luxurious hotel is the Four Seasons on Via Gesù. The neoclassical facade hides a 15th-century Renaissance convent complete with frescoes and a tranquil arcaded cloister. Dine here at one of the nine outdoor tables of **La Veranda** (☎02 7 70 88; www.fourseasons.com/milan; Via Gesù 6/8; meals €80-90; ⏰noon-4.30pm & 7-11pm; Ⓟ; Ⓜ Montenapoleone). Opposite is the **Museo Bagatti Valsecchi** (☎02 7600 6132; www.museobagattivalsecchi.org; Via Gesù 5; adult/reduced €9/6; ⏰1-5.45pm Tue-Sun; Ⓜ Montenapoleone), stuffed with Renaissance furnishings and paintings.

The Walk ›› Retrace your steps and head northwest to the top of Via Monte Napoleone to the intersection with bigger, busier Via Alessandro

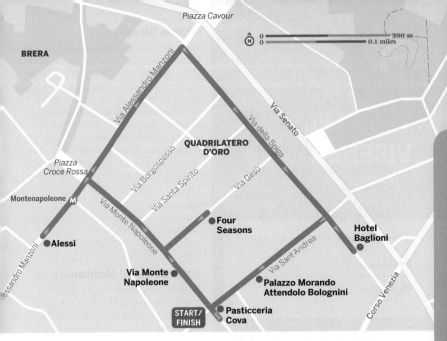

Manzoni. Turn left here and after a few metres you'll find Alessi on your left.

Alessi

Established on the shores of Lago d'Orta in Omegna in 1921, **Alessi** (📞02 79 57 26; www.alessi.com; Via Manzoni 14-16; 🕐10am-2pm & 3-7pm Mon, 10am-7pm Tue-Sat; Ⓜ️Montenapoleone) has gone on to transform modern homes with over 22,000 crafted utensils. Some of the best examples now reside in the V&A in London and New York's MoMA, but you can just pop into the flagship store refitted by Martí Guixé.

The Walk » Exit Alessi and turn right, retracing your footsteps. Continue past Via Monte Napoleone, past the Teatro Manzoni and take the next right down Via della Spiga. Walk almost the whole length of it, past Sermoneta and Tiffany, to reach the back door of the Baglioni.

Hotel Baglioni

Who wouldn't love shopping on pedestrianised Via della Spiga, once the domain of bakeries. But if the cobbles are making those killer heels pinch, take the back door into **Hotel Baglioni** (📞02 7 70 77; www.baglionihotels.com; Via Senato 5; 🕐7-1am; Ⓜ️San Babila) for a Campari and soda in its cafe, decked out like a 19th-century drawing room.

The Walk » Exit the Baglioni back onto Via della Spiga, turn right and walk to Via Sant'Andrea and take a left. Walk a few metres down Via Sant'Andrea and you'll see the board for the Museo di Milano.

Palazzo Morando Attendolo Bolognini

For a glimpse of the Quad as it was during its 18th-century heyday, wander around the **Palazzo Morando Attendolo Bolognini**. Its **Costume Moda Immagine** (📞02 8846 5735; www.costumemodaimmagine. mi.it; Via Sant'Andrea 6; adult/reduced €5/3; 🕐9am-1pm & 2-5.30pm Tue-Sun; Ⓜ️San Babila) exhibits the collections of Contessa Bolognini in her personal apartments, while other rooms house the **Museo di Milano** civic art collection, which provides a picture of the city as it was during Napoleonic times.

The Walk » It's a short walk back to Cova from the Museo di Milano. Turn left down Via Sant'Andrea and you'll find it just past Via Bagutta on your left.

STRETCH YOUR LEGS
VICENZA

Start/Finish: Teatro Olimpico

Distance: 3km

Duration: 1½ hours

When Palladio escaped an oppressive employer in his native Padua, few knew the humble stonecutter would transform not only his adoptive city of Vicenza, but also the history of European architecture. It's no wonder Vicenza has been declared one grand Unesco World Heritage Site.

Take this walk on Trip

14

Teatro Olimpico

Palladio's **Teatro Olimpico** (☎0444 22 28 00; www.teatroolimpicovicenza.it; Piazza Matte-otti 11; adult/reduced €11/8, or with MuseumCard; ☺9am-5pm Tue-Sun, to 6pm early Jul-early Sep), which he began in 1580, was inspired by Roman amphitheatres. Vincenzo Scamozzi finished the theatre, adding a stage set modelled on the ancient Greek city of Thebes; check online for opera, jazz and classical performances. The ticket also gets you into the Museo Civico.

The Walk » Pick up the main Corso Palladio and walk southwest. Then turn right up Contrà Santa Corona, and proceed past the red-brick Dominican church. Shortly afterwards you'll arrive at the Palazzo Leoni Montanari on your left.

Palazzo Leoni Montanari

Outside it may look like a bank, but a treasure beyond accountants' imaginings awaits inside the **Palazzo Leoni Montanari** (☎800 578875; www.gallerie ditalia.com; Contrà di Santa Corona 25; adult/reduced €5/3, or with MuseumCard; ☺10am-6pm Tue-Sun). Grand salons are adorned with Canaletto's lagoon landscapes and Pietro Longhi 18th-century society satires. Up another flight, 400 Russian icons are spotlit in darkened galleries.

The Walk » Retrace your steps to Corso Palladio and walk its length, lined with mansions and notable buildings. Turn right up Via Fogazzaro and after a short distance arrive in Piazza San Lorenzo.

Tempio di San Lorenzo

Not everything in Vicenza is Palladian, not least the **Tempio di San Lorenzo** (Piazza San Lorenzo 6). In the Middle Ages Franciscan friars tended to the sick here and guarded the relics of St Lawrence. Now the facade is a Gothic extravagance. Sadly much of the interior decoration was damaged when Napoleon's troops set up barracks here, although the flower-filled 14th-century cloister remains.

The Walk » Make your way back to Corso Palladio via Contrà Cordenons and turn right. A short walk further west will bring you to the end of the Corso in front of Torrione di Porta Castello. Pass under it to the gardens.

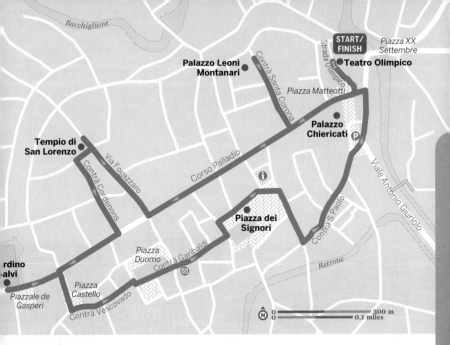

Giardino Salvi

Just beyond the city walls, Luigi Valmarana commissioned the **Giardino Salvi** (Corso S Felice Fortunato; ⊙8am-8pm) as a meeting place for intellectuals and academics. Silver firs, Himalayan cedars and tulip trees line its neatly tended lawns, which sit between two Palladian lodges: the **Loggia Longhena**, built by Baldassare Longhena, and the **Loggia Valmarana**, a Doric temple, attributed to a student of Andrea Palladio.

The Walk ⟫ Head south, through morning market stalls, out of Piazza Castello on Contrà Vescovado. After a few steps you'll pass through Piazza Duomo and continue along Contrà Garibaldi until you reach Piazza dei Signori.

Piazza dei Signori

The heart of historic Vicenza is Piazza dei Signori, where Palladio lightens the mood of government buildings with his trademark play of light and shadow. Dazzling white Piovene stone arches frame shady double arcades in the **Basilica Palladiana** (☎0444 22 21 22; www. museicivicivicenza.it; Piazza dei Signori; tempo-

rary exhibitions €10-13; ⊙ temporary exhibitions only). Across the piazza, white stone and stucco grace the exposed red-brick colonnade of the 1571-designed **Loggia del Capitaniato**.

The Walk ⟫ From Piazza dei Signori head south and pick up Contrà S Paolo, which bears left (northeast) back to Piazza Matteotti.

Palazzo Chiericati

Built in 1550, **Palazzo Chiericati** (☎0444 22 28 11; www.museicivicivicenza.it; Piazza Matteotti 37/39; adult/reduced €5/3; ⊙10am-6pm Tue-Sun early Jul-early Sep, 9am-5pm Tue-Sun rest of year) is one of Palladio's finest buildings and now houses the **Museo Civico**. The frescoed ground floor includes the Sala dal Firmamento (Salon of the Skies), with Domenico Brusasorci's ceiling fresco of Diana galloping across the sky to meet the sun.

The Walk ⟫ Exit the palazzo onto Piazza Matteotti and you'll see the Teatro Olimpico to your left at the end of the square.

Central Italy

AS FLORENCE'S RENAISSANCE SKYLINE FADES INTO THE BACKGROUND the open road beckons. Motoring through Tuscany's voluptuous, wine-rich hills is one of Italy's great driving experiences and one of the many on offer in this fascinating part of the country.

To the north of Tuscany, Emilia-Romagna is a mecca for foodies, its handsome medieval towns supplying many of Italy's most revered delicacies. Travel to Italy's green, rural heart where you'll come across artistic treasures by Renaissance heroes, ancient Roman ruins and Etruscan tombs.

And all the while the road leads inexorably, often tortuously, towards Rome, the Eternal City.

Tuscany Val d'Orcia
RANK BIENEWALD/CONTRIBUTOR/GETTY IMAGES ©

 DON'T MISS

Necropolis Tarquinia

The frescoed Etruscan tombs at Tarquinia's Unesco-listed Necropolis are remarkable, yet they rarely attract big crowds. Visit on Trip 20

Santo Stefano di Sessanio

It's a thrilling drive up to this atmospheric *borgo* in Abruzzo's Parco Nazionale del Gran Sasso e Monti della Laga. Try it on Trip 19

Palazzo Ducale, Urbino

The palatial residence of an art-loving Renaissance aristocrat dominates Urbino's charming historic centre, as you'll discover on Trip 23

Ostia Antica

Overshadowed by the more famous ruins in Rome, this is one of central Italy's most compelling archaeological sites. See it on Trip 18

Montalcino

Crowned by a 14th-century fort, this hilltop town produces one of Italy's top red wines. Indulge yourself on Trip 24

Roaming Around Rome

18

Rome's little-explored hinterland is a real eye-opener, with verdant scenery and thrilling cultural treasures – haunting ancient ruins, hilltop villas and landscaped Renaissance gardens.

TRIP HIGHLIGHTS

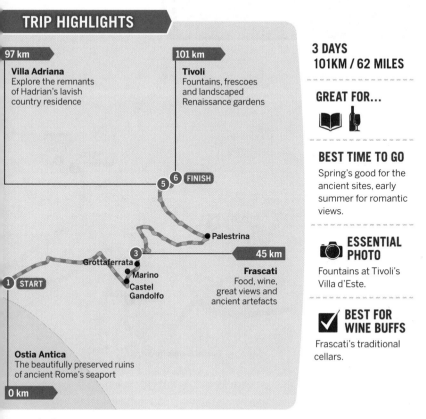

97 km

Villa Adriana
Explore the remnants of Hadrian's lavish country residence

101 km

Tivoli
Fountains, frescoes and landscaped Renaissance gardens

5 6 **FINISH**

● **Palestrina**

45 km

3

Grottaferrata ●
● **Marino**
Castel Gandolfo

Frascati
Food, wine, great views and ancient artefacts

1 **START**

Ostia Antica
The beautifully preserved ruins of ancient Rome's seaport

0 km

3 DAYS
101KM / 62 MILES

GREAT FOR...

BEST TIME TO GO
Spring's good for the ancient sites, early summer for romantic views.

ESSENTIAL PHOTO
Fountains at Tivoli's Villa d'Este.

BEST FOR WINE BUFFS
Frascati's traditional cellars.

18 Roaming Around Rome

While Rome (Roma) hogs the limelight, the area around the capital makes for an absorbing drive with its wealth of historic sights. Headline acts include the remarkably well-preserved ruins of ancient Rome's port at Ostia Antica, and Emperor Hadrian's vast palace complex at Tivoli. Tivoli is one of several hilltop towns that feature on this trip, along with the wine town of Frascati and the papal retreat of Castel Gandolfo.

TRIP HIGHLIGHT

❶ Ostia Antica

The remarkably well-preserved ruins of Ostia Antica, ancient Rome's main seaport, form one of Italy's most compelling and under-appreciated archaeological sites. The city was founded in the 4th century BC at the mouth of the Tiber and developed into a major port with a population of around 50,000. Decline set in after the 5th century when barbarian invasions and outbreaks

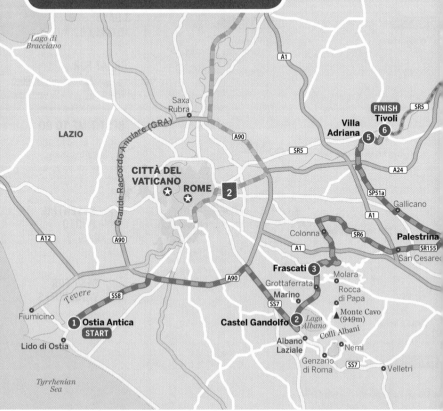

of malaria led to its abandonment and slow burial in river silt, and thanks to the silt it has survived very well.

The **Scavi Archeologici di Ostia Antica** (📞06 5635 0215; www.ostiaantica.beniculturali.it; Viale dei Romagnoli 717; adult/reduced €8/4, exhibitions €3; ⏰8.30am-6.15pm Tue-Sun summer, shorter hr winter) are spread out and you'll need a few hours to do them justice. The main thoroughfare, the **Decumanus Maximus**, leads from the city's entrance (the Porta Romana) to highlights such as the **Terme di Nettuno** (Baths of Neptune), whose floor features a famous mosaic of Neptune driving his seahorse chariot. Next door, the steeply stacked **amphitheatre** was built by Agrippa and later enlarged to hold 3000 people. Behind the theatre, the **Piazzale delle Corporazioni** (Forum of the Corporations) housed Ostia's merchant guilds and is decorated with well-preserved mosaics. Further towards Porta Marina, the **Thermopolium** is an ancient cafe complete with a bar and fresco advertising the bill of fare.

✗ p219

The Drive » Head back towards Rome and take the Grande Raccordo Anulare (GRA; A90) for Naples. Exit at the Ciampino Airport turn-off and continue up Via Appia (SS7), until you come to traffic lights halfway up a long climb. Make a left turn to Lago Albano and follow this road up under the towering umbrella pines to Castel Gandolfo at the top. All told, it takes about 35 minutes.

- - - - - - - - - - - - - -

❷ Castel Gandolfo

One of the prettiest towns in the Castelli Romani, an area of wooded wine-rich hills just south of Rome, Castel Gandolfo makes for a memorable stop. It's not a big place but what it lacks in size it makes up for in atmosphere, and on a warm summer's evening there's no better place for a romantic tête-à-tête. Action is centred on **Piazza della Libertà**, a refined baroque square overlooked by the **Palazzo Apostolico** (http://biglietteriamusei.vatican.va/musei/tickets/do; Piazza della Libertà, Castel Gandolfo; adult/reduced €10/5; ⏰9am-noon Mon-Fri, 9-11am & 2.30pm, 3.30pm, 4.30pm Sat), the pope's impressive summer residence. But a stop here is as much about lapping up the gorgeous views over Lago

ABRUZZO

A24

p218

Subiaco

A1

160km to 27

Segni

0 ——— 10 km
0 ——— 5 miles

LINK YOUR TRIP

2 World Heritage Wonders

From Ostia Antica head into Rome along Via Ostiense to join up with this tour of Italy's greatest hits.

27 Shadow of Vesuvius

Take the A1 autostrada from near Frascati and head down to Naples (Napoli), the starting point for this exploration of Vesuvius, Pompeii and other classic sites.

Albano and enjoying a leisurely al fresco meal as sightseeing.

✕ p219

The Drive 》 To Frascati, it's a pretty straightforward 20-minute drive. From Castel Gandolfo follow the road for Marino, enjoying glimpses of the lake off to your right, and then Grottaferrata. Here you'll come to a roundabout. Take the third exit and Frascati is 4km further on.

TRIP HIGHLIGHT

❸ Frascati

Best known for its crisp white wine, Frascati is a popular day-trip destination. On hot summer weekends Romans pile into town to hang out in the elegant historic centre and fill up on *porchetta* (herb-roasted pork) and local wine. You can follow suit by filling up from the food stalls on **Piazza del Mercato** or searching out the traditional *cantinas* (originally wine and olive-oil cellars, now informal restaurants) that pepper the centre's narrow lanes. Once you've explored the town and admired the sweeping views from the tree-lined avenue at the bottom of Piazza Marconi, head up to **Villa Aldobrandini**. Designed by Giacomo della Porta and built by Carlo Maderno, this regal 16th-century villa sits haughtily above town in a stunning hillside

position. The villa itself is closed to the public but you can visit the impressive early baroque **gardens** (Via Cardinal Massai 18; ☺9am-5.30pm Mon-Fri) dramatically landscaped into the wooded hill.

✕ ⬛ p219

The Drive 》 Take Viale Catone from the top of Piazza Marconi, following the green signs for the autostrada. Continue, passing through Colonna, until soon afterwards you hit the fast-flowing SR6 (Via Casilina). Turn right onto the Casilina and after San Cesareo turn left onto the SR155 for a twisting climb up to Palestrina. Plan on about half an hour from Frascati.

❹ Palestrina

The pretty town of Palestrina stands on the slopes of Monte Ginestro, one of the foothills of the Apennines. In ancient times Praeneste, as it was then known, was a favourite summer retreat for wealthy Romans and the site of a much-revered temple dedicated to the goddess of fortune. Little remains intact of the 2nd-century-BC **Santuario della Fortuna Primigenia**, but much of what is now the historic centre was built over its six giant terraces. Nowadays, the town's main act is the fantastic **Museo Archeologico Nazionale di Palestrina** (☏06 953 81 00; Piazza della Cortina; admission incl sanctuary €5; ☺9am-8pm, sanctuary 9am-

1hr before sunset), housed in the 17th-century **Palazzo Colonna Barberini**. The museum's collection comprises ancient sculpture, funerary artefacts, and some huge Roman mosaics, but its crowning glory is the breathtaking Mosaico Nilotico, a 2nd-century-BC mosaic depicting the flooding of

Ostia Antica Ruins of the theatre and the Piazzale delle Corporazioni

the Nile and everyday life in ancient Egypt.

🍴 p219

The Drive » It takes just over half an hour to get to Villa Adriana. Exit Palestrina and head northwest towards Gallicano. Here, follow the signs to Tivoli, continuing past the shrubbery and under the Castello di Passerano until you see Villa Adriana signposted a few kilometres short of Tivoli.

- - - - - - - - - - - - - -

TRIP HIGHLIGHT

⑤ Villa Adriana

Emperor Hadrian's sprawling 1st-century summer residence, **Villa Adriana** (☎0774 38 27 33; www.villaadriana.benicul-turali.it; adult/reduced €8/4; ⏰9am-1hr before sunset) was one of ancient Rome's grandest properties, lavish even by the decadent standards of the day. Hadrian personally designed much of the complex, taking inspiration from buildings he'd seen around the world. The pecile, the large pool area near the walls, is a reproduction of a building in Athens.

DETOUR: SUBIACO

Start: ⑥ Tivoli

Remote-feeling and dramatic, Subiaco is well worth the trip to see its two breathtaking Benedictine monasteries. The **Monastero di San Benedetto** (www.benedettini-subiaco.org; ⊙9.30am-12.15pm & 3.30-6.15pm) is carved into the rock over the cave where St Benedict holed up for three years to meditate and pray. Apart from its stunning setting, which inspired Petrarch to comparisons with the edge of Paradise, it's adorned with rich 13th- to 15th-century frescoes.

Halfway down the hill from San Benedetto is the **Monastero di Santa Scolastica** (📞0774 8 55 69; www.benedettini-subiaco.org; ⊙9.30am-12.15pm & 3.30-6.15pm), the only one of the 13 monasteries built by St Benedict still standing in the Valley of the Amiene. If you decide to stay, its **Foresteria** (📞0774 8 55 69; www.benedettini-subiaco.org; per person half-board €37) is a great place to spend a contemplative night. But book ahead, as Benedictine clergy from around the world often make the pilgrimage here to work in the monastery's famous library and archive. There's also a restaurant offering set menus for €19 and €23.

Similarly, the canopo is a copy of a sanctuary in the Egyptian town of Canopus, with a narrow 120m-long pool flanked by sculptural figures.

To the northeast of the pecile, the **Teatro Marittimo** is one of the villa's signature buildings, a mini-villa built on an island in an artificial pool. Originally accessible only by swing bridges, it's currently off-limits due to ongoing restoration.

There are also several bath complexes, temples and barracks.

Parking (€3) is available at the site.

The Drive » Pick up Via Tiburtina (SR5), the main Rome–Tivoli road, and head up to Tivoli *centro*. It's a short, steep, twisting climb up to the town centre that should take about 15 minutes.

TRIP HIGHLIGHT

⑥ Tivoli

Tivoli's elevated historic centre is an attractive,

if often busy, spot. Its main attraction is the Unesco-protected **Villa d'Este** (📞0774 33 29 20; www.villadestetivoli.info; Piazza Trento; adult/reduced €8/4; ⊙8.30am-1hr before sunset Tue-Sun), a one-time Benedictine convent that Lucrezia Borgia's son, Cardinal Ippolito d'Este, transformed into a pleasure palace in the late-16th century. From 1865 to 1886 it was home to Franz Liszt and inspired his 1877 piano composition *The Fountains of the Villa d'Este*.

Before heading out to the gardens, take time to admire the villa's rich Mannerist frescoes. Outside, the manicured **gardens** feature water-spouting gargoyles and shady lanes flanked by lofty cypresses and extravagant fountains, all powered by gravity alone. Look out for the Bernini-designed **Fountain of the Organ**, which uses water pressure to play music through a concealed organ, and the 130m-long **Avenue of the Hundred Fountains**.

✖ p219

Eating & Sleeping

Ostia Antica ❶

✗ Ristorante
Monumento   Ristorante €€

(📞06 565 00 21; www.ristorantemonumento.
it; Piazza Umberto I 8; fixed-price lunch menu
€14, meals €25-30; 🕐12.30-3.30pm & 8-11pm
Tue-Sun) This historic restaurant started life in
the 19th century, catering to the men working
on reclaiming the local marshlands. Nowadays,
it feeds sightseers fresh out of the nearby
ruins, serving homemade pastas and excellent
seafood. A fixed-price lunch menu is available.

Castel Gandolfo ❷

✗ Antico Ristorante
Pagnanelli   Ristorante €€€

(📞06 936 00 04; www.pagnanelli.it; Via Antonio
Gramsci 4, Castel Gandolfo; meals €60-70;
🕐noon-3.30pm & 6.30-11.45pm) Housed in a
wisteria-clad villa, this celebrated restaurant is
a great place for a romantic meal. It's no casual
trattoria, erring on the formal and touristy side,
but the seasonally driven food is excellent,
there's a colossal wine list and the views over
Lago Albano are unforgettable.

Frascati ❸

✗ Cantina Simonetti   Osteria €

(Piazza San Rocco 4; meals €25; 🕐7.45pm-
midnight Wed-Sun, 1-4pm Sat & Sun, longer hours
summer) For an authentic dining experience,
search out this traditional *cantina* and sit down
to a casual meal of *porchetta*, cold cuts and
cheese, accompanied by local white wine. In
keeping with the food, the decor is rough-and-
ready rustic with plain wooden tables and
simple white tablecloths.

✗ Cacciani   Ristorante €€€

(📞06 942 03 78; www.cacciani.it; Via Armando
Diaz 13; fixed-price lunch menu €25, meals €50;

🕐12.15-3pm & 7-11pm Tue-Sat, 12.15-3pm Sun)
Frascati's most renowned restaurant offers fine
food and twinkling terrace views over Rome.
The menu lists various modern creative dishes,
but it's the classics like *cannelloni con ragù*
(cannelloni with meat sauce) that really stand
out. There's also a weighty wine list and a couple
of fixed-price menus, including a €25 weekday
lunch option.

🛏 Cacciani   Hotel €

(📞06 940 19 91; www.cacciani.it; Via Armando
Diaz 13; d €85-95; ❄ 🤍) The hotel of the
Cacciani restaurant. Rooms are simple but
comfortable enough and most have views down
to Rome.

Palestrina ❹

✗ Zi' Rico   Ristorante €€

(📞06 8308 2532; www.zirico.it; Via Enrico Toti
2; meals €35-40; 🕐12.30-3pm & 8-11.30pm
Tue-Sat, 12.30-3pm Sun) Hidden away on a side
alley in the *centro storico*, this highly regarded
restaurant serves contemporary Italian fare in
an intimate setting near the cathedral.

Tivoli ❻

✗ Trattoria del Falcone   Trattoria €€

(📞0774 31 23 58; Via del Trevio 34; meals
€30; 🕐noon-4pm & 6.30-11pm) Near Villa
d'Este, this cheerful, family run trattoria has
been serving pizzas, classic pastas, meat and
seafood since 1918. Boasting exposed stone
decor and a small internal courtyard, it's
popular with both tourists and locals.

✗ Sibilla   Ristorante €€€

(📞0774 33 52 81; www.ristorantesibilla.com; Via
della Sibilla 50; meals €50; 🕐12.30-3pm & 7.30-
10.30pm Tue-Sun) With tables set out by two
ancient Roman temples and water cascading
down the green river gorge below, the Sibilla's
outdoor terrace sets a romantic stage for
seasonally driven food and superlative wine.

Abruzzo's Wild Landscapes

19

This stunning mountain region offers superb driving and spectacular scenery. Roads snake through silent valleys and stone-clad villages, over highland plains and past thick forests.

TRIP HIGHLIGHTS

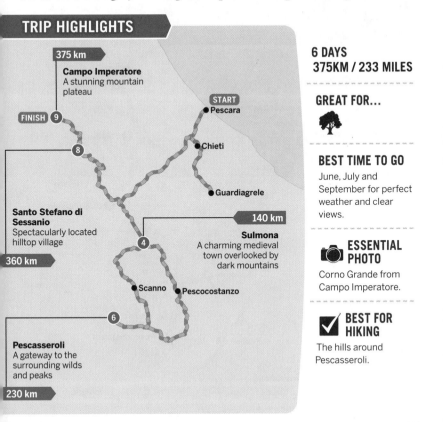

375 km

Campo Imperatore
A stunning mountain plateau

FINISH ⑨

START
●Pescara

●Chieti

●Guardiagrele

Santo Stefano di Sessanio
Spectacularly located hilltop village

360 km

④

140 km

Sulmona
A charming medieval town overlooked by dark mountains

●Scanno ●Pescocostanzo

⑥

Pescasseroli
A gateway to the surrounding wilds and peaks

230 km

6 DAYS
375KM / 233 MILES

GREAT FOR...

BEST TIME TO GO
June, July and September for perfect weather and clear views.

ESSENTIAL PHOTO
Corno Grande from Campo Imperatore.

BEST FOR HIKING
The hills around Pescasseroli.

19 Abruzzo's Wild Landscapes

Although little more than an hour's drive from Rome (Roma), Abruzzo is largely unknown to foreign visitors. Yet with its thrilling mountain scenery and rural, back-country charm, it's ideal for a road trip. This route takes in the best of the region's three national parks, winding past ancient beech woods populated by wolves and bears, as stark snow-capped summits shimmer in the distance. Cultural gems also await, such as the charming medieval town of Sulmona.

1 Pescara

Before heading into the wild interior spend a day relaxing on the beach in Pescara, Abruzzo's largest city. Action centres on the animated seafront although there are a couple of small museums worth a look – the **Museo delle Genti d'Abruzzo** (☏085 451 00 26; www.gentidabruzzo.it; Via delle Caserme 24; adult/reduced €6/3; ⊗8.30am-2pm Mon-Sat), which illustrates local rural culture, and the **Museo Casa Natale Gabriele D'Annunzio**

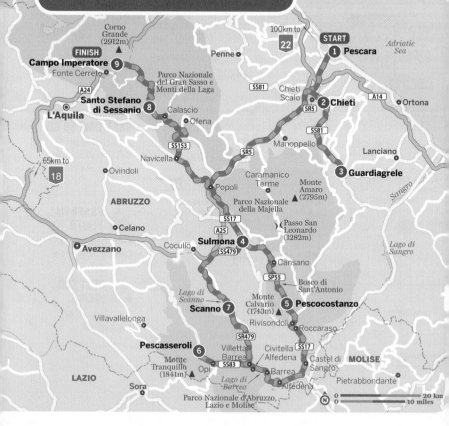

(📞0865 6 03 91; Corso Manthonè 116; €2; ⏰9am-1.30pm), birthplace of controversial fascist poet Gabriele D'Annunzio.

 p227

The Drive » From central Pescara it's about half an hour to Chieti. Follow the green signs to the autostrada, which direct you onto the Raccordo Pescara-Chieti, a fast-moving dual carriageway that runs past factories and warehouses towards the distant mountains. Exit for Chieti and follow signs for Chieti *centro* and then the Civetta and Museo Archeologico Nazionale.

- - - - - - - - - - - -

② Chieti

Overlooking the Aterno valley, hilltop Chieti dates back to pre-Roman times, as you'll discover in its two archaeol-

LINK YOUR TRIP

18 Roaming Around Rome

From Fonte Cerreto take the A24 for about 105km southwest to Tivoli, one of the gems in Rome's fascinating hinterland.

22 Green Heart of Italy

Pick up the A14 at Pescara and follow the coast north for the 100km or so to Ascoli Piceno and a tour of Umbria and Le Marche's verdant valleys.

ogy museums. The most important of these is the **Museo Archeologico Nazionale d'Abruzzo Villa Frigerj** (📞0871 40 43 92; www.archeoabruzzo. beniculturali.it; Villa Comunale; adult/reduced €4/2; ⏰9am-8pm Tue-Sun), home to the 6th-century-BC *Warrior of Capestrano*, the most important pre-Roman find in central Italy and a much-publicised regional icon. Uphill from the museum, the **Museo Archeologico Nazionale d'Abruzzo La Civitella** (📞0871 6 31 37; www.archeo abruzzo.beniculturali.it; Via Pianell; adult/reduced €4/2; ⏰9am-2pm Mon-Sat & 1st Sun of month) is built around a Roman amphitheatre.

The Drive » Descend from Chieti's centre until you see signs for Guardiagrele and the SS81 off to the left. The road twists and turns slowly for the first few kilometres but eventually broadens out and becomes quicker as it runs past woods and vineyards up to Guardiagrele, about 26km (40 minutes) away.

- - - - - - - - - - - -

③ Guardiagrele

Described as Abruzzo's terrace by poet Gabriele D'Annunzio, this ancient

borgo (medieval town) on the eastern flank of the **Parco Nazionale della Majella** (www.parco majella.it) commands sweeping views. Admire these and the striking **Chiesa di Santa Maria Maggiore** (Piazza di Santa Maria Maggiore, Guardiagrele; ⏰7am-noon & 4-7pm Mon-Fri) with its 14th-century arched portico and austere Romanesque facade.

 p227

The Drive » To Sulmona it's about two hours from Guardiagrele. Double back to Chieti on the SS81, then follow signs for the autostrada towards L'Aquila then the SR5 to Chieti Scalo and Manoppello. Pass through Popoli and continue on the SS17 until you see Sulmona signposted about 18km on.

- - - - - - - - - - - -

TRIP HIGHLIGHT

④ Sulmona

Overlooked by the grey Morrone massif, Sulmona is an atmospheric medieval town famous for its *confetti* (sweets traditionally given to guests at Italian weddings). Life is focused on **Corso Ovidio**, named after local boy Ovid, and **Piazza Garibaldi**, a striking piazza

---

✓ TOP TIP: ARRIVING IN SULMONA

Try to time your arrival in Sulmona between 1.30pm and 5.30pm, when traffic restrictions are lifted and you can drive into the historic centre. It makes getting to your hotel much easier.

accessed through a 13th-century **aqueduct**. Here on the square, you can peruse religious and contemporary art at the **Museo Diocesano di Arte Sacra** (☎0864 21 29 62; Piazza Garibaldi; €3.15, incl Museo Civico €5.25; ☉9am-1pm & 3.30-6.30pm Tue-Sun).

At the other end of Corso Ovidio, **Palazzo dell'Annunziata** sits above a 1st-century-BC Roman *domus* (villa), remains of which can be seen at the **Museo Civico** (☎0864 21 02 16; €3.15, incl Museo Diocesano di Arte Sacra €5.25; ☉9am-1pm & 3.30-6.30pm Tue-Sun).

✕ ⊨ p227

The Drive » The 50-minute run over to Pescocostanzo takes you through some beautiful mountain terrain, via the Bosco di Sant'Antonio (ideal for a picnic). From Sulmona head towards Cansano and follow the road as it ascends the increasingly rocky landscape. At Cansano take the SP55 for Pescocostanzo.

⑤ Pescocostanzo

Surrounded by lush highland meadows, Pescocostanzo (elevation 1400m) is a characteristic hilltop town whose historical core has changed little in over 500 years. Of particular note is the **Collegiata di Santa Maria del Colle**, an atmospheric Romanesque church with a lavish baroque interior. Nearby, **Piazza del Municipio** is flanked by a number of impressive *palazzi* (mansions), including **Palazzo Comunale** with its distinctive clock tower, and **Palazzo Fanzago**, designed by the great baroque architect Cosimo Fanzago in 1624.

History apart, Pescocostanzo also offers skiing on **Monte Calvario** and summer hiking in the **Bosco di Sant'Antonio**.

The Drive » Reckon on about 75 minutes to Pescasseroli. Continue past Rivisondoli to the SS17, then turn south towards Roccaraso. After Castel di Sangro head right onto the SS83. This beautiful road swoops and dips its way through Alfedena, Barrea, past the artificial Lago di Barrea, and on to Villetta Barrea, Opi and Pescasseroli.

Campo Imperatore Views across the plain to Corno Grande mountain

TRIP HIGHLIGHT

6 Pescasseroli

Deep in the heart of the Marsican mountains, Pescasseroli is the main centre of the **Parco Nazionale d'Abruzzo, Lazio e Molise** (www.parcoabruzzo.it), the oldest and most popular of Abruzzo's national parks. Hiking oppor-tunities abound with clearly marked paths for all levels and in winter there's popular downhill skiing. If you're travelling with kids, you can see a bear at the **Centro Visita** (☎0863 911 32 21; Viale Colli d'Oro; adult/reduced €6/4; ☺10am-5.30pm) and learn about wolves in Civitella Alfedena at the **Museo del Lupo Appenninico** (Wolf Centre; ☎0864 89 01 41; Via Santa Lucia; adult/reduced €3/2; ☺10am-1.30pm & 3-6.30pm).

🛏 p227

The Drive ❱❱ To Scanno it takes about an hour. Double back to Villetta Barrea and turn left onto the SR479. Wind your way up through a pine forest and past grassy slopes to the Passo Godi at about 1500m, from where the road starts its slow, tortuous descent to Scanno.

ABRUZZO WILDLIFE

Abruzzo's three national parks – Parco Nazionale del Gran Sasso e Monti della Laga; Parco Nazionale della Majella; and Parco Nazionale d'Abruzzo, Lazio e Molise – are home to thousands of animal species. Most famous of all is the Marsican brown bear, of which there are an estimated 50 or so in the Parco Nazionale d'Abruzzo, Lazio e Molise. Apennine wolves also prowl the deep woods, sometimes emerging in winter when thick snow forces them to approach villages in search of food. Other notable animals include the Abruzzi chamois and red deer, and, overhead, golden eagles and peregrine hawks.

7 Scanno

A tangle of steep alleyways and sturdy, grey-stone houses, picture-pretty Scanno is an atmospheric *borgo* known for its finely worked filigree gold jewellery. Explore the pint-sized historic centre and then head down to Lago di Scanno – a couple of kilometres out of town on the road to Sulmona – for a cool lakeside drink.

✖ p227

The Drive » This two-hour leg can be broken up by overnighting in Sulmona, 31km from Scanno through the breathtaking Gole di Sagittario. From Sulmona pick up the SS17 to Popoli and then follow signs for L'Aquila, climbing steadily to Navicella. Here, take the SS153 towards Pescara. Exit for Ofena and climb the snaking road past Calascio and on to Santo Stefano di Sessanio.

TRIP HIGHLIGHT

8 Santo Stefano di Sessanio

If you really want to get away from it all, you can't get much more remote than this picturesque village high in the **Parco Nazionale del Gran Sasso e Monti della Laga** (www.gransassolagapark. it). Once a 16th-century Medici stronghold, it suffered damage in the 2009 earthquake and many of its stone buildings are now under scaffolding. That said, it's still a memorable experience to explore its steeply sloping streets and enjoy the great panoramas. For information, ask at the helpful **Centro Visite** (www.centrovisitesantostefano disessanio.it; Via del Municipio; ⌚10am-7pm summer, 10am-3pm Sat & Sun winter).

🛏 p227

The Drive » From Santo Stefano, Campo Imperatore is signposted as 13km. It's actually more like 20km (20 minutes), but you'll forget about such things as the awesome scenery unfolds ahead of you. Just follow the road and its continuation, the SS17bis, and admire the views.

TRIP HIGHLIGHT

9 Campo Imperatore

The high point – quite literally – of this trip is the highland plain known as Campo Imperatore (average elevation 1800m). Often referred to as Italy's Little Tibet, this magnificent grassy plateau provides spectacular views of **Corno Grande** (2912m), the highest mountain in the Apennines. But as daunting as it might appear, the Corno Grande is not an especially arduous climb, and the 11.5km *via normale* (normal route) from the Hotel Campo Imperatore is one of the area's most popular trekking routes.

From Campo Imperatore, signs direct you down to **Fonte Cerreto**, a small cluster of hotels set around a *funivia* (cable car) station, and the nearby A24 autostrada.

Eating & Sleeping

Pescara ❶

✕ Ristorante Marechiaro da Bruno
Seafood, Pizza €€

(☎085 421 38 49; www.ristorantemarechiaro.
eu; Lungomare Matteotti 70; meals €25-40;
⏱noon-3pm & 7-11pm) With a prime position
on the seafront, the speciality here is bound to
be seafood – in all shapes and sizes. It's a lively
place, smarter than its neighbours, with suited
waiters and white linen, and there's an impressive
array of pizzas at night.

⊨ Hotel Alba
Hotel €

(☎085 38 91 45; www.hotelalba.pescara.it; Via
Michelangelo Forti 14; s €60-110, d €65-120, tr
€90-150, q €110-180; P ❄ @) A glitzy three-
star place, the Alba provides comfort and a
central location. Rooms vary but the best sport
polished wood, firm beds and plenty of sunlight.
Rates are lowest at weekends and garage parking
costs €10.

Guardiagrele ❸

✕ Antichi Sapori
Sandwiches €

(www.saporidabruzzo.com; Via Tripio 135; panino
€2; ⏱8am-1pm & 5-8pm Tue-Sat, 8am-1pm
Sun) An old-fashioned deli in the historic centre,
this is a great place for a doorstopper panino
(filled bread) and regional delicacies – honey,
marinated vegetables and local red wine.

Sulmona ❹

✕ Il Vecchio Muro
Abruzzese €

(☎0864 5 05 95; www.vecchiomuro.it; Via M
D'Eramo 20; meals €25; ⏱12.45-2.30pm &
7.45-10.30pm, closed Wed Oct-Apr) Possibly
Sulmona's best restaurant (no mean feat), the
'old wall' is notable for its fantastic pizza
(dinner only) and unique cacio e pepe (spaghetti
with cheese and black pepper), served in an
edible basket made from Parmesan. Other
dishes, especially those involving sausage and
mushroom, offer a good back-up. You can eat
either inside, or outside in a covered garden.

⊨ Albergo Ristorante Stella
Hotel €

(☎0864 5 26 53; www.albergostella.info;
Via Panfilo Mazara 18; s €50-65, d €70-85;
P ❄ @ ☎) A bright little three-star place in the
centro storico, the Stella offers nine airy, modern
rooms and a smart, ground-floor restaurant-
wine-bar (meals €15 to €25). For small groups,
it also has a nearby apartment that sleeps up
to eight people. Discounts of around 20% are
available for stays of more than one night.

Pescasseroli ❻

⊨ Pensione Al Castello
Pension €

(☎0863 91 07 57; www.pensionecastello.it; Viale
D'Annunzio 1; r €45-60, half-board per person
€40-60; ⏱year-round) Just off the main square
in Pescasseroli, this family-run pensione has
large, sunny rooms decorated with white tiled
floors and pleasant wooden furniture. Breakfast
is an extra €4.

Scanno ❼

✕ Pizzeria Trattoria Vecchio Mulino
Trattoria €

(☎0864 74 72 19; Via Silla 50; pizzas/meals
€7/25; ⏱noon-3pm & 7pm-midnight, closed Wed
winter) This old-school eatery is a good bet for a
classic wood-fired pizza, lentil soups and pasta
liberally sprinkled with local saffron. In summer
the pretty street-side terrace provides a good
perch from which to people-watch.

Santo Stefano di Sessanio ❽

⊨ Sextantio
Design Hotel €€

(☎0862 89 91 12; www.sextantio.it; Via Principe
Umberto; d from €165; ☎) This enchanting
albergo diffuso has some 27 rooms and suites
scattered throughout the village. These marry
traditional handmade bedspreads and rustic
furniture with under-floor heating, mood
lighting and divinely deep bath-tubs. The hotel's
restaurant, **Locanda Sotto gli Archi** (Via
degli Archi; meals €35-50; ⏱7.30-11pm Mon, Thu-
Sun & noon-2pm Sun), serves quality regional fare
in a 16th-century dining room.

Etruscan Tuscany & Lazio

20

From Tuscan seascapes and rugged hilltop towns to tufa-carved tombs and raunchy frescoes, this tour takes you into the heart of ancient Etruria, the land the Etruscans once called home.

TRIP HIGHLIGHTS

73 km

Sovana
Explore monumental tombs and ancient Etruscan roads

80 km

Pitigliano
A rocky dramatically sited hill town

• Bolsena

② ③

• Viterbo

Porto Ercole
START

⑥

175 km

Tarquinia
Delve into amazing frescoed tombs

⑦ **FINISH**

Cerveteri
Walk around a veritable town of the dead

224 km

3–4 DAYS
224KM / 139 MILES

GREAT FOR...

BEST TIME TO GO
Early summer is good for sightseeing and the sea.

ESSENTIAL PHOTO
Pitigliano rising out of the rock.

BEST FOR HIKING
Etruscan trails around Sovana and Pitigliano.

20 Etruscan Tuscany & Lazio

Long before Rome came into existence, the Etruscans had forged a great civilisation in the pitted, rugged hills of southern Tuscany, Umbria and northern Lazio. This trip leads through these little-known parts of the country, opening the window onto dramatic natural scenery and spectacular Etruscan treasures. From Tuscany's pock-marked peaks to the haunting tombs that litter Lazio's soft green slopes, it's a beguiling ride.

Parco
Regionale
della
Maremma

SS1

*Laguna di
Ponente*
Albinia

Porto Santo
Stefano

Orbete

Monte
Argentario

Porto Ercole ❶

START

❶ Porto Ercole, Monte Argentario

To warm you up for the road ahead, spend some time exploring Monte Argentario, a rugged promontory just off the southern Tuscan coast. The more appealing of its two towns is Porto Ercole, an attractive harbour nestled between three Spanish forts on the promontory's less-crowded eastern side. This is where Caravaggio died in 1610, and although it's fairly short on traditional attractions its hillside *centro storico* (historic centre) is a charming place for a stroll. Continue to the top, past the **Chiesa di Sant'Erasmo** to the **Rocca fort** and you're rewarded with magnificent views.

✗ p235

The Drive » Reckon on about 1¾ hours for this first leg. Cross the water over to Albinia and join the eastbound SR74. Follow this through expanses of farmland until, shortly after Manciano, you'll see Sovana signposted off to the left. Follow this narrow, leafy road to connect with the SP22 for the final few kilometres.

TRIP HIGHLIGHT

❷ Sovana

Tuscany's most significant Etruscan tombs are concentrated in the **Parco Archeologico della Città del Tufa** (Necropoli di Sovana; www.leviecave.it; €5; ◷10am-7pm summer, to 6pm Oct, to 5pm Sat & Sun Nov & Mar), an archaeological park encompassing land around the villages of Sovana, Sorano and Vitozza. At Sovana, the best finds are in the **Necropoli**, just 1.5km west of the village. Here you'll find four major

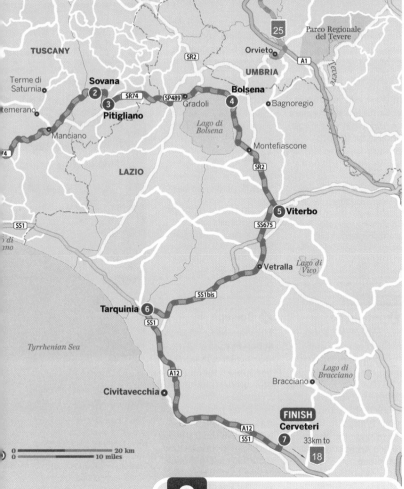

tombs, including the monumental **Tomba Ildebranda**, with traces of carved columns and stairs, as well as two stretches of original Etruscan road – **Via del Cavone** and **Via Cava di Poggio Prisca**.

The village itself boasts a pretty main street and two beautiful

LINK YOUR TRIP

18 Roaming Around Rome

At Cerveteri, pick up the A12 autostrada and continue south 45km, via Fiumicino, to Ostia Antica, Rome's very own Pompeii.

25 Tuscan Landscapes

From Bolsena, head northeast to join the SR71 for the 20km drive to Orvieto, one of the stars of this fabulously scenic trip.

Romanesque churches – the **Duomo** (Concattedrale dei Santi Pietro e Paolo; ⏰9am-1pm & 3-8pm summer, 10am-1pm & 3-6pm winter), with its austere vaulted interior, and the **Chiesa di Santa Maria Maggiore** (Piazza Pretorio; ⏰9am-5pm), notable for its 16th-century apse frescoes.

✗ p235

The Drive » Head east out of Sovana and after a couple of kilometres go right on the SP46. This winding road twists through scorched open peaks and occasional pockets of woodland as it wends its way to Pitigliano, about 10 minutes away.

- - - - - - - - - - - -

TRIP HIGHLIGHT

❸ Pitigliano

Sprouting from a towering tufa outcrop and surrounded by dramatic gorges on three sides, Pitigliano is a lovely knot of twisting stairways, cobbled alleys and quaint stone houses. In the middle of it all, the **Museo Civico Archeologico di Pitigliano** (📞0564 61 40 67; Piazza della Fortezza; adult/reduced €3/2; ⏰10am-5pm Mon, Thu & Fri, to 6pm Sat & Sun Jun-Aug, to 5pm Sat & Sun Easter-May) has a small but rich collection of local Etruscan finds, including some huge *bucchero* (black earthenware pottery) dating from the 6th century BC.

The town also has an interesting Jewish history – at one point it was dubbed 'Little

Jerusalem' – which you can find out about at **La Piccola Gerusalemme** (Little Jerusalem; 📞0564 61 42 30; www.lapiccola gerusalemme.it; Vicolo Manin 30; adult/reduced €5/4; ⏰10am-1pm & 2.30-6pm Sun-Fri summer, 10am-noon & 3-5pm Sun-Fri winter).

✗ 🛏 p235

The Drive » Head east on the SR74 until the road forks. Bear right for Gradoli and follow through the increasingly lush countryside until you hit the fast-flowing SR2 (Via Cassia). Go right and skirt the lake's northern banks into Bolsena. All told it should take just over half an hour.

- - - - - - - - - - - -

❹ Bolsena

The main town on **Lago di Bolsena**, Italy's largest volcanic lake, Bolsena was a major medieval pilgrimage destination after a miracle supposedly took place here in 1263, leading Pope Urban IV to establish the festival of Corpus Domini. Other than the lake, the main reason to stop by is to visit the **Rocca Monaldeschi**, a 13th-century fortress that dominates the skyline and houses a small collection of locally unearthed artefacts in the **Museo Territoriale del Lago di Bolsena** (📞0761 79 86 30; www. simulabo.it; Piazza Monaldeschi 1; adult/reduced €5/3.50; ⏰10am-1pm & 3-6pm Mon, Tue, Thu, Fri, 10am-1pm Wed,

10am-6pm Sat & Sun winter, longer hrs summer).

The Drive » It's a straightforward 50-minute drive to Viterbo along the SR2. This takes you down Lago di Bolsena's eastern side, past orchards, vineyards and olive groves through the medieval town of Montefiascone and on to Viterbo.

- - - - - - - - - - - -

❺ Viterbo

Founded by the Etruscans and eventually taken over by Rome (Roma), Viterbo was an important medieval centre, and in the 13th century became the residence of the popes. Its Etruscan

Tarquinia Frescoes in the Tomba dei Leopardi

past is chronicled at the **Museo Nazionale Etrusco** (☎0761 32 59 29; Piazza della Rocca; adult/reduced €6/3; ☺8.30am-7.30pm Tue-Sun), one of several interesting sights in the walled *centro storico*. To the south, the Renaissance **Piazza del Plebiscito** is overlooked by **Palazzo dei Priori** (Via Ascenzi 1; ☺9am-1pm & 3-6.30pm Mon-Fri, 9am-noon & 4-7pm Sat, 9am-noon Sun), Viterbo's city hall, which boasts some fine 16th-century frescoes. Southwest of here, **Piazza San Lorenzo** was the medieval city's religious heart, where cardinals came to vote for their popes and pray in the 12th-century **Cattedrale di San Lorenzo** (www.archeoares.it; Piazza San Lorenzo; ☺10am-1pm & 3-7pm Tue-Sun, to 6pm winter).

Next door, the **Museo del Colle del Duomo** (☎320 7911328; www.archeoares.it; Piazza San Lorenzo 8; admission €3, incl guided visit to cathedral & Palazzo dei Papi €9; ☺10am-1pm & 3-7pm Tue-Sun, to 6pm winter) displays a small collection of religious artefacts, including a reliquary said to contain the chin (!) of John the Baptist. Also on the piazza is the **Palazzo dei Papi** (☎320 7911328; www.archeoares.it; Piazza San Lorenzo; incl cathedral & Museo Colle del Duomo €9; ☺ guided tours only), **built for the popes who lived in Viterbo from 1257 to 1281. Its main feature is the Sala del Conclave, scene of the first and longest papal conclave.**

✗ 🛏 p235

The Drive » Exit Viterbo and pick up the SS675 heading towards Rome. Continue on this fast dual carriageway until the turn-off for SR2 (Via Cassia). Take this and continue to Vetralla, where you should go right onto the SS1bis (Via Aurelia bis) and continue on to Tarquinia. Allow 50 minutes all told.

THE ETRUSCANS

Of the many Italic tribes that emerged from the Stone Age, the Etruscans left the most enduring mark. By the 7th century BC their city-states – places such as Caere (modern-day Cerveteri), Tarquinii (Tarquinia), Veii (Veio), Perusia (Perugia), Volaterrae (Volterra) and Arretium (Arezzo) – were the dominant forces in central Italy.

Debate rages about their origins – Roman historian Herodotus claimed they came to Italy from Asia Minor to escape famine – but what is not disputed is that they gave rise to a sophisticated society based on agriculture, trade and mineral mining. They were skilled architects, and although little remains of their buildings, archaeologists have found evidence of aqueducts, bridges and sewers, as well as temples. In artistic terms, they were known for their jewellery and tomb decoration, producing elaborate stone sarcophagi and bright, vivid frescoes.

For much of their existence, the Etruscans were rivals of the Greeks, who had colonised much of southern Italy from the 8th century BC, but in the end it was the Romans who finally conquered them. In 396 BC they lost the key town of Veii, and by the 2nd century BC they and their land had largely been incorporated into the rapidly expanding Roman Republic.

✖ p235

The Drive ›› The easiest way to Cerveteri, about 45 minutes away, is by the A12 autostrada. Take this towards Rome/Civitavecchia and exit at the Cerveteri/Ladispoli turn-off. After the toll booth, head left into town.

- - - - - - - - - - - -

TRIP HIGHLIGHT

❼ Cerveteri

Cerveteri, or Kysry to the Etruscans and Caere to Latin-speakers, was one of the most important commercial centres in the Mediterranean from the 7th to the 5th century BC. The main sight is the Unesco-listed **Necropoli di Banditaccia** (☑06 994 06 51; www.tarquinia-cerveteri. it; Via della Necropoli 43/45; adult/reduced €8/5, incl museum €10/6; ⏰8.30am-1hr before sunset) just outside town. This 12-hectare site is laid out like a town of the dead, with streets, squares and terraces of *tumuli* (circular tomb structures cut into the earth and capped with turf). Some of the major tombs, including the 6th-century-BC **Tomba dei Rilievi**, are decorated with painted reliefs.

Back in Cerveteri, the **Museo Nazionale Cerite** (☑06 994 13 54; www. tarquinia-cerveteri.it; Piazza Santa Maria 4; adult/reduced €8/5, incl necropolis €10/6; ⏰8.30am-7.30pm Tue-Sun) displays treasures from the tombs.

✖ p235

- - - - - - - - - - - -

TRIP HIGHLIGHT

❻ Tarquinia

The pick of Lazio's Etruscan towns, Tarquinia is a gem. Its highlight is the 7th-century-BC **Necropoli di Monterozzi** (☑0766 84 00 00; www.tarquinia-cerveteri.it; Via Ripagretta; adult/reduced €6/3, incl museum €8/4; ⏰8.30am-7.30pm Tue-Sun summer, to 1hr before sunset winter), one of Italy's most important Etruscan sites. Some 6000 tombs have been excavated here since 1489, of which 21 are open to the public, including the **Tomba della Caccia e della Pesca**, the richly decorated **Tomba dei Leopardi**, and the **Tomba della Fustigazione** with its erotic depiction of ancient S&M.

In the *centro storico*, the **Museo Archeologico Nazionale Tarquiniense** (☑0766 85 00 80; www. tarquinia-cerveteri.it; Via Cavour 1; adult/reduced €6/3, incl necropoli €8/4; ⏰8.30am-7.30pm Tue-Sun) is a delightful museum, showcasing some wonderful Etruscan artefacts, including a breathtaking terracotta frieze of winged horses (the *Cavalli Alati*).

Eating & Sleeping

Porto Ercole, Monte Argentario ❶

✗ Il Pellicano   Seafood €€€

(☎0564 85 82 75; www.ilpellicanorestaurant.
com; Località Lo Sbarcatello, Porto Ercole;
tasting menu €160; ⏰from 8pm Apr-Oct; 🛜)
The proud possessor of a Michelin star, the
classy restaurant at the five-star hotel of the
same name specialises in intricate, impeccably
presented seafood creations and has two
outdoor terraces with spectacular views. There's
also a more casual and slightly cheaper poolside
grill that serves lunch and dinner.

Sovana ❷

✗ La Tavernetta   Trattoria €

(www.latavernettasovana.it; Via del Pretorio
3; meals €20-25, pizzas €4-7; ⏰noon-3pm &
7-10.30pm daily summer, Wed-Mon winter; 🛜)
Bag a table on the street-side terrace of this
casual eatery near the tourist office for simple,
traditional local dishes by day (try the *tortelli alla
Maremmana* or *salumi Toscana*) and pizzas from
a wood-fired oven by night.

Pitigliano ❸

✗ Il Tufo Allegro   Tuscan €€

(☎0564 61 61 92; www.iltufoallegro.com; Vicolo
della Costituzione 5; meals €22-70; ⏰noon-
2.30pm & 7.30-9.30pm Thu-Mon, 7.30-9.30pm
Wed Mar-Dec) The aromas emanating from the
kitchen door off Via Zuccarelli should be enough
to draw you down the stairs and into the cosy
dining rooms, which are carved out of tufa. Chef
Domenico Pichini's menus range from traditional
to modern and all of his creations rely heavily on
local produce for inspiration.

🛏 Le Camere del Ceccottino   Pension €€

(☎0564 61 42 73; www.ceccottino.com; Via Roma
159; r €80-150; ❄🛜) This *pensione* boasts
an excellent location near the *duomo* and five
immaculately maintained and well-equipped

rooms. Opt for the superior or prestige room
if possible, as the standard versions are a little
small. No breakfast.

Viterbo ❺

✗ Ristorante Tre Re   Trattoria €€

(☎0761 30 46 19; Via Gattesco 3; meals €30;
⏰12.30-2.30pm & 7.30-10pm Fri-Wed) Viterbo's
oldest trattoria is a cosy spot for steaming
plates of seasonally driven dishes and earthy
specialities such as *pollo alla viterbese* (roast
chicken with spiced potato and olives).

🛏 Tuscia Hotel   Hotel €

(☎0761 34 44 00; www.tusciahotel.com; Via
Cairoli 41; s €40-64, d €62-82; 🅿❄🛜) The
best of the city's central hotels, this businesslike three-star has large and light rooms in a
convenient and easy-to-find location. There's
also a sunny roof terrace and parking (€8). Note
that not all rooms have air-con.

Tarquinia ❻

✗ Il Cavatappi   Italian €€

(☎0766 84 23 03; www.cavatappirestaurant.
it; Via dei Granari 2; meals €30; ⏰7-10pm Wed-
Mon, 12.30-2pm Fri-Sun, longer hours summer)
This family run restaurant in the *centro storico*
specialises in traditional regional dishes, so
expect cheese and local salamis, flavoursome
grilled meats and *acquacotta*, a soup thickened
with bread and vegetables.

Cerveteri ❼

✗ Antica Locanda le Ginestre   Italian €€

(☎06 994 33 65; www.anticalocandaleginestre.
com; Piazza Santa Maria 5; fixed-price menus
€20-30, meals €40-45; ⏰12.30-2.30pm &
7.30-10.30pm) On a delightful *centro storico*
piazza, this family run restaurant is a top choice
for quality regional food. Dishes such as risotto
with asparagus tips and saffron are prepared
with seasonal local produce and served in an
elegant dining room and flower-filled courtyard.
Book ahead.

Monasteries of Tuscany & Umbria

21

This trip takes in world-famous basilicas, remote hermitages and secluded sanctuaries as it leads from Assisi to medieval monasteries in the windswept woodlands of eastern Tuscany.

TRIP HIGHLIGHTS

150 km

Poppi ● ④

Santuario della Verna
Remote sanctuary in stunning surroundings

Arezzo ●

75 km

③

Cortona & Eremo Francescano Le Celle
A classic Tuscan hilltop town and hermitage

● Asciano
⑦ FINISH

Perugia ● **START**
①

Abbazia di Monte Oliveto Maggiore
Frescoes in a 14th-century monastery

315 km

Assisi
Fabulous church art in St Francis' hometown

0 km

5 DAYS
315KM / 196 MILES

GREAT FOR...

BEST TIME TO GO
Summer and early autumn are best for monastic visits.

ESSENTIAL PHOTO
The towered castle at Poppi.

BEST FOR HIKING
The forests around the Santuario della Verna.

Monasteries of Tuscany & Umbria

Away from the crowds and bright lights, an austere 11th-century monastery sits in silence surrounded by forest and rocky mountainsides. Welcome to the Monastero & Sacro Eremo di Camaldoli, one of the remote, art-rich monasteries that you'll discover on this tour of central Umbria and Tuscany's northeastern Casentino region. Most people don't venture up here, but with its ancient forests and dark peaks, it makes for a gripping drive.

TRIP HIGHLIGHT

1 Assisi

Both the birthplace and the final resting place of St Francis, this medieval hilltop town is a major destination for millions of pilgrims. Its biggest drawcard is the **Basilica di San Francesco** (www.sanfrancescoassisi.org; Piazza di San Francesco; ☺ upper church 8.30am-6.50pm, lower church & tomb 6am-6.50pm summer, upper & lower church to 6pm winter), **which comprises two gloriously frescoed churches – the**

Gothic **upper church**, which was built between 1230 and 1253 and features a celebrated fresco cycle by Giotto, and the dimly lit **lower church**, with frescoes by Simone Martini, Cimabue and Pietro Lorenzetti.

At the other end of the *centro storico* (historic centre), the 13th-century **Basilica di Santa Chiara** (Piazza Santa Chiara; ☺6.30am-noon & 2-7pm summer, to 6pm winter) is the last resting place of St Clare, a contemporary of St Francis and founder of the Order of the Poor Ladies, aka the Poor Clares.

✕ ⛺ p243

The Drive » From Assisi you can get to Perugia in about 40 minutes, but if you've got time it's worth stopping off to admire the basilica at Santa Maria degli Angeli. From Assisi head down the snaking road to Santa Maria degli Angeli and pick up the fast-running SS75 to Perugia.

- - - - - - - - - - - - -

❷ Perugia

With its hilltop medieval centre and international student population, Perugia is as close as Umbria gets to a heaving metropolis – which isn't all that close. Action is focused on the main strip, **Corso Vannucci**, and **Piazza IV Novembre**, home to the austere 14th-century **Cattedrale di San Lorenzo** (Piazza IV Novembre; ☺7.30am-12.30pm & 3.30-7pm Mon-Sat, 8am-12.45pm & 4-7pm Sun) with its unfinished two-tone facade.

Over the square, the 13th-century **Palazzo dei Priori** houses Perugia's best museums, including the **Galleria Nazionale dell'Umbria** (📞075 5866 8410; Palazzo dei Priori, Corso Vannucci 19; adult/reduced €6.50/3.25; ☺8.30am-7.30pm Tue-Sun, 9.30am-7.30pm Mon summer), with a collection containing works by local heroes Perugino and Pinturicchio. Close to the *palazzo* (mansion), the impressive **Nobile Collegio del Cambio** (Exchange Hall; www.collegiodelcambio.it; Palazzo dei Priori, Corso Vannucci 25; €4.50, incl Nobile Collegio della Mercanzia €5.50; ☺9am-12.30pm & 2.30-5.30pm Mon-Sat, 9am-1pm Sun) also has some wonderful frescoes by Perugino.

✕ ⛺ p243, p253

The Drive » From Perugia it's just under an hour's drive to Cortona. Pick up the RA6 Raccordo Autostradale Bettolle-Perugia and head west, skirting Lago Trasimeno before joining the northbound SR71 at the lake's northwestern corner. From there the pace slackens as the road cuts through vineyards and sunflower fields up to Cortona.

Urbino

Metauro

E MARCHE

0 — 20 km
0 — 10 miles

Parco Regionale del Monte Cucco

Gubbio

Monte Cucco (1566m)

p242

SR298

Chiascio

Parco Regionale del Monte Subasio

START ❶ Assisi

SS75

Santa Maria degli Angeli

Monte Subasio (1290m)

Topino

LINK YOUR TRIP

❷ World Heritage Wonders

From the Abbazia di Monte Oliveto Maggiore, head 30km north to Siena, one of the stars of this classic trip.

㉓ Piero della Francesca Trail

Push north from Cortona to Arezzo and join up with this art-based trail that runs from Urbino to Florence.

TRIP HIGHLIGHT

❸ Cortona & Eremo Francescano Le Celle

A stunning hilltop town, and setting for the film *Under the Tuscan Sun,* Cortona has a remarkable artistic pedigree. Fra' Angelico lived and worked here in the late 14th century, and fellow artists Luca Signorelli and Pietro da Cortona were both born within its walls – all three are represented in the excellent **Museo Diocesano** (Piazza del Duomo 1; adult/reduced €5/3; ⏰10am-7pm daily summer, to 5pm Tue-Sun winter).

Three kilometres north of town in dense woodland, the Franciscan hermitage called **Eremo Francescano Le Celle** (☎0575 60 33 62; Strada dei Cappuccini 1; ⏰7am-7pm) sits next to a picturesque stream. It's a wonderfully tranquil spot, disturbed only by the bells calling the resident friars to mass in the cave-like **Chiesa Cella di San Francesco**.

🍴 🛏 p243

The Drive » The 1¾-hour drive to the Santuario della Verna takes you deep into the heart of the Casentino hills. From Cortona head north on the SR71. About 25km beyond Arezzo, in Rassina, follow signs right and continue up the densely wooded slopes to Chiusi della Verna. The sanctuary is about 3km above Chiusi.

TRIP HIGHLIGHT

❹ Santuario della Verna

St Francis of Assisi is said to have received the stigmata at the **Santuario della Verna** (☎0575 53 41; www.laverna. it; Via del Santuario 45, Chiusi della Verna; ⏰Sanctuary 6.30am-10pm summer, to 7.30pm winter, Cappella delle Stimmate 8am-7pm summer, to 5pm winter, Museo della Verna 10am-noon & 1-4pm Sat & Sun) on the southeastern edge of the **Parco Nazionale delle Foreste Casentinesi Monte Falterona e Campigna** (www.parco forestecasentinesi.it). The sanctuary, which is dramatically positioned on a windswept mountainside, holds some fine works by Andrea Della Robbia, including ceramics in the **basilica** and a magnificent *Crucifixion*

ST FRANCIS OF ASSISI

The son of a wealthy merchant and a French noblewoman, Francesco was born in Assisi in 1181. He enjoyed a carefree youth, but in his mid-20s he went off to fight against Perugia and spent a year in an enemy prison. Illness followed and after a series of holy visions he decided to renounce his possessions and live a humble life in imitation of Christ, preaching and helping the poor. He travelled widely, performing miracles (curing the sick, communicating with animals) and establishing monasteries until his death in 1226. He was canonised two years later.

Today, various places claim links with the saint, including Gubbio where he supposedly brokered a deal between the townsfolk and a man-eating wolf, and Rome where Pope Innocent III allowed him to found the Franciscan order at the Basilica di San Giovanni in Laterano.

Assisi The upper church of the Basilica di San Francesco

in the **Cappella delle Stimmate**, the 13th-century chapel built on the spot where the saint supposedly received the stigmata.

The Drive » Allow about 40 minutes to Poppi from the sanctuary. The first leg, along the SP208, winds through the lush tree-covered mountains to Bibbiena, from where it's an easy 5km north on the SR71. You'll know you're near when you see Poppi's castle up on your left.

⑤ Poppi

Perched high above the Arno plain, Poppi is crowned by the **Castello**

dei Conti Guidi (☎0575 52 05 16; www.buonconte.com; Piazza Repubblica 1; adult/reduced €6/5; ◷10am-7.30pm summer, to 5pm Thu-Sun winter). Inside the 13th-century structure, you'll find a fairytale courtyard, a library full of medieval manuscripts, and a chapel with frescoes by Taddeo Gaddi, including a gruesome depiction of *Herod's Feast* with a dancing Salome and headless John the Baptist.

✖ 🛏 p243

The Drive » Camaldoli is about 18km from Poppi. Take SP67 (Via Camaldoli) and follow

it up through the forest until you come to a fork in the road – the hermitage is uphill to the right; the monastery is downhill to the left.

⑥ Monastero & Sacro Eremo di Camaldoli

The 11th-century **Monastero & Sacro Eremo di Camaldoli** (www.camaldoli. it; ◷monastery 8am-1pm & 3.30-6pm, hermitage 9am-noon & 3-5pm, pharmacy 9am-12.30pm & 2.30-6pm) sits immersed in thick forest on the southern fringes of the Parco Nazionale delle Foreste Casentinesi Monte Falterona

241

DETOUR:
GUBBIO

Start: ❷ Perugia (p239)

Stacked on the steep slopes of an Umbrian mountainside, the medieval town of Gubbio is well worth a visit. Highlights include **Piazza Grande**, with grandstand views over the surrounding countryside, and the **Museo Civico** (Piazza Grande; adult/reduced €5/3; ⊙10am-1.30pm & 3-6pm summer, 10am-1pm & 2.30-5.30pm winter), where you'll find Gubbio's most famous treasures – the Eugubian Tablets. Dating to between 300 BC and 100 BC, these bronze tablets are the best existing examples of ancient Umbrian script.

For a change of scene, and yet more views, take the **Funivia Colle Eletto** (www.funiviagubbio.it; adult/reduced return €6/5; ⊙9am-8pm daily summer, 10am-1.15pm & 2.30-5pm Thu-Tue winter) up to the **Basilica di Sant'Ubaldo** high above up on Monte Ingino.

Gubbio is just over an hour's drive northeast of Perugia on the SR298. See also p253.

e Campigna. Home to about 20 Benedictine monks, it boasts some wonderful art: in the monastery's **church** you'll find three paintings by Vasari: *Deposition from the Cross; Virgin with Child, St John the Baptist and St Girolamo;* and a Nativity; while at the hermitage, the small church harbours an

exquisite altarpiece by Andrea Della Robbia.

For a souvenir, pop into the 16th-century **pharmacy** and pick up soap, perfumes and other items made by the resident monks.

The Drive >> From the Monastero, it's a 2½-hour haul down to the Abbazia di Monte Oliveto Maggiore, 10km south of Asciano. From Camaldoli double

back to the SR71 and head south for Arezzo and the A1. Come off the autostrada at the Valdichiana exit and follow for Siena until the Rapolano Terme turn-off. Take this and continue on to Asciano and the Abbazia.

TRIP HIGHLIGHT

❼ Abbazia di Monte Oliveto Maggiore

Dating to the late 14th century, the red-brick **Abbazia di Monte Oliveto Maggiore** (☏0577 70 76 11; www.monteolivetomaggiore. it; Monte Oliveto Maggiore; ⊙9am-noon & 3-5pm Mon-Sat, to 6pm summer, to 12.30pm Sun) is still a retreat for Benedictine monks who live the contemplative life while tending vines and olives and studying in one of Italy's most important medieval libraries. For visitors, the highlight is the Great Cloister's magnificent **fresco series**, painted by Luca Signorelli and Il Sodoma, illustrating the life of St Benedict. You can also visit the church, frescoed refectory, magnificent 16th-century library, and a small museum.

Eating & Sleeping

Assisi ❶

✖ Osteria Eat Out   Umbrian €€

(☎075 81 31 63; www.nunassisi.com; Via Eremo delle Carceri 1a; meals €35-50; ☻7.30-10.30pm Tue-Thu, 12.30-2.30pm & 7.30-10.30pm Fri-Sun) With such astounding views and minimalist-chic interiors, you might expect this glass-fronted restaurant to prefer style over substance. Not so. Polished service and an exciting wine list are well matched with seasonal Umbrian cuisine flavoured with home-grown herbs. Dishes such as *umbricelli* pasta with fresh truffle and fillet of Chianina beef are big on flavour.

🛏 Hotel Alexander   Hotel €€

(☎075 81 61 90; www.hotelalexanderassisi. it; Piazza Chiesa Nuova 6; s €60-80, d €72-140; ❋🛜) On a small cobbled piazza by the Chiesa Nuova, Hotel Alexander offers nine spacious rooms and a communal terrace with wonderful rooftop views. The modern decor – pale wooden floors and earthy brown tones – contrasts well with the wood-beamed ceilings and antiques.

Perugia ❷   see also p253

✖ La Taverna   Italian €€

(☎075 572 41 28; www.ristorantelataverna.com; Via delle Streghe 8; meals €30-40; ☻12.30-3pm & 7.30-11pm) Way up there on the Perugia dining wish list, La Taverna consistently wins the praise of local foodies. Chef Claudio cooks market-fresh produce with flair and precision, while waiters treat you like one of the *famiglia*.
Brick vaults and candlelit tables create an intimate backdrop for season-rooted dishes, from homemade pasta with black truffles to herb-crusted lamb, all paired with superb wines.

🛏 Primavera Minihotel   Hotel €

(☎075 572 16 57; www.primaveraminihotel. it; Via Vincioli 8; s €50-55, d €72-100; ❋🛜) This petite, welcoming hotel is tucked in a quiet corner of the *centro storico*. Magnificent views complement the bright rooms, decorated with period furnishings and characterful features like exposed stone, beams and wood floors. Breakfast costs €8 extra. There's no lift, so be prepared to schlep your bags up steps.

Cortona & Eremo Francescano Le Celle ❸

✖ La Bucaccia   Tuscan €€

(☎0575 60 60 39; www.labucaccia.it; Via Ghibellina 17; meals €28-35; ☻12.45-3pm & 7-10.30pm Tue-Sun) Cortona's finest address, this gourmet gem is at home in the old medieval stable of a Renaissance *palazzo*. Cuisine is Tuscan and Cortonese – much meat and handmade pasta (chestnut ravioli!) – and the cheese course is superb, thanks to owner Romano Magi who ripens his own. Reservations essential.

🛏 Casa Chilenne   B&B €

(☎338 7727427, 0575 60 33 20; www.casa chilenne.com; Via Nazionale 65; s/d €85/110; ❋@🛜) Run by San Francisco–born Jeanette and her Cortonese husband Luciano, this welcoming B&B scales a narrow townhouse on Cortona's main pedestrian street. Five spacious rooms have access to a small rooftop terrace, complete with bijou cooking area and chairs to lounge on. Breakfast is a feast, served around beautifully dressed tables with exquisitely folded napkins.

Poppi ❺

✖ L'Antica Cantina   Tuscan €€

(☎0575 52 98 44; www.anticacantina.com; Via Lapucci 2; meals €40; ☻noon-2.30pm & 8-11pm Tue-Sun, closed Jan) This old-fashioned dining experience cooks up traditional Tuscan beneath an atmospheric vaulted ceiling. Find it on a steep side street off Via Cesare Battisti in Poppi Alta.

🛏 Borgo Corsignano   Agriturismo €€

(☎0575 50 02 94; www.borgocorsignano.it; Località Corsignano; d €100, weekly €500-700; 🅿@🛜🞰) At home in a *borgo* (medieval village) once home to Camaldoli monks, this gorgeous country hotel is the Casentino's finest accommodation option. A 5km drive from Poppi, it has a mix of self-catering apartments and houses spread lavishly among 13 old stone properties. Voluptuous sculptures collected by the art-loving owners pepper the vast grounds and weeping mountain views are magnificent.

Green Heart of Italy

22

From handsome hill towns to otherworldly caves and the wild green peaks of the Monti Sibillini, this trip weaves through the rural heartland of Umbria and Le Marche.

TRIP HIGHLIGHTS

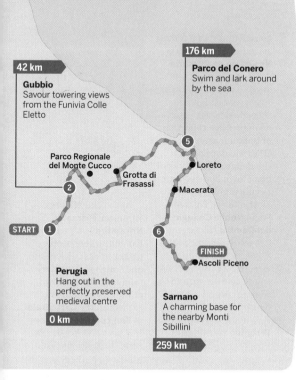

42 km

Gubbio
Savour towering views from the Funivia Colle Eletto

Parco Regionale del Monte Cucco

2

Grotta di Frasassi

176 km

Parco del Conero
Swim and lark around by the sea

5

Loreto

Macerata

START **1**

6

FINISH
Ascoli Piceno

Perugia
Hang out in the perfectly preserved medieval centre

0 km

Sarnano
A charming base for the nearby Monti Sibillini

259 km

4–5 DAYS
309KM / 192 MILES

GREAT FOR...

BEST TIME TO GO
June to September for wild flowers, arts festivals and hiking.

ESSENTIAL PHOTO

Gubbio's medieval rooftops from the Funivia Colle Eletto.

BEST FOR FOOD
Veal-stuffed *olive all'ascolana* in their hometown, Ascoli Piceno.

245

co Nazionale dei Monti Sibillini Medieval town of Preci, Valnerina

22 Green Heart of Italy

Few places are as off the beaten track as this swath of central Italy. Here small rural roads run past sun-ripened wheat fields while dark mountains brood in the distance and medieval hill towns cling onto wooded slopes. But it's not all nature and stunning scenery – there's also culture aplenty with several fine art galleries, striking basilicas and opera in the summer sun.

TRIP HIGHLIGHT

❶ Perugia

Lifted by a hill above a valley patterned with fields, where the River Tiber runs swift and clear, Perugia is Umbria's petite, likeable capital. Its *centro storico* (historic centre) rises in a helter-skelter of cobbled alleys, arched stairways and piazzas framed by magnificent *palazzi*. History seeps through every shadowy corner of these streets and a wander can feel like time travel.

Flanking **Corso Vannucci**, the main strip, the 14th-century Gothic **Palazzo dei Priori** was the headquarters of the local magistracy, but now houses Umbria's foremost art gallery, the **Galleria Nazionale dell'Umbria** (Palazzo dei Priori; adult/reduced €6.50/3.25; ⊙8.30am-7.30pm Tue-Sun, 9.30am-7.30pm Mon summer) and its impressive collection of Italian masterpieces. Of particular note are the Renaissance works of hometown heroes Pinturicchio and Perugino.

Also in the Palazzo is the **Nobile Collegio del Cambio** (Exchange Hall; www.collegiodelcambio. it; Palazzo dei Priori, Corso Vannucci 25; €4.50, incl Nobile Collegio della Mercanzia €5.50; ⊙9am-12.30pm & 2.30-5.30pm Mon-Sat, 9am-1pm Sun), home to yet more Perugino paintings.

At the end of Corso Vannucci, **Piazza IV Novembre** is a local hangout where people gather to chat, lick gelato and watch street entertainers in the shadow of the city's landmark cathedral, the **Cattedrale di San Lorenzo** (⊙7.30am-12.30pm & 3.30-7pm Mon-Sat, 8am-12.45pm & 4-7pm Sun).

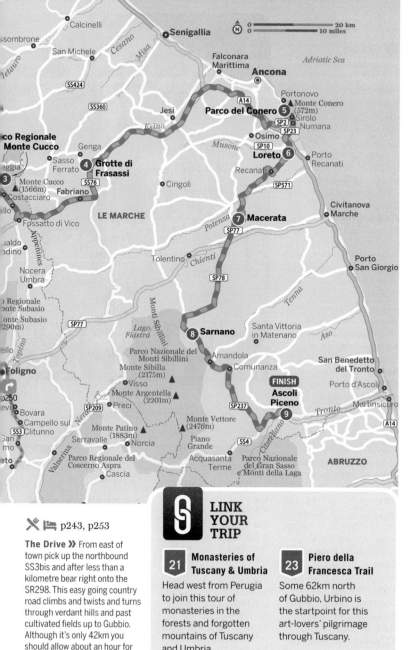

✕ 🛏 p243, p253

The Drive » From east of
town pick up the northbound
SS3bis and after less than a
kilometre bear right onto the
SR298. This easy going country
road climbs and twists and
turns through verdant hills and past
cultivated fields up to Gubbio.
Although it's only 42km you
should allow about an hour for
the drive.

LINK YOUR TRIP

21 Monasteries of Tuscany & Umbria

Head west from Perugia
to join this tour of
monasteries in the
forests and forgotten
mountains of Tuscany
and Umbria.

23 Piero della Francesca Trail

Some 62km north
of Gubbio, Urbino is
the startpoint for this
art-lovers' pilgrimage
through Tuscany.

❷ Gubbio

While most of Umbria feels soft, warm and rounded by the millennia, Gubbio is angular, imposing and medieval through and through. Perched on the steep slopes of Monte Ingino, the Gothic buildings wend their way up the hill towards the closest thing Umbria has to a theme-park ride: the **Funivia Colle Eletto** (www. funiviagubbio.it; adult/reduced return €6/5; ⏰9am-8pm daily summer, 10am-1.15pm & 2.30-5pm Thu-Tue winter). This cable car – more like a glorified ski lift with a precarious-looking metal basket – hauls you up to the **Basilica di Sant'Ubaldo** (⏰8am-7pm), a fine medieval church displaying the body of St Ubaldo, offering huge views of the town and valley beyond.

Once back on terra firma, head over to **Piazza Grande**, Gubbio's show-stopping square, to enjoy yet more panoramas and to visit the **Museo Civico** (adult/reduced €5/3; ⏰10am-1.30pm & 3-6pm summer, 10am-1pm & 2.30-5.30pm winter). Occupying the 14th-century **Palazzo dei Consoli**, this museum boasts a picture gallery, archaeological artefacts and most notably, seven bronze tablets known as the Eugubian Tablets. These are considered the best existing examples of ancient Umbrian script.

ROSMARIE WIRZ/GETTY IMAGES ©

✗ p253

The Drive » The 19km drive to Costacciaro takes you east to the Parco Regionale del Monte Cucco, via the SR298 and spectacular SS3. This scenic road winds down the eastern fringes of the park, affording mood-lifting views on almost every corner, passing quaint mountain hamlets and woods where wolves, lynx and wild boar roam.

❸ Parco Regionale del Monte Cucco

Up on the Umbria–Le Marche border, the **Parco Regionale del Monte Cucco** (www.discover montecucco.it) is a gorgeous swath of wildflower-speckled meadows, gentle slopes brushed with beech, yew and silver fir trees,

Gubbio National Liberation Day (25 April) is marked by flag throwers in traditional costume

deep ravines splashed by waterfalls and karst cave systems, all topped off by the oft-snowcapped hump of **Monte Cucco** (1566m). Outdoor escapades beckon, and if you have the time, there's everything from hiking on 120km of marked trails to mountain biking, horse riding, hanggliding and cross-country skiing.

For cavers, the highlight is the **Grotta Monte Cucco** (☏075 917 10 46; www.grottamontecucco.umbria. it; Via Valentini 39, Costacciaro; tour adult/reduced €12/10; ⏱info point 9am-12.30pm & 3-5pm daily summer, shorter hr spring & autumn), one of Europe's most spectacular limestone caves, with a 30km maze of galleries reaching a depth of 900m. Those up for a

challenge can delve into its underground forest of stalactites and stalagmites on a guided two- to three-hour discovery tour. For more details on the caves and park, stop by the info point in the nearby village of **Costacciaro**.

The Drive » Push on down the park's eastern flank on the SS3 to pick up the eastbound SS76 near Fossato di Vico. Continue

DETOUR:
SPOLETO

Start: ❶ Perugia (p246)

Presided over by a formidable medieval fortress and backed by the broad-shouldered Apennines, their summits iced with snow in winter, the hill town of Spoleto is visually stunning.

At its heart is the pretty, pale-stone **Duomo** (Piazza del Duomo; ⏰8.30am-6pm), originally built in the 11th century using huge blocks of salvaged stones from Roman buildings for its slender bell tower. Inside, marvel at a rainbow swirl of mosaic frescoes by Filippo Lippi and assistants.

For a different view of things, head up to the **Rocca Albornoziana** (Piazza Campello; adult/reduced €7.50/3.75; ⏰9.30am-7pm Tue-Sun, to 2pm Mon), a glowering 14th-century former papal fortress that now houses the **Museo Nazionale del Ducato**, a small museum dedicated to the Duchy of Spoleto.

Before leaving town, make sure to photo the medieval **Ponte delle Torri**, a 10-arch bridge that leaps spectacularly across a steeply wooded gorge – a scene beautifully captured by Turner in his 1840 oil painting.

Spoleto is worth visiting any time, but come in summer and you'll find it a hive of cultural activity as it hosts the mammoth, 17-day **Festival dei Due Mondi**.

To get to Spoleto, it's a 65km drive south from Perugia via the SS75 and SS3.

on this fast road, exiting beyond Fabriano at Valtreara. Follow the brown signs to the Grotte, which will take you to Camponocecchio and then off to the left. All in, it's 40km to the Grotte.

- - - - - - - - - - - -

❹ Grotte di Frasassi

Further subterranean displays await at the **Grotte di Frasassi** (☎800 166 250; www.frasassi.com; adult/reduced €15.50/13.50; ⏰10am-6pm summer, to 5pm winter), Le Marche's unmissable geological marvel near the village of Genga.

Discovered by a team of climbers in September 1971, this vast cave system is one of the biggest in Europe. The fast-flowing River Sentino has gouged out a karst wonderland, which can be admired on a 70-minute tour through its warren of chambers and tunnels. This takes in the cave's rock stars. First up is the **Ancona Abyss**, a cavernous 200m-high, 180m-long chamber, which – as your guide will point out – would

comfortably accommodate Milan Cathedral. Your gaze will be drawn to a fairy forest of dripping stalactites and giant stalagmites, some 1.4 million years in the making. Highlights here include the **Niagara**, a petrified cascade of pure calcite, and a crystallised lake. In the so-called **Gran Canyon**, look out for parallel stalactites resembling pipe organs and waxy stalagmites that rise up like melted candles.

The Drive ≫ From the caves return to Camponocecchio to rejoin the SS76. Continue northeast on this double-carriageway as it traverses lush farmland to pick up the A14 autostrada near Chiaravalle. Push on towards Pescara until the Ancona-Sud Osimo exit. From here take the SP2 to Sirolo in the Parco del Conero, some 75km from the Grotte.

- - - - - - - - - - - -

`TRIP HIGHLIGHT`

❺ Parco del Conero

Just south of Ancona, Le Marche's main city and port, the Parco del Conero is a stunning pocket of coastal countryside. Limestone cliffs soar above the cobalt-blue Adriatic as crescent-shaped, white pebble bays hide behind fragrant woods of pine, oak, beech, broom and oleander trees. Walking trails thread through the 60 sq km park, which is a conservation area. Remarkably still off the radar, the park retains a peaceful, unspoilt air found nowhere else along Le Marche's coastline. Its highest peak is 572m **Monte Conero**, which takes a spectacular nosedive into the sea and provides fertile soil for the vineyards that taper down its slopes, giving rise to the excellent Rosso Conero red wine.

In its southern reaches, the cliff-backed resort of **Sirolo** is one of several that makes a fine base for exploring the area. A boat trip is the best way to cove hop.

🛏 p253

The Drive » It's a short 15km haul down to Loreto. South of Sirolo pick up the SP23 and head inland towards Castelfidardo. It's a slow, country drive, past hedgerows and sunflower fields, to Crocette where you should go left onto the SP10 and follow signs to Loreto.

----

6 Loreto

Straddling a hilltop and visible from miles around, Loreto is absorbed entirely by its bauble-domed **Basilica della Santa Casa** (http://santuarioloreto.it; Piazza della Madonna; ⏰6.15am-7.30pm). While the original basilica started in 1468 was Gothic, Renaissance additions have made today's basilica an architectural masterpiece, with its riot of gold-leafed halos, impressive frescoes and religious triptychs. Inside stands the elaborate marble Santa Casa di Loreto, or the Holy House shrine, where pilgrims flock to

glimpse a jewel-encrusted black statue of the Virgin and pray in the candlelit twilight. The chapel is allegedly where Jesus was raised as a child. Legend has it a host of angels winged the chapel over from Nazareth in 1294 after the Crusaders were expelled from Palestine.

🍴 p253

The Drive » More back country roads await on the 28km stretch to Macerata. From Loreto head south to pick up the SP571. Continue on to Fontenoce where you should bear left on to the SP77 which will take you on to the village of Sambucheto. Go left here and continue through the bucolic green scenery to Macerata.

----

7 Macerata

Straddling low-rise hills, Macerata combines charming hill-town scenery with the verve of student life – its university is one of Europe's oldest, dating to 1290. Its old town, a jumbled maze of cobblestone streets and honey-coloured *palazzi,*

springs to life in summer for the month-long **Macerata Opera Festival**, one of Italy's foremost musical events during which big name opera stars take to the stage at the stunning outdoor **Arena Sferisterio** (www.sferisterio.it; Piazza Mazzini 10; adult/reduced €3/2, incl guided tour €5/4; ⏰9am-4pm Mon, 9am-1pm & 3-7pm Tue-Sun, shorter hours winter).

Of the numerous Renaissance *palazzi* in the *centro storico,* the **Loggia dei Mercanti** (Piazza della Libertà) stands out. An arcaded building built in 1505, it originally housed travelling merchants selling their wares. A short walk away, the **Musei Civici di Palazzo Buonaccorsi** (www.maceratamusei.it; Via Don Minzoni 24; adult/reduced €3/2; ⏰10am-6pm Tue-Sun) harbours an eclectic collection of 18th- to 20th-century coaches and artworks. Of particular note are the paintings of Ivo Pannaggi, one of the driving forces behind Italian futurism in the 1920s and '30s.

THE 2016 EARTHQUAKE

More than 290 people were killed when a strong earthquake struck central Italy on 24 August 2016. The 6.2-magnitude quake, whose epicentre was near Norcia in Umbria, caused widespread damage in the mountainous area between Umbria, Lazio and Le Marche, and devastated the towns and villages of Amatrice, Accumoli, Arquata del Tronto and Pescara del Tronto. At the time of writing, aftershocks were still being felt and buildings were being checked for structural damage in towns across the area, including Macerata, Sornano and Ascoli Piceno.

PARCO NAZIONALE DEI MONTI SIBILLINI

Straddling the Le Marche–Umbria border in rugged splendour, the **Parco Nazionale dei Monti Sibillini** (www.sibillini.net) never looks less than extraordinary, whether visited in winter, when its peaks are dusted with snow, or in summer, when its meadows are carpeted with poppies and cornflowers.

The 70,000-hectare national park covers some of the most dramatic landscapes in central Italy, with glacier-carved valleys, beautifully preserved hilltop hamlets, quiet beech forests where deer roam, and mountains, 10 of which tower above 2000m.

The park is a magnet for anyone seeking outdoor adventure or a brush with wildlife, with an expansive network of walking trails crisscrossing the area. *Rifugi* (mountain huts) welcome hikers every few kilometres with hearty meals and warm beds; most open summer only and details are available at all local tourist offices.

✖ p253

The Drive ›› Exit Macerata and head south on the SP77 to Sforzacosta where you'll need to hook up with the SP78. Continue southwards, past the ancient Roman ruins of Urbs Salvia, and on to Sarnano, 40km away.

TRIP HIGHLIGHT

⑧ Sarnano

Spilling photogenically down a hillside, its medieval heart a maze of narrow cobbled lanes, Sarnano looks every inch the prototype Italian hill town, particularly when its red-brick facades glow warmly in the late-afternoon sun. There are no great must-see sights but it makes a charming, hospitable base for exploring the Monti Sibillini range, much of which is encompassed in the **Parco Nazionale dei Monti Sibillini** (www.sibillini.net).

For a taste of the park's natural treasures, head south towards Montefortino and take the road to Madonna dell'Ambro. This will eventually lead you to the **Gola dell'Infernaccio**, a waterfall formed by the river Tenna coursing through the limestone rock. Adding to the atmosphere are the local legends which claim that ancient rites of necromancy were once performed at the waterfall.

🛏 p253

The Drive ›› Driving this 50km leg you'll understand why this part of Italy is referred to as the country's green heart. The SP237 runs past overhanging trees and overgrown hedgerows before opening up to reveal wooded peaks as far as the eye can see. Continue for about 46km and then join the eastbound SS4 for the last few kilometres into Ascoli.

---

⑨ Ascoli Piceno

The charming town of Ascoli Piceno marks the end of the road. With a continuous history dating from the Sabine tribe in the 9th century, Ascoli (as it's known locally) is like the long-lost cousin of ancient Rome and a small Marchigiani village, heavy on history and food – it's famous for its calorific veal-stuffed fried olives, aka *olive all'ascolana*.

Right in the centre of town, the harmonious and lovely **Piazza del Popolo** has been Ascoli's *salotto* (sitting room) since Roman times. It's flanked by the 13th-century **Palazzo dei Capitani del Popolo** and the beautiful **Chiesa di San Francesco** (⊙7am-12.30pm & 3.30-8pm). Virtually annexed to the church is the Loggia dei Mercanti, built in the 16th century by the powerful guild of wool merchants to hide their rough-and-tumble artisan shops.

Ascoli's fine **pinacoteca** (www.ascoli musei.it; Piazza Arringo; adult/reduced €8/5; ⊙10am-7pm Tue-Sun summer, to 5pm winter) holds an outstanding display of art, sculpture, and religious artefacts including paintings by Van Dyck, Titian and Rembrandt.

✖ p253

Eating & Sleeping

Perugia ① see also p243

✖ Osteria a Priori — Osteria €€

(📞075 572 70 98; www.osteriaapriori.it; Via dei Priori 39; meals €30; ⏱12.30-2.30pm & 7.30-10pm Mon-Sat) This fashionable *osteria* (tavern) specialises in local wines and fresh regional cuisine prepared with seasonal ingredients. Umbrian cheeses and cured meats feature alongside truffles, roast meats and autumnal mushrooms. Weekday lunch is a snip at €9.

🛏 B&B San Fiorenzo — B&B €

(📞393 386 99 87; www.sanfiorenzo.com; Via Alessi 45; r €70-120; 🛜) Buried in Perugia's medieval maze of a centre is this charming 15th-century *palazzo* with three unique rooms. Mod cons and marble bathrooms are carefully incorporated into spacious quarters with brick vaulting, lime-washed walls and antique furnishings, including an apartment with a 13th-century tower room.

Gubbio ②

✖ Taverna del Lupo — Umbrian €€

(📞075 927 43 68; www.tavernadellupo.it; Via Ansidei 21; meals €35-45; ⏱noon-3pm & 7-11pm; 🍴) Soft light casts flattering shadows across the barrel-vaulted interior of Gubbio's most sophisticated restaurant, serving Umbrian cuisine with a pinch of creativity and a dash of medieval charm. Flavours ring true in specialities like ravioli in asparagus-porcini sauce and tender capon with truffles, expertly matched with wines.

Parco del Conero ⑤

🛏 Acanto Country House — Guesthouse €€

(📞071 933 11 95; www.acantocountryhouse. com; Via Ancarano 18, Sirolo; s €70, d €90-140, ste €100-150; 🅿❄🛜🏊) Set back from Sirolo's beaches and surrounded by cornfields and olive groves, this converted farmhouse is a gorgeous country escape, taking in the full sweep of the coast. Rooms have been designed with the utmost attention to detail, with gleaming wood floors, exposed stone and embroidered bedspreads.

Loreto ⑥

✖ Ristorante Andreina — Italian €€€

(📞071 97 01 24; www.ristoranteandreina.it; Via Buffolareccia 14; menus €55-85; ⏱noon-3pm & 8-10.30pm, closed dinner Tue & Wed) Foodie pilgrims won't want to miss out on the grilled meats prepared with a gourmet twist at Michelin-starred Ristorante Andreina.

Macerata ⑦

✖ L'Enoteca — Ristorante €€€

(📞0733 23 18 97; www.enotecalecase.it; Via Mozzavinci 16/17; meals €50-60, tasting menus €45-90; ⏱8-10.30pm Wed-Sat) Worth the trek to the countryside this Michelin-starred restaurant has foodies coming from afar. Meat reared on the organic farm, foraged herbs and flowers and garden veg all go into menus created with love, precision and a razor-sharp eye for detail.

Sarnano ⑧

🛏 Agriturismo Serpanera — Agriturismo €€

(📞334 1220242; www.serpanera.com; Contrada Schito 447; apt €85-210, per week €479-1499; 🅿❄🛜🏊) Quite the rural idyll, this 17th-century farmhouse snuggles deep among 10 hectares of orchards, vines and woodlands. Besides its spotless apartments, the eco-savvy *agriturismo* has a pool overlooking rolling hills, a spa, barbecue area, nature trails and horse riding. Your hosts, Marco and Cristiana, whip up delicious breakfasts with farm-fresh produce.

Ascoli Piceno ⑨

✖ Il Desco — Mediterranean €€

(📞0736 25 07 57; www.ildescoristorante.it; Via Vidacilio 10; meals €30-40; ⏱12.30-2.30pm & 7.30-10.30pm Tue-Sat, 12.30-2.30pm Sun) Funky chandeliers and white distressed wood create a country-chic backdrop at this gorgeously styled *palazzo*. In warm weather diners spill out into the garden courtyard, lit by tealights. A clever use of herbs elevates seasonal specialities, from homemade fettucine with artichokes and bacon to fillet of sea bass with zucchini and almonds.

Piero della Francesca Trail

23

Follow in the footsteps of the Renaissance painter Piero della Francesca as you wind your way from the medieval centre of Urbino to Florence, stopping en route to admire his greatest works.

TRIP HIGHLIGHTS

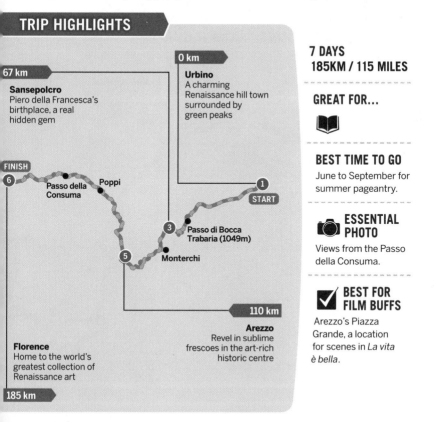

7 DAYS
185KM / 115 MILES

GREAT FOR...

BEST TIME TO GO
June to September for summer pageantry.

ESSENTIAL PHOTO
Views from the Passo della Consuma.

BEST FOR FILM BUFFS
Arezzo's Piazza Grande, a location for scenes in *La vita è bella*.

0 km

Urbino
A charming Renaissance hill town surrounded by green peaks

67 km

Sansepolcro
Piero della Francesca's birthplace, a real hidden gem

FINISH
6

Passo della Consuma   **Poppi**

START
1

3   **Passo di Bocca Trabaria (1049m)**

5   **Monterchi**

110 km

Arezzo
Revel in sublime frescoes in the art-rich historic centre

Florence
Home to the world's greatest collection of Renaissance art

185 km

23 Piero della Francesca Trail

The Piero della Francesca trail was first advocated by the British author Aldous Huxley in *The Best Picture*, a 1925 essay he wrote in praise of della Francesca's *Resurrezione* (Resurrection). The roads have improved since Huxley's day but the trail remains a labour of love for art fans — it leads through dramatic Apennine scenery, over mountain passes and onto bustling medieval towns, culminating in Italy's revered Renaissance city, Florence.

TRIP HIGHLIGHT

❶ Urbino

Hidden away in hilly Le Marche, the charming town of Urbino was a key player in the Renaissance art world. Its ruler, the Duca Federico da Montefeltro, was a major patron and many of the top artists and intellectuals of the day spent time here at his behest. Piero della Francesca arrived in 1469 and, along with a crack team of artists and architects, worked on the duke's palatial residence,

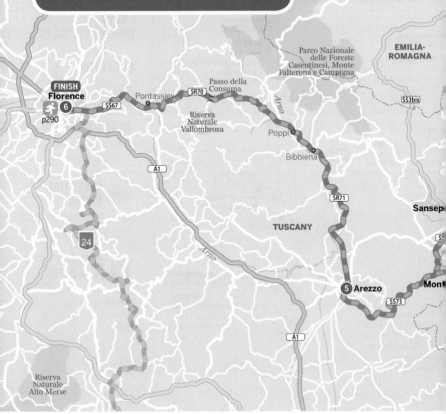

the **Palazzo Ducale**
(www.palazzoducaleurbino.it;
Piazza Rinascimento 13; adult/
reduced €6.50/4; ⏰8.30am-
7.15pm Tue-Sun, to 2pm Mon).
This magnificent palace
now houses the Galleria
Nazionale delle Marche
and its rich collection
of Renaissance paint-
ings, including Piero
della Francesca's great
Flagellazione di Cristo
(Flagellation of Christ).

A short walk away, you
can pay homage to Urbi-
no's greatest son at the
Casa Natale di Raffaello
(www.palazzoducaleurbino.it;
Via Raffaello 57; adult/reduced

€3.50/2.50; ⏰9am-7pm Mon-
Sat, 10am-1pm & 3-6pm Sun
summer, 9am-2pm Mon-Sat,
10am-1pm Sun winter), the
house where superstar
painter Raphael was
born in 1483.

✖️ 🛏️ p261

The Drive » The 50km (1½-
hour) drive up to the Passo
di Bocca Trabaria involves
hundreds of hairpin bends and
tortuous climbing as it traverses
a magnificent swath of Apennine
mountains. From Urbino pick up
the SS73bis and head through
Montesoffio and Urbania before
climbing up to the pass.

- - - - - - - - - - -

❷ Passo di Bocca Trabaria

The Bocca Trabaria
mountain pass (1049m)
divides the Valtiberina
(Tiber Valley), on the
Urbino side, from the
upper Valle del Metauro
(Metauro Valley). It's a
spectacular spot, well
worth a quick pause,
with sweeping views over
the Apennines and sev-
eral hiking trails heading
into the surrounding
mountains.

The Drive » Allow about
half an hour for the 20km
descent from Bocca Trabaria to
Sansepolcro. For the first 15km
or so the winding road plunges
down the valley slopes to San
Giustino, from where it's an easy
hop northwest to Sansepolcro.

🔗 LINK YOUR TRIP

24 **Tuscan Wine Tour**
From Florence head
south on the SR222 to the
Castello di Verrazzano,
one of the historic Chianti
vineyards on this classic
wine tour.

26 **Foodie Emilia-Romagna**
Head 125km north
from Urbino via the A14
autostrada to connect with
Ravenna and this tasty trip
through Emilia-Romagna.

TRIP HIGHLIGHT

❸ Sansepolcro

Birthplace of Piero della Francesca and home to three of his great works, Sansepolcro is an authentic hidden gem. Its unspoiled historic centre is littered with *palazzi* (mansions) and churches harbouring great works of art, including the 14th-century **Cattedrale di San Giovanni Evangelista** (Duomo di Sansepolcro; Via Giacomo Matteotti 4; ☺10am-noon & 4-7pm), which contains an *Ascension* by Perugino. The highlight, though, is the **Museo Civico** (www.museocivicosansepolcro.it; Via Niccolò Aggiunti 65; adult/reduced €8/5; ☺10am-1.30pm & 2.30-7pm summer, 10am-1pm & 2.30-6pm winter), whose small but top-notch collection boasts three Piero della Francesca masterpieces: *Resurrezione* (Resurrection; c 1460), the *Madonna della Misericor-dia* (c 1445–62) and *San Giuliano* (Saint Julian; c1455).

🍴 p261

The Drive » Head southwest from Sansepolcro along the SS73 following signs for Arezzo. After roughly 12km of easy driving through pleasant green countryside, turn left onto the SP42 and continue for 3km to Monterchi. It takes about 25 minutes.

❹ Monterchi

This unassuming village boasts one of Piero della Francesca's best-loved works, the *Madonna del Parto* (Pregnant Madonna, c 1460). Housed in its own museum, the **Museo della Madonna del Parto** (Pregnant Madonna Museum; ☎0575 7 07 13; www.madonnadelparto.it; Via della Reglia 1, Monterchi; adult/reduced €6.50/5; ☺9am-1pm & 2-7pm summer, to 5pm Wed-Mon winter), it depicts a heavily pregnant Madonna wearing a simple blue gown and standing in a tent, flanked by two angels who hold back the tent's curtains as a framing device. In a nice touch, pregnant women get free entry to the museum.

The Drive » Take the SP221 out of Monterchi until you hit the SS73. Turn left and follow the fast-running road, which opens to four lanes in certain tracts, as it snakes through thickly wooded hills up to Arezzo.

TRIP HIGHLIGHT

❺ Arezzo

The biggest town in eastern Tuscany, Arezzo has a distinguished cultural history. Petrarch and art historian Giorgio Vasari were both born here, and, between 1452 and 1466, Piero della Francesca painted one of his greatest works, the *Leggenda della Vera Croce* (Legend of the True Cross) fresco cycle in the Basilica di San Francesco's **Cappella Bacci** (☎0575 35 27 27; www.pierodellafrancesca.it; Piazza San Francesco; adult/reduced €8/5; ☺9am-6pm Mon-Fri, to 5.30pm Sat, 1-5.30pm Sun).

Once you've seen that, take time to admire the magnificent Romanesque facade of the **Chiesa di Santa Maria della Pieve** (Corso Italia 7; ☺8am-12.30pm & 3-6.30pm) en route to the **Duomo** (Cattedrale di SS Donato e Pietro; Piazza del Duomo; ☺7am-12.30pm & 3-6.30pm) and yet another della

---

PIERO DELLA FRANCESCA

Though many details about his life are hazy, it's believed that Piero della Francesca was born around 1415 in Sansepolcro and died in 1492. Trained as a painter from the age of 15, his distinctive use of perspective, mastery of light and skilful synthesis of form and colour set him apart from his artistic contemporaries. His most famous works are the *Leggenda della Vera Croce* (Legend of the True Cross) in Arezzo, and *Resurrezione* (Resurrection) in Sansepolcro, but he is most fondly remembered for his luminous *Madonna del Parto* (Pregnant Madonna) in Monterchi.

Monterchi *Madonna del Parto* (Pregnant Madonna) on display in the Museo della Madonna del Parto

Francesca fresco – the exquisite *Mary Magdalene* (c 1460).

Film buffs should also stop by **Piazza Grande**, where scenes were filmed for Roberto Benigni's *La vita è bella* (Life is Beautiful), and where the city celebrates its big annual festival, the **Joust of the Saracino**, on the third Saturday in June and first Sunday in September.

✗ 🛏 p261

The Drive » The quickest route to Florence is via the A1 autostrada, but you'll enjoy the scenery more if you follow the SR71 up the Casentino valley and on to the medieval castle town of Poppi. At Poppi pick up the SR70 to tackle the heavily forested Passo della Consuma (1050m) and descend to Pontassieve and the SS67 into Florence. Allow about 2¾ hours.

- - - - - - - - - - -

TRIP HIGHLIGHT

❻ Florence

The last port of call is Florence, the city where the Renaissance kicked off in the late 14th century. Paying the way was the Medici family, who sponsored the great

259

THE RENAISSANCE

Bridging the gap between the Middle Ages and the modern world, the Renaissance (*il Rinascimento*) emerged in 14th-century Florence and quickly spread throughout Italy.

The Early Days

Giotto di Bondone (1267–1337) is generally considered the first great Renaissance artist, and with his exploration of perspective and a new interest in realistic portraiture, he inspired artists such as Lorenzo Ghiberti (1378–1455) and Donatello (c 1382–1466). In architectural terms, the key man was Filippo Brunelleschi (1377–1446), whose dome on Florence's Duomo was one of the era's blockbuster achievements. Of the following generation, Sandro Botticelli (c 1444–1510) was a major player and his *Birth of Venus* (c 1485) was one of the most successful attempts to resolve the great conundrum of the age – how to give a painting both a realistic perspective and a harmonious composition.

The High Renaissance

By the early 16th century, the focus had shifted to Rome and Venice. Leading the way in Rome was Donato Bramante (1444–1514), whose classical architectural style greatly influenced the Veneto-born Andrea Palladio (1508–80). One of Bramante's great rivals was Michelangelo Buonarrotti (1475–1564), whose legendary genius was behind the Sistine Chapel frescoes, the dome over St Peter's Basilica, and the *David* sculpture. Other headline acts included Leonardo da Vinci (1452–1519), who developed a painting technique (sfumato) enabling him to modulate his contours using colour; and Raphael (1483–1520), who more than any other painter mastered the art of depicting large groups of people in a realistic and harmonious way.

artists of the day and whose collection today graces the **Galleria degli Uffizi** (Uffizi Gallery; www. uffizi.beniculturali.it; Piazzale degli Uffizi 6; adult/reduced €8/4, incl temporary exhibition €12.50/6.25; ☺8.15am-6.50pm Tue-Sun). Here you can admire Piero della Francesca's famous portrait of the red-robed *Duke and Duchess of Urbino* (1465–72) alongside works by Renaissance giants, from Giotto and Cimabue to Botticelli, Leonardo da Vinci, Raphael and Titian.

Elsewhere in town, you'll find spiritually uplifting works by Fra' Angelico in the wonderful **Museo di San Marco** (☎055 238 86 08; Piazza San Marco 3; adult/reduced €4/2; ☺8.15am-1.50pm Mon-Fri, 8.15am-4.50pm Sat & Sun, closed 1st, 3rd & 5th Sun & 2nd & 4th Mon of month), and superb frescoes by Masaccio, Masolino da Panicale and Filippino Lippi at the **Cappella Brancacci** (☎055 276 82 24; http://museicivicifiorentini. comune.fi.it; Piazza del Carmine 14; adult/reduced €6/4.50; ☺10am-5pm Wed-Sat & Mon, 1-5pm Sun), over the river in the Basilica di Santa Maria del Carmine. The historic centre is a great place to explore on foot (p290).

✗ ⏟ p47, p60, p261, p271

Eating & Sleeping

Urbino ❶

✖ Antica Osteria da la Stella
Osteria €€

(☏0722 32 02 28; www.anticaosteriadalastella.com; Via Santa Margherita 1; meals €30-40; ◷12.30-2.15pm & 7.30-10.30pm Tue-Sat, 7.30-10.30pm Mon) Duck down a quiet side street to this rustically elegant, beamed 15th-century inn once patronised by the likes of Piero della Francesca. Legendary in these parts, Osteria de la Stella puts its own inventive twist on seasonal food. Every dish strikes perfect balance, be it gnocchi with porcini and quail sauce or venison with wild berries and polenta.

⌑ Albergo Italia
Hotel €€

(☏0722 27 01; www.albergo-italia-urbino.it; Corso Garibaldi 32; s €50-75, d €80-130; ❋ 🤶) Set behind the Palazzo Ducale, the Italia could not be better positioned. Modern and well designed, the shuttered townhouse is restfully quiet and staff are genuinely friendly. In warmer months, take breakfast on the balcony.

Sansepolcro ❸

✖ Ristorante Da Ventura
Tuscan €€

(☏0575 74 25 60; www.albergodaventura.it; Via Niccolò Aggiunti 30; meals €25-30; ◷12.30-2.15pm & 7.30-9.45pm Tue-Sat) This old-world eatery is a culinary joy. Trolleys laden with fiesty joints of pork, beef stewed in Chianti Classico and roasted veal shank are pushed from table to table, bow-tied waiters intent on piling plates high. The veal fillet topped with wafer-thin slices of *lardo di colonnata* (cured pork fat) and the veal carpaccio with black truffle shavings are glorious.

Arezzo ❺

✖ La Torre di Gnicche
Tuscan €

(☏0575 35 20 35; www.latorredignicche.it; Piaggia San Martino 8; soup €7, meat & cheese platters €10; ◷noon-3pm & 6pm-midnight Thu-Tue) This cosy bottle-lined room just off Piazza Grande offers a huge choice of Tuscan wine (by the glass or bottle), platters of cheese and meat, and rustic tummy-fillers including *pappa al pomodoro* (a thick bread-and-tomato soup served in summer) and *ribollita* (a 'reboiled' bean, vegetable, cabbage and bread soup served in winter).

⌑ Graziella Patio Hotel
Boutique Hotel €€

(☏0575 40 19 62; www.hotelpatio.it; Via Cavour 23; s €120-165, d €150-180, ste €270-285; ❋ @ 🤶) A delightful mix of ancient (15th-century cellars) and contemporary design, this 10-room hotel has themed rooms named after Bruce Chatwin's travel books – with decor to match. Pink-kissed Arkady is the 'Australia room', Fillide exudes a distinctly Moroccan air, and Cobra Verde is a green Amazon-inspired loft. Every room has a Macbook for guests to go online and service is first-class.

Florence ❻ see also p47, p60 and p271

✖ Trattoria Mario
Tuscan €

(www.trattoria-mario.com; Via Rosina 2; meals €20; ◷noon-3.30pm Mon-Sat, closed 3 weeks Aug; ❋) Arrive by noon to ensure a stool around a shared table at this noisy, busy, brilliant trattoria – a legend that retains its soul (and allure with locals) despite being in every guidebook. Charming Fabio, whose grandfather opened the place in 1953, is front of house while big brother Romeo and nephew Francesco cook with speed in the kitchen.

⌑ Hotel Torre Guelfa
Historic Hotel €€€

(☏055 239 63 38; www.hoteltorreguelfa.com; Borgo SS Apostoli 8; d €170-369, tr €197-389; ❋ @ 🤶) If you want to kip in a real McCoy Florentine *palazzo* without breaking the bank, this 31-room hotel with fortress-style facade is the address. Scale its 13th-century, 50m-tall tower – Florence's tallest privately owned *torre* – for a sundowner overlooking Florence and you'll be blown away. Rates are practically halved in low season.

Classic Trip

Tuscan Wine Tour

24

Tuscany has its fair share of highlights, but few can match the indulgence of a drive through its wine country – an intoxicating blend of scenery, acclaimed restaurants and ruby-red wine.

TRIP HIGHLIGHTS

START
Florence

34 km

Greve in Chianti
Taste Tuscany's best at Greve's vast cellar

4 ③

Panzano in Chianti

Radda in Chianti

Badia a Passignano
Idyllically located wine estate and top restaurant

⑥

41 km

67 km

Castello di Ama
Marvel at modern art and Chianti Classico

Siena

138 km

FINISH
Montepulciano

Montalcino
A fortified hilltown, home of Brunello di Montalcino

⑦

4 DAYS
185KM / 115 MILES

GREAT FOR...

BEST TIME TO GO
Autumn for earthy hues and the grape harvest.

📷 ESSENTIAL PHOTO
Panoramas from Montalcino's Fortezza.

✔ BEST FOR GOURMETS
Tuscan *bistecca* (steak) in Panzano in Chianti.

Classic Trip

24 Tuscan Wine Tour

Meandering through Tuscany's bucolic wine districts, this classic Chianti tour offers a taste of life in the slow lane. Once out of Florence (Firenze), you'll find yourself on quiet back roads driving through wooded hills and immaculate vineyards, stopping off at wine estates and hilltop towns to sample the local vintages. En route, you'll enjoy soul-stirring scenery, farmhouse food and some captivating Renaissance towns.

80 km to
26

Arno
START
Florence ❶
A1
p290

SR222

Castello di Verrazzano ❷
Badia a Passignano ❹
Greve in Chianti   SP118
Panzano in Chianti

Riserva
Naturale
Alto Merse

E78

ⓝ 0 ──────────── 10 km
   0 ──────────── 5 miles

❶ Florence

Whet your appetite for the road ahead with a one-day cooking course at the **Food & Wine Academy** (☎055 28 11 03; www.florencecookingclasses. com; Via de' Lamberti 1; 1-day class with market visit & lunch €89), one of Florence's many cookery schools. Once you're done at the stove, sneak out to visit the **Chiesa e Museo di Orsanmichele** (Via dell'Arte della Lana; ⏰ church 10am-5pm, museum 10am-5pm Mon), an inspirational 14th-century church and one of Florence's lesser-known gems. Over the river, you can stock up on Tuscan wines and gourmet foods at **Obsequium** (☎055 21 68 49; www.obsequium. it; Borgo San Jacopo 17-39; ⏰11am-9pm Mon-Sat), a well-stocked wine shop on the ground floor of a medieval tower. Or, explore the old town on foot (p290) before you hit the road.

✕ 🛏 p47, p60, p261, p271

The Drive >> From Florence it's about an hour to Verrazzano. Head south along the scenic SR222 (Via Chiantigiana) towards Greve. When you get to Greti, you'll see a shop selling wine from the Castello di Verrazzano and, just before it, a right turn up to the castle.

----

❷ Castello di Verrazzano

Some 26km south of Florence, the **Castello di Verrazzano** (☎055 85 42 43; www.verrazzano.com; Via Citille, Greti; tours €16-115) lords it over a 230-hectare estate where Chianti Classico, Vin Santo, grappa, honey, olive oil and balsamic vinegar are produced. In a previous life, the castle was home to Giovanni di Verrazzano (1485–1528), an adventurer who explored the North American coast and is commemorated in New

🔗 LINK YOUR TRIP

23 Piero della Francesca Trail

Starting in Florence, you can join this trail of revered Renaissance frescoes.

26 Foodie Emilia-Romagna

Also from Florence, continue 120km north on the A1 to Bologna and a tour of Emilia-Romagna's great food towns.

York by the Verrazano-Narrows bridge linking Staten Island to Brooklyn.

At the Castello, you can choose from a range of guided tours, including a Classic Wine Tour (1½ hours; adult €18; 10am to 3pm Monday to Friday) and Wine & Food Experience (three hours, adult €58; noon Monday to Friday), which includes a tasting and lunch with the estate wines. Book ahead.

The Drive » From the Castello it's a simple 10-minute drive to Greve in Chianti. Double back to the SR222 in Greti, turn right and follow for about 3km.

TRIP HIGHLIGHT

③ Greve in Chianti

The main town in the Chianti Fiorentino, the northernmost of the two Chianti districts, Greve in Chianti has been an important wine centre for centuries. It has an amiable market-town air, and several eateries and *enoteche* (wine bars) that showcase the best Chianti food and drink. To stock up on picnic-perfect cured meats, the **Antica Macelleria Falorni** (www. falorni.it; Piazza Matteotti 71; ⊙9.30am-1pm & 3.30-7.30pm Mon-Sat, from 10am Sun), is an atmospheric butcher's shop-cum-bistro that the Bencistà Falorni family have been running since the early 19th century and which specialises in delicious *finocchiona briciolona* (pork salami made with fennel seeds and Chianti wine). The family also run the Enoteca Falorni (p270), the town's top cellar, where you can sample all sorts of local wine.

The Drive » From Greve turn off the main through road, Viale Giovanni di Verrazzano, near the Esso petrol station, and head up towards Montefioralle. Continue on as the road climbs past olive groves and through woods to Badia a Passignano, about 15 minutes away.

TRIP HIGHLIGHT

④ Badia a Passignano

Encircled by cypress trees and surrounded by swaths of olive groves and vineyards, the 11th-century **Badia a Passignano** (☎055 807 12 78; www.osteriadipassignano. com; Badia a Passignano) sits at the heart of a historic wine estate. It's run by the Antinoris, one of Tuscany's oldest and most prestigious winemaking families, and offers a range of guided tours, tastings and cookery courses. Most require a minimum of four people and prior booking, but you can just turn up at the estate's wine shop, **La Bottega** (www.osteria dipassignano.com; Badia di Passignano; ⊙10am-7.30pm Mon-Sat), to taste and buy Antinori wines and olive oil.

✕ 🖺 p271

The Drive » From Badia a Passignano, double back towards Greve and pick up the signposted SP118 for a pleasant 15-minute drive along the narrow tree-shaded road to Panzano.

⑤ Panzano in Chianti

The quiet medieval town of Panzano is an essential stop on any gourmet's tour of

---

✓ **TOP TIP:**
DRIVING IN CHIANTI

To cut down on driving stress, purchase a copy of *Le strade del Gallo Nero* (€2.50), a useful map that shows major and secondary roads and has a comprehensive list of wine estates. It's available at newsstands across the region.

TUSCAN REDS

Something of a viticultural powerhouse, Tuscany excites wine buffs with its myriad of full-bodied, highly respected reds. Like all Italian wines, these are classified according to strict guidelines, with the best denominated *Denominazione di Origine Controllata e Garantita* (DOCG), followed by *Denominazione di Origine Controllata* (DOC) and *Indicazione di Geografica Tipica* (IGT).

Chianti
Cheery, full and dry, contemporary Chianti gets the thumbs up from wine critics. Produced in eight subzones from Sangiovese and a mix of other grape varieties, Chianti Classico is the best known, with its Gallo Nero (Black Cockerel) emblem that once symbolised the medieval Chianti League. Young, fun Chianti Colli Senesi from the Siena hills is the largest subzone; Chianti delle Colline Pisane is light and soft in style; and Chianti Rùfina comes from the hills east of Florence.

Brunello di Montalcino
Brunello is up there at the top with Italy's most prized wines. The product of Sangiovese grapes, it must spend at least two years ageing in oak. It is intense and complex with an ethereal fragrance, and is best paired with game, wild boar and roasts. Brunello grape rejects go into Rosso di Montalcino, Brunello's substantially cheaper but wholly drinkable kid sister.

Vino Nobile di Montepulciano
Prugnolo Gentile grapes (a clone of Sangiovese) form the backbone of the distinguished Vino Nobile di Montepulciano. Its intense but delicate nose and dry, vaguely tannic taste make it the perfect companion to red meat and mature cheese.

Super Tuscans
Developed in the 1970s, the Super Tuscans are wines that fall outside the traditional classification categories. As a result they are often made with a combination of local and imported grape varieties, such as Merlot and Cabernet. Sassacaia, Solaia, Bolgheri, Tignanello and Luce are all super-hot Super Tuscans.

Tuscany. Here you can stock up on meaty picnic fare at **L'Antica Macelleria Cecchini** (www.dariocecchini.com; Via XX Luglio 11; 🕙9am-4pm), a celebrated butcher's shop run by the poetry-spouting guru of Tuscan meat, Dario Cecchini. Alternatively, you can eat at one of his three eateries: the **Officina della Bistecca** (📞055 85 21 76; www.dariocecchini.com;

Via XX Luglio 11; set menu €50; 🕙sittings at 1pm & 8pm), which serves a simple set menu based on *bistecca*; **Solociccia** (📞055 85 27 27; www.dariocecchini.com; Via Chiantigiana 5; set menus €30 & €50; 🕙sittings at 1pm, 7pm & 9pm), where guests share a communal table to sample meat dishes other than *bistecca;* and **Dario DOC** (www.dario cecchini.com; Via XX Luglio 11; menus €10-20; 🕙noon-3pm Mon-Sat), a casual

daytime eatery. Book ahead for the Officina and Solociccia.

The Drive ⟫ From Panzano, it's about 20 kilometres to the Castello di Ama. Strike south on the SR222 towards Radda in Chianti, enjoying views off to the right as you wend your way through the green countryside. At Croce, just beyond Radda, turn left and head towards Lecchi and San Sano. The Castello di Ama is signposted after a further 7km.

ATLANTIDE PHOTOTRAVEL/GETTY IMAGES ©

CULTURA RM EXCLUSIVE/PHILIP LEE HARVEY/GETTY IMAGES ©

WHY THIS IS A CLASSIC TRIP
DUNCAN GARWOOD, WRITER

The best Italian wine I've ever tasted was a Brunello di Montalcino. I bought it directly from a producer after a tasting in the Val d'Orcia and it was a revelation. It was just so thrilling to be drinking wine in the place it had been made. And it's this, combined with the inspiring scenery and magnificent food, that makes this tour of Tuscan wineries so uplifting.

Top: Wine cellar, Castello di Ama
Left: Wine shop, Montalcino
Right: Badia a Passignano

TRIP HIGHLIGHT

❻ Castello di Ama

To indulge in some contemporary-art appreciation between wine tastings, make for the **Castello di Ama** (☎0577 74 60 69; www.castellodiama.com; Località Ama; guided tours €15, with wine & oil tasting €35-110; ☺by appointment) near Lecchi. The highly regarded Castello di Ama estate produces a fine Chianti Classico and has an original sculpture park showcasing 14 site-specific works by artists including Louise Bourgeois, Chen Zhen, Anish Kapoor, Kendell Geers and Daniel Buren. Book ahead.

The Drive ❯❯ Reckon on about 1½ hours to Montalcino from the Castello. Double back to the SP408 and head south to Lecchi and then on towards Siena. Skirt around the east of Siena and pick up the SR2 (Via Cassia) to Buonconvento and hilltop Montalcino, off to the right of the main road.

TRIP HIGHLIGHT

❼ Montalcino

Montalcino, a pretty medieval town perched above the Val d'Orcia, is home to one of Italy's great wines, Brunello di Montalcino (and the more modest, but still very palatable, Rosso di Montalcino). There are plenty of *enoteche* where

you can taste and buy, including one in the **Fortezza** (Piazzale Fortezza; courtyard free, ramparts adult/reduced €4/2; ⏰9am-8pm Apr-Oct, 10am-6pm Nov-Mar), the 14th-century fortress that dominates the town's skyline.

For a historical insight into the town's winemaking past, head to the **Museo della Comunità di Montalcino e del Brunello** (☎0577 84 60 21; www.museodelbrunello.it; c/o Fattoria dei Barbi, Località Podernovi 170; €5, with wine tasting €8-10; ⏰3.30-7pm Tue-Fri, 11am-1pm & 3.30-7pm Sat & Sun), a small museum off the road to the Abbazia di Sant'Antimo.

WINE TASTING GOES HIGH TECH

One of Tuscany's biggest cellars, the **Enoteca Falorni** (☎055 854 64 04; www.enotecafalorni.it; Piazza delle Cantine 6; ⏰10.30am-7.30pm) in Greve in Chianti stocks more than 1000 labels, of which around 100 are available for tasting. It's a lovely, brick-arched place, but wine tasting here is a very modern experience, thanks to a sophisticated wine-dispensing system that preserves wine in an open bottle for up to three weeks and allows tasters to serve themselves by the glass. The way it works is that you buy a prepaid wine card costing from €10 and then use it at the various 'tasting islands' dotted around the cellar. Any unused credit is then refunded when you return the card.

✖ 🛏 p271

The Drive ⟫ From Montalcino, head downhill and then, after about 8km, turn onto the SR2. At San Quirico d'Orcia pick up the SP146, a fabulously scenic road that weaves along the Val d'Orcia through rolling green hills, past the pretty town of Pienza, to Montepulciano. Allow about an hour.

↱ DETOUR: ABBAZIA DI SANT'ANTIMO

Start: ❼ Montalcino (p269)

The striking Romanesque **Abbazia di Sant'Antimo** (www.antimo.it; Castelnuovo dell'Abate; ⏰10am-1pm & 3-6pm) lies in an isolated valley just below the village of Castelnuovo dell'Abate, 10.5km from Montalcino. According to tradition, Charlemagne founded the original monastery in 781. The exterior, built in pale travertine stone, is simple but for the stone carvings, which include various fantastical animals. Inside, study the capitals of the columns lining the nave, especially the one representing Daniel in the lions' den.

Music lovers should plan their visit to coincide with the daily services, which include Gregorian chants. Check the website for times.

❽ Montepulciano

Set atop a narrow ridge of volcanic rock, the Renaissance centre of Montepulciano produces the celebrated red wine Vino Nobile. For a drop, head up the main street, called in stages Via di Gracciano nel Corso, Via di Voltaia del Corso and Via dell'Opio nel Corso, to the **Cantine Contucci** (www.contucci. it; Via del Teatro 1; ⏰8.30am-12.30pm & 2.30-6.30pm), housed underneath the *palazzo* (mansion) of the same name. A second cellar, the **Cantina de' Ricci** (☎0578 75 71 66; www.dericci.it; Via Collazzi 7; wine tasting plus food €15; ⏰9.30am-6pm), occupies a grotto-like space underneath **Palazzo Ricci** near **Piazza Grande**, the town's highest point.

✖ 🛏 p271, p279

Eating & Sleeping

Florence ❶ <small>see also p47, p60 and p261</small>

✗ Il Santo Bevitore   Tuscan €€

(☎055 21 12 64; www.ilsantobevitore.com; Via di Santo Spirito 64-66r; meals €40; ⊗12.30-2.30pm & 7.30-11.30pm, closed Sun lunch & Aug) Reserve or arrive dot on 7.30pm to snag the last table at this ever-popular address, an ode to stylish dining where gastronomes eat by candlelight in a vaulted, whitewashed, bottle-lined interior. The menu is a creative reinvention of seasonal classics: purple cabbage soup with mozzarella cream and anchovy syrup, acacia honey *bavarese* (firm, creamy mousse) with Vin Santo–marinated dried fruits.

Badia a Passignano ❹

✗ Osteria di Passignano   Tuscan €€€

(☎055 807 12 78; www.osteriadipassignano. com; Via di Passignano 33, Badia a Passignano; meals €85, tasting menu €80, with wine €130; ⊗12.15-2.15pm & 7.30-10pm Mon-Sat) Badia a Passignano sits amid a landscape scored by row upon row of vines, and the elegant Michelin-starred eatery in the centre of the village has long been one of Tuscany's most glamorous dining destinations. Intricate, Tuscan-inspired dishes fly the local-produce flag and the wine list is mightily impressive, with Antinori offerings aplenty (by the glass €7 to €35).

🛏 Fattoria di Rignana   Agriturismo €€

(☎0558 5 20 65; www.rignana.it; Via di Rignana 15, Rignana; d fattoria €110-120, without bathroom €95, d villa €140; P@🛜🏊) A chic, historic farmhouse with its very own bell tower rewards you for the drive up the long, rutted road. You'll also find glorious views, a large swimming pool and a very decent eatery. Choose between elegant rooms in the 17th-century villa and rustic ones in the *fattoria* (farmhouse). It's 4km from Badia a Passignano and 10km west of Greve.

Montalcino ❼

✗ Ristorante di Poggio Antico   Modern Italian €€€

(☎0577 84 92 00; www.poggioantico.com; Loc Poggio Antico, Montalcino; meals from €50; ⊗noon-2.30pm & 7-9.30pm, closed Mon summer, closed Sun dinner & Mon winter) Located 4.5km outside town on the road to Grosseto, the Poggio Antico vineyard makes award-winning wines, conducts tastings and offers guided tours. Its fine-dining restaurant is one of the best in the area, serving a menu of creative, contemporary Italian cuisine.

🛏 Hotel Vecchia Oliviera   Hotel €€

(☎0577 84 60 28; www.vecchiaoliviera.com; Via Landi 1; s €70-85, d €120-190; P❄🛜🏊) Chandeliers, elegant armchairs, polished wooden floors and rich rugs lend this converted oil mill a refined air. The pick of the 11 rooms comes with hill views and a jacuzzi, the pool is in an attractive garden setting, and the terrace has wraparound views.

Montepulciano ❽ <small>see also p279</small>

✗ Osteria Acquacheta   Tuscan €€

(☎0578 71 70 86; www.acquacheta.eu; Via del Teatro 2; meals €25-30; ⊗12.30-3pm & 7.30-10.30pm Wed-Mon) Hugely popular with locals and tourists alike, this bustling *osteria* specialises in *bistecca alla fiorentina* (chargrilled T-bone steak), which comes to the table in huge, lightly seared and exceptionally flavoursome slabs (don't even *think* of asking for it to be served otherwise). Book ahead.

🛏 Locanda San Francesco   B&B €€

(☎0578 75 87 25; www.locandasanfrancesco. it; Piazza San Francesco 3; d €180-250; P❄@🛜) There's only one downside to this B&B: once you check into the supremely welcoming, 14th-century *palazzo*, you might never want to leave. The feel is elegant but also homely: refined furnishings meet well-stocked bookshelves; restrained fabrics are teamed with fluffy bathrobes. The best room has superb views over Val d'Orcia on one side and Val di Chiana on the other.

Tuscan Landscapes

25

Rolling hills capped by medieval towns, golden wheat fields and snaking lines of cypress trees – immerse yourself in Tuscan scenery on this trip through the region's southern stretches.

TRIP HIGHLIGHTS

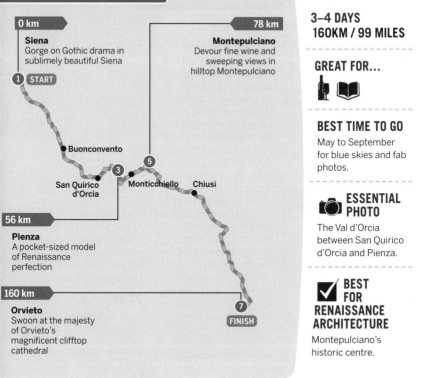

0 km

Siena
Gorge on Gothic drama in sublimely beautiful Siena

1 START

78 km

Montepulciano
Devour fine wine and sweeping views in hilltop Montepulciano

Buonconvento

3

5

San Quirico d'Orcia

Monticchiello

Chiusi

56 km

Pienza
A pocket-sized model of Renaissance perfection

160 km

Orvieto
Swoon at the majesty of Orvieto's magnificent clifftop cathedral

7 FINISH

3–4 DAYS
160KM / 99 MILES

GREAT FOR...

BEST TIME TO GO
May to September for blue skies and fab photos.

ESSENTIAL PHOTO
The Val d'Orcia between San Quirico d'Orcia and Pienza.

BEST FOR RENAISSANCE ARCHITECTURE
Montepulciano's historic centre.

l d'Orcia Farmhouse in the countryside near San Quirico d'Orcia

273

START
1 Siena
SP438
TUSCANY
Buonconvento
Riserva
Naturale
Alto Merse
E78

25 Tuscan Landscapes

Ever since medieval pilgrims discovered Tuscany en route from Canterbury to Rome, the region has been captivating travellers. This trip strikes south from Siena, running through the Crete Senesi, an area of clay hills scored by deep ravines, to the Unesco-listed Val d'Orcia, whose soothing hills and billowing plains are punctuated by delightful Renaissance towns. The end of the road is Orvieto, home to one of Italy's most feted Gothic cathedrals.

TRIP HIGHLIGHT

1 Siena

With its medieval *palazzi* (mansions) and humbling Gothic architecture, Siena's historic centre is a sight to compare with any in Tuscany. To admire it from above, climb to the top of the **Torre del Mangia** (☎0577 29 26 15; Palazzo Comunale, Piazza del Campo 1; €10; ⊙10am-7pm summer, to 4pm winter), the slender 14th-century tower that rises above **Piazza del Campo**, and look down on a sea of red-tiled roofs and, beyond, to the green, undulating countryside that awaits you on this trip.

At the foot of the tower, **Palazzo Pubblico** (Palazzo Comunale) is a magnificent example of Sienese Gothic architecture and home to the city's best art museum, the **Museo Civico** (☎0577 29 26 15; Palazzo Comunale, Piazza del Campo 1; adult/reduced €9/8; ⊙10am-7pm summer, to 6pm winter).

To the southwest of Palazzo Pubblico, another inspiring spectacle awaits. Siena's 13th-century **Duomo** (www.operaduomo.siena.it; Piazza del Duomo; summer/winter €4/free, when floor displayed €7; ⊙10.30am-7pm Mon-Sat,1.30-6pm Sun summer, 10.30am-5.30pm Mon-Sat, 1.30-5.30pm Sun winter) is one of Italy's greatest

Gothic churches, and its magnificent facade of white, green and red polychrome marble is one you'll remember long after you've left town.

✕ ⊨ p60, p279

The Drive » The first leg down to San Quirico d'Orcia, about an hour's drive, takes you down the scenic SR2 via the market town of Buonconvento. En route

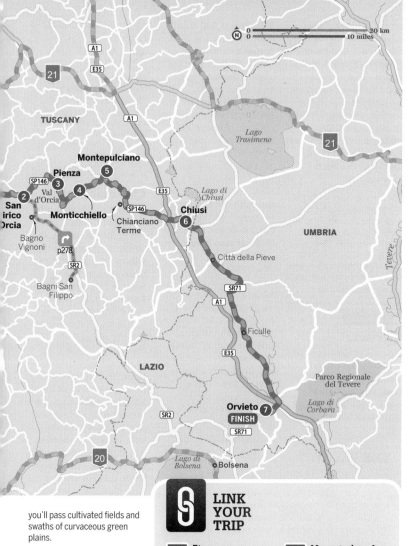

you'll pass cultivated fields and swaths of curvaceous green plains.

- - - - - - - - - - - -

② San Quirico d'Orcia

First stop in the Unesco-protected Val d'Orcia is San Quirico d'Orcia. A fortified medieval town and one-time stopover

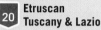 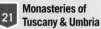

🔗 LINK YOUR TRIP

20 Etruscan Tuscany & Lazio

From Orvieto continue 20km southwest to Bolsena and join up with this Etruscan treasure hunt.

21 Monasteries of Tuscany & Umbria

Head southeast from Siena along the SP438 to the Abbazia di Monte Oliveto Maggiore to tour monasteries.

on the Via Francigena pilgrim route between Canterbury and Rome, it's now a lovely, low-key village. There are no great must-see sights but it's a pleasant place for a stroll, with a graceful Romanesque **Colle-giata** (church) and formal Renaissance gardens known as the **Horti Leononi**.

The Drive » From San Quirico d'Orcia it's a quick 15-minute drive to Pienza along the SP146. This is one of the trip's most beautiful stretches, offering unfettered views over seas of undulating grasslands peppered by stone farmhouses and lines of elegant cypress trees.

❸ Pienza

One of the most popular hill towns in the Val d'Orcia, pint-sized Pienza boasts a Renaissance centre that has changed little since local boy

Pope Pius II had it built between 1459 and 1462. Action is centred on Piazza Pio II, where the solemn **Duomo** (Piazza Pio II; 8.30am-1pm & 2.15-6.30pm) is flanked by two Renaissance *palazzi* – on the right, **Palazzo Pic-colomini** (www.palazzo piccolominipienza.it; Piazza Pio II; adult/reduced with guided tour €7/5; 10am-6.30pm Tue-Sun summer, to 4.30pm winter), the former papal residence; on the left, Palazzo Vescovile, home to the **Museo Diocesano** (0578 74 99 05; http:// palazzoborgia.it; Corso Rossellino 30; adult/reduced €4.50/3; 10.30am-1.30pm & 2.30-6pm Wed-Mon summer, 10am-4pm Sat & Sun winter) and an intriguing miscellany of artworks, manuscripts, tapestries and miniatures. Before leaving town make sure you pick up some local *pecorino* cheese for

which the area is justly famous.

✗ p279

The Drive » From Pienza strike south on the SP18 and head into the heart of the countryside, enjoying more bucolic scenery as you go. After 6km or so you'll see a sign to Monticchiello off to the left. Take this and continue for another 4km.

- - - - - - - - - - - - -

❹ Monticchiello

A 15-minute drive south-east from Pienza brings you to Monticchiello, a sleepy medieval hilltop village. Just inside the main gate, the highly regarded **Osteria La Porta** (0578 75 51 63; www.osterialaporta.it; Via del Piano 3; meals €40; cafe 9am-12.30pm & 3-7pm, restaurant 12.30-3pm & 7.30-10.30pm, closed Thu winter) has a small terrace with panoramic views of the Val d'Orcia and a reputa-tion for food and service that behoves a reserva-tion, even in low season. The €23 fixed-price menu at lunchtime offers great value, and *spuntini* (snacks) such as brus-chetta, olives and cheese plates are served outside usual meal hours.

The Drive » Take the SP88 and follow it as it ploughs on through fields and light woodland to the main SP146. Go left and continue past orderly vineyards and olive groves up to San Biagio and 2km further on to Montepulciano. All told it's about 20 minutes.

THE PALIO

Siena's Palio is one of Italy's most spectacular annual events. Dating from the Middle Ages, it comprises a series of colourful pageants and a wild horse race on 2 July and 16 August. Ten of Siena's 17 *contrade* (town districts) compete for the coveted *palio* (silk banner).

From about 5pm, representatives from each *contrada* parade around the Campo in historical costume, all bearing their individual banners. Then, at 7.30pm in July and 7pm in August, the race gets the green light. For scarcely one exhilarating minute, the 10 horses and their bareback riders tear three times around the temporarily constructed dirt racetrack with a speed and violence that makes spectators' hair stand on end.

Orvieto View towards the Duomo di Orvieto

5 Montepulciano

Famous for its Vino Nobile wine, Montepulciano is a steeply stacked hill town harbouring a wealth of *palazzi* and fine buildings, as well as grandstand views over the Val di Chiana and Val d'Orcia. The main street, aka the Corso, climbs steeply, passing **Caffè Poliziano**, which has been operating since 1868, as it leads to the **Cantine Contucci** (www.contucci.it; Via del Teatro 1; ⊘8.30am-12.30pm & 2.30-6.30pm), one of two historic wine cellars in town. Nearby **Piazza Grande** is flanked by the 14th-century **Palazzo Comunale** (Piazza Grande; terrace/tower €2.50/5; ⊘10am-6pm) and late-16th-century **Duomo** (Piazza Grande; ⊘8am-7pm).

✗ p271, p279

The Drive » Reckon on about 40 minutes to cover the 25km to Chiusi. From Montepulciano head southeast along the SP146 to Chianciano Terme, a popular spa town. Continue on towards the A1 autostrada, and Chiusi is just on the other side of the highway.

DETOUR: BAGNO VIGNONI & BAGNI SAN FILIPPO

Start: ② San Quirico d'Orcia (p275)

Some 9km south of San Quirico d'Orcia along the SP53, hot sulphurous water (around 49°C) bubbles up into a picturesque pool in the centre of **Bagno Vignoni**. You can't actually enter the pool but there are various spa complexes offering a full range of treatments. For free hot-water frolics continue 18km further along the SR2 to the tiny village of **Bagni San Filippo**, where there are thermal cascades in an open-air reserve. You'll find these just uphill from Hotel le Terme – follow a sign marked 'Fosso Bianco' down a lane for about 150m and you'll come to a series of mini pools, fed by hot, tumbling cascades of water. Not unlike a free, al fresco spa. It's a pleasant if slightly whiffy spot for a picnic.

⑥ Chiusi

Once an important Etruscan centre, Chiusi is now a sleepy country town. Its main attractions are the Etruscan tombs dotted around the surrounding countryside, two of which are included in the ticket price of the **Museo Archeologico Nazionale** (☎0578 2 01 77; Via Porsenna 93; adult/reduced €6/3; ⊘9am-8pm). In town, you can go underground in the **Labirinto di Porsenna** (Museo della Cattedrale, Piazza Duomo 7; adult/reduced €5/3.50; ⊘10am-12.45pm Mon-Fri, 10am-12.45pm & 3.20-6.15pm Sat & Sun late Mar-Oct), a series of tunnels dating to Etruscan times that formed part of the town's water-supply system.

The Drive » You have two choices for Orvieto. The quick route is on the A1 autostrada (about 45 minutes), but it's a more interesting drive along the SR71 (1½ hours). This passes through Città della Pieve, birthplace of the painter Perugino, and Ficulle, known since Roman times for its artisans.

TRIP HIGHLIGHT

⑦ Orvieto

Over the regional border in Umbria, the precariously perched town of Orvieto boasts one of Italy's finest Gothic cathedrals. The **Duomo di Orvieto** (☎0763 34 24 77; www.opsm.it; Piazza Duomo 26; €3; ⊘9.30am-7pm summer, shorter hr & closed Tue winter) took 30 years to plan and three centuries to complete. Work began in 1290, originally to a Romanesque design, but as construction proceeded, Gothic features were incorporated into the structure. Highlights include the richly coloured facade, and, in the **Cappella di San Brizio**, Luca Signorelli's fresco cycle *The Last Judgement*.

Across the piazza from the cathedral, the **Museo Claudio Faina e Civico** (www.museofaina. it; Piazza Duomo 29; adult/reduced €4.50/3; ⊘9.30am-6pm summer, 10am-5pm Tue-Sun winter) houses an important collection of Etruscan archaeological artefacts.

✕ 🛏 p279

Eating & Sleeping

Siena ① see also p60

✕ Morbidi   Deli €

(www.morbidi.com; Via Banchi di Sopra 75; lunch buffet €12; ⏱8am-10pm Mon-Sat) Possibly the classiest cheap feed in Siena: set in the stylish basement of Morbidi's deli, the lunch buffet on offer here is excellent. For a mere €12, you can join the well-dressed locals sampling antipasti, salads, risottos, pastas and a dessert of the day. Bottled water is supplied, wine and coffee cost extra. Buy your ticket upstairs before heading down.

🛏 Campo Regio Relais   Boutique Hotel €€€

(☎0577 22 20 73; www.camporegio.com; Via della Sapienza 25; d €190-450; ❄🤶) The decor in each of the six, individually styled rooms here is exquisite – expect anything from old mahogany to fine linen, 18th-century antiques to art nouveau. Breakfast is served in the sumptuously decorated lounge or on the terrace, with a sensational view across a valley of higgledy-piggledy rooftops to Torre del Mangia and the *duomo*.

Pienza ③

✕ Osteria Sette di Vino   Tuscan €

(☎0578 74 90 92; Piazza di Spagna 1; meals €20; ⏱noon-2.30pm & 7.30-10pm Thu-Tue) Known for its *zuppa di pane e fagioli* (bread and white-bean soup), *bruschette* and range of local *pecorino* cheese, this simple place is run by the exuberant Luciano, who is immortalised as Bacchus in a copy of Caravaggio's famous painting hanging above the main counter. There's a clutch of tables inside and a scattering outside – book ahead.

Montepulciano ⑤ see also p271

✕ La Grotta   Ristorante €€€

(☎0578 75 74 79; www.lagrottamontepulciano. it; Via di San Biagio 15; meals €45, 6-course tasting menu €50; ⏱12.30-2pm & 7.30-10pm Thu-Tue, closed mid-Jan–mid-Mar) The ingredients, and sometimes dishes, may be traditional, but the presentation is full of refined flourishes – artfully arranged Parmesan shavings and sprigs of herbs crown delicate towers of pasta, vegetables and meat. The service is exemplary and the courtyard garden divine. It's just outside town on the road to Chiusi.

Orvieto ⑦

✕ I Sette Consoli   Italian €€€

(☎0763 34 39 11; www.isetteconsoli.it; Piazza Sant'Angelo 1a; meals around €45, 6-course tasting menu €45; ⏱12.30-3pm & 7.30-10pm, closed Wed & dinner Sun) This refined restaurant walks the culinary high wire in Orvieto, with inventive, artfully presented dishes, from pasta so light it floats off the fork to beautifully cooked pigeon casserole with minced hazelnuts and cherry beer sauce. In good weather, try to get a seat in the garden, with the *duomo* in view. Dress for dinner and reserve ahead.

🛏 B&B La Magnolia   B&B €

(☎349 4620733, 0763 34 28 08; www. bblamagnolia.it; Via del Duomo 29; d €60-90; ❄) Tucked down a side street north of the *duomo* (the sign is easily missed), this light-filled Renaissance residence has delightful rooms and apartments, an English-speaking owner, a large shared kitchen and a balcony overlooking the rooftops. The owner Serena can tell you all about Orvieto – whatever you want to know, just ask.

Foodie Emilia-Romagna

26

Experience the best of cucina italiana on this tour of Italy's culinary heartland. As well as great food and wine, you'll also come across artistic treasures and medieval cities at every turn.

TRIP HIGHLIGHTS

0 km

Parma
Ham and cheese top Parma's gourmet menu

100 km

Bologna
Eat, drink and shop in this handsome, hedonistic city

Abbazia di Pomposa

Ferrara

Comacchio

Reggio Emilia

1
START

3

4

7
FINISH

Modena
A foodie hot spot with a magnificent medieval heart

Ravenna
Feast your eyes on lavish Byzantine mosaics

55 km

255 km

7 DAYS
255KM / 158 MILES

GREAT FOR...

BEST TIME TO GO
Autumn is ideal for fresh seasonal produce.

ESSENTIAL PHOTO
Food stalls and delis in Bologna's Quadrilatero district.

BEST FOR ART LOVERS
Ravenna's sparkling mosaics.

26 Foodie Emilia-Romagna

Sandwiched between Tuscany and the Veneto, Emilia-Romagna is a foodie's dream destination. Many of Italy's signature dishes originated here, and its regional specialities are revered across the country. This tasty trip takes in the region's main culinary centres of Parma, Modena and Bologna, as well as the charming Renaissance town of Ferrara, and art-rich Ravenna, celebrated for its glorious Byzantine mosaics.

TRIP HIGHLIGHT

❶ Parma

Handsome and prosperous, Parma is one of Italy's culinary hotspots, producing the country's finest ham *(prosciutto di Parma)* and its most revered cheese *(parmigiano reggiano)*. To stock up on these, as well as local Lambrusco wines and other regional delicacies, head to the **Salumeria Garibaldi** (Via Garibaldi 42; ⏲8am-8pm Mon-Sat), a divine deli in the historic centre.

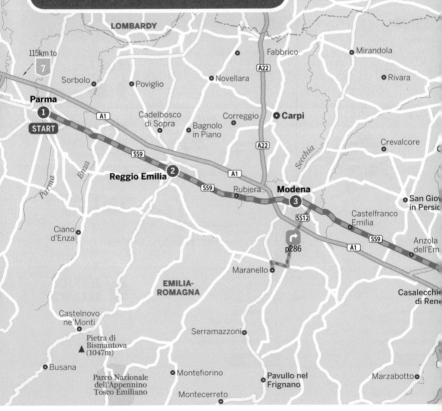

Once you've fed your appetite, feed your soul at the city's 12th-century **Duomo** (www.piazza duomoparma.com; Piazza del Duomo; ◷10am-6.30pm), with its classic Lombard-Romanesque facade and ornate baroque interior. Nearby, the octagonal **Battistero** (www.piazza duomoparma.com; Piazza del Duomo; adult/reduced incl Museo Diocesano €8/6; ◷10am-6.30pm summer, to 4.30pm winter) displays a hybrid Romanesque-Gothic look in pink and white marble. Parma's main art collection, which includes

works by locals Parmigianino and Correggio alongside paintings by Fra' Angelico, El Greco and a piece attributed to Leonardo da Vinci, are in the **Galleria Nazionale** (www.gallerianazionaleparma. it; adult/reduced incl Teatro

Farnese & Museo Archeologico Nazionale €10/5; ◷8.30am-7pm Tue-Sat, to 2pm Sun), one of several museums in the monumental **Palazzo della Pilotta.** (Piazza della Pilotta)

✂ 🛏 p287

LINK YOUR TRIP

7 Cinematic Cinque Terre

From Parma head 120km along the A15 autostrada to La Spezia, gateway to the spectacular Cinque Terre coastline.

8 Northern Cities

From Ferrara take the A13 autostrada for 80km to Padua, home of one of Italy's great Renaissance masterpieces.

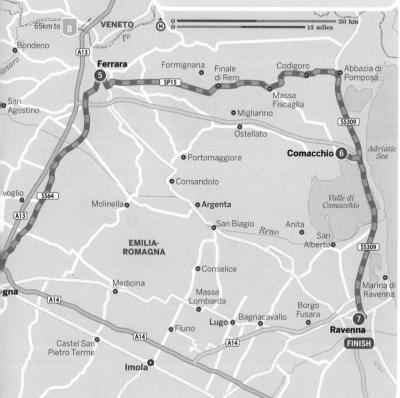

The Drive » From Parma, it's a straightforward 50-minute drive southeast on the SS9 (Via Emilia) through fairly uninspiring flat farmland to Reggio Emilia. If you're in a hurry, the quicker A1 autostrada covers the same route.

❷ Reggio Emilia

Genteel Reggio Emilia puts the *reggiano* in *parmigiano reggiano* (Parmesan cheese). Apart from its cheese, the city is best known as the birthplace of the Italian flag – the famous red, white and green tricolour – whose history is chronicled at the **Museo del Tricolore** (www.musei.re.it/sedi/museo-del-tricolore; Piazza Prampolini 1; ⏰9am-noon Tue-Fri, 10am-1pm & 4-7pm Sat & Sun Sep-Jun, 9-11pm Tue-Sun Jul & Aug). There are several other museums and galleries in town, including the **Galleria Parmeggiani** (www.musei. re.it/sedi/galleria-parmeggiani;

Corso Cairoli 2; ⏰9am-noon Tue-Fri, 10am-1pm & 4-7pm Sat & Sun Jun-Sep, 9-11pm Tue-Sun late Jul-Aug), which has some interesting Italian, Flemish and Spanish paintings.

🍴 p287

The Drive » The run down to Modena takes about an hour on the SS9. The scenery is much like the first leg from Parma – flat fields, petrol stations, agricultural buildings and the occasional stone farmhouse. At Modena head for the *centro*.

❸ Modena

Modena is one of Italy's great gastronomic centres, the creative force behind *aceto balsamico* (balsamic vinegar), *zamponi* (pig's trotters), *cotechino* (stuffed pork sausage) and sparkling Lambrusco wines. You'll find shops all over town selling local delicacies, including the **Enoteca Ducale** (www.enotecaducale.

it; Corso Vittorio Emanuele II 15; ⏰9am-7pm Tue-Sun), which has a comprehensive selection of aged balsamic vinegars.

Modena is not just about food, though. It boasts a wonderfully suggestive medieval core, centred on **Piazza Grande** and the **Duomo** (www.duomodimodena.it; Corso Duomo; ⏰7am-7pm Tue-Sun, 7am-12.30pm & 3.30-7pm Mon), considered by many to be the finest Romanesque church in Italy. Inseparable from the cathedral is the early-13th-century tower, the **Torre Ghirlandina** (Corso Duomo; €3; ⏰9.30am-1pm & 3-7pm Tue-Fri, 9.30am-7pm Sat & Sun summer, 9.30am-1pm & 2.30-5.30pm Tue-Fri, 9.30am-5.30pm Sat & Sun winter).

🍴 p61, p287

The Drive » From Modena take the SS9 southeast to Bologna. It's only about 40km away but traffic is often heavy and it can take up to 1½ hours to get there. Bologna's centre is closed to most traffic, so if you're staying downtown contact your hotel to ask about parking.

❹ Bologna

Emilia-Romagna's vibrant regional capital, Bologna is a city with serious culinary credentials. Its most famous creation is the eponymous bolognese sauce (known as *ragù* in Italian), but it also gifted the world lasagne, *mortadella* and *tortellini*

VIA EMILIA

For the first half of the trip from Parma to Bologna you follow the region's most famous road, the ruler-straight Via Emilia. Built by the Romans in the 2nd century BC, it ran for 206km through the Po river valley connecting the region's main cities – Placentia (Piacenza), Parma, Regium (Reggio Emilia), Mutina (Modena), Bononia (Bologna) and Ariminum (Rimini). Within decades of completion it had opened up Italy's fertile northern hinterland to economic expansion, and converted the rich river plain into the empire's proverbial breadbasket – a position it still enjoys today.

KEN SCICLUNA/GETTY IMAGES ©

Modena Via Emilia Centro in the historic town centre

(pockets of meat-stuffed pasta). These and other local goodies appear on menus across the city, but for a real gastro treat, sniff out the fabulous old-style delis in the bustling **Quadrilatero** district.

Overshadowing the Quadrilatero's medieval streets are **Le Due Torri**, Bologna's two leaning towers. If vertigo's not a problem, you can climb the taller of the two, the 97.6m-high **Torre degli Asinelli** (Piazza di Porta Ravegnana; €3; ⌚9am-7pm Apr-Sep, to 5pm Oct-Mar), and survey the historic centre from on high. The big barn-like structure you'll see to the northwest is the **Basilica di San Petronio** (www.basilicadisanpetronio.it; Piazza Maggiore; ⌚7.45am-2pm & 3-6pm), the world's fifth-largest basilica, which lords over **Piazza Maggiore**, Bologna's striking showpiece square. Also on the piazza is **Palazzo Comunale** (Town Hall), home of the interesting **Collezioni Comunali d'Arte** (☎051 219 39 98; Palazzo Comunale; adult/reduced €5/3; ⌚9am-6.30pm Tue-Fri, from 10am Sat & Sun).

✕ 🛏 p47, p287

The Drive » Head north out of Bologna along Via Stalingrado and follow the SS64. This leads through orderly farmland and neat villages to Ferrara, about 1½ hours away. In Ferrara, turn left after the river and head for the *centro storico* (historic centre) car park on Via Darsena.

5 Ferrara

Ferrara was once the seat of the powerful Este family (1260–1598) and although it is often bypassed by travellers, it's an attractive place with an austere Renaissance cityscape and compact historic centre. In food terms, specialities include the town's uniquely shaped bread, known as *coppia ferra-*

DETOUR: MARANELLO

Start: ❸ Modena (p284)

A mecca for petrol heads, Maranello is the home town of Ferrari. The world's sportiest cars have been manufactured here since the early 1940s and although the factory is off-limits (unless you happen to own a Ferrari), you can get your fix ogling the flaming red autos on display at the **Museo Ferrari** (http://museomaranello.ferrari.com; Via Ferrari 43; adult/reduced €15/13; ⊘9.30am-7pm Apr-Oct, to 6pm Nov-Mar). Maranello is 17km south of Modena on the SS12.

rese, and *cappellacci di zucca* (hat-shaped pasta stuffed with pumpkin, herbs and nutmeg).

The town centre, which is easily explored on foot, is focused on **Castello Estense** (www.castelloestense.it; Viale Cavour; adult/reduced €8/6; ⊘9.30am-5.30pm daily Mar-May & Sep, 9.30am-5.30pm Tue-Sun Jan, Feb & Oct, 9am-1.30pm & 3-7pm daily Jun, 9am-1.30pm & 3-7pm Tue-Sun Jul & Aug), a martial 14th-century castle complete with moat and drawbridge. Linked to the castle by an elevated passageway is the 13th-century crenellated **Palazzo Municipale** (⊘9am-1pm Mon-Fri), now largely occupied by administrative offices. Opposite, Ferrara's pink-and-white, 12th-century **Duomo** (Piazza Cattedrale; ⊘7.30am-noon & 3.30-6.30pm Mon-Sat, 7.30am-12.30pm & 3.30-7pm Sun) sports a graphic three-tier facade, combining Romanesque and Gothic styles.

The Drive » Head east out of Ferrara on the SP15 and continue on the straight road past immaculate vineyards onto the tiny village of Massa Fiscaglia. Bear left here and continue on to Codigoro and the Abbazia di Pomposa (well worth a quick stop). From the abbey it's a straight 20-minute run down the SS309 to Comacchio.

---

❻ Comacchio

Resembling a mini-Venice with its canals and brick bridges, Comacchio is the main centre in the Po Delta (Foci del Po). This area of dense pine forests and extensive wetlands, much of it protected in the **Parco del Delta del Po** (www.parcodeltapo.it), offers superlative bird-watching and excellent cycling. Foodies can try the prized local speciality, eel, which is served with great relish at the many restaurants and trattorias on Comacchio's canals.

The Drive » From Comacchio, Ravenna is only an hour's drive away, 40km south on the SS309. The road spears down a narrow strip of land between a lagoon and the Adriatic coast, but you won't see much water thanks to lengthy curtains of verdant trees and heavy foliage.

TRIP HIGHLIGHT

❼ Ravenna

No tour of Emilia-Romagna would be complete without a stop at Ravenna to see its remarkable Unesco-protected mosaics. Relics of the city's golden age as capital of the Western Roman and Byzantine Empires, they are described by Dante in his *Divine Comedy,* much of which he wrote here.

The mosaics are spread over several sites, five of which are covered by a single ticket (5-site combo ticket €9.50, plus summer-only surcharge €2; ⊘9am-7pm Apr-Sep, 9am-5.30pm Mar & Oct, 9.30am-5pm Nov-Feb) – **Basilica di San Vitale** (Via Fiandrini), **Mausoleo di Galla Placidia** (Via Fiandrini), **Basilica di Sant'Apollinare Nuovo** (Via di Roma), **Museo Arcivescovile** (Piazza Arcivescovado) and **Battistero Neoniano** (Piazza del Duomo). Outside town you'll find more mosaics at the **Basilica di Sant'Apollinare in Classe** (Via Romea Sud; adult/reduced €5/2.50; ⊘8.30am-7.30pm).

For more information check www.ravenna mosaici.it.

🛏 p287

Eating & Sleeping

Parma ❶

✖ Trattoria del Tribunale — Trattoria €

(www.trattoriadeltribunale.it; Vicolo Politi 5; meals €25; ☺ noon-3pm & 7-11pm) Run the gauntlet of ham slicers and waiters gouging lumps of *parmigiano reggiano* and settle in for a memorable meal. Start with a plate of Parma ham, proceed to the *degustazione di tortelli* (pasta pockets stuffed with chard, pumpkin and artichokes), and finish with *parmigiana di melanzane* (eggplant Parmesan). Pure Parma!

🛏 B&B Pio — B&B €

(☏ 347 776 90 65; www.piorooms.it; Borgo XX Marzo 14; s/d €70/80; 📶) Location, comfort and hospitality all come together at this B&B run by a gregarious owner with a passion for local food and wine. Four lower-floor doubles and a kitchenette-equipped upper floor suite share attractive features such as beamed ceilings, antique textiles and ultra-modern fixtures. All guests share access to a small but bright top-floor breakfast room.

Reggio Emilia ❷

✖ Caffè Arti e Mestieri — Gastronomy €€€

(☏ 0522 43 22 02; www.giannidamato.it; Via Emilia San Pietro 14; meals €50, 5-course tasting menu €65; ☺ noon-2.30pm & 7.30-10.30pm Tue-Sat, noon-2.30pm Sun) Tucked back off the street around a lovely interior garden, this is Reggio's best spot for an elegant dinner. Chef Gianni d'Amato launched this new venture after his Michelin-starred Rigoletto was destroyed by the region's 2012 earthquake. Weekday lunch specials offer the rare chance for gourmet dining with a €10 price tag (main course, water and coffee; €13 with wine).

Modena ❸ see also p61

✖ Ristorante da Danilo — Italian €€

(☏ 059 21 66 91; www.ristorantedadanilo modena.it; Via Coltellini 31; meals €30; ☺ noon-3pm & 7pm-midnight Mon-Sat) Speedy waiters glide around balancing bread baskets, wine bottles and pasta dishes in this deliciously traditional dining room where first dates mingle with animated families and office groups on a birthday jaunt. Antipasti of salami, *pecorino* and fig marmalade are followed by delicious *secondi* of *bollito misto* (mixed boiled meats) or a vegetarian *risotto al radicchio trevigiano* (with red chicory).

Bologna ❹ see also p47

✖ Drogheria della Rosa — Trattoria €€

(☏ 051 22 25 29; www.drogheriadellarosa. it; Via Cartoleria 10; meals €35-40; ☺ 1-3pm & 7.30-11.45pm) With its wooden shelves and apothecary jars, it's not difficult to picture this place as the pharmacy it once was. Nowadays it's a charming, high-end trattoria, run by a congenial owner who gets round to every table to explain the day's short, sweet menu of superbly prepared Bolognese classics, and often bestows roses upon guests at evening's end.

Ravenna ❼

🛏 Albergo Cappello — Boutique Hotel €€

(☏ 0544 21 98 13; www.albergocappello.it; Via IV Novembre 41; r €139-189; 🅿 ❄ @ 📶) Colour-themed rooms come in three categories (deluxe, suite and junior suite) at this finely coiffed seven-room boutique hotel smack in the town centre. Murano glass chandeliers, original 15th-century frescoes and coffered ceilings are set against modern fixtures and flat-screen TVs. The ample breakfast features pastries from Ravenna's finest *pasticceria*. There's also an excellent restaurant and wine bar attached.

STRETCH YOUR LEGS
ROME

Start/Finish: Largo di Torre Argentina

Distance: 1.7km

Duration: Three hours

The best way to explore Rome's historic centre, much of which is closed to unauthorised traffic, is on foot. Park near Stazione Termini, then head into the centre by bus. As you walk you'll discover picturesque cobbled lanes, showboating piazzas, basilicas and ancient ruins.

Take this walk on Trips

Largo di Torre Argentina

Start in **Largo di Torre Argentina**, a busy square easily reached by bus. In its sunken central area, the Republican-era templesdate to between the 2nd and 4th centuries BC. On the piazza's western flank, **Teatro Argentina**, Rome's premier theatre, stands near the spot where Julius Caesar was assassinated in 44 BC.

The Walk » From the square, head east along Corso Vittorio Emanuele II to Piazza del Gesù.

Chiesa del Gesù

The landmark **Chiesa del Gesù** (www. chiesadelgesu.org; Piazza del Gesù; ⊘7am-12.30pm & 4-7.45pm, St Ignatius rooms 4-6pm Mon-Sat, 10am-noon Sun) is Rome's most important Jesuit church. Behind its imposing facade is an awe-inspiring baroque interior. Headline works include the swirling vault fresco by Il Baciccia and Andrea del Pozzo's opulent tomb for Ignatius Loyola, the Jesuits' founder.

The Walk » Cross Corso Vittorio Emanuele II and follow Via del Gesù north. Then turn left onto Via Santa Caterina da Siena.

Basilica di Santa Maria Sopra Minerva

Trumpeted by Bernini's much-loved **Elefantino** statue, this **basilica** (www. santamariasopraminerva.it; Piazza della Minerva 42; ⊘7.30am-7pm Mon-Fri, 7.30am-12.30pm & 3.30-7pm Sat, 8am-12.30pm & 3.30-7pm Sun) is Rome's only Gothic church. However, little remains of the original 13th-century structure and these days the main drawcard is a minor Michelangelo sculpture and its colourful, art-rich interior.

The Walk » From the basilica, it's an easy stroll up Via della Minerva to Piazza della Rotonda.

Pantheon

A remarkable 2000-year-old temple, now church, the **Pantheon** (www.pantheon roma.com; Piazza della Rotonda; ⊘8.30am-7.30pm Mon-Sat, 9am-6pm Sun) is the best preserved of Rome's ancient monuments. Built by Hadrian over Marcus Agrippa's earlier 27 BC temple, it has stood since around AD 125. t's an exhilarating

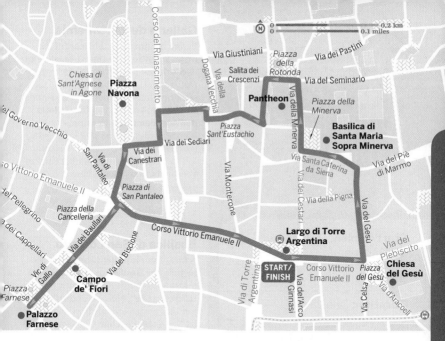

experience to pass through its vast bronze doors and gaze up at the largest unreinforced concrete dome ever built.

The Walk » Follow the signs to Piazza Navona, stopping en route for a quick coffee at **Caffè Sant'Eustachio** (Piazza Sant'Eustachio 82; ⏰8.30am-1am Sun-Thu, to 1.30am Fri, to 2am Sat).

Piazza Navona

With its ornate fountains, baroque *palazzi* (mansions) and colourful cast of street artists, hawkers and tourists, **Piazza Navona** is central Rome's elegant showpiece square. Its grand centrepiece is Bernini's **Fontana dei Quattro Fiumi**, an ornate, showy fountain featuring personifications of the rivers Nile, Ganges, Danube and Plate.

The Walk » Exit the piazza to the south, cross Corso Vittorio Emanuele II and continue up Via dei Baullari.

Campo de' Fiori

Noisy, colourful **Campo de' Fiori** is a major focus of Roman life: by day it hosts one of Rome's best-known markets, while at night it morphs into a raucous open-air pub. Amidst the chaos look out for a sinister statue of a hooded monk. This is the heretic philosopher Giordano Bruno who was burned at the stake here in 1600.

The Walk » Head up to Piazza Farnese, a matter of metres away.

Palazzo Farnese

The formidable **Palazzo Farnese** (www.inventerrome.com; Piazza Farnese; €9; ⏰guided tours 3pm, 4pm & 5pm Mon, Wed & Fri) is one of Rome's finest Renaissance buildings. Now home to the French Embassy, it can only be visited on a guided tour (for which you need to pre-book; see the website for details), but it's worth it to marvel at a series of frescoes by Annibale Carracci that are said by some to rival Michelangelo's in the Sistine Chapel.

The Walk » To get back to Largo di Torre Argentina, double back to Corso Vittorio Emanuele II and head right.

STRETCH YOUR LEGS
FLORENCE

Start/Finish: Galleria dell'Accademia

Distance: 2.5km

Duration: One day

To get the best out of Florence (Firenze), park your car at Piazza della Libertà, and head into the city's historic centre on foot. This tour provides a great introduction to the city, passing through its headlining piazzas, basilicas and galleries.

Take this walk on Trips

Galleria dell'Accademia

Before heading into the heart of the historic centre, take time to salute Florence's fabled poster boy. Michelangelo's *David* (1504), arguably the most famous sculpture in the Western world, stands in all his naked glory in the **Galleria dell'Accademia** (www.firenzemusei.it; Via Ricasoli 60; adult/reduced €8/4, incl temporary exhibition €12.50/6.25; ☺8.15am-6.50pm Tue-Sun). He originally guarded Palazzo Vecchio but was moved here in 1873.

The Walk › From the gallery, head south along Via Ricasoli, past the Carabé gelateria, down to Via de' Pucci. Turn right, skirting past Palazzo Pucci, as you continue on to Piazza San Lorenzo.

Basilica di San Lorenzo

A fine example of Renaissance architecture, the **Basilica di San Lorenzo** (Piazza San Lorenzo; €5, incl Biblioteca Medicea Laurenziana €7.50; ☺10am-5.30pm Mon-Sat, plus 1.30-5pm Sun winter) is best known for its **Sagrestia Vecchia** (Old Sacristy). Around the corner, at the rear of the basilica, the **Museo delle Cappelle Medicee** (Medici Chapels; www.firenzemusei. it; Piazza Madonna degli Aldobrandini 6; adult/ reduced €6/3; ☺8.15am-1.50pm, closed 2nd & 4th Sun & 1st, 3rd & 5th Mon of month) has some exquisite Michelangelo sculptures.

The Walk › From Piazza Madonna degli Aldobrandini, head down Via de' Conti and its continuation Via F Zanetti to Via de' Cerretani. Hang a left and soon you'll see Piazza del Duomo ahead.

Duomo

Florence's 14th-century **Duomo** (www. operaduomo.firenze.it; Piazza del Duomo; ☺10am-5pm Mon-Wed & Fri, to 4pm Thu, to 4.45pm Sat, 1.30-4.45pm Sun) is the city's most iconic landmark with its pink, white and green marble facade and red-tiled **dome** (adult/reduced incl cupola, baptistry, campanile, crypt & museum €15/3; ☺8.30am-7pm Mon-Fri, to 5.40pm Sat). Nearby, you can climb the **campanile** (☺8.30am-7.30pm) and admire the bas-reliefs on the 11th-century **Battistero** (Baptistry; ☺11.15am-7pm Mon-Sat, 8.30am-2pm Sun & 1st Sat of month).

The Walk » It's a straightforward 400m or so down Via dei Calzaiuoli to Piazza della Signoria.

Piazza della Signoria

This lovely cafe-lined piazza is overlooked by the **Torre d'Arnolfo**, the high point of **Palazzo Vecchio** (www.musefirenze .it; museum adult/reduced €10/8, tower €10/8, museum & tower €14/12, guided tour €4; ⊗ museum 9am-11pm Fri-Wed, to 2pm Thu, tower 9am-9pm Fri-Wed, to 2pm Thu, shorter hours winter), Florence's medieval City Hall. It still houses the mayor's office but you can visit its lavish apartments.

The Walk » To get to the Galleria degli Uffizi takes a matter of seconds, although we can't vouch for how long it'll take to get inside. The gallery is just off the piazza's southeastern corner, in a grey porticoed *palazzo* (mansion).

Galleria degli Uffizi

The **Uffizi** (www.uffizi.beniculturali.it; Piazzale degli Uffizi 6; adult/reduced €8/4, incl temporary exhibition €12.50/6.25; ⊗8.15am-6.50pm Tue-Sun) boasts one of Italy's greatest art collections, bequeathed to Florence in 1743 by the Medici family on condition that it never leave the city. The highlight is the stash of Renaissance art, including Botticelli's *La nascita di Venere* (Birth of Venus), Leonardo da Vinci's *Annunciazione* (Annunciation) and Michelangelo's *Tondo doni* (Holy Family).

The Walk » Pick up Via Lambertesca, over the way from the gallery entrance, and follow it to Via Por Santa Maria. Go left and it's a short hop to the river.

Ponte Vecchio

Florence's celebrated bridge has twinkled with the wares of jewellers since the 16th century when Ferdinando I de' Medici ordered them to replace the the town butchers, who were wont to toss malodorous unwanted leftovers into the river. The bridge as it stands was built in 1345 and was the only one in Florence saved from destruction by the retreating Germans in 1944."

The Walk » To get back to the Galleria dell'Accademia, pick up bus C1 from Lungarno Generale Diaz and head up to Piazza San Marco.

Southern Italy

NATURE ITSELF SEEMS A LITTLE WILDER IN SOUTHERN ITALY, where a single landscape can encompass smoking volcanoes, fertile green valleys, steep sea cliffs and cobalt seas. Italy's greatest hits may lie further to the north, but the south may actually tug harder at the heartstrings, with its friendly and voluble people, piquant culinary traditions, wild backcountry and splendorous, palm-fanned cities.

With the exception of Naples' notorious traffic, this is also perfect driving country. Naples, Vesuvius and the Amalfi Coast are Grand Tour musts. But lesser-known routes reward for their pure surprise factor, from Cilento's pristine coast to the ski slopes of Sicily's Madonie Mountains.

Amalfi Coast The village of Amalfi
LEOKS/SHUTTERSTOCK ©

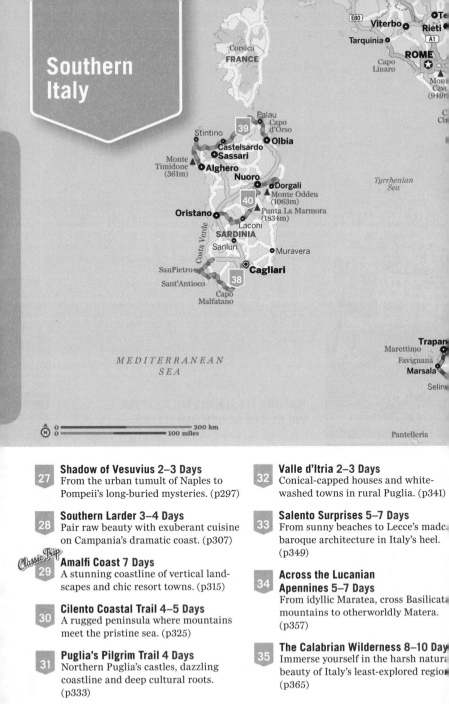

Southern Italy

 DON'T MISS

Vietri sul Mare

Bring back a piece of the Amalfi Coast from this seaside centre, renowned for its bright-hued ceramics, on Trip 29

Capo Palinuro

Hike this rocky promontory for gorgeous views of the Cilento coast, followed by a snorkel in its cobalt waters, on Trip 30

Matera

Visit Matera, where ancient cave dwellings have been transformed into cool wine bars and boutique sleeps, on Trip 34

Noto

Stroll one of Italy's most beautiful town centres, admiring golden baroque buildings in the southern Sicilian sun on Trips 36 37

Isola della Maddalena

Crystalline waters lap onto weird, wind-whipped rock formations on this small Sardinian island, one of the stars of Trip 39

Shadow of Vesuvius

27

Beginning in the tumult that is Naples, this trip winds around the Bay of Naples to the ruins of Herculaneum and Pompeii and on to seaside Sorrento – even daring the slopes of Vesuvius itself.

TRIP HIGHLIGHTS

0 km

Naples
Incomparable city of bombastic baroque and electrifying street life

1 START

27 km

Mt Vesuvius
The crater offers views into the lofty menace

5

10 km

3

Herculaneum
Superbly preserved ruins, from ancient advertisements to skeleton remains of the terror-struck

Oplontis

8

60 km

Pompeii
These celebrated ruins still conjure visions of Vesuvius

Castellammare di Stabia

Sorrento
FINISH

2–3 DAYS
90KM / 56 MILES

GREAT FOR...

BEST TIME TO GO
Spring and autumn for best weather; ˙ December for stunning Christmas displays.

ESSENTIAL PHOTO
Capture Vesuvius' brooding majesty from Naples' waterfront.

BEST FOR HISTORY

Relive history amid Herculaneum's ruins.

27 Shadow of Vesuvius

This trip begins in Naples (Napoli), a city that rumbles with contradictions – grimy streets hit palm-fringed boulevards; crumbling facades mask golden baroque ballrooms. Rounding the Bay of Naples and the dense urban sprawl, you quickly reach some of the world's most spectacular Roman ruins including Pompeii and Herculaneum, as well as lesser-known jewels, from ancient villas to Portici's royal getaway. Above it all looms Vesuvius' dark beauty.

TRIP HIGHLIGHT

❶ Naples

Italy's most misunderstood city is also one of its finest – an exhilarating mess of bombastic baroque churches, bellowing baristas and electrifying street life. Contradiction is the catchphrase here. It's a place where anarchy, pollution and crime sidle up to lavish palaces, mighty museums and aristocratic tailors.

The Unesco-listed *centro storico* (historic

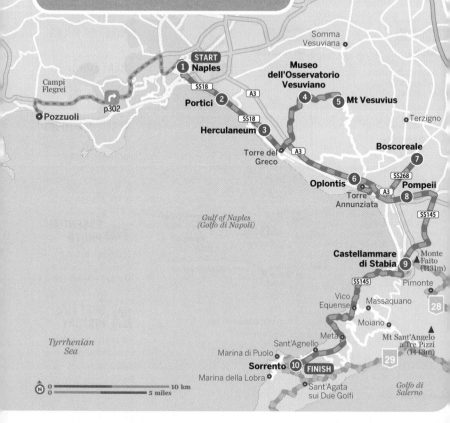

centre) is an intoxicating warren of streets packed with ancient churches, citrus-filled cloisters and first-rate pizzerias. It's here, under the washing lines, that you'll find classic Neapolitan street life – overloaded Vespas hurtling through cobbled alleyways and clued-up *casalinghe* (housewives) bullying market vendors. Move towards the sea and the cityscape opens up. Imperious palaces flank show-off squares where Gucci-clad shoppers strut their stuff, then lunch in chandeliered cafes. This is Royal Naples, the Naples of the Bourbons that so impressed the 18th-century grand tourists.

To buff up for Pompeii and Herculaneum, head

LINK YOUR TRIP

28 **Southern Larder** From Sorrento, you can embark on this culinary adventure along the Amalfi Coast and the Golfo di Salerno, where mozzarella rules the roost.

29 **Amalfi Coast** Sorrento kicks off this week-long adventure of hairpin turns and vertical landscapes amid the world's most glamorous stretch of coastline.

to the **Museo Archeologico Nazionale** (☏081 442 21 49; http://cir.campania.beniculturali.it/museo archeologiconazionale; Piazza Museo Nazionale 19; adult/reduced €8/4; ☺9am-7.30pm Wed-Mon; Ⓜ Museo, Piazza Cavour). With one of the world's finest collections of Graeco-Roman artefacts, it stars a series of stunning sculptures, mosaics from Pompeii, and a room full of ancient erotica.

✗ 🛏 p47, p305

The Drive ❯❯ A straight 8km drive along the SS18 provides an easy journey from central Naples straight to the Palazzo Reale di Portici – if the other drivers behave, of course.

- - - - - - - - - -

❷ Portici

The town of Portici lies at the foot of Mt Vesuvius and had to be rebuilt in the wake of its ruin by the 1631 eruption. Charles III of Spain, king of Naples and Sicily, erected a stately royal palace here between 1738 and 1748. Known as the **Reggia di Portici** (☏081 253 20 16; www.centro musa.it; Via Università 100; museum & botanic garden €7; ☺ Herculanense Museum 9am-6.30pm; Botanic Garden 9am-1hr before sunset), the palace today houses a couple of worthwhile museums, most notably the **Herculanense Museum** with artefacts from Pompeii and Herculaneum. Outside,

the exquisite **botanic gardens** are operated by the University of Naples Federico II.

The Drive ❯❯ The entrance to the ruins of Herculaneum lie just down the street, a couple of kilometres down the SS18.

- - - - - - - - - -

❸ Herculaneum

Superbly conserved, the ruins of ancient **Herculaneum** (☏081 857 53 47; www.pompeiisites.org; Corso Resina 187, Ercolano; adult/reduced €11/5.50, incl Pompeii €22/12; ☺8.30am-7.30pm summer, to 5pm winter; 🚉 Circumvesuviana to Ercolano-Scavi) are smaller, less daunting and easier to navigate than Pompeii. They also include some of the area's richest archaeological finds, from ancient advertisements and mosaics to carbonised furniture and skeletons of people who died cowering in terror.

Destroyed by an earthquake in AD 63, Herculaneum was completely submerged by the AD 79 eruption of Mt Vesuvius. However, because it was much closer to the volcano than Pompeii, it drowned in a sea of mud, essentially fossilising the town and ensuring that even delicate items were discovered remarkably well preserved.

Look out for the **Casa d'Argo** (Argus House) a well-preserved example of a Roman noble family's house, complete

Mt Vesuvius View over the Bay of Naples to the volcano

DETOUR: CAMPI FLEGREI

Start: ❶ Naples (p298)

Stretching west of Posillipo Hill to the Tyrrhenian Sea, the oft-overlooked Campi Flegrei (Phlegrean Fields) counterbalances its ugly urban sprawl with steamy active craters, lush volcanic hillsides and priceless ancient ruins. While its Greek settlements are Italy's oldest, its Monte Nuovo is Europe's youngest mountain. It's not every week that a mountain just appears on the scene. At 8pm on 29 September 1538, a crack appeared in the earth near the ancient Roman settlement of Tripergole, spewing out a violent concoction of pumice, fire and smoke over six days. By the end of the week, Pozzuoli had a new 134m-tall neighbour.

Today, Europe's newest mountain is a lush and peaceful nature reserve. Before exploring the Campi Flegrei, stop at the helpful **tourist office** (☏081 526 14 81; www.infocampiflegrei.it; Largo Matteotti 1a; ⏰9am-3pm Mon-Fri; Ⓜ Pozzuoli, Ⓡ Cumana to Pozzuoli) in Pozzuoli to get local information and purchase a €4 cumulative ticket to four of the area's key sites: the **Anfiteatro Flavio**, the **Parco Archeologico di Cuma**, the **Terme di Baia**, and the **Castello Aragonese di Baia**.

with porticoed garden and *triclinium* (dining area). **Casa dei Cervi** (House of the Stags; closed at time of writing) is an imposing example of a Roman nobleman's villa, with two storeys ranged around a central courtyard and animated with murals and still-life paintings. And don't miss the 1st-century-AD **Terme Suburbane** (Suburban Baths; closed at time of writing), with deep pools, stucco friezes and bas-reliefs looking down upon marble seats and floors.

✖ p305

The Drive ⟫ The museum is only 10km from Herculaneum. Keep heading down the SS18 until you reach the centre of Torre del Greco, where you will turn left on Via Vittorio Veneto, which will quickly turn into Via Guglielmo Marconi. Follow the signs as you wind your way up the lower elevations of Mt Vesuvius, and the Bay of Naples comes into view.

- - - - - - - - - - - -

❹ Museo dell'Osservatorio Vesuviano

Halfway up Mt Vesuvius, this **museum** (Museum of the Vesuvian Observatory; ☏081 610 85 60; www.ov.ingv. it; Via dell'Osservatorio; ⏰by reservation 9.30am-4pm Mon-Sat, from 10am Sun) contains an interesting array of artefacts telling the history of 2000 years of Vesuvius-watching. Founded in 1841 to monitor Vesuvius' moods, it is the oldest volcanic observatory in the world. To this day, scientists are still constantly monitoring the active volcanoes at Vesuvius, Campi Flegrei and Ischia.

The Drive ⟫ It's many more hairpin turns as you make your way along the same road almost to Vesuvius' crater, about 7km away. Views across the Bay of Naples and Campania are magnificent.

- - - - - - - - - - - -

TRIP HIGHLIGHT

❺ Mt Vesuvius

Since exploding into history in AD 79, **Mt Vesuvius** (adult/reduced €10/8; ⏰9am-6pm Jul & Aug, to 5pm Apr-Jun & Sep, to 4pm Mar & Oct, to 3pm Nov-Feb, ticket office closes 1hr before crater) has blown its top more than 30 times. The most devastating of these was in 1631, and the most recent was in 1944. It is the only volcano on the European mainland to have erupted within the last hundred years. What redeems this lofty menace is the spectacular view from its **crater** – a breathtaking panorama that takes in Naples, its world-famous bay, and part of the Apennine mountains.

The end of the road is the summit car park and the ticket office. From here, a relatively easy 860m path leads up to the summit (allow 25 minutes), best tackled in sneakers and with a jacket in tow (it can be chilly up top, even in summer). Note that when the weather is bad the summit path is shut.

The Drive » The first part of this 21km stretch heads back down Vesuvius the same way you came up. Head all the way down to the A3 highway, turn left onto it and head southeast. The villas of Oplontis are just off the Torre Annunziata exit.

➏ Oplontis

Buried beneath the unappealing streets of modern-day Torre Annunziata, **Oplontis** (☎081 857 53 47; www.pompeiisites. org; Via dei Sepolcri, Torre Annunziata; adult/reduced incl Boscoreale & Stabiae €5.50/2.75, incl Pompeii & Herculaneum €22/12; ☺8.30am-7.30pm Apr-Oct, to 5pm Nov-Mar; ℞Circumvesuviana to Torre Annunziata) was once a seafront suburb under the administrative control of Pompeii. First discovered in the 18th century, only two of its houses have been unearthed, and only one, **Villa Poppaea**, is open to the public. This villa is a magnificent example of an *otium* villa (a residential building used for rest and recreation), and may once have belonged

to Emperor Nero's second wife.

The Drive » This brief 5km jaunt has you once again heading south on the SS18 to SS268 (Via Settetermini), which leads through scruffy Neapolitan suburbs to Boscoreale.

➐ Boscoreale

Some 3km north of Pompeii, the archaeological site of **Boscoreale** (☎081 857 53 47; www.pompei isites.org; Via Settetermini, Boscoreale; adult/reduced incl Oplontis & Stabiae €5.50/2.75, incl Pompeii & Herculaneum €22/12; ☺8.30am-7.30pm Apr-Oct, to 5pm Nov-Mar; ℞Circumvesuviana to Pompeii-Scavi-Villa dei Misteri) consists of a rustic country villa dating back to the 1st century BC, and a fascinating antiquarium showcasing artefacts from Pompeii, Herculaneum and the surrounding region. Note that the villa was closed to visits at the time of writing but the antiquarium was open to visitors.

The Drive » Head straight back down the SS268 for about 4km all the way back to the SS18, which will take you through about 2km of scruffy suburbs

right up next to the ruins of Pompeii.

➑ Pompeii

Nothing piques human curiosity like a mass catastrophe, and few beat the ruins of **Pompeii** (☎081 857 53 47; www. pompeiisites.org; entrances at Porta Marina, Piazza Esedra & Piazza Anfiteatro; adult/reduced €13/7.50, incl Herculaneum €22/12; ☺9am-7.30pm summer, to 5pm winter), a stark reminder of Vesuvius' malign forces.

Of Pompeii's original 66 hectares, 44 have now been excavated. However, expect a noticeable lack of clear signage, areas cordoned off for no apparent reason, and the odd stray dog. Audio-guides (€6.50) are a sensible investment, and a detailed guidebook will help – try *Pompeii* published by Electa Napoli. To do justice to the site, allow at least three hours.

Highlights include the site's main entrance at **Porta Marina**, the most impressive of the seven gates that punctuated the

PASS TO THE PAST

You can visit all five key sites around Pompeii, including the ruins of Pompeii and Herculaneum as well as Boscoreale, Oplontis and Stabiae, with a single pass that costs adult/reduced €22/12 and is valid for three days. It is available at the ticket offices of all five sites.

VESUVIAN WINES

Vesuvian wine has been relished since ancient times. The rare combination of rich volcanic soil and a favourable microclimate created by its slopes make the territory one of Italy's most interesting viticultural areas. Lacryma Christi (literally 'tears of Christ') is the name of perhaps the most celebrated wine produced on the slopes of Mt Vesuvius.

Further afield, other top regional wines include Taurasi, Fiano di Avellino, Aglianico del Taburno, and Greco del Tufo.

ancient town walls, and the 1st-century BC **Terme Suburbane**, famous for its risqué frescoes. Ancient Pompeii's main piazza was the **foro**, now a grassy rectangle flanked by limestone columns. To the northeast of the foro, the **Lupanare** (brothel) boasts a series of raunchy frescoes which originally served as a menu for clients. In the far east of the site, the **Anfiteatro** is the oldest known Roman amphitheatre in existence. Over on the opposite side of town, the **Villa dei Misteri**, one of the site's most complete structures, contains the remarkable fresco *Dionysiac Frieze*. One of the world's largest ancient paintings, it depicts the initiation of a bride-to-be into the cult of Dionysus, the Greek god of wine.

✗ p305

The Drive » The 9km trip from Pompeii begins heading south along the SS145 (Corso Italia). It will take you through a mixture of suburbs and small farms. Ahead, you will see the mountains of the Amalfi Coast rear up. The ancient villas of Stabiae are just east of Corso Italia, off Via Giuseppe Cosenza.

⑨ Castellammare di Stabia

South of Oplontis in modern-day Castellammare di Stabia, **Stabiae** (☏081 857 53 47; www.pompeii sites.org; Via Passeggiata Archeologica, Castellammare di Stabia; ⊗8.30am-7.30pm Apr-Oct, to 5pm Nov-Mar; 🚆Circumvesuviana to Via Nocera) was once a popular resort for wealthy Romans. It stood on the slopes of the Varano hill overlooking the entire Bay of Naples, and according to ancient historian Pliny it was lined for miles

with extravagant villas. You can visit two villas: the 1st-century-BC Villa Arianna and the larger Villa San Marco, said to measure more than 11,000 sq metres.

The Drive » This stretch is a bit longer, at 21km, than the last few. Head back to the SS145, which will soon head over to the coast. Enjoy beautiful views over the Bay of Naples as you wind your way past Vico Equense, Meta and Piano di Sorrento to Sorrento.

⑩ Sorrento

For an unabashed tourist town, Sorrento still manages to preserve the feeling of a civilised coastal retreat. Even the souvenirs are a cut above the norm, with plenty of fine old shops selling ceramics, lacework and marquetry items. It is also the spiritual home of *limoncello,* a delicious lemon liqueur traditionally made from the zest of Femminello St Teresa lemons, also known as Sorrento lemons. Its tart sweetness makes the perfect nightcap, as well as a brilliant flavouring for both sweet and savoury dishes.

✗ 🛏 p305, p313, p323

Eating & Sleeping

Naples ❶ see also p47

✖ Pizzeria Gino Sorbillo   Pizza €

(☎081 44 66 43; www.sorbillo.it; Via dei Tribunali 32; pizzas from €3.30; ☻noon-3.30pm & 7pm-1am Mon-Sat; Ⓜ Dante) Day in, day out, this cult-status pizzeria is besieged by hungry hordes. While debate may rage over whether Gino Sorbillo's pizzas are the best in town there's no doubt that they will have you licking fingertips. Head in super early or queue.

✖ Ristorantino dell'Avvocato   Neapolitan €€

(☎081 032 00 47; www.ilristorantinodellavvocato. it; Via Santa Lucia 115-117; meals €40; ☻noon-3pm & 7-11pm Tue-Sat, noon-3pm Mon & Sun; ☎; ☒128 to Via Santa Lucia) This elegant yet welcoming restaurant has quickly won the respect of Neapolitan gastronomes. Chef Raffaele Cardillo's passion for Campania's culinary heritage merges with a knack for subtle, refreshing twists – think gnocchi with fresh mussels, clams, crumbed pistachio, lemon, ginger and garlic.

🛏 Hotel Piazza Bellini   Boutique Hotel €€

(☎081 45 17 32; www.hotelpiazzabellini.com; Via Santa Maria di Costantinopoli 101; d €58-148; ✳ @ ☎; Ⓜ Dante) Only steps from buzzing Piazza Bellini, this contemporary hotel occupies a 16th-century *palazzo*, its mint white spaces spiked with original majolica tiles and the work of emerging artists. Rooms offer pared-back cool, with designer fittings; rooms on the 5th and 6th floors have panoramic terraces.

🛏 Hotel San Francesco al Monte   Hotel €€

(☎081 423 91 11; www.sanfrancescoalmonte. it; Corso Vittorio Emanuele I 328; d €117-189; Ⓟ ✳ @ ☎ ☒; ☒Centrale to Corso Vittorio Emanuele I) Occupying a 16th-century monastery, this hotel is magnificent. The monks' cells have become classically elegant rooms, the ancient cloisters house an open-air bar, and the barrel-vaulted corridors are lined with contemporary art. Capping it all is a lofty outdoor swimming pool with views of Capri and Vesuvius.

Herculaneum ❸

✖ Viva Lo Re   Modern Italian €€

(☎081 739 02 07; www.vivalore.it; Corso Resina 261, Ercolano; meals €35; ☻noon-4pm & 7-11pm Tue-Sat, noon-4pm Sun) Located 500m southeast of the ruins of Herculaneum Viva Lo Re is a stylish, inviting *osteria*, where vintage prints and bookshelves meet a superb wine list, gracious staff and gorgeous regional cooking.

Pompeii ❽

✖ Melius   Neapolitan €

(☎081 850 25 98; Via Lepanto 156-160, Pompeii; meals €20; ☻9am-8pm Mon, to 10.30pm Tue-Sat, to 3pm Sun; ☒FS to Pompei, Circumvesuviana to Pompei-Scavi-Villa dei Misteri) Stop by this luscious gourmet deli to revel in the taste of Campania. There's a small in-house restaurant to try local delicacies such as fresh *mozzarella di bufala* (buffalo mozzarella), Graniano pasta, smoked Cilento salamis, and anchovies from Cetara, or you can take away.

✖ President   Campanian €€

(☎081 850 72 45; www.ristorantepresident.it; Piazza Schettini 12; meals from €40; ☻noon-4pm & 7pm-midnight, closed Mon Oct-Apr; ☒FS to Pompei, Circumvesuviana to Pompei Scavi-Villa dei Misteri) With its chandeliers and gracious service, the Michelin-starred President feels like a private dining room in an Audrey Hepburn film. At the helm is charming owner-chef Paolo Gramaglia, whose passion for local produce, history and culinary creativity translates into bread made to ancient Roman recipes and deconstructed *pastiera* (sweet Neapolitan tart).

Sorrento ❿ see also p313 and p323

🛏 Casa Astarita   B&B €

(☎081 877 49 06; www.casastarita.com; Corso Italia 67; d €70-130, tr €95-150; ✳ ☎) Housed in a 16th-century *palazzo* on Sorrento's main strip, this charming B&B has a colourful, eclectic look with original vaulted ceilings, brightly painted doors and majolica-tiled floors. Its six simple but well-equipped rooms surround a central parlour, where breakfast is served on a large rustic table.

Southern Larder

28

From the Amalfi Coast to Paestum, this trip packs in both jaw-dropping natural beauty and mouth-watering cuisine built on fresh fish, sun-kissed veggies and the world's finest mozzarella.

TRIP HIGHLIGHTS

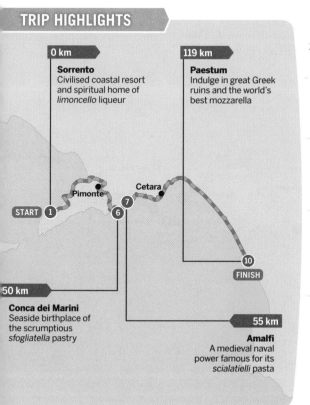

0 km

Sorrento
Civilised coastal resort and spiritual home of *limoncello* liqueur

119 km

Paestum
Indulge in great Greek ruins and the world's best mozzarella

Pimonte

Cetara

START 1

6 **7**

10

FINISH

50 km

Conca dei Marini
Seaside birthplace of the scrumptious *sfogliatella* pastry

55 km

Amalfi
A medieval naval power famous for its *scialatielli* pasta

3–4 DAYS
119KM / 74 MILES

GREAT FOR…

BEST TIME TO GO

Spring for sunny, clear weather; early autumn for abundant produce.

ESSENTIAL PHOTO

Capture the terraced cliffs of Agerola at sunset.

BEST FOR FOODIES

Going to mozzarella's source in Paestum.

alfi Coast A serving of *spaghetti ai frutti di mare* (spaghetti with seafood)

28

Southern Larder

Besides the natural beauty of the Amalfi Coast and Gulf of Sorrento, this trip is a gourmand's dream. Foodies flock here for local specialities such as *limoncello* (lemon liqueur), ricotta-stuffed *sfogliatella* pastries, and a wildly creamy concoction made from water-buffalo milk that gives the word 'mozzarella' a whole new meaning. Burn off the extra calories hiking the Amalfi's jaw-dropping coastal trails or clambering over Paestum's Greek ruins.

TRIP HIGHLIGHT

1 Sorrento

Most people come to seaside Sorrento as a pleasant stopover between Capri, Naples and the Amalfi Coast. It boasts dramatic views of the Bay of Naples and a festive holiday feel. However, foodies converge here for a very specific treat: *limoncello*, a simple lemon liqueur made from the zest of lemons (preferably the local Femminello St Teresa lemons), plus sugar and grain alcohol. It is

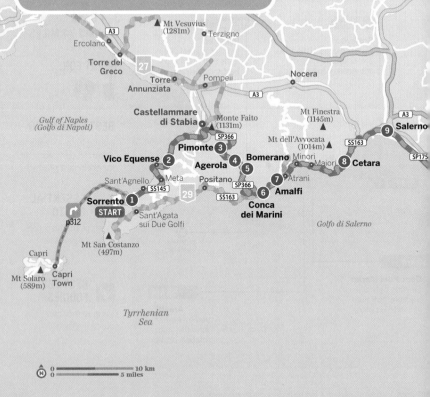

traditionally served after dinner in chilled ceramic cups, and its combination of sweetness and biting tartness make the perfect end to a meal.

✗ 🛏 p305, p313, p323

The Drive ›› Head north on the SS145, including a beautiful stretch along the Bay of Naples, for 12km to Vico Equense.

❷ Vico Equense

Known to the Romans as Aequa, Vico Equense is a small clifftop town east of Sorrento. Largely bypassed by international tourists, it's a laid-back, authentic place worth a quick stopover, if only to experience some of the famous pizza served by the metre at the justly celebrated **Ristorante & Pizzeria da Gigino** (📞081 879 83 09; www.pizzametro. it; Via Nicotera 15; pizza per metre from €30, meals €15-20; 🕐 noon-1.30am). This is no tourist trap but a beloved local institution due to its fresh ingredients and fluffy dough.

The Drive ›› From Vico Equense to Pimonte is 18km. You'll again hug the beautiful Bay of Naples for a while, reaching the turn-off for the SP ex SS366 in Castellammare di Stabia. From here, head inland and uphill as you wind your way to Pimonte.

❸ Pimonte

Tucked into the mountains in the easternmost end of the Amalfi peninsula, this small rural town is a far cry from the high-rolling coast, with tractors trundling through the narrow streets. Make a point of stopping at Piazza Roma for the delicious almond-based speciality *torta palummo* at the **Bar Pasticceria Palummo**. Expect curious stares; tourists are a rarity here.

The Drive ›› The 8km drive from Pimonte to Agerola takes you along a winding road through forested countryside along the SP ex SS366.

❹ Agerola

Agerola is located amid a wide green valley approximately 600m above sea level. It is surrounded by forests and offers amazing views of the nearby mountains and Mediterranean Sea. Be sure to make a stop here for the legendary *fior di latte* (cow's-milk mozzarella) and *cacio-cavallo* (gourd-shaped traditional curd cheese) produced on the fertile slopes around town.

Acerno

Montecorvino

Eboli

Battipaglia

SP175

Paestum ❿
FINISH

Capaccio Scalo

Parco Nazionale del Cilento e Vallo di Diano

LINK YOUR TRIP

27 **Shadow of Vesuvius**

From Sorrento, strike northeast around the Bay of Naples to conquer Naples (Napoli), wander the ruins of Pompeii and Herculaneum, and brave the slopes of Vesuvius.

29 **Amalfi Coast**

Sorrento kicks off this week-long adventure of hairpin turns and vertical landscapes amid the world's most glamorous stretch of coastline.

The Drive ≫ From Agerola to Bomerano, hop back on the SP ex SS366 for a quick 3km jaunt to Bomerano, enjoying a forest of beech trees and a backdrop of mountains thickly quilted with pines. You are now in the depths of the verdant Parco Regionale dei Monti Lattari.

---

⑤ Bomerano

Just a stone's throw from Agerola, you can easily follow your nose to tiny Bomerano for delicious buffalo-milk yoghurt, an ultra-rich, mildly tangy and creamy treat. While in town, you can also feast your eyes on the ornate ceiling frieze in the 16th-century **Chiesa San Matteo Apostolo**.

The Drive ≫ From Bomerano to Conca Dei Marini, continue on the same road, SP ex SS366, for 9km as it winds dramatically down to the sea, with strategically placed lookouts along the way. From the SP ex SS366, you will do more switchbacking down to the town of Conca dei Marini itself.

TRIP HIGHLIGHT

⑥ Conca dei Marini

This charmingly picturesque fishing village has been beloved by everyone from Princess Margaret to Gianni Agnelli, Jacqueline Onassis and Carlo Ponti. Work up an appetite with an excursion to the **Grotta dello Smeraldo** (€5; ⊙9.30am-4pm), a seaside cavern where the waters glow an eerie emerald green. Then head back to the town for a *sfogliatella,* a scrumptious shell-shaped, ricotta-stuffed pastry that was probably invented here in the 18th century in the monastery of Santa Rosa. The local pastry is even honoured with its own holiday: the first Sunday in August.

The Drive ≫ Head northeast on the SS163 to the town of Amalfi.

TRIP HIGHLIGHT

⑦ Amalfi

A picturesque ensemble of whitewashed buildings and narrow alleyways set around a sun-kissed central piazza, Amalfi is the main centre on the Amalfi Coast. To glean a sense of its medieval history, be sure to explore the hidden lanes that run parallel to the main street, with their steep stairways, covered porticos and historic shrine niches. And of course, gourmets shouldn't miss *scialatielli*. A fresh pasta resembling short, slightly widened strips of tagliatelle, it is a local speciality, most commonly accompanied by zucchini and mussels or clams, or a simple sauce of fresh cherry tomatoes and garlic.

✕ ⌖ p313, p323

The Drive ≫ It's about 15km on the SS163 from Amalfi to Cetara. Silver birches and buildings draped in bougainvillea add to the beauty of the drive.

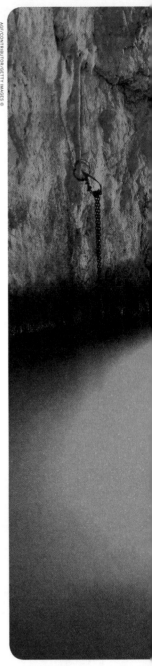

Conca dei Marini Grotta dello Smeraldo

DETOUR: CAPRI

Start: ❶ Sorrento (p308)

A mass of limestone rock that rises sheer through impossibly blue water, Capri (ca-pri) is the perfect microcosm of Mediterranean appeal – a smooth cocktail of chichi piazzas and cool cafes, Roman ruins and rugged seascapes. Need any more reason to go?

OK, here's one more: the *torta capresa*. Back in the 1920s, when an absent-minded baker forgot to add flour to the mix of a cake order, a great dessert was born. Now a traditional Italian chocolate-and-almond or -walnut cake, it is named for the island of Capri from which it originated. The cake has a thin hard shell covering a moist interior. It is usually covered with a light dusting of fine powdered sugar, and sometimes made with a small amount of Strega or other liqueur. It's even gluten-free.

Gescab (☏ 081 807 18 12; www.gescab.it) runs up to 18 daily hydrofoils from Sorrento to Capri (€18.30, 20 minutes).

❽ Cetara

A picturesque tumble-down fishing village, Cetara is also a gastronomic highlight. Tuna and anchovies are the local specialities, especially the sauce from the latter, appearing in various guises at Al Convento (p313), a sterling seafood restaurant near the small harbour. For your money, you'll probably not eat better anywhere else on the coast; the *puttanesca con alici fresche* (pasta with fresh anchovy sauce, chilli and garlic) sings with flavour.

✕ p313

The Drive » Head northeast on SS163 for Salerno. En route, colourful wildflowers spill over white stone walls as you travel the sometimes hair-raising 11km along the coast.

❾ Salerno

Salerno may seem like a bland big city after the Amalfi Coast's glut of pretty towns, but the place has a charming, if gritty, individuality, especially around its vibrant *centro storico* (historic centre). Don't miss the **Duomo** (Piazza Alfano; ⏰ 8.30am-8pm Mon-Sat, 8.30am-1pm & 4-8pm Sun), built in the 11th century and graced by a magnificent main entrance, the 12th-century **Porta dei Leoni**. And for *torta di ricotta e pera* (ricotta-and-pear tart), Salerno is unsurpassed. This dessert is an Amalfi Coast speciality, deriving its unique tang from the local sheep's-milk ricotta.

🛏 p313

The Drive » Head south on the SP175 and hug the coast all the way. Lush palm and lemon trees and the sparkling sea are your escorts for this 38km drive to Paestum.

TRIP HIGHLIGHT

❿ Paestum

Work up an appetite amid Paestum's Unesco-listed Greek **temples** (Area Archeologica di Paestum; ☏ 0828 81 10 23; www.museopaestum.beniculturali.it; adult/reduced incl museum €7/3.50; ⏰ 8.30am-half hr before sunset), some of the best-preserved in the world. Then head to **Tenuta Vannulo** (☏ 0828 72 78 94; www.vannulo.it; Via G Galilei 101, Capaccio Scalo; 1hr group tour €4, incl lunch €20-25), a 10-minute drive from Paestum, for a superbly soft and creamy mozzarella made from the organic milk of water buffalo. Group tours are available (reservations are essential) but you can also stop just to buy the cheese. Be warned, though, it usually sells out by early afternoon.

🛏 p313

Eating & Sleeping

Sorrento ❶ see also p305 and p323

✗ Inn Bufalito   Italian €€

(☎081 365 69 75; www.innbufalito.it; Vico
Fuoro 21; meals €25-30; ☺noon-3pm & 6-11pm;
📶🚲) Owner Franco Coppola (no relation
to the movie man) exudes a real passion for
showcasing local produce – the restaurant
is a member of the Slow Food movement. A
mozzarella bar as well as a restaurant, this
effortlessly stylish place boasts a menu
including delights such as Sorrento-style
cheese fondue and buffalo-meat carpaccio.

✗ Aurora Light   Italian €

(☎081 877 26 31; www.auroralight.it; Piazza
Tasso 3-4; meals €15-25; ☺noon-midnight)
At first glance the menu here looks more
Californian than Campanian, with such
imaginative salads as spicy chickpea and
spinach, and fennel with beetroot and orange.
The enthusiastic young owner has tapped into
traditional dishes and given them an innovative
twist: white-bean soup with baby squid,
aubergine parmigiana with swordfish sauce,
stuffed-pepper roulade and so on.

Amalfi ❼ see also p323

✗ Ristorante La Caravella   Italian €€€

(☎089 87 10 29; www.ristorantelacaravella.it;
Via Matteo Camera 12; tasting menus €50-150;
☺noon-2.30pm & 7-11pm Wed-Mon; ❄)
The regional food here recently earned the
restaurant a Michelin star, with dishes that offer
nouvelle zap, like black ravioli with cuttlefish
ink, scampi and ricotta, or that are unabashedly
simple, like the catch of the day served grilled
on lemon leaves. Wine aficionados are likely
to find something to try on the seriously
impressive *carta dei vini*. Reservations are
essential.

⬛ Hotel Lidomare   Hotel €€

(☎089 87 13 32; www.lidomare.it; Largo Duchi
Piccolomini 9; s €55-65, d €103-145; ❄📶)
Family run, this old-fashioned hotel has real
character. The large rooms have an air of
gentility, with their appealingly haphazard

decor, vintage tiles and fine antiques. Some
have jacuzzi bath-tubs, others have sea
views and a balcony, some have both. Rather
unusually, breakfast is laid out on top of a grand
piano.

Cetara ❽

✗ Al Convento   Seafood, Pizza €€

(☎089 26 10 39; www.alconvento.net; Piazza
San Francesco 16; meals €30; ☺12.30-3pm &
7-11pm summer, closed Wed winter) Al Convento
enjoys an evocative setting in former church
cloisters with original, albeit faded, 17th-
century frescoes. This is an excellent spot to
tuck into some local fish specialities: you can
eat *tagliata di tonna alle erbe* (lightly grilled tuna
with herbs) as an antipasto, and the spaghetti
with anchovies and wild fennel is particularly
delicious.

Salerno ❾

⬛ Hotel Montestella   Hotel €€

(☎089 22 51 22; www.hotelmontestella.it;
Corso Vittorio Emanuele II 156; s €72-108, d
€88-122, tr €112-140; ❄@📶) Within walking
distance of just about anywhere worth going
to, the Montestella is on Salerno's main
pedestrian thoroughfare, halfway between
the *centro storico* and train station. The rooms
are spacious and comfortable while the public
spaces have a fresh, modern look. It's one of the
best midrange options in town.

Paestum ❿

⬛ Casale Giancesare   B&B €

(☎0828 72 80 61, 333 1897737; www.casale-
giancesare.it; Via Giancesare 8; s & d €65-140,
apt per week €600-1300; 🅿❄@📶🏊) A
19th-century former farmhouse, this elegantly
decorated stone-clad B&B is run by the
delightful Voza family, who will happily ply you
with their homemade wine and *limoncello*. It's
located 2.5km from the glories of Paestum and
surrounded by vineyards and olive and mulberry
trees; views are stunning, particularly from the
swimming pool.

Classic Trip

Amalfi Coast

29

Not for the fainthearted, this trip along the Amalfi Coast tests your driving skill on a 100km stretch, featuring dizzying hairpin turns and pastel-coloured towns draped over sea-cliff scenery.

TRIP HIGHLIGHTS

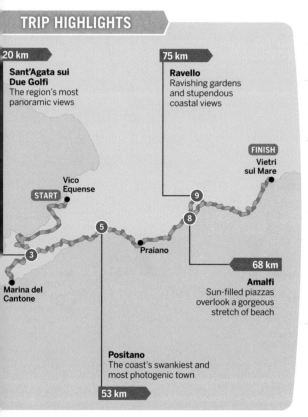

20 km

Sant'Agata sui Due Golfi
The region's most panoramic views

75 km

Ravello
Ravishing gardens and stupendous coastal views

FINISH
Vietri sul Mare

Vico Equense

START

Praiano

Marina del Cantone

68 km

Amalfi
Sun-filled piazzas overlook a gorgeous stretch of beach

Positano
The coast's swankiest and most photogenic town

53 km

7 DAYS
100KM / 62 MILES

GREAT FOR...

BEST TIME TO GO
Summer for best beach weather, but also peak crowds.

ESSENTIAL PHOTO
Positano's vertiginous stack of pastel-coloured houses cascading down to the sea.

BEST FOR OUTDOORS
Hiking Ravello and its environs.

itano Spiaggia Grande

Classic Trip

29 Amalfi Coast

The Amalfi Coast is about drama, and this trip takes you where mountains plunge seaward in a stunning vertical landscape of precipitous crags, forests and resort towns. Positano and Amalfi are fabulously picturesque and colourful, while mountain-top Ravello is a serenely tranquil place with a tangible sense of history. Cars are useful for inland exploration, as are your own two legs. Walking trails provide a wonderful escape from the coastal clamour.

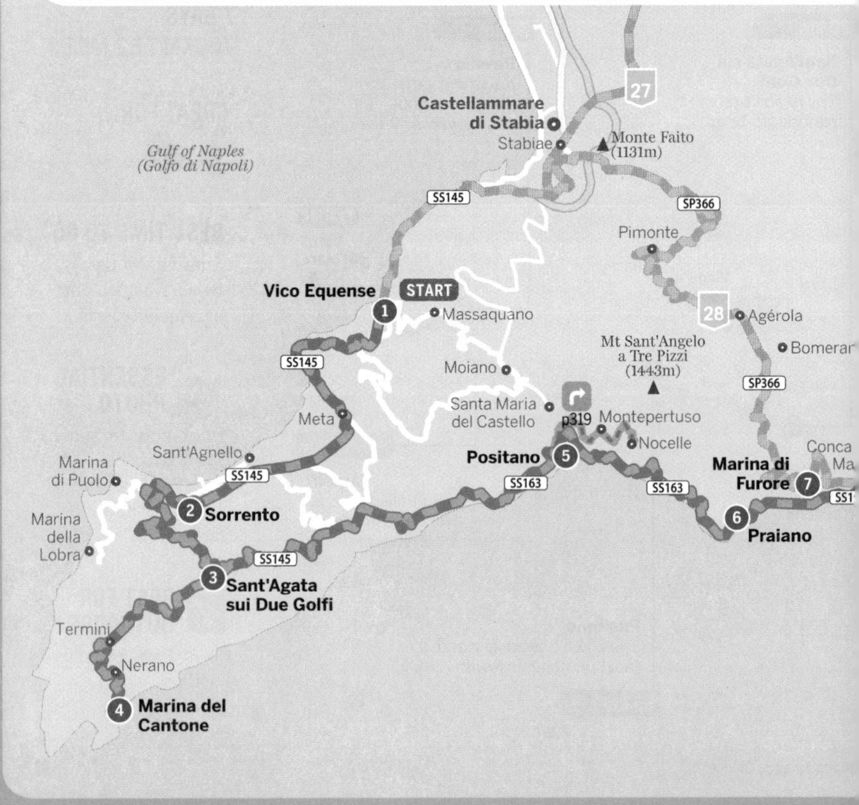

❶ Vico Equense

The Bay of Naples is justifiably famous for its pizza, which was invented here as a savoury way to highlight two local specialties: mozzarella and sun-kissed tomatoes. Besides its pretty little *centro storico* (historic centre), this little clifftop town overlooking the Bay of Naples boasts some of the region's best pizza, including a by-the-metre version at **Ristorante & Pizzeria da Gigino** (📞081 879 83 09; www.pizzametro. it; Via Nicotera 15; pizza per metre from €30, meals €15-20; ⏱noon-1.30am; 🚻).

The Drive ›› From Vico Equense to Sorrento, your main route will be the SS145 roadway for 12km. Expect to hug the sparkling coastline after Marina di Equa before venturing inland around Meta.

TRIP HIGHLIGHT

❷ Sorrento

On paper, cliff-straddling Sorrento is a place to avoid – a package-holiday centre with few sights, no beach to speak of and a glut of brassy English-style pubs. In reality, it's strangely appealing, its laid-back southern Italian charm resisting all attempts to swamp it in souvenir tat and graceless development.

According to Greek legend, it was in Sorrento's waters that the mythical sirens once lived. Sailors of antiquity were powerless to resist the beautiful song of these charming maidens-cum-monsters, who would lure them to their doom.

🍴 🛏 p305, p313, p323

The Drive ›› Take the SS145 for 8km to Sant'Agata sui Due Golfi. Sun-dappled village streets give way to forest as you head further inland.

TRIP HIGHLIGHT

❸ Sant'Agata sui Due Golfi

Perched high in the hills above Sorrento, sleepy Sant'Agata sui Due Golfi commands spectacular

LINK YOUR TRIP

27 **Shadow of Vesuvius**

Follow the curve of the Bay of Naples, from simmering Vesuvius to roiling Naples.

28 **Southern Larder**

From Sorrento to Paestum, this trip takes you to the heart of mozzarella country.

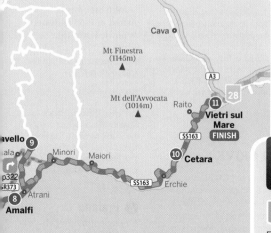

views of the Bay of Naples on one side and the Bay of Salerno on the other (hence its name, Saint Agatha on the Two Gulfs). The best viewpoint is the **Convento del Deserto** (📞081 878 01 99; Via Deserto; ⏰gardens 8am-7pm, lookout 10am-noon & 5-7pm summer, 10am-noon & 3-5pm winter), a Carmelite convent 1.5km uphill from the village centre. It's a knee-wearing hike, but make it to the top and you're rewarded with fabulous 360-degree vistas.

The Drive ›› From Sant'Agata sui Due Golfi to Marina del Cantone it's a 9km drive, the last part involving some serious hairpin turns. Don't let the gorgeous sea views distract you.

④ Marina del Cantone

From **Nerano**, where you'll park, a beautiful hiking trail leads down to the stunning Bay of Ieranto and one of the coast's top swimming spots, Marina del Cantone. This unassuming village with its small pebble beach is a lovely, tranquil place to stay as well as a popular diving destination. The village also has a reputation as a gastronomic hotspot and VIPs regularly catch a boat over from Capri to dine here.

✗ p323

The Drive ›› First, head back up that switchback to Sant'Agata sui Due Golfi. Catch the SS145 and then the SS163 as they weave their way along bluffs and cliff sides to Positano. Most of the 24km involve stunning sea views.

TRIP HIGHLIGHT

⑤ Positano

The pearl in the pack, Positano is the coast's most photogenic and expensive town. Its steeply stacked houses are a medley of peaches, pinks and terracottas, and its near-vertical streets (many of which are, in fact, staircases) are lined with voguish shop displays, elegant hotels and smart restaurants. Look closely, though, and you'll find reassuring signs of everyday reality – crumbling stucco, streaked paintwork and occasionally a faint whiff of problematic drainage.

John Steinbeck visited in 1953 and was so bowled over that he wrote of its dream-like qualities in an article for *Harper's Bazaar*.

🛏 p323

The Drive ›› From Positano to Praiano it's a quick 6km spin on the SS163, passing Il San Pietro di Positano at the halfway point, then heading southeast along the peninsula's edge.

⑥ Praiano

An ancient fishing village, a low-key summer resort and, increasingly, a popular centre for the arts, Praiano is a delight. With no centre as such, its whitewashed houses pepper the verdant ridge of Monte Sant'Angelo as it slopes towards

---

THE BLUE RIBBON DRIVE

Stretching from Vietri sul Mare to Sant'Agata sui Due Golfi near Sorrento, the SS163 nicknamed the Nastro Azzurro (Blue Ribbon) remains one of Italy's most stunning roadways. Commissioned by Bourbon king Ferdinand II and completed in 1853, it wends its way along the Amalfi Coast's entire length, snaking round impossibly tight curves, over deep ravines and through tunnels gouged out of sheer rock. It's a magnificent feat of civil engineering – although it can be challenging to drive – and in certain places it's not wide enough for two cars to pass, a fact John Steinbeck alluded to in a 1953 essay.

Capo Sottile. Exploring involves lots of steps and there are several trails that start from town, including the legendary **Sentiero degli Dei**.

For those willing to take the plunge, the **Centro Sub Costiera Amalfitana** (☎089 81 21 48; www.centrosub.it; Via Marina di Praia; dives from €80; 🚗) runs beginner to expert dives exploring the area's coral, marine life and grottoes.

The Drive ⟫ From Praiano, Marina di Furore is just 3km further on, past beautiful coves that cut into the shoreline.

⑦ Marina di Furore

A few kilometres further on, Marina di Furore sits at the bottom of what's known as the fjord of Furore, a giant cleft that cuts through the Lattari mountains. The main village, however, stands 300m above, in the upper Vallone del Furore. A one-horse place that sees few tourists, it breathes a distinctly rural air despite the presence of colourful murals and unlikely modern sculpture.

The Drive ⟫ From Marina di Furore to Amalfi, the sparkling Mediterranean Sea will be your escort as you drive westward along the SS163 coastal road for 6km. Look for Vettica Minore and Conca dei Marini along the way, along with fluffy bunches of fragrant cypress trees.

WALK OF THE GODS

Probably the best-known walk on the Amalfi Coast is the three-hour, 12km **Sentiero degli Dei**, which follows the high ridge linking Praiano to Positano. The walk commences in the heart of **Praiano**, where a thigh-challenging 1000-step start takes you up to the path itself. The route proper is not advised for vertigo sufferers: it's a spectacular, meandering trail along the top of the mountains, with caves and terraces set dramatically in the cliffs and deep valleys framed by the brilliant blue of the sea. You'll eventually emerge at Nocelle, from where a series of steps will take you through the olive groves and deposit you on the road just east of **Positano**.

TRIP HIGHLIGHT

⑧ Amalfi

It is hard to grasp that pretty little Amalfi, with its sun-filled piazzas and small beach, was once a maritime superpower with a population of more than 70,000. For one thing, it's not a big place – you can easily walk from one end to the other in about 20 minutes. For another, there are very few historical buildings of note. The explanation is chilling – most of the old city, along with its populace, simply slid into the sea during an earthquake in 1343.

One happy exception is the striking **Cattedrale di Sant'Andrea** (☎089 87 10 59; Piazza del Duomo; ⏰7.30am-7pm), parts of which date from the early

DETOUR: NOCELLE

Start: ⑤ Positano

A tiny, still relatively isolated mountain village above Positano, Nocelle (450m) commands some of the most spectacular views on the entire coast. A world apart from touristy Positano, it's a sleepy, silent place where not much ever happens, nor would its few residents ever want it to. If you want to stay, consider delightful **Villa della Quercia** (☎089 812 34 97; www.villadellaquercia.com; Via Nocelle 5; r €70-80; ⏰Apr-Oct; 🛜), a former monastery with spectacular views. Nocelle lies eight very windy kilometres northeast of Positano.

Classic Trip

WHY THIS IS A CLASSIC TRIP
DUNCAN GARWOOD, WRITER

With its plunging cliffs, shimmering azure waters and picture-book villages, Italy's most celebrated coastline lives up to expectations in spectacular style. The scenery is amazing and its vivid colours are brilliant in the sharp Mediterranean sunlight. Most attention is focussed on the seafront hotspots, but you can always escape the clamour by heading into the hills to take on some of Italy's most jaw-dropping hikes.

Top: Traditional ceramics, Vietri sul Mare
Left: Villa Rufolo, Ravello
Right: Interior of Cattedrale di Sant'Andrea, Amalfi

PATRICE HAUSER/GETTY IMAGES ©

10th century. Between 10am and 5pm entrance to the cathedral is through the adjacent **Chiostro del Paradiso** (☎089 87 13 24; Piazza del Duomo; adult/reduced €3/1; ⏲9am-6pm), a 13th-century Moorish-style cloister.

Be sure to take the short walk around the headland to neighbouring **Atrani**, a picturesque tangle of whitewashed alleys and arches centred on a lively, lived-in piazza and popular beach.

✕ ⊨ p313, p323

The Drive » Start the 7km trip to Ravello by heading along the coast to Atrani. Here turn inland and follow the SR 373 as it climbs the steep hillside in a series of second-gear hairpin turns up to Ravello.

TRIP HIGHLIGHT

❾ Ravello

Sitting high in the hills above Amalfi, refined Ravello is a polished town almost entirely dedicated to tourism. Boasting impeccable artistic credentials – Richard Wagner, DH Lawrence and Virginia Woolf all lounged here – it's known today for its ravishing gardens and stupendous views, the best in the world according to former resident Gore Vidal.

To enjoy these views, head south of Ravello's cathedral to the 14th-century tower that marks the entrance to

Villa Rufolo (☎089 85 76 21; www.villarufolo.it; Piazza Duomo; adult/reduced €5/3; ☺9am-8pm summer, to 4pm winter). Created by Scotsman Scott Neville Reid in 1853, these gardens combine celestial panoramic views, exotic colours, artistically crumbling towers and luxurious blooms.

Also worth seeking out is the wonderful **Camo** (☎089 85 74 61; Piazza Duomo 9, Ravello; ☺10am-noon & 3-5pm Mon-Sat). Squeezed between tourist-driven shops, this very special place is, on the face of it, a cameo shop. And exquisite they are too, crafted primarily out of coral and shell.

But don't stop here; ask to see the treasure trove of a museum beyond the showroom.

✗ ⌂ p323

The Drive » Head back down to the SS163 for a 19km journey that twists and turns challengingly along the coast to Cetara. Pine trees and a variety of flowering shrubs line the way.

---

⑩ Cetara

Cetara is a picturesque, tumbledown fishing village with a reputation as a gastronomic delight. Since medieval times it has been an important fishing centre, and today its deep-sea tuna fleet is considered one of the Mediterranean's most important. At night, fishermen set out in small boats armed with powerful lamps to fish for anchovies. No

surprise then that tuna and anchovies dominate local menus, especially at **Al Convento** (☎089 26 10 39; www.alconvento. net; Piazza San Francesco 16; meals €30; ☺12.30-3pm & 7-11pm summer, closed Wed winter), a sterling seafood restaurant near the small harbour.

The Drive » From Cetara to Vietri sul Mare, head northeast for 6km on the SS163 for more twisting, turning and stupendous views across the Golfo di Salerno.

---

⑪ Vietri sul Mare

Marking the end of the coastal road, Vietri sul Mare is the ceramics capital of Campania. Although production dates back to Roman times, it didn't take off as an industry until the 16th and 17th centuries. Today, ceramics shopaholics find their paradise at the **Ceramica Artistica Solimene** (☎089 21 02 43; www.ceramicasolimene. it; Via Madonna degli Angeli 7; ☺9am-8pm Mon-Fri, 9am-1.30pm & 4-8pm Sat), a vast factory outlet with an extraordinary glass and ceramic facade.

For a primer on the area's ceramics past, devotees should seek out the **Museo della Ceramica** (☎089 21 18 35; Villa Guerriglia, Via Nuova Raito; ☺9am-3pm Tue-Sat, 9.30am-1pm Sun) in the nearby village of Raito.

↱ **DETOUR: RAVELLO WALKS**

Start: ⑨ Ravello (p321)

Ravello is the starting point for numerous walks that follow ancient paths through the surrounding Lattari mountains. If you've got the legs for it, you can walk down to **Minori** via an attractive route of steps, hidden alleys and olive groves, passing the picturesque hamlet of **Torello** en route. Alternatively, you can head the other way, to Amalfi, via the ancient village of **Scala**. Once a flourishing religious centre with more than a hundred churches and the oldest settlement on the Amalfi Coast, Scala is now a pocket-sized sleepy place where the wind whistles through empty streets, and gnarled locals go patiently about their daily chores.

Eating & Sleeping

Sorrento ② see also p305 and p313

✖ L'Antica Trattoria — Italian €€

(☏081 807 10 82; www.lanticatrattoria.com; Via Padre Reginaldo Giuliani 33; lunch menu €19.50, fixed-price menus €45-80; ☺noon-11pm) **Head to the upstairs terrace with its traditional tiles and trailing grape vines and you seem miles away from the alleyways outside. With a deserved reputation as the finest restaurant in town, it has a mainly traditional menu, with homemade pasta, a daily fish special and vegetarian options.**

☻ Hotel Cristina — Hotel €€

(☏081 878 35 62; www.hotelcristinasorrento. it; Via Privata Rubinacci 6, Sant'Agnello; s €130, d €150-200, tr €220, q €240; ☺Mar-Oct; P ❋ ⛱ @ ⛱) Located high above Sant'Agnello, this hotel has superb views, particularly from the swimming pool. The spacious rooms have sea-view balconies and combine inlaid wooden furniture with contemporary flourishes like Philippe Starck chairs. There's an in-house restaurant and a free shuttle bus to/from Sorrento's Circumvesuviana train station.

Marina del Cantone ④

✖ Lo Scoglio — Seafood €€€

(☏081 808 10 26; www.hotelloscoglio.com; Piazza delle Sirene 15, Massa Lubrense; meals €60; ☺12.30-5pm & 7.30-11pm) Lo Scoglio is a favourite of visiting celebs and the food is top notch (and priced accordingly). Although you can eat *fettucine al bolognese* and steak here, you'd be sorry to miss the superb seafood. Options include a €30 antipasto of raw seafood and *spaghetti al riccio* (spaghetti with sea urchins).

Positano ⑤

☻ Pensione Maria Luisa — Pension €

(☏089 87 50 23; www.pensionemarialuisa.com; Via Fornillo 42; r €55-120; ☺Mar-Oct; @ ⛱) The Maria Luisa is a friendly old-school *pensione*. Rooms feature shiny blue tiles and simple, no-frills decor; those with private balconies are well worth the extra €15 for the bay views. If you can't bag a room with a view, there's a small communal terrace offering the same sensational vistas.

Amalfi ⑧ see also p313

✖ Marina Grande — Seafood €€€

(☏089 87 11 29; www.ristorantemarinagrande. com; Viale Delle Regioni 4; tasting menu lunch/dinner €28/60, meals €50; ☺noon-3pm & 6.30-11pm Wed-Mon Mar-Oct) Run by the third generation of the same family, this beachfront restaurant prides itself on its use of locally sourced organic produce, which, in Amalfi, means high-quality seafood.

☻ Hotel Luna Convento — Hotel €€€

(☏089 87 10 02; www.lunahotel.it; Via Pantaleone Comite 33; s €270-370, d €290-390, ste €490-590; ☺Easter-Oct; P ❋ @ ⛱ ⛱) This former convent was founded by St Francis in 1222 and has been a hotel for some 170 years. Rooms in the original building are in the former monks' cells, but there's nothing poky about the bright tiles and seamless sea views. The newer wing is equally beguiling, with religious frescoes. The cloistered courtyard is magnificent.

Ravello ⑨

✖ Ristorante Pizzeria Vittoria — Pizza €€

(☏089 85 79 47; www.ristorantepizzeriavittoria. it; Via dei Rufolo 3; meals €30, pizza from €5; ☺12.15-3pm & 7.15-11pm) Come here for exceptional pizza, including the Ravellese, with cherry tomatoes, mozzarella, basil and courgettes. Other dishes include lasagne with red pumpkin, smoked mozzarella and porcini mushrooms, and an innovative chickpea-and-cod antipasto. The atmosphere is one of subdued elegance, with a small outside terrace and grainy historical pics of Ravello on the walls.

☻ Agriturismo Monte Brusara — Agriturismo €

(☏089 85 74 67; www.montebrusara.com; Via Monte Brusara 32; s/d €45/90; ☺year-round) A working farm, this mountainside *agriturismo* is located a tough half-hour walk of about 1.5km from Ravello's centre (call ahead to arrange to be picked up). It is especially suited to families – children can feed the pony while you sit back and admire the views – or to those who simply want to escape the crowds.

Cilento Coastal Trail

30

Following the wild and rugged coastline of the Cilento peninsula, this trip takes in pristine coastline, fascinating hilltop towns, ancient Greek ruins and atmospheric fishing villages.

TRIP HIGHLIGHTS

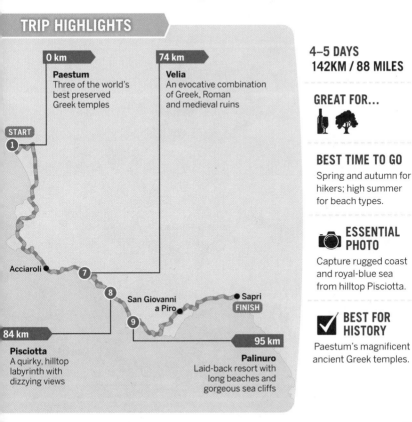

0 km

Paestum
Three of the world's best preserved Greek temples

74 km

Velia
An evocative combination of Greek, Roman and medieval ruins

START
1

Acciaroli ●
7
8
San Giovanni ● Sapri
a Piro ● FINISH
9

84 km

Pisciotta
A quirky, hilltop labyrinth with dizzying views

95 km

Palinuro
Laid-back resort with long beaches and gorgeous sea cliffs

4–5 DAYS
142KM / 88 MILES

GREAT FOR...

BEST TIME TO GO
Spring and autumn for hikers; high summer for beach types.

ESSENTIAL PHOTO
Capture rugged coast and royal-blue sea from hilltop Pisciotta.

BEST FOR HISTORY
Paestum's magnificent ancient Greek temples.

f of Salerno Coastal scenery on the Cilento peninsula

30 Cilento Coastal Trail

Barely accessible by road until the 20th century, the jagged cliff-bound Cilento peninsula is one of Italy's least-explored stretches of coastline. After flourishing under the Greeks and Romans, the Cilento was abandoned for centuries to the vagaries of Mediterranean pirates. Today, its fishing villages and pretty hill towns remain largely free of mass development, despite long, sandy beaches, pristine blue waters, and exquisite local seafood.

TRIP HIGHLIGHT

❶ Paestum

The three stately, honey-coloured **temples** (Area Archeologica di Paestum; ☎0828 81 10 23; www.museo paestum.beniculturali.it; adult/reduced incl museum €7/3.50; ⏱8.30am-half hr before sunset) at Paestum are among the best preserved in Magna Graecia – the Greek colonies that once held sway over much of southern Italy. The Greeks capitulated to the Romans in 273 BC, and Poseidonia, as it was

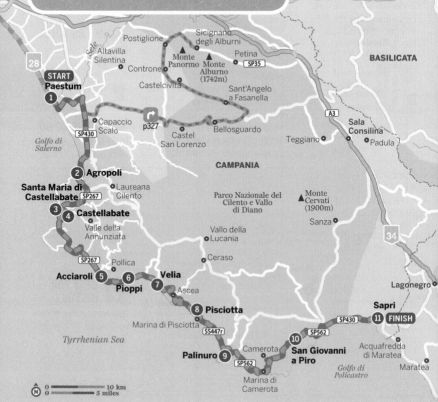

known, remained a thriving trading port until the fall of the Roman Empire.

Buy tickets to the temples at the **museum**, itself a fascinating repository of frescoes, statues and archaeological artefacts, before entering the site's main entrance.

The first structure you encounter is the 6th-century-BC **Tempio di Cerere** (Temple of Ceres), the smallest of the three temples, which later served as a Christian church. As you head south, you can pick out the remnants of the Roman city, including an amphitheatre, housing complexes and the **foro** (forum). Beyond lies the **Tempio di Nettuno**

LINK YOUR TRIP

28 Southern Larder
Join this culinary adventure through Campania where this trips begins – amid the ancient ruins of Paestum.

34 Across the Lucanian Apennines
A stunning 20km from Sapri along Basilicata's coastline, Maratea kicks off this journey over the gorgeous Lucanian Apennines to otherworldly Matera.

DETOUR: PARCO NAZIONALE DEL CILENTO E VALLO DI DIANO

Start: ❶ Paestum

Italy's second-largest national park, the **Parco Nazionale del Cilento e Vallo di Diano** (www.cilentoediano.it) occupies the lion's share of the Cilento peninsula. Some of the most interesting and accessible parts lie within an hour's drive northeast of Paestum, in the park's northwest corner. Near the town of **Castelcivita**, you can explore the **Grotte di Castelcivita** (☑0828 77 23 97; www.grottedicastelcivita.com; Piazzale N Zonzi, Castelcivita; adult/reduced €10/8; ◷standard tours 10.30am, noon, 1.30pm & 3pm Mar-Oct, plus 4.30pm & 6pm Apr-Sep; [P][🚻]), a complex of otherworldly prehistoric caves. For hikers, the town of **Sicignano degli Alburni**, capped by a medieval castle, makes a good base for the tough trek up 1742m-high **Monte Panormo**. Finally, the medieval centre of **Postiglione**, crowned by an 11th-century Norman castle, makes for a lovely stroll.

(Temple of Neptune), the largest and best preserved of the three temples.

Almost next door, the equally beautiful **basilica** (in reality, a temple to the goddess Hera) is Paestum's oldest surviving monument, dating from the middle of the 6th century BC.

🛏 p313

The Drive ⟩⟩ Heading 10km south down the SP430 from Paestum, you quickly start winding into the foothills of the Cilento. Agropoli's historic centre will loom up on the right. Follow signs to the 'Centro Storico'.

- - - - - - - - - - -

❷ Agropoli

Guarding the northern flank of the Cilento

peninsula, the ancient town of Agropoli proffers stunning views across the Gulf of Salerno to the Amalfi Coast. The outskirts are made up of a rather faceless grid of shop-lined streets, but the historic kernel, occupying a rocky promontory, is a charming tangle of cobbled streets with ancient churches, the remains of a **castle** and superlative views up and down the coast.

🍴 p331

The Drive ⟩⟩ South of Agropoli, the 13km stretch of the SR ex SS267 turns inland, giving a taste of Cilento's rugged interior, but you'll quickly head west and to the sea.

③ Santa Maria di Castellabate

Because of the danger of sudden pirate attacks, all the coastal towns on the Cilento once consisted of a low-lying coastal fishing community and a nearby highly defended hilltop town where the peasants and fishing families could find quick refuge.

These days, the fishing district of Castellabate – known as Santa Maria di Castellabate – has outgrown its hilltop protector, thanks to the town's 4km beach of golden sand. Despite the development, the town's historic centre preserves a palpable southern Italian feel, with dusky-pink and ochre houses blinkered by traditional green shutters. The little harbour is especially charming, with its 19th-century *palazzi* (mansions) and the remnants of a much older castle. Note that these charms can diminish quickly when summer crowds overwhelm the scant parking.

🍴 🛏 p331

The Drive » Just past Santa Maria di Castellabate along the SR ex SS267 is the turn-off to Castellabate. The road then winds through orchards and olive groves for 8km.

ANDREY LEBEDEV/SHUTTERSTOCK ©

④ Castellabate

One of the most endearing towns on the Cilento coast, medieval Castellabate clings to the side of a steep hill 280m above sea level. Its summit is marked by the broad **Belvedere di San Costabile**, from where there are sweeping coastal views, and the shell of a 12th-century castle. The surrounding labyrinth of narrow streets is punctuated by ancient archways, small piazzas and the occasional *palazzo*.

The Drive » Head back down to the SR ex SS267 and follow for 21km. The road leads inland, but you'll see the sea soon enough as you twist down to Acciaroli.

Paestum Tempio di Cerere (Temple of Ceres)

5 Acciaroli

Despite a growing number of concrete resorts on its outskirts, the tastefully restored historic centre of this fishing village makes it worth a stop, especially for Hemingway lovers. The author spent time here in the early 1950s, and some say he based *The Old Man and the Sea* on a local fisherman.

The Drive » After Acciaroli, the coastal highway climbs quickly for 8km to Pioppi, proffering stunning views down the Cilento coast to Capo Palinuro.

6 Pioppi

A tiny, seaside hamlet, Pioppi enjoys culinary fame as the spiritual home of the Mediterranean diet. For more than 30 years, the American medical researcher Dr Ancel Keys lived here, observing the vigorous residents and studying the health benefits of their diet. Join the latest generation of locals on lovely Piazza de Millenario, before heading to the pristine, pale pebble beach a few steps away for a picnic.

The Drive » By Cilento standards, it's a straight shot for 8km along the coastal highway to the archaeological site of Velia. Some 6km further southeast is Ascea, where coastal mountains make way for the small but rich plains that once fed ancient Velia.

TRIP HIGHLIGHT

7 Velia

Founded by the Greeks in the mid-6th century BC, and subsequently a popular resort for wealthy Romans, Velia (formerly Elea) was once home to philosophers Parmenides and Zeno. Today, you can wander around the town's evocative ruins at the **Parco Archeologico di Elea Velia** (☎0974 97 23 96; Contrada Piana di Velia; adult/ reduced €3/1.50; ☺8.45am-1hr before sunset), and explore intact portions of the original city walls, plus remnants of thermal baths, an Ionic temple, a Roman theatre and even a medieval castle.

The Drive » You are now headed into the most hair-raising stretch of the Cilento's coastal highway, but spectacular views are your reward. Olive trees start multiplying as you near Pisciotta. The total distance is about 10km.

TRIP HIGHLIGHT

8 Pisciotta

The liveliest town in the Cilento and also its most dramatic, hilltop Pisciotta consists of a steeply pitched maze of medieval streets. Life centres on the lively main square, Piazza Raffaele Pinto, where the town's largely elderly residents rule the roost. The hills surrounding the town are terraced into rich olive groves and produce particularly prized oil, while local fishermen specialise in anchovies. When their catch is marinated in the local oil, the result is mouth-wateringly good.

✕ 🛏 p331

The Drive » The 11km trip begins with a steep descent from Pisciotta, and a straight road to Palinuro. Before reaching town, you'll see its beautiful, miles-long beach.

TRIP HIGHLIGHT

9 Palinuro

The Cilento's main resort, Palinuro remains remarkably low-key (and low rise), with a tangible fishing-village feel, though its beaches become crowded in August. Extending past its postcard-pretty harbour, the remarkable 2km-long promontory known as **Capo Palinuro** proffers wonderful walking trails and views up and down the coast. Better yet, you can visit its sea cliffs and hidden caves, including Palinuro's own version of Capri's famous Grotta Azzurra, with a similarly spectacular display of water, colour and light. To arrange an excursion, **Da Alessandro** (☎347 654 09 31; www.costieradelcilento.

it; Spiaggia del Porto di Palinuro; trips from €15; ☺mid-Mar–mid-Nov) runs two-hour trips to the Grotta and four other local caves.

✕ p331

The Drive » Begin the 27km drive with a beautiful jaunt along the water before heading inland at Marina di Camerota. Get ready for plenty of sharp turns as you wind up the stunning SR ex SS562.

10 San Giovanni a Piro

With its tight-knit historic centre and jaw-dropping views across the Gulf of Policastro to the mountains of Basilicata and Calabria, this little agricultural town makes a worthy stop as you wind your way around the wild, southern tip of the Cilento peninsula.

The Drive » The final 20km of this trip begins with a winding descent from San Giovanni a Piro to the pretty port town of Scario; the road flattens out as you make your way around the picturesque Golfo di Policastro.

11 Sapri

Set on an almost perfectly round natural harbour, Sapri is the ideal place to wave goodbye to the Cilento. The peninsula's dramatic interior mountains rear up across the beautiful Golfo di Policastro. Admire the views from the town's seafront promenade or from one of its nearby beaches.

Eating & Sleeping

Agropoli ❷

✖ Il Gambero — Seafood €€

(📞0974 82 28 94; www.gambero.it; Via Lungomare San Marco 234; meals from €25; 🕐12.15-3.30pm & 7pm-midnight, closed Tue winter) Il Gambero is located across from Agropoli's long sandy beach – get here early to grab a table out front and enjoy the sun setting over Sorrento with Capri twinkling in the distance. Specialities include seafood mixed salad, pasta with clams and pumpkin, and fried mixed fish. Although there are some non-seafood dishes, the fish has star billing. Reservations recommended.

Santa Maria di Castellabate ❸

✖ I Due Fratelli — Seafood €€

(📞0974 96 80 04; www.ristoranteiduefratelli. net; Via San Andrea 13; meals €40; 🕐noon-2.30pm & 7-11pm Thu-Tue) Run by two brothers, this long-standing roadside restaurant is renowned for its top-notch seafood. Enjoy dishes such as *risotto alla pescatora* (fisherman's risotto) and relaxing views from the panoramic terrace.

✖ Perbacco — Campanian €€

(📞0974 96 18 32; Via Andrea Guglielmini 19; meals €35-40; 🕐5.30-11pm Wed-Mon, closed Nov) Set on the charming town beach, foodie favourite Perbacco proffers a long wine list and creative takes on local seafood specialities, like *tortino di alici* (anchovies with smoked cheese, creamed potatoes and eggplant) and ravioli stuffed with sea urchin. Reservations recommended.

🛏 Residenza d'Epoca 1861 — Guesthouse €

(📞0974 96 14 54; http://residenzadepoca1861. it; Lungomare Perrotti; d €50-90; 🕸🛜) Occupying an 18th-century mansion on Santa Maria di Castellabate's historic waterfront, this small, impeccably run guesthouse offers sea views from every room, plus whitewashed interiors with discreet splashes of modernist colour. Reserve ahead at weekends and in summer.

Pisciotta ❽

✖ I Tre Gufi — Italian €€

(📞0974 97 30 42; Via Roma, Pisciotta; meals €30-35; 🕐noon-3pm & 7-11pm) Follow the signs from Pisciotta's sweeping Piazza Raffaele Pinto to this restaurant in a star setting, its long, wide terrace overlooking the pine-forested hillside stretching down to the sea. The menu has plenty of choice, with seafood the speciality. There's also a good choice of salads, plus pasta, *fagiolini* (green beans), risotto and specials like sea bass with porcini mushrooms and olives.

🛏 Marulivo Hotel — Boutique Hotel €€

(📞0974 97 37 92; www.marulivohotel.it; Via Castello, Pisciotta; d €80-170, ste €140-210; 🕐Easter-Oct; 🕸🛜) Great for romance, or just a stress-free break in idyllic surroundings. Located in the narrow web of lanes behind medieval Pisciotta's main piazza, rooms feature earthy colours, antique furnishings, crisp white linen and exposed stone walls. The rooftop terrace with sea views and an adjacent small bar are unbeatable for lingering over a long, cold drink.

Palinuro ❾

✖ Ristorante Core a Core — Italian €€

(📞0974 93 16 91; www.coreacorepalinuro.it; Via Piano Faracchio 13; meals €30-40; 🕐12.45-2.45pm & 8pm-midnight) Ignore the cheesy heart-shaped sign: with its glorious garden setting and great reputation for seafood, Core a Core is your best bet in Palinuro. The *antipasti al mare* (€19.50) is superb, and there's a menu of proper kids' food. Book in advance – it's popular.

Puglia's Pilgrim Trail

31

From basilicas in Bari to pilgrimage sites on the wild Promontorio del Gargano, this trip spotlights the medieval castles and churches that bequeathed by Puglia's Norman and German conquerors.

TRIP HIGHLIGHTS

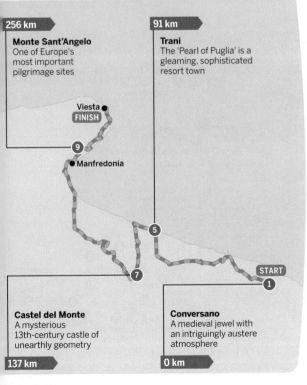

256 km

Monte Sant'Angelo
One of Europe's most important pilgrimage sites

Viesta ●
FINISH

⑨

● Manfredonia

91 km

Trani
The 'Pearl of Puglia' is a gleaming, sophisticated resort town

⑤

⑦

START
①

Castel del Monte
A mysterious 13th-century castle of unearthly geometry

137 km

Conversano
A medieval jewel with an intriguingly austere atmosphere

0 km

4 DAYS
312KM / 194 MILES

GREAT FOR...

BEST TIME TO GO
April to June for hiking amid wildflowers. Fall for mushrooms and mild weather.

ESSENTIAL PHOTO
Capture the isolated mountain-top splendour of the Monte Sant'Angelo.

BEST FOR HISTORY
Conversano's restrained medieval splendour.

31 Puglia's Pilgrim Trail

Both pilgrims and princes have long been partial to this stretch of the Adriatic coast, and you'll understand why as you weave your way from the sun-kissed seaside to fertile inland plains, which together form the basis for Puglia's extraordinary cuisine. All the way to the dramatic Promontorio del Gargano, you'll see splendid evidence of Puglia's medieval golden age, when Norman and Swabian overlords built castles and distinctive Romanesque churches.

TRIP HIGHLIGHT

① Conversano

Conversano's historic centre is a medieval jewel that generates its own austerely intriguing atmosphere. The main attraction is the Norman-Swabian **Castello di Conversano**, which commands views over the coastal plains all the way to Bari. And don't miss the beautiful Romanesque **cathedral** (Largo Cattedrale). Built between the 9th and the 14th centuries, it has a

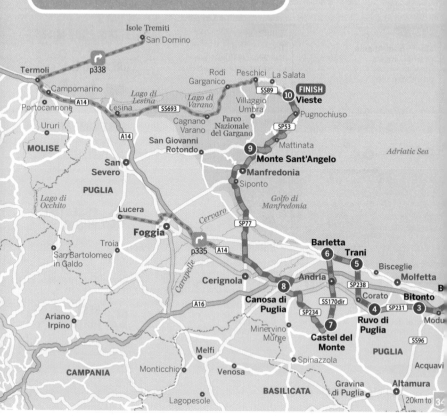

typical graven portal, large rose window and pointy gabled roof.

The Drive » Head northwest through Puglia's rich agricultural flatlands along the SP240 for the 31km to Bari.

② Bari

A lively university town and regional transport hub, Bari is often overlooked by time-poor travellers. But Puglia's capital, and southern Italy's second largest city, deserves more than a cursory glance. The most interesting area is **Bari**

0 ——— 30 km
0 ——— 15 miles

Vecchia (Old Bari), an atmospheric warren of tight alleyways, unfussy trattorias and graceful piazzas. In the heart of the district, the 12th-century **Basilica di San Nicola** (www.basilicasannicola.it; Piazza San Nicola; ⊙7am-8.30pm Mon-Sat, to 10pm Sun) was one of the first Norman churches built in southern Italy. A splendid example of Puglian-Romanesque architecture, it's best known for housing the

DETOUR: LUCERA

Start: ❽ Canosa di Puglia (p338)

About 85km north of Canosa di Puglia, Lucera has one of Puglia's most impressive castles and a handsome old town centre of mellow sand-coloured brick and stone, with chic shops lining wide, shiny stone streets. Frederick II's enormous **castle** (adult/reduced €3/1; ⊙9am-1pm & 3.30-7.30pm Tue-Sun), built in 1233, lies 14km northwest of the town on a rocky hillock surrounded by a perfect 1km-long pentagonal wall, guarded by 24 towers.

bones of St Nicholas (aka Santa Claus).

✕ 🛏 p339

The Drive » A not-very-interesting 19km drive leads to Bitonto. From Bari, follow the SS96 through the city's flat, industrial suburbs to the town of Modugno, where you should connect with the SP231 to Bitonto.

③ Bitonto

Surrounded as it is by olive groves, it's no surprise Bitonto produces a

§ LINK YOUR TRIP

33 Salento Surprises
From Bari, head 153km along coastal highways SS16, SS379 and SS613 until you reach jewel-like Lecce, then along the fascinating, beach-lined high heel of the Italian boot.

34 Across the Lucanian Apennines
About 67km south of Bari via the SS96 and SS99 lies Matera, the culmination of this trip over the gorgeous and little-explored Lucanian Apennines.

ggiano
SS16
SP240 **Conversano**
① START   90km to
SP101 Castellana   33
Grotte
Putignano
Valle d'Itria
p336
Locorotondo

celebrated extra-virgin oil. However, it is the town's medieval core that makes it worth seeking out. Its magnificent 12th-century **cathedral** is romantically dedicated to St Valentine. There's also an impressive 14th-century **tower**, and some smaller medieval churches to refresh the spirit.

The Drive ›› Heading along the SP231, the flat Puglia landscape becomes increasingly rural, until you reach the outskirts of Ruvo di Puglia, 19km to the west.

- - - - - - - - - - - - - -

❹ Ruvo di Puglia

Situated on the eastern slopes of the Murgia plateau and surrounded by olive and almond orchards, Ruvo is an attractive country town. Its historic core is dominated by a famous 13th-century **cathedral**, a gorgeous example of Puglia's distinctive version of Romanesque architecture. A short walk away, the **Museo Nazionale Jatta** (www.palazzojatta.org; Piazza Bovio 35; ⊙8.30am-1.30pm Mon-Wed, Fri & Sun, to 7.30pm Thu & Sat) showcases an interesting collection of ancient Greek ceramics. And don't leave town without trying the exquisite cakes and pastries made with Ruvo's prized local almonds.

DETOUR: VALLE D'ITRIA

Start: ❶ Conversano (p334)

Just south of Conversano rises the great limestone plateau of the Murgia (473m), a strange landscape riddled with holes and ravines through which small streams and rivers gurgle. At the heart of the Murgia lies the idyllic Valle d'Itria, famous for its *trulli* (see also p340). Unique to Puglia, these Unesco-protected circular stone-built houses boast curious conical roofs.

The Murgia is also famous for its *masserie*. Modelled on the classical Roman villa, these fortified farmhouses – equipped with oil mills, storehouses, chapels and accommodation for workers and livestock – functioned as self-sufficient communities. These days, many offer stylish country accommodation, including lovely **Biomasseria Lama di Luna** (☑0883 56 95 05; www.lamadiluna.com; Montegrosso; d €160-210; P✳), a working farm redesigned according to principles of green architecture.

The Drive ›› Head through fields and olive orchards along the SP2 for 8km to Corato, where you'll catch the SP238 – a straight shot north for 14km through dozens of olive groves to seaside Trani.

- - - - - - - - - - - - - -

TRIP HIGHLIGHT

❺ Trani

Known as the 'Pearl of Puglia', Trani has a sophisticated feel, particularly in summer when well-heeled visitors pack the bars on the marina. The marina is the place to promenade and watch the boats, while the historic centre, with its medieval churches, glossy limestone streets

Castel del Monte The castle of Frederick II

and faded yet charming *palazzi* (mansions), is enchanting. The most arresting sight is the austere, 12th-century **cathedral** (www.cattedrale trani.it; Piazza del Duomo; campanile €5; ⏰8.30am-12.30pm & 3.30-7pm Mon-Sat, 9am-12.30pm & 4-9pm Sun), white against the deep-blue sea.

✕ 🛏 p339

The Drive » Following the coastline, the SS16 heads quickly into agricultural land until you reach Barletta's suburbs after 15km.

⑥ Barletta

Barletta's crusading history is a lot more exotic than the modern-day town, although the historic centre is pretty enough with its **cathedral, colossus**, and fine **castle**. However, the history of the town is closely linked with the nearby archaeological site of **Canne della Battaglia** (☎0883 51 09 93; ⏰8.30am-7pm Tue-Sat, to 1.30pm Sun & Mon), where Carthaginian Hannibal whipped the Romans. Barletta also boasts some of the nicest beaches along this stretch of coast.

The Drive » From Barletta it's a straight drive south to Andria along the SS170dir. Continue on the same road and follow as the land begins to rise near Castel del Monte. In all, it's approximately 31km.

TRIP HIGHLIGHT

⑦ Castel del Monte

With its unearthly geometry and hilltop location, this 13th-century, Unesco-protected **castle** (☎0883 56 99 97; www.casteldelmonte.beniculturali.it; adult/reduced €5/2.50; ⏰9am-6.30pm Oct-Mar, 10.15am-7.30pm Apr-Sep) is visible for miles around. No one knows why Frederick II built this

DETOUR: ISOLE TREMITI

Start: ⑩ Vieste

This three-island archipelago is a picturesque vision of rugged cliffs, medieval structures, lonesome caves, sandy coves and thick pine woods – all surrounded by a glittering, dark-blue sea. It's packed to the gills in July and August, but makes a wonderful off-season getaway. Ferries depart in summer from Vieste, and year-round from Termoli, about a three-hour drive up the Adriatic coast.

mysterious structure – there's no nearby town or strategic crossroads, and it lacks typical defensive features like a moat or arrow slits. Some theories claim that, in accordance with mid-13th-century beliefs, the octagon represented the union between the circle (representing the sky and the infinite) and square (the Earth and the temporal).

The Drive ≫ From Castel del Monte this leg is 34km, heading northeast along the SS170dir, then picking up the SP234 and SP149 at Montegrosso. The road winds through a hilly and rather barren stretch until you reach the SP231 and the flatter lands around Canosa di Puglia.

- - - - - - - - - - - - - -

⑧ Canosa di Puglia

Predating the arrival of the Romans by many centuries, this rather drab provincial town was once rich and powerful Canusium, Roman capital of the region. Today you can see remnants of this prosperity in the

massive **Arco Traiano**, the **Roman Bridge**, and the **Basilica di San Leucio**. Once a huge Roman temple, it was converted into a massive Christian basilica in the 4th and 5th centuries. Today only tantalising fragments remain at the **Parco Archeologico di San Leucio**.

The Drive ≫ From Canosa head toward Cerignola on the A14 autostrada. Exit at Cerignola Est and follow the SP77 past olive groves to Manfredonia at the southern end of the Promontorio del Gargano. Join the SS89 and then the SP55 for the climb to hilltop Monte Sant'Angelo. Allow two hours for the 85km drive.

- - - - - - - - - - - - - -

TRIP HIGHLIGHT

⑨ Monte Sant'Angelo

One of Europe's most important pilgrimage sites; it was here in AD 490 that St Michael the Archangel is said to have appeared in a grotto. During the Middle Ages, the **Santuario**

di San Michele (Via Reale Basilica; ⊙7am-8pm Jul-Sep, 7am-1pm & 2.30-8pm Apr-Jun & Oct, 7am-1pm & 2.30-7pm Nov-Mar) marked the end of the Route of the Angel, which began in Mont St-Michel in Normandy and passed through Roma (Rome). Today the sanctuary is a remarkable conglomeration of Romanesque, Gothic and baroque elements. Etched bronze and silver doors, cast in Constantinople in 1076, open into the grotto itself. Inside, a 16th-century statue of the archangel covers a sacred spot: the site of St Michael's footprint.

✕ p339

The Drive ≫ From Monte Sant'Angelo, you head back towards the sea, eventually reaching SS89 and then the fiercely winding SP53 as you head to the tip of the peninsula. This 56km drive is the most scenic of the trip.

- - - - - - - - - - - - - -

⑩ Vieste

Jutting off the Gargano's easternmost promontory into the Adriatic, Vieste is an attractive white-washed town overlooking a lovely sandy beach – a gleaming wide strip flanked by sheer white cliffs and overshadowed by the towering rock monolith, **Scoglio di Pizzomunno**. It's packed in summer and ghostly quiet in winter.

✕ 🛏 p339

Eating & Sleeping

Bari ❷

✖ Terranima — Puglian €€

(☎080 521 97 25; www.terranima.com; Via Putignani 213/215; meals €25-30; ☺11.30am-3.30pm & 6.30-10.30pm Mon-Sat, 11.30am-3.30pm Sun) Peep through the lace curtains into the cool interior of this rustic trattoria where worn flagstone floors and period furnishings make you feel like you're dining in someone's front room. The menu features fabulous regional offerings such as veal, lemon and caper meatballs, and *sporcamuss*, a sweet flaky pastry.

✖ La Locanda di Federico — Puglian €€

(☎080 522 77 05; www.lalocandadifederico.com; Piazza Mercantile 63-64; meals €30-40; ☺noon-3.30pm & 7.30pm-12.30am) With domed ceilings, archways and medieval-style artwork on the walls, this restaurant oozes atmosphere. The menu is typical Puglian, starring dishes such as *orecchiette con le cime di rape* ('little ears' pasta with turnip tops) and prawns with pancetta. The people-watching is equally good – if you can take your eyes off the food.

⭐ B&B Casa Pimpolini — B&B €

(☎080 521 99 38; www.casapimpolini.com; Via Calefati 249; s €45-60, d €70-80; ❉ 📶) This lovely B&B in the new town is within easy walking distance to shops, restaurants and Bari Vecchia. The rooms are warm and welcoming, and the homemade breakfast is a treat. Great value.

Trani ❺

✖ Corteinfiore — Seafood €€

(☎0883 50 84 02; www.corteinfiore.it; Via Ognissanti 18; meals €35; ☺noon-2.15pm & 8-10.15pm, closed Sun evening & Mon) Romantic, urbane, refined. The wooden decking, buttercup-yellow tablecloths and marquee-conservatory setting are refreshing, while the wines are excellent and the cooking delicious. It also has modern and attractive rooms (from €100) decked out in pale colours.

⭐ Albergo Lucy — Hotel €

(☎0883 48 10 22; www.albergolucy.com; Piazza Plebiscito 11; d/tr/q from €75/95/115; ❉ 📶)

Located in a restored 17th-century *palazzo* overlooking a leafy square and close to the shimmering port, this family run place oozes charm and is great value. Bike hire and guided tours are available. Breakfast isn't served, but there are plenty of cafes a short stroll away.

Monte Sant'Angelo ❾

✖ Casa li Jalantuúmene — Trattoria €€

(☎0884 56 54 84; www.li-jalantuumene.it; Piazza de Galganis 5; meals €40; ☺12.15-2.45pm & 7.30-10.30pm Wed-Mon) This renowned restaurant has an entertaining and eccentric chef, Gegè Mangano, and serves excellent fare. It's intimate, there's a select wine list and, in summer, tables spill onto the piazza. There are also four suites on site (from €100), decorated in traditional Puglian style.

Vieste ❿

✖ Taverna Al Cantinone — Italian €€

(☎0884 70 77 53; Via Mafrolla 26; meals €35; ☺noon-3pm & 7-11pm) Run by a charming Italian-Spanish couple who have a passion for cooking. The food is exceptional and exquisitely presented, and the menu changes with the seasons.

⭐ Relais Parallelo 41 — B&B €

(☎0884 35 50 09; www.bbparallelo41.it; Via Forno de Angelis 3; r from €50; ❉ 📶) Beautiful small B&B in the midst of the old town where five renovated rooms have been decorated with hand-painted ceilings, luxurious beds and super-modern bathrooms. Breakfasts consist of a substantial buffet, and the reception area acts as a mini information centre for a slew of local activities. Note that there are minimum stays in July and August.

⭐ Hotel Seggio — Hotel €€

(☎0884 70 81 23; www.hotelseggio.it; Via Veste 7; d €90-160, half-board per person €60-105; ☺Apr-Oct; 🅿 ❉ @ 📶 🏊) A butter-coloured, 17th-century, family run *palazzo* in the town's historic centre. Steps spiral down to a dreamy pool and sunbathing terrace with an ocean backdrop. The 30 rooms are plain but modern.

Valle d'Itria

32

With its grey drystone walls, endless groves of olive trees, and Hobbit-like trulli homes, Puglia's rural heartland sets the backdrop to this tour of the Valle d'Itria.

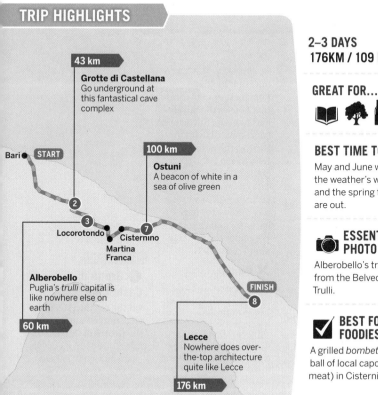

Bari START

43 km

Grotte di Castellana
Go underground at this fantastical cave complex

100 km

Ostuni
A beacon of white in a sea of olive green

Locorotondo Cisternino

Martina Franca

Alberobello
Puglia's *trulli* capital is like nowhere else on earth

60 km

FINISH

Lecce
Nowhere does over-the-top architecture quite like Lecce

176 km

2–3 DAYS
176KM / 109 MILES

GREAT FOR...

BEST TIME TO GO

May and June when the weather's warm and the spring flowers are out.

ESSENTIAL PHOTO

Alberobello's trulli from the Belvedere Trulli.

BEST FOR FOODIES

A grilled *bombetta* (a ball of local capocollo meat) in Cisternino.

32 Valle d'Itria

It might only be an hour's drive from big-city Bari but the Valle d'Itria is another world. This is farming country, where quiet backroads run past orderly fruit orchards and gnarled, centuries-old olive trees writhe out of the rusty red soil. Attractive hilltop towns harbour whitewashed historic centres and strange *trulli* (circular stone-built houses) litter the rock-strewn landscape. Marking the end of the road is Lecce, Puglia's great baroque city.

❶ Bari

Start your trip with a blast of urban grit in Bari. Pugila's regional capital and main transport hub is a city of busy, shop-lined boulevards and grand municipal buildings, its large student population ensuring there's always plenty of life in its piazzas, bars and cafes.

Much of the city's grid-patterned centre dates to the 19th century but it's in the tightly-packed Old Town, known as **Bari Vecchia**, that you'll find the city's greatest treasures. Chief among these is the mighty **Basilica di San Nicola** (www.basilicasannicola.it; Piazza San Nicola; ⊗7am-8.30pm

Mon-Sat, to 10pm Sun), a towering Puglian-Romanesque cathedral that houses the miraculous bones of St Nicholas (aka Santa Claus). Nearby, the hulking **Castello Svevo** (Swabian Castle; ☎080 521 37 04; Piazza Federico II di Svevia; adult/reduced €3/1.50; ⊗8.30am-7.30pm, closed Wed winter) harks back to Puglia's golden age under the Swabian king Frederick II.

✖ ▭ 339

The Drive ❯❯ From Bari pick up the SS100, following signs for Taranto. Exit at Casamassima and push on to Turi on the SS172. The road traverses typical Pugliese countryside, drystone walls and orchards of fruit and olive trees. After Turi, head left on the SP32 for the Grotte, some 43km from Bari.

TRIP HIGHLIGHT

❷ Grotte di Castellana

On the northwestern edge of the Valle d'Itria, the **Grotte di Castellana** (☎080 499 82 21; www.grottedicastellana.it; Piazzale Anelli; short/full tour €10/15; ⊗9am-6pm summer, by appointment

winter) are a series of spectacular limestone caves that link to form Italy's longest natural subterranean network. The galleries, first discovered in 1938, contain an incredible range of underground landscapes, with extraordinary stalactite and stalagmite formations – look out for

LINK YOUR TRIP

31 **Puglia's Pilgrim Trail**

Instead of turning south at Bari, head north to join this tour of Puglia's architectural splendours and medieval castles.

33 **Salento Surprises**

Lecce is the starting point for this trip through the fashionable summer hotspots of Puglia's deep south.

343

the jellyfish, the bacon and the stocking. The highlight is the **Grotta Bianca** (White Grotto), visitable on the full tour only, an eerie white alabaster cavern hung with stiletto-thin stalactites.

The Drive >> On this short 17km drive up to Alberobello via the SP237 to Putignano and then the SS172, you'll catch sight of the Valle d'Itria's unique *trulli* houses dotted amidst the roadside fields and olive groves.

TRIP HIGHLIGHT

3 Alberobello

The Unesco-listed town of Alberobello is Puglia's *trulli* capital. There are more than 1000 of these gnomic conical-capped houses spread across town, many huddled together on the hillside in the **Rione Monti** district southwest of the central strip, Via Indipendenza.

Alberobello, which was named after a primitive oak forest, Arboris Belli (beautiful trees), that once covered the area, is an amazing sight, but it does get very touristy – from May to October busloads of tourists pile into *trullo* homes, have a drink in *trullo* bars and go shopping in *trullo* shops.

To get the best views of the whole higgledy-piggledy scene, park in Lago Martellotta and follow the steps up to Piazza del Popolo and the **Belvedere Trulli** lookout.

✗ 🛏 p347

The Drive >> It's a straightforward 9km drive up along the SS172 to Locorotondo. Once arrived, don't attempt to take your car into the *centro storico* (historic centre) but park on the road downhill from the centre.

4 Locorotondo

Perched on a ridge overlooking the valley, Locorotondo boasts one of Puglia's most beautiful historic centres. There are few 'sights' as such, rather, the town is a sight in itself with its circular *centro storico* – the name Locorotondo is a derivation of the Italian for 'round place' – where everything is a shimmering white and blood-red geraniums tumble down from pretty window boxes. The streets are paved with smooth ivory-coloured stones, with the church of **Santa Maria della Greca** as their sun-baked centrepiece.

You can enjoy inspiring views of the surrounding valley from the **Villa Comunale**, whilst for inspiration of another kind, make sure to try some of the town's celebrated white wine.

✗ p347

The Drive >> Yet another short drive. Follow the southbound SS172 as it undulates to Martina Franca, passing more *trulli*, rock walls, and giant *fichi d'India* (prickly pears).

FREEARTIST/GETTY IMAGES ©

5 Martina Franca

The main town in the Valle d'Itria, Martina Franca is known for its graceful baroque buildings and lovely old quarter, a picturesque ensemble of winding alleys, blinding white houses and curlicue wrought-iron balconies.

Passing under the **Arco di Sant'Antonio** at the western end of pedestrianised Piazza XX Settembre, you emerge into Piazza Roma, dominated by the 17th-century rococo **Palazzo Ducale** (📞080 480 57 02; Piazza Roma 32; 🕓9am-1pm Mon-Fri & 4-7pm Tue, Thu & Fri,

Ostuni View towards the cathedral

10am-noon & 5-7pm Sat & Sun), whose upper rooms have semi-restored frescoed walls and host temporary art exhibitions.

From the piazza, Corso Vittorio Emanuele leads to Piazza Plebiscito, the centre's baroque heart. The square is overlooked by the 18th-century **Basilica di San Martino** and at its centre a statue of city patron, St Martin, swings a sword and shares his cloak with a beggar.

The Drive » This quick 9km leg takes you off the main roads onto the quiet back-country SP61 and its continuation the SP13. All around you extends bucolic farmland littered with rocks and the ubiquitous olive trees.

- - - - - - - - - - - - -

⑥ Cisternino

An appealing, white-washed hilltop town, slow-paced Cisternino has been designated as one of Italy's *borghi più belli* (most beautiful towns). Beyond its bland modern outskirts it harbours a charming kasbah-like *centro storico*. Highlights include the 13th-century **Chiesa Matrice** and the **Torre Civica**, a defensive tower dating to the Norman-Swabian period (11th to 12th centuries). There's also a pretty communal garden with rural views. If you take Via Basilioni next to the tower you can amble along an elegant route right to the central piazza, **Vittorio Emanuele**.

Cisternino is also famous for its *fornelli pronti* (literally 'ready ovens') and in many butchers' shops and trattorias you can select a cut of meat and have it grilled to eat straight away.

✘ p347

The Drive » From Cisternino, the SP17 makes for an attractive

345

TRULLI

Unique to this part of Puglia, the white-grey, conical-capped *trulli* (circular stone-built houses) are a characteristic part of the Valle d'Itria's landscape. They first appeared in the late-15th century when they were built without mortar, making them easy to dismantle and allowing their wily owners to avoid local taxes. But while their design looks simple, it is well suited to the local climate – they are made out of whitewashed limestone and have thick walls that keep them cool in the baking summers.

drive as it passes though yet more typically Puglian countryside as it heads to Ostuni, 15km away.

TRIP HIGHLIGHT

❼ Ostuni

Surrounded by an ocean of olive trees, chic Ostuni shines like a pearly white tiara, extending across three hills. The town, which marks the end of the *trulli* region and the beginning of the hot, dry Salento, heaves in summer as crowds flock to its excellent restaurants and stylish bars.

The historic centre is a great place to hang out, but if you're in the mood for exploring there are a couple of worthy sights. First up, there's the dramatic 15th-century **cathedral** (Via Cattedrale; €1; ☺9am-noon & 3.30-7pm) with an unusual Gothic-Romanesque facade.

Then there's the **Museo di Civiltà Preclassiche della Murgia** (☎0831 33 63 83; Via Cattedrale 15; adult/reduced €5/3; ☺10am-noon & 4.30-10pm daily summer, 10am-1pm daily & 4-7pm Sat & Sun winter), a small museum showcasing finds from a nearby Paleolithic burial ground, including the skeleton of a 25,000-year-old woman nicknamed Delia.

✗ ⨤ p347

The Drive ≫ This last 76km leg takes you south of the Valle d'Itria to the sun-scorched Salento district and the handsome city of Lecce. From Ostuni head seawards on the SP21 to join up with the SS379, which parallels the coast down to Brindisi. Continue south, following signs to Lecce and hook up with the fast-flowing SS613 for the final push.

TRIP HIGHLIGHT

❽ Lecce

Lecce, the so-called Florence of the South, is a lively, laid-back university city celebrated for its extraordinary 17th-century baroque architecture. Known as *barocco leccese* (Lecce baroque), this local style is an expressive and hugely decorative incarnation of the genre replete with gargoyles, asparagus columns and cavorting gremlins. Swooning 18th-century traveller Thomas Ashe thought Lecce was Italy's most beautiful city, but the less-impressed Marchese Grimaldi said the facade of the **Basilica di Santa Croce** (☎0832 24 19 57; Via Umberto I; ☺9am-noon & 5-8pm) made him think a lunatic was having a nightmare. For a taste head to **Piazza del Duomo**, the city's prized focal square overlooked by a 12th-century **cathedral** (crypt €1; ☺7am-noon & 4-6.30pm) and 15th-century **Palazzo Vescovile** (Episcopal Palace; Piazza del Duomo) with an arched arcade loggia.

✗ ⨤ p347, p355

Eating & Sleeping

Alberobello ③

✕ Trattoria Terra Madre   Italian €

(☎080 432 38 29; www.trattoriaterramadre.it; Piazza Sacramento 17; meals €17-30; ⏱12.15-2.45pm & 7.15-9.45pm Tue-Sat, 12.15-2.45pm Sun; 🍴) Run by the charming people from Charming Tours, this ambitious venture slavishly honours the farm-to-table ethos – most of what you eat will have been plucked from the organic garden outside. The vegetable antipasto is epic, ditto the chickpea soup and stuffed artichokes. The place is educational too: various alcoves in the restaurant explain the harvesting and processing techniques.

🛏 Trullidea   Rental House €€

(☎080 432 38 60; www.trullidea.it; Via Monte Sabotino 24; 2-person trullo €99-160; 🛜) Trullidea has numerous renovated, quaint, cosy and atmospheric *trulli* (circular stone-built houses) in Alberobello's historic centre available on a self-catering, B&B, half- or full-board basis.

Locorotondo ④

✕ La Taverna del Duca   Trattoria €€

(☎080 431 30 07; www.tavernadelducascatigna.it; Via Papadotero 3; meals €30-35; ⏱noon-3pm & 7.30pm-midnight Tue-Sat, noon-3pm Sun & Mon) In a narrow side street off Piazza Vittorio Emanuele, this well-regarded trattoria serves local classics such as *orecchiette* ('little ears' pasta) with various vegetable sidekicks.

Cisternino ⑥

✕ Rosticceria L'Antico Borgo   Barbecue €€

(☎080 444 64 00; www.rosticceria-lanticoborgo.it; Via Tarantini 9; meals €20-30; ⏱6.30-11pm daily summer, Mon-Sat winter) A classic *fornello pronto* (half butcher's shop, half trattoria), this is the place for a cheerful, no-frills meat fest. The menu is brief and to the point, listing a few simple pastas and various meat options (priced per kilo), including Cisternino's celebrated *bombette* (skewered pork wrapped around cheese).

Ostuni ⑦

✕ Osteria del Tempo Perso   Puglian €€

(☎0831 30 33 20; www.osteriadeltempoperso.com; Gaetano Tanzarella Vitale 47; meals €30-40; ⏱12.30-3pm & 7.30-11pm Tue-Sun) A sophisticated rustic restaurant in a cave-like former bakery, this laid-back place serves great Puglian food, specialising in roasted meats. To get here, face the cathedral's south wall and turn right through the archway into Largo Giuseppe Spennati, then follow the signs to the restaurant.

🛏 Il Frantoio   Agriturismo €€€

(☎0831 33 02 76; www.masseriailfrantoio.it; SS16, Km 874; d €133-250; 🅿❄@🛜) Stay at this charming, whitewashed farmhouse, where the owners still live and work producing high-quality organic olive oil. Owner Armando takes guests for a tour of the farm each evening in his 1949 Fiat. Il Frantoio lies 5km outside Ostuni along the SS16 in the direction of Fasano. You'll see the sign on your left-hand side when you reach the Km 874 marker.

Lecce ⑧   see also p355

✕ Trattoria Il Rifugio della Buona Stella   Puglian €

(☎0832 181 05 11; www.ilrifugiodellabuonastella.it; Via Prato 28; meals €20; ⏱noon-3pm & 7-11.45pm Wed-Mon) A third-generation family restaurant in a gorgeous Leccese building with sandy stone walls and medieval decor, this wonderful trattoria serves fine food at sale-of-the-century prices (*secondi* from €6.50!). Start off with the homemade bread, proceed to pasta with swordfish and rapini, and hit the jackpot with the grilled sausages.

🛏 Palazzo Belli B&B   B&B €

(☎348 094 68 02; www.palazzobelli.it; Corso Vittorio Emanuele II 33; s/d €60/80; ❄🛜) A wonderfully central, elegant and well-priced option located in a fine mansion near the cathedral. Rooms have marbled floors and wrought-iron beds. Breakfast is served in your room.

Salento Surprises

33

This journey into Italy's heel takes you to a land of crickets and cacti. You'll find Greek, Roman and much older relics, but also gorgeous beaches lined by a new generation of sun worshippers.

TRIP HIGHLIGHTS

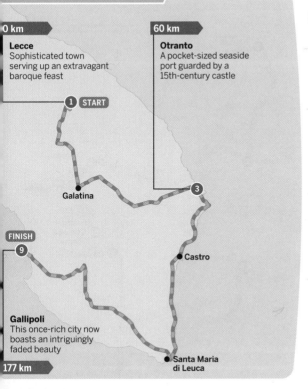

0 km

Lecce
Sophisticated town serving up an extravagant baroque feast

1 START

Galatina

FINISH
9

Gallipoli
This once-rich city now boasts an intriguingly faded beauty

177 km

60 km

Otranto
A pocket-sized seaside port guarded by a 15th-century castle

3

Castro

Santa Maria di Leuca

5–7 DAYS
177KM / 110 MILES

GREAT FOR...

BEST TIME TO GO

Summers are scorching and crowded, but good for beach lovers.

ESSENTIAL PHOTO

Lecce's Basilica di Santa Croce illuminated at night.

✓ BEST FOR HISTORY

Gape at Lecce's hypnotic baroque treasures.

anto Palascia lighthouse

33 Salento Surprises

Until quite recently the Salento was a poor, isolated region littered with the broken relics of a better past, from crumbling Greek ports to Bronze Age dolmens. Nowadays, it's a fashionable summer destination, attracting crowds of sun-seeking Italians and VIP holidaymakers such as Meryl Streep and Helen Mirren. This trip highlights the area's great cultural and natural treasures, taking you from Lecce's baroque splendours to some of Italy's finest beaches.

TRIP HIGHLIGHT

❶ Lecce

As you stare open-mouthed at Lecce's madcap baroque architecture, it's almost hard not to laugh. It's so joyously extravagant that it can be considered either grotesquely ugly or splendidly beautiful. The 18th-century traveller Thomas Ashe called it the most beautiful city in Italy, while the Marchese Grimaldi called the facade of Santa Croce the nightmare of a lunatic.

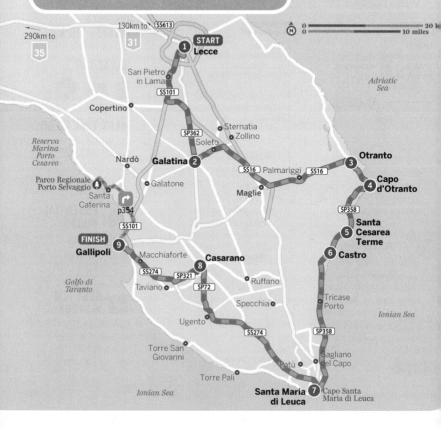

What is certain is that, with more than 40 churches and at least as many *palazzi* (mansions) from the 17th and 18th centuries, the city has an extraordinary cohesion.

A baroque feast, **Piazza del Duomo** is the city's focal point and a sudden open space amid the surrounding enclosed lanes. However, the most hallucinatory spectacle has to be the **Basilica di Santa Croce** (📞0832 24 19 57; Via Umberto I; ⏰9am-noon & 5-8pm), a swirling allegorical feast of sheep, dodos, cherubs and unidentified beasties. A short walk away, the **Museo Faggiano** (📞0832 30 05 28; www.museo

LINK YOUR TRIP

31 Puglia's Pilgrim Trail

From Lecce, head about 130km north along the SS613, SS379 and SS16 to Conversano, which kicks off this exploration of northern Puglia's great castles and churches.

35 The Calabrian Wilderness

From the wild snow-capped peaks of the Pollino to Tropea's violet-coloured seas, get lost in Italy's least-explored region – about 290km from Lecce along the SS106, SP653 and SP4.

LOCAL KNOWLEDGE: PUGLIA ON YOUR PLATE

Puglia's bold, brawny cuisine adheres very closely to its roots in *cucina povera* – literally, 'cooking of the poor'. Yet that cuisine is built on an incredibly rich set of raw ingredients: seafood from the long coastline; durum wheat, olives and extraordinary produce from its rich plains; abundant grapes that are being turned into rapidly improving wines; and some of the world's best almonds. For pasta, Puglians tend to favour broccoli or *ragù* (meat sauce) topped with the pungent local *ricotta forte*. Like their Greek forebears, they're also partial to lamb and kid. Also, raw fish (such as anchovies or baby squid) are marinated to perfection in olive oil and lemon juice.

faggiano.it; Via Grandi 56/58; €3; ⏰9.30am-8pm) is an archaeological treasure trove revealing layers of local history dating back to the 5th century BC.

🍴 🛏 p347, p355

The Drive » Head south for 26km, first on the SS101, then on the SS367 and SP362 through fertile plains to Galatina.

- - - - - - - - - - - - - -

② Galatina

With a charming historic centre, Galatina is the capital of the Salento's Greek-inflected culture. It is almost the only place where the ritual of tarantism – a folk cure for the bite of a tarantula – is still remembered. The *taranta* folk dance evolved from it, and each year the ritual is performed on the feast day of Sts Peter and Paul (29 June). However, most people come to Galatina

to see the incredible 14th-century **Basilica di Santa Caterina d'Alessandria** (⏰8.30am-12.30pm & 4-6.30pm Mon-Sat, 4-6.30pm Sun Apr-Sep, 8.30am-12.30pm & 3.30-5.30pm Mon-Sat, 3.30-5.30pm Sun Oct-Mar), its interior a kaleidoscope of Gothic frescoes set off by the serenity of a pure-white altarpiece

🛏 p355

The Drive » Head back to the SS16 and strike east for a total of 34km, mostly through flat agricultural fields and olive orchards.

- - - - - - - - - - - - - -

TRIP HIGHLIGHT

③ Otranto

Overlooking a pretty harbour on the blue Adriatic, whitewashed Otranto is today a pocket-sized resort town, but for 1000 years it was Italy's main port to the East. The small historic centre is watched over by a beautiful 15th-century **castle** (Piazza Castello; adult/reduced €3/2; ⏰10am-6pm). Long a target of jealous neighbours, Otranto was besieged by Turks, in league with Venezia (Venice), in 1480. They brutally murdered 800 of Otranto's faithful who refused to convert to Islam. Their bones are preserved in a chapel of the 11th-century Norman **cathedral** (☎0836 80 27 20; Piazza Basilica; ⏰7am-noon daily, plus 3-7pm Apr-Sep, 3-5pm Oct-Mar). The cathedral also features a vast 12th-century mosaic of a stupendous tree of life balanced on the back of two elephants. The town itself has a pretty beach, though there are much longer strands just outside of town.

✕ 🛏 p355

The Drive ❭❭ It is a fairly straight shot for 7km through the farmland south of Otranto to Capo d'Otranto. As you get close, you'll see the white lighthouse against the blue Adriatic.

- - - - - - - - - - - - -

❹ Capo d'Otranto

As you head down Salento's dreamy coast, take a pit stop on this small peninsula, which serves as the official division between the Ionian and Adriatic Seas. Its recently restored 19th-century **lighthouse** sits picturesquely at its tip. On clear days you can see the mountains of Albania

across a sparkling blue Adriatic Sea.

The Drive ❭❭ Heading south for 13km, the coastal road (the SP87 and its continuation the SP358) suddenly starts twisting and turning as the coastline turns more rugged, with broad rocky flatlands.

- - - - - - - - - - - - -

❺ Santa Cesarea Terme

Santa Cesarea Terme boasts a number of Liberty-style (art nouveau) villas, reminiscent of the days when spa-going was all the rage. There are still hotels that cater to the summer crowds of Italians who come to bathe in the thermal spas. But don't have visions of stylish hammams and soothing massages; here spa-going is a serious medical business, and the **Terme di Santa Cesarea** (☎0836 94 43 14; www.termesantacesarea.it; Via Roma 40; swimming pool €5, beauty treatments & massages from €20; ⏰Mar-Nov) feels a like a fusty old hospital with a lingering smell of sulphur about it. Still, this makes a great stop to ease the aches and pains of life on the road.

The Drive ❭❭ From Santa Cesarea Terme to Castro, it is a quick 7km drive along the coastal SP358.

- - - - - - - - - - - - -

❻ Castro

Almost midway between Santa Maria and Otranto

Santa Cesarea Terme A resort town popular for its thermal spas

DETOUR:
PARCO REGIONALE
PORTO SELVAGGIO

Start: ❾ Gallipoli

The Ionian coast can be holiday hell in July and August, but head about 25km north from Gallipoli and you'll soon find the real belle of the region, the **Parco Regionale Porto Selvaggio**, a protected area of rocky coastline covered with umbrella pines, eucalyptus trees and olives. Right in the middle of the park is elegant **Santa Caterina**, a summer seaside centre.

lies the town of Castro, which is dominated by an austere, Romanesque **cathedral** and forbidding **castle**. Just downhill, its marina serves as a popular boating and diving hub for the rocky coastline, which is riddled with fascinating sea caves. Most famous is the **Grotta Zinzulusa**, which is filled with stalactites that hang like sharp daggers from the ceiling. It can only be visited on a guided tour. Note that in summer it gets maniacally busy. Details at www.castropromozione.it.

The Drive ›› Keep hugging the coastline south along SP358 for 31km as you pass pine and eucalyptus groves, farmland and a series of small resort towns until you reach the southernmost point of the peninsula.

❼ Santa Maria di Leuca

At the very tip of Italy's high heel, the resort town of Santa Maria di Leuca occupies what Romans called *finibus terrae,* the end of the earth. The spot is marked by the **Basilica Santuario di Santa Maria di Leuca**, an important place of pilgrimage built over an older Roman temple dedicated to Minerva. These days, with its Gothic- and Liberty-style villas, this is a holiday resort, pure and simple. Many people come here to take one of the boat trips to visit sea grottoes like the **Grotta del Diavolo**, the **Grotta della Stalla** and the **Grotta Grande di Ciolo**. Trips depart from the little *porto* (port) between June and September.

The Drive ›› Head 29km inland on the SS274 through seemingly endless olive groves and sunburnt farms to around Ugento, then 10km along the SP72 to Casarano.

❽ Casarano

Sitting amid the Salento's rich olive groves, laid-back Casarano is home of **Chiesa di Santa Maria della Croce**. One of the oldest sites in Christendom, it holds mosaics that date to the 5th century as well as Byzantine frescoes.

The Drive ›› From Casarano to Gallipoli, head west on the SP321 and SS274 roadways. You'll drive 20km through olive trees and ochre-coloured fields, passing Taviano and Macchiaforte en route.

TRIP HIGHLIGHT

❾ Gallipoli

Kallipolis, the 'beautiful city' of the Greeks, may be a faded beauty now, but it still retains its island charm. The Salentines see it as a kind of southern Portofino, and its weathered white *borgo* (historic centre) has a certain grungy chic: part fishing village, part fashion model. In the 16th and 17th centuries, Gallipoli was one of the richest towns in the Salento, exporting its famous olive oil to Napoli (Naples), Paris and London to illuminate their street lamps. That explains the rather elegant air of the old town, which is divided into two distinct halves: the patrician quarter, which housed the wealthy merchant class, to the north of Via Antonietta de Pace; and the popular quarter, with its rabbit-warren of streets to the south.

✕ ⊨ p355

Eating & Sleeping

Lecce ❶ see also p347

✖ Gelateria Natale
Gelateria €

(www.natalepasticceria.it; Via Trinchese 7a; ice cream €2; ☺7.30am-11pm Mon-Fri, 7.30am-1am Sat & Sun) Lecce's best ice-cream parlour also has an array of fabulous confectionery.

✖ Trattoria le Zie – Cucina Casareccia
Trattoria €€

(☎0832 24 51 78; Viale Costadura 19; meals €25-30; ☺12.30-2.30pm & 7.45-10.30pm Tue-Sat, 7.45-10.30pm Sun) Ring the bell to gain entry to this place that feels like a private home, with its patterned cement floor tiles, desk piled high with papers, and charming owner Carmela Perrone. In fact, it's known locally as simply le Zie (the aunts). Here you'll taste true *cucina povera*, including horse meat done in a *salsa piccante* (spicy sauce). Booking is a must.

🛏 Palazzo Rollo
B&B, Apartment €

(☎0832 30 71 52; www.palazzorollo.it; Corso Vittorio Emanuele II 14; s €60-70, d €85-95; P ✳ @) Stay in a 17th-century palace – the Rollo family seat for more than 200 years. The grand B&B suites (with kitchenettes) have high curved ceilings and chandeliers. Downstairs, contemporary-chic studios open onto an ivy-hung courtyard. The rooftop garden has wonderful views.

🛏 Risorgimento Resort
Hotel €€

(☎0832 24 63 11; www.risorgimentoresort.it; Via Imperatore Augusto 19; d €115-220, ste from €250; P ✳ @ 🛜) A warm welcome awaits at this stylish five-star hotel in the centre of Lecce. The rooms are spacious and refined with high ceilings, modern furniture and contemporary details reflecting the colours of the Salento, and the bathrooms are enormous. There's a restaurant, wine bar and rooftop garden.

Galatina ❷

🛏 Samadhi
Agriturismo €

(☎0836 60 02 84; www.agricolasamadhi.com; Via Stazione 116, Zollino; d €59-109, without bathroom €44-104; ✳ 🛜 ⛱) Soothe the soul with a stay at Samadhi, located around 7km east of Galatina in tiny Zollino. It's on a 10-hectare organic farm and the owners are multilingual. As well as ayurvedic treatments and yoga courses, there's a vegan restaurant offering organic meals.

Otranto ❸

✖ La Bella Idrusa
Pizza €

(☎0836 80 14 75; Via Lungomare degli Eroi 1; pizzas from €5; ☺7pm-midnight) You can't miss this pizzeria right by the huge Porta Terra in the historic centre. Despite the tourist-trap location, the food doesn't lack authenticity. And it's not just pizzas on offer: seafood standards are also served.

🛏 Palazzo Papaleo
Hotel €€

(☎0836 80 21 08; www.hotelpalazzopapaleo. com; Via Rondachi 1; r €79-590; P ✳ @ 🛜) Located next to the town cathedral, this sumptuous hotel was the first to earn the EU Eco-label in Puglia. Aside from its ecological convictions, the hotel has magnificent rooms with original frescoes, exquisitely carved antique furniture and walls washed in soft greys, ochres and yellows. Soak in the panoramic views while enjoying the rooftop spa.

Gallipoli ❾

✖ La Puritate
Seafood €€€

(☎0833 26 42 05; Via Sant'Elia 18; meals €45; ☺12.30-3pm & 8-11.30pm, closed Wed winter) *The* place for fish in the old town, with large windows and sea views. Follow the practically obligatory seafood antipasti with delicious *primi* (first courses). Anything involving fish is good, especially the prawns, swordfish and tuna. It's popular and quite formal. Reservations are recommended.

🛏 Insula
B&B €

(☎329 8070056, 0833 20 14 13; www. bbinsulagallipoli.it; Via Antonietta de Pace 56; s €40-80, d €60-150; ☺Apr-Oct; ✳ @) A magnificent 15th-century building houses this memorable B&B. The five rooms are all different but share the same princely atmosphere with exquisite antiques, vaulted high ceilings and cool pastel paintwork.

Across the Lucanian Apennines

34

From seaside Maratea to otherworldly Matera, this trip crosses the hinterlands of Basilicata, a gorgeous region of hilltop towns, purple peaks, fertile valleys and possibly the world's best cheese.

TRIP HIGHLIGHTS

63 km

Padula
Wander through this sprawling, splendid and impossibly grand monastery

288 km

Matera
Haunting cave dwellings overlay a ruggedly unforgiving landscape

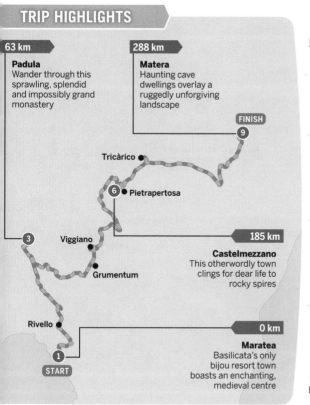

FINISH
9

Tricàrico

6 Pietrapertosa

3

Viggiano

185 km

Castelmezzano
This otherwordly town clings for dear life to rocky spires

Grumentum

Rivello

0 km

Maratea
Basilicata's only bijou resort town boasts an enchanting, medieval centre

1
START

5–7 DAYS
288KM / 179 MILES

GREAT FOR...

BEST TIME TO GO

Spring and autumn for sunny weather without summer heat and crowds.

📷 ESSENTIAL PHOTO

Capture Matera's ancient cave dwellings at sunset.

✓ BEST FOR FOODIES

Try the heavenly local cheeses in Castelmezzano's Al Becco della Civetta.

---

atea *Christ the Redeemer of Maratea by sculptor Bruno Innocenti*

34

Across the Lucanian Apennines

This trip begins on Basilicata's Tyrrhenian coast, which may be diminutive but rivals Amalfi for sheer drama. It ends in a completely different world — the chalky, sunburnt landscape around Matera, a strange and remarkable city with troglodyte dwellings that are Unesco-protected. In between, you'll cross the dramatic peaks of the Lucanian Apennines, a gorgeous land of alpine forests, green valleys and bristling hilltop downs.

TRIP HIGHLIGHT

❶ Maratea

Sitting in stately fashion above the cliffs and pocket-sized beaches of the Golfo di Policastro, Maratea is Basilicata's only bijou resort town. Uphill, the enchanting medieval centre boasts elegant hotels, pint-sized piazzas, wriggling alleys and startling coastal views. Still further up, a 22m-high statue of **Christ the Redeemer** lords it over the rugged landscape. Down at sea

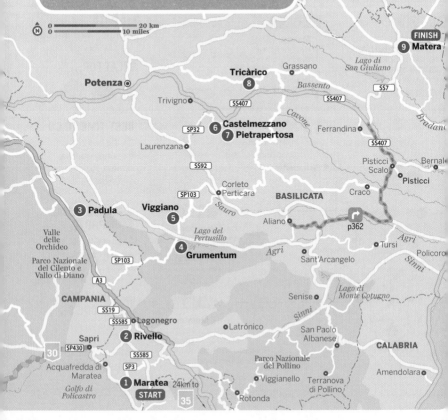

level, the town's **harbour** shelters sleek yachts and bright-blue fishing boats. The deep green hillsides that encircle this tumbling conurbation offer excellent walking trails, while the surrounding coastline hides dozens of tiny beaches.

 p363

The Drive ›› The 23km to Rivello takes you into the heights of the coastal range. From Maratea, follow signs north to Trecchina. Expect great sea views along the way. At Trecchina, head down to a short but blessedly straight stretch of highway SS585. Rivello will appear quickly on your left.

- - - - - - - - - - - -

❷ Rivello

Perched on a high ridge and framed by the southern Apennines, Rivello is not just another picture-pretty medieval village. Due to its strategic posi-

LINK YOUR TRIP

30 **Cilento Coastal Trail**

From Maratea, take the coastal SS18 north to Sapri to explore this wild coastline.

35 **The Calabrian Wilderness**

From Rivello take the A3 south to Mormanno to get lost in Italy's least-explored region.

tion, it was contested for centuries by both Lombards and Byzantines. Eventually, they reached an unlikely compromise – the Lombards settled in the lower part of town, the Byzantines in the upper. This resulted in two separate centres with two diverse cultures developing in a single town. Today, Rivello's charm lies in its narrow alleys, where homes both grand and humble are graced with wrought-iron balconies.

The Drive ›› For the 40km to Padula, return to the SS585 and head to the northbound A3 autostrada. Rugged mountains will suddenly open out into the wide, fertile Vallo di Diano. Take the Padula exit and follow signs to the abbey.

- - - - - - - - - - - -

`TRIP HIGHLIGHT`

❸ Padula

In the plains just below hilltop Padula lies one of southern Italy's most extraordinary sites. The **Certosa di San Lorenzo** (📞0975 77 74 45; adult/reduced €4/2; ⏰9am-7pm Wed-Mon) is among the largest monasteries in southern Europe, with 320 rooms and halls, 13 courtyards, 100 fireplaces, 52 stairways, 41 fountains and the world's largest cloisters. Founded in 1306, its buildings represent more than four centuries of construction, though primarily it is a 17th- and 18th-century baroque creation.

The Drive ›› From Padula, double back along the SS19. Just past Montesano Scalo, follow signs to Sarconi along the SP ex SS103. Here begins a beautiful, winding ascent into the Lucanian Apennines, then a descent towards the verdant Val d'Agri. Reckon on just over an hour for the 44km journey.

- - - - - - - - - - - -

❹ Grumentum

Set amid the fertile Val d'Agri, Grumentum was once an important enough Roman city that the invading Hannibal made it his headquarters. Eventually it was abandoned for hilltop Grumento Nova in the 9th century. Today, its **ruins** (Contrada Spineta, Grumento Nova; admission incl museum €2.50; ⏰9am-1hr before sunset) sit humbly amid agricultural fields and leave much to the imagination. Still, they make for a fascinating and atmospheric ramble, especially the miniature version of the Colosseum.

The Drive ›› Head back to the SP ex SS103 for a 15km drive along the pastoral valley floor following signs to Viggiano. The last few kilometres are pure switchback.

- - - - - - - - - - - -

❺ Viggiano

Hilltop Viggiano stands guard above the beautiful Val d'Agri. Aside from its fine views, the town has an illustrious music history. Since the 18th century, it has been celebrated for its harp

BLUE4XPHOTO/GETTY IMAGES ©

makers and players, and has a long tradition of producing lively street musicians.

Viggiano is also a historic pilgrimage destination thanks to its ancient statue of the Black Madonna, the *Madonna Nera del Sacro Monte*.

🛏 p363

The Drive ›› The 63km ride to Castelmezzano is breathtaking. Head back down the switchback and look for the SP ex SS103 and signs to the town Corleto Perticara. At Corleto Perticara, pick up the SS92 and wind past Laurenzana with its beautiful Romanesque church and castle. Then catch the SP32 and head north. After passing a pretty reservoir signs will lead to Castelmezzano.

TRIP HIGHLIGHT

⑥ Castelmezzano

Clinging to a series of impossibly narrow ledges, the houses of tiny Castelmezzano look like something out of a fairytale, bounded on one side by rocky spires and on the other by the vertigo-inducing gorges of the Caperrino river.

Matera View of the new town topped by the cathedral

When the mist swirls in (as it often does) the effect is otherworldly.

For an adrenaline rush, fly across the gorge to neighbouring Pietrapertosa at 120km/h attached to a steel cable via **Il Volo dell'Angelo.** (The Angel Flight; ☎Pietrapertosa 0971 98 31 10, Castelmezzano 0971 98 60 42; www.volodellangelo.com; singles €35-40, couples €63-72; ⏱9.30am-6.30pm May-Oct)

This region is also know for its incomparable goat's and sheep's milk cheese, the best of which is on the menu at Al Becco della Civetta (p363).

🍴 p363

The Drive » Though you could practically throw a stone across the gorge separating Castelmezzano from Pietrapertosa, the 10km drive requires dozens of hairpin turns and a strong stomach. But views of the gorges are gorgeous indeed. The way is well marked.

- - - - - - - - - - -

❼ Pietrapertosa

As the highest town in Basilicata, Pietrapertosa is possibly even more dramatically situated than neighbouring

DETOUR:
CARLO LEVI COUNTRY

Start: ❾ Matera

Aliano, a tiny and remote village about 80km south of Matera, would still languish unknown had not writer, painter and political activist Carlo Levi been exiled here in the 1930s during Mussolini's regime. In his extraordinary book *Christ Stopped at Eboli,* Levi graphically describes the aching hardship of peasant life in 'Gagliano' (in reality, Aliano) where 'there is no definite boundary between the world of human beings and that of animals and even monsters'. Today, Aliano is a sleepy town that only seems to come alive late in the afternoon when old men congregate on the park benches in the pleasant tree-lined Via Roma, and black-shrouded women exchange news on the streets.

Castelmezzano. Pietrapertosa literally translates as 'perforated stone' and, indeed, the village sits in the midst of bizarrely shaped rocky towers. Literally carved into the mountainside, its 10th-century **Saracen fortress** is difficult to spot, but once you've located it you won't regret the long climb up. The views are breathtaking.

The Drive 》 After the winding descent from Pietrapertosa, take SS407 to the Tricàrico exit, 29km from Pietrapertosa. You'll notice the peaks of the Dolomiti Lucani disappear in favour of the chalky plains and gorges that define the landscape around Matera.

❽ Tricàrico

Perched on a ridge above the Basento river valley, Tricàrico may not be as dazzlingly odd

as Castelmezzano and Pietrapertosa, but it does have one of the best-preserved medieval cores in Basilicata, with Gothic and Romanesque religious buildings capped by a picturesque Norman tower. Its ramparts also proffer lovely views over the surrounding countryside.

The Drive 》 Head back to the SS407 and continue east along the snaking Bassento river valley, until you see the castle of Migliònico far off on your left. Shortly after, exit the main road onto the SS7 and follow the signs to Matera.

- - - - - - - - - - - - - - -
TRIP HIGHLIGHT

❾ Matera

Haunting and beautiful, Matera's unique *sassi* (districts of cave houses and churches) sprawl below the rim of the steep-

sided Gravina gorge like a giant nativity scene. The houses' rock-grey facades once hid grimy abodes, but in recent years many have being converted into restaurants and swish cave-hotels. Overlooking the *sassi* – divided into the **Sasso Barisano** and **Sasso Caveoso** – the new town is a lively place, with its elegant baroque churches, exquisite Romanesque **cathedral**, and elegant *palazzi* (mansions).

Matera is said to be one of the world's oldest towns, dating back to the Paleolithic Age and continuously inhabited for around 7000 years. The simple natural grottoes that dotted the gorge were adapted to become homes, and an ingenious system of canals regulated the flow of water and sewage. In his great book, *Christ Stopped at Eboli,* Carlo Levi describes the appalling poverty he saw in the city in the 1930s. Such publicity finally galvanised the authorities into action and in the late 1950s about 15,000 inhabitants were forcibly relocated to new government housing schemes. For a fascinating glimpse into Matera's past, search out the **Casa Noha** (📞0835 33 54 52; Recinto Cavone 9; adult/reduced €4/2; ⏰9am-6pm Wed-Sun Apr-Oct, 10am-4.30pm Nov-Mar) in the Sasso Caveoso.

✕ 🛏 p363

Eating & Sleeping

Maratea ❶

✗ Lanterna Rossa   Seafood €€
([☎]0973 87 63 52; Via Arenile, Porto; meals
€40; [🕐]11am-3pm & 7-11.30pm) Head for this
terrace overlooking the port to dine on exquisite
seafood. Highly recommended is the signature
dish, *zuppa di pesce* (fish soup). The Bar del
Porto sits beneath it serving ice cream and
coffee.

🛏 Hotel Villa Cheta Elite   Hotel €€
([☎]0973 87 81 34; www.villacheta.it; Via Timpone
46; r €124-264; [🕐]Apr-Oct; [P][❄][🛜]) Set in an
art nouveau villa at the entrance to the hamlet
of Acquafredda, this hotel is like a piece of plush
Portofino towed several hundred kilometres
south. Enjoy a broad terrace with spectacular
views, a fabulous restaurant and large
rooms where antiques mix seamlessly with
modernities. Bright Mediterranean foliage fills
sun-dappled terraced gardens.

🛏 Locanda delle Donne
Monache   Hotel €€
([☎]0973 87 61 39; www.locandamonache.
com; Via Mazzei 4; r €115-335; [🕐]Apr-Oct;
[P][❄][@][🛜][🏊]) Overlooking the medieval
borgo, this exclusive hotel is in a converted
18th-century convent with a suitably lofty
setting. It's a hotchpotch of vaulted corridors,
terraces and gardens fringed with bougainvillea
and lemon trees. The rooms are elegantly
decorated in pastel shades and – bonus –
there's a panoramic outdoor pool and tempting
offers of cooking classes.

Viggiano ❺

🛏 Hotel dell'Arpa   Hotel €
([☎]0975 31 13 03; www.hoteldellarpa.it; Corso
Giorgio Marconi 34; s/d €62/77; [P][❄][@][🛜])
Sitting conveniently at the foot of historic
Viggiano, this modern hotel is more comfortable
than charming, but most rooms have fantastic
views across the Val d'Agri.

Castelmezzano ❻

✗ Al Becco della Civetta   Ristorante €€
([☎]0971 98 62 49; www.beccodellacivetta.
it; Vico I Maglietta 7; meals €35; [🕐]1-3pm &
8-9.30pm) Don't miss the high-up, authentic
Lucano restaurant Al Becco della Civetta in
Castelmezzano, which serves excellent regional
cuisine based on seasonal local ingredients.
It also offers traditionally furnished, simple
whitewashed rooms (doubles €75 to €105) with
lots of dark wood and fabulous views. Booking
recommended.

Matera ❾

✗ Le Botteghe   Trattoria €
([☎]0835 34 40 72; www.lebotteghematera.it;
Piazza San Pietro Barisano 22; meals €20-30;
[🕐]1-2.30pm & 8-11pm Mon, Sat & Sun, 8-11pm
Tue, Thu & Fri) In Sasso Barisano, this is a
classy but informal restaurant set in arched
whitewashed rooms. Try delicious local
specialities like *fusilli mollica e crusco* (pasta
and fried bread with local sweet peppers).

🛏 Hotel Il Belvedere   Hotel €€
([☎]0835 31 17 02; www.hotelbelvedere.matera.it;
Via Casalnuovo 133; d from €134; [🛜]) Looks can
be deceptive – especially in Matera. This cave
boutique looks unremarkable from its streetside
perch on the edge of the Sasso Caveoso, but
you'll feel your jaw start to drop as you enter
its luxurious entrails and spy the spectacle of
Old Matera sprawling below a jutting terrace.
Cavernous rooms sport mosaics, mood lighting
and curtained four-poster beds.

🛏 Sassi Hotel   Hotel €€
([☎]0835 33 10 09; www.hotelsassi.it; Via San
Giovanni Vecchio 89; s €70, d €94-130; [❄][@])
The first hotel in the *sassi* is set in an 18th-
century rambling edifice in Sasso Barisano with
some rooms in caves and some not. Singles are
small but doubles are gracefully furnished. The
balconies have superb views of the cathedral.

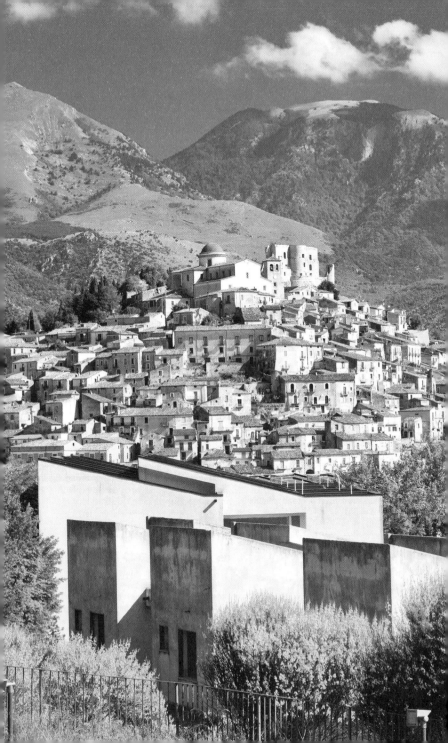

The Calabrian Wilderness

35

From the peaks of the Pollino to the crystalline waters of the Tropea peninsula, this trip immerses you in the natural beauty of Calabria, one of Italy's wildest and least explored regions.

TRIP HIGHLIGHTS

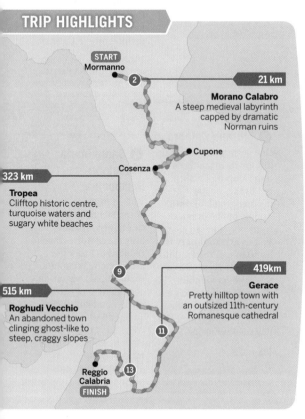

START
Mormanno

2

21 km

Morano Calabro
A steep medieval labyrinth capped by dramatic Norman ruins

● **Cupone**

Cosenza ●

323 km

Tropea
Clifftop historic centre, turquoise waters and sugary white beaches

9

419km

Gerace
Pretty hilltop town with an outsized 11th-century Romanesque cathedral

11

515 km

Roghudi Vecchio
An abandoned town clinging ghost-like to steep, craggy slopes

13

Reggio Calabria
FINISH

8–10 DAYS
606KM / 376 MILES

GREAT FOR...

BEST TIME TO GO

Spring and autumn for sunny weather without summer heat and crowds.

ESSENTIAL PHOTO

Sweeping views of mountains and sea from Capo Vaticano.

BEST FOR OUTDOORS

From Cupone, strike out into the wilds of Calabria's Sila mountain range.

35 The Calabrian Wilderness

From the alpine Pollino to the thickly forested slopes of the Aspromonte, Calabria possesses some of Italy's wildest landscapes. Avoid the overbuilt coast and you'll often have the place to yourself. Plagued by earthquakes, poverty and organised crime, its artistic heritage is limited, yet its rough beauties are gripping. Besides three sprawling national parks, ancient towns grow out of craggy hilltops, while amethyst waters wash Tropea's beaches.

❶ Mormanno

In the heart of the **Parco Nazionale del Pollino** (www.parcopollino.gov.it), this bristling hilltop town of 3000 souls stands guard over the narrow Lao river valley. Mormanno makes a convenient base to explore the peaks and forests of the surrounding national park. Don't miss its prized local lentils, best served in a deliciously simple soup loaded with oregano.

✖ p372

The Drive » Instead of the A3 autostrada, take the pleasant SP241, which winds its way for 21km through forested hills and green valleys as you sneak up on the back side of Morano Calabro.

TRIP HIGHLIGHT

❷ Morano Calabro

One of the most dramatic hill towns in southern Italy, Morano Calabro is a dense, steeply rising medieval labyrinth capped by the dramatic ruins of a **Norman castle**. Just as extraordinary is its setting at the foothills of a dramatic stretch of the Pollino mountain range. Morano makes a good jumping-off point for the beautiful Gole del Raganello canyon.

🛏 p372

The Drive » Head down the A3, dramatically framed by the Pollino mountain range, until you reach the exit for Altomonte, which is about 30km from Morano Calabro. The town itself sits at the end of a series of well-marked country roads, a further 10km away.

❸ Altomonte

The views from this well-preserved hilltop town encompass the snowy heights of the Pollino range, the rich patchwork of farms that cover its foothills and even a glimpse of the blue Mediterranean off to the east. Don't miss the 14th-century **Chiesa di Santa Maria della Consolazione**, one of the finest examples of Gothic architecture in Calabria.

The Drive » For this 51km leg, head back to the A3, then south to the Montalto exit, where you'll then twist and turn along SS559 as you head for Santa Maria Assunta in Sambucina.

❹ Santa Maria Assunta in Sambucina

Tucked in the foothills of the Sila mountains, this once-vast **abbey** has, over the centuries, been reduced to just a few atmospheric remnants, thanks to a devastating combination of earthquakes and landslides. Today, all that is left is a transept of the original church, which incorporates both Romanesque and Gothic elements.

The Drive » Back on the SS559, you will soon wind your way up to the SP247, then along a high plain, where pastureland alternates with pine and oak forests offering a distinct alpine flavour. Signs lead you the 38km to Camigliatello Silano.

❺ Camigliatello Silano

A popular ski-resort town with 6km of trails, Camigliatello Silano looks much better under snow – think Swiss chalets in poured concrete. However, even in the summer it makes a comfortable base to explore the Sila mountains, with their upland meadows, pine and oak forests and well-marked hiking trails.

🍴 🛏 p372

LINK YOUR TRIP

34 Across the Lucanian Apennines

From Mormanno, head north 66km to seaside Maratea to begin your adventure into the beautiful interior of Basilicata.

36 Wonders of Ancient Sicily

From Reggio Calabria sail over to Messina and head 50km south to Taormina to join this fascinating journey into Sicily's ancient past.

DETOUR:
GOLE DEL RAGANELLO

Start: ❷ Morano Calabro (p366)

Located just outside the town of Civita, about 20km east of Morano Calabro, the dramatic gorges carved by the Raganello river are well worth seeking out. In addition to the majesty of their sheer limestone walls, the gorges are also home to rich flora and fauna, from foxes and martens to soaring golden eagles. Note also that the towns in this region still preserve traces of Albanian culture more than five centuries after their ancestors fled to Calabria when Turks invaded Albania.

The Drive ›› As you gently wind you way along the 10km jaunt on the SP250 to Cupone, you will soon see the blue waters of Lago Cecita appear through the trees.

❻ Cupone

Home to the headquarters of the **Parco Nazionale della Sila** (www.parcosila.it), Cupone sits on the edge of pretty, meandering Lago Cecita. Well-marked hikes into the surrounding heights radiate out from here, and there is a helpful **visitors centre** and small **museum** devoted to the local ecology and geology.

The Drive ›› Head back to Camigliatello Silano then catch the SS107, which winds its way down to Cosenza, for a total distance of 43km. The last part of the drive is particularly beautiful.

❼ Cosenza

Though surrounded by uninspiring sprawl, Cosenza's medieval core is one of the best-preserved historic centres in Calabria, one of the few areas to have survived the constant earthquakes that have ravaged the region over the centuries. Its narrow, winding lanes have a gritty feel with their antiquated shopfronts and fading, once-elegant *palazzi* (mansions). Follow **Corso Telesio** and you eventually reach **Piazza XV Marzo**, an appealing square fronted by the Renaissance-style **Palazzo del Governo** and the neoclassical **Teatro Rendano**. Behind the piazza, the lovely **Villa Vecchia** park provides some welcome shade.

✕ ⊨ p372

The Drive ›› Head south on the A3 until you reach sweeping views of the Golfo di Sant'Eufemia. Pizzo sits at its southern end, 90km away.

❽ Pizzo

Stacked high on a sea cliff with sweeping views down to the Tropean peninsula, Pizzo has a distinct ramshackle charm. On its main square, cafes compete to offer the town's best *tartufo,* a death-by-chocolate ice-cream ball. A kilometre north of town, the **Chiesa di Piedigrotta** (€2.50; ⊙9am-1pm & 3-7.30pm, shorter hr winter) is a rock church that was first carved into the tufa rock by Neapolitan shipwreck survivors in the 17th century. It has since been filled with tufa saints as well as less godly figures like Fidel Castro and JFK.

✕ ⊨ p372

The Drive ›› Head 30km south along coastal route SS522, which winds its way through uninspired beach resorts that alternate with farmland.

TRIP HIGHLIGHT

❾ Tropea

Much of the Calabrian coast has been decimated by poorly planned mass development. Tropea is a jewel-like exception. Set on a rocky promontory, the town's small but well-preserved historic centre sits above a sugary, white-sand beach. At sunset, the clear turquoise waters are known to turn garish shades of purple. And don't miss the sweet fire of the region's prized red onions, which come from the surrounding peninsula.

Note that the town's attractions are compromised in high summer by teeming crowds, when parking can become a blood sport.

✗ 🛏 p373

The Drive » It is a lovely drive to Capo Vaticano for 13km along SP22, mostly following the coastline. When you reach the little town of San Nicoló, follow signs to Faro Capo Vaticano.

⑩ Capo Vaticano

Even if you don't have time to explore its beaches, ravines and limestone sea cliffs, stop at this cape on the southwestern corner of the Promontorio di Tropea for its jaw-dropping views. On a clear day, you can see past the Aeolian Islands all the way to Sicily.

The Drive » For this 83km drive, wind your way along the coastal SP23, skirting Rosarno until you reach the SS682. Take this and head across the pretty northern reaches of the Aspromonte to the Ionian coast. Push on south to Locri, from where hilltop Gerace is a short inland hop – follow signs from Via Garibaldi and follow the torturously winding SP1.

TRIP HIGHLIGHT

⑪ Gerace

A spectacular medieval hill town, Gerace is worth a detour for the views alone. On one side lies the Ionian Sea, and on the other the dark, dramatic heights of the Aspromonte mountains. It also boasts Calabria's largest Romanesque **cathedral** (Piazza Tribuna; ☉9.30am-1.30pm & 3-6pm, closed Mon winter), a majestically simple structure that dates from 1045 and incorporates columns pilfered from nearby Roman ruins.

✗ 🛏 p373

The Drive » After heading back down the SP1, turn south on the SS106 which parallels the blue Ionic coast. At the town of Bova Marina, follow signs inland along the sharply twisting road to hilltop Bova. The total distance is 77km.

⑫ Bova

Perched at 900m above sea level, this mountain eyrie possesses a photogenic ruined **castle**, plus stupendous surf-and-turf views that rival Gerace's. Don't miss the bilingual signage – the townspeople are among the few surviving speakers of Griko, a Greek dialect that dates at least to the Byzantine period and possibly to the times when ancient Greeks ruled here.

The Drive » The 19km road from Bova to Roghudi Vecchio boasts the most stunning stretch of driving on this trip, though it's also the most tortuous – and has some pretty rough patches. Note that it's important to ask about road conditions before setting out as roads can be washed out. It may be advisable to skip Roghudi and head straight to Gambarie.

DREADED 'NDRANGHETA

While the Sicilian mafia, known as Cosa Nostra, and Naples' Camorra gets more press, Calabria's 'ndrangheta is one of the world's most feared organised crime networks. EURISPES, an independent Italian think tank, estimated its annual income reached more than €40 billion in 2007, much of it coming from drug trafficking, usury, construction and skimming off public-works contracts. Estimates of its strength vary but the *Guardian* has reported that the loosely organised group, which is cemented by actual family bonds, has up to 7000 members worldwide. The Aspromonte mountains have long served as the group's traditional refuge.

TRIP HIGHLIGHT

⓭ Roghudi Vecchio

The wild, winding ride to Roghudi Vecchio takes you through a stunning stretch of the Aspromonte mountains. This ghostly town clings limpet-like to a steep, craggy slope above an eerily white bed of the Amendolea river, which is formed by limestone washed down from the surrounding peaks. The river is barely a trickle most of the year, but two terrible floods in the 1970s caused the town itself to be abandoned.

Note that the town is still uninhabited and unpoliced, so wandering off the main road is not recommended.

The Drive » On the 59km drive to Gambarie, it's more dramatic switchbacks down to the Amendolea river and back up, past the very poor town of Roccaforte del Greco and eventually back to the SS183, which climbs quickly from the olive trees and cacti of the lower altitudes to pines, oaks and chestnut trees along the flat peaks of the Aspromonte.

⓮ Gambarie

Headquarters of the **Parco Nazionale dell'Aspromonte** (www. parcoaspromonte.gov. it) and the park's largest town, faux-Swiss Gambarie is more convenient than charming. It does make a great base to explore the pine-covered heights that surround it.

This is wonderful walking country, and the park has several colour-coded trails. There is also skiing in winter, with a lift right from the town centre.

🛏 p373

The Drive » It's now time to return to sea level. This 32km leg begins on the SP7 as it winds its way down through the towns of San Stefano and Sant'Alessio in Aspromonte, all the way to the A3. On the way down, gape at the views across the Strait of Messina to Sicily, weather permitting.

⓯ Reggio Calabria

Reggio is the main launching point for ferries to Sicily, which sparkles temptingly across the Strait of Messina. Though the city's grid of dusty streets have the slightly dissolute feel shared by most port cities, Reggio's wide, sea-front promenade, lined with art-deco palaces, is delightful.

The city is also home to what are, probably, the world's finest examples of ancient Greek sculpture: the spectacular **Bronzi di Riace**. Dating from around 450 BC, these two full-sized Greek bronze nudes now reside at the **Museo Nazionale di Reggio Calabria** (📞0965 81 22 55; www.archeocalabria. beniculturali.it; Piazza de Nava 26; adult/reduced €8/6; ⊘9am-8pm Tue-Sun).

✕ 🛏 p373

Capo Vaticano Coastal landscape of limestone sea cliffs, beaches and ravines

Eating & Sleeping

Mormanno ❶

✖ Osteria del Vicolo
Calabrian €

(☎0981 8 04 75; www.osteriadelvicolo.it; Vico Primo San Francesco 5; meals €25; ⊗noon-3pm & 7.30-11.30pm Thu-Tue) Follow signs from Mormanno's church to this humble but much-lauded eatery. The menu stars the region's highly prized lentils, which accompany local grilled meats, form the base for pasta sauce, or come infused with oregano in a divinely simple soup. There's also wood-fired pizza in the evenings. The family runs a B&B nearby, too.

Morano Calabro ❷

🛏 Albergo Villa San Domenico
Hotel €€

(☎0981 39 99 91; www.albergovillasandomenico.it; Via Sotto gli Olmi; s/d/tr/q €80/110/135/160; ᴘ❄🛜) This handsome four-star hotel occupies an 18th-century palace that sits picturesquely next to Santa Magdalena church at the foot of the old town. Rooms are furnished in traditional style, but fitted out with all the modern comforts.

Camigliatello Silano ❺

✖ La Tavernetta
Calabrian €€€

(☎0984 57 90 26; www.latavernetta.info; Campo San Lorenzo 14; meals €50; ⊗12.30-2.30pm & 7.45-10pm Tue-Sun) Among Calabria's best eats, La Tavernetta marries rough country charm with citified elegance in warmly colourful dining rooms. The food is first-rate and based on the best local ingredients, from wild anise seed and mushrooms to mountain-raised lamb and kid. Reserve ahead on Sundays and holidays.

🛏 Albergo San Lorenzo
Hotel €

(☎0984 57 08 09; www.sanlorenzosialberga.it; Campo San Lorenzo 14; d €80-110, tr €110-130, q €130-160; ᴘ❄🛜) Above their famous restaurant, the owners of La Tavernetta have opened the area's most stylish sleep, with 21 large, well-equipped rooms done up in colourful, modernist style.

Cosenza ❼

✖ Ristorante Calabria Bella
Calabrian €€

(☎0984 79 35 31; www.ristorantecalabriabella.it; Piazza del Duomo 20; meals €25; ⊗noon-3pm & 7pm-midnight) Traditional Calabrian cuisine, such as homemade pasta with sausage and porcini mushrooms, and *grigliata mista di carne* (mixed grilled meats), is regularly dished up at this cosy restaurant in the old town.

🛏 Royal Hotel
Hotel €

(☎0984 41 21 65; www.hotelroyalsas.it; Via delle Medaglie d'Oro 1; s/d/t €64/79/84; ᴘ❄🛜) Probably the best all-round hotel, the four-star Royal is a short stroll from Corso Mazzini right in the heart of town. Rooms are fresh and businesslike, if a little bland.

Pizzo ❽

✖ Bar Gelateria Ercole
Gelateria €

(☎0963 53 11 49; www.barercole.com; Piazza della Repubblica; tartufo €5; ⊗8am-midnight Thu-Tue) Pizzo enjoys something of a reputation for its gelato, and, on the main square, Ercole is reckoned by many to serve the best in town. The most admired flavours include *tartufo* (chocolate and hazelnut) and *cassata* (egg cream with candied fruit).

🛏 Piccolo Grand Hotel
Boutique Hotel €€

(☎0963 53 32 93; www.piccolograndhotel.com; Via Leoluca Chiaravalloti 32; s €95-110, d €138-173; ❄🛜) This shining four-star boutique hotel is hidden on an unlikely and rather dingy side street. But its exuberant blue-and-white design, upscale comforts and panoramic rooftop breakfasts make it one of the town's top sleeps.

Tropea ➒

✗ Pimm's   Seafood €€

(☎0963 66 61 05; Largo Migliarese; meals
€40-45; ☺noon-2.30pm & 7-11pm) Set on the
lip of Tropea's stunning cliffs, Pimm's serves
up simple but excellent local seafood, as well
as wonderful salads starring the town's prized
red onions. Adding to the experience are the
memorable beach views from the panoramic
terrace.

🛏 Donnaciccina   B&B €€

(☎0963 6 21 80; www.donnaciccina.com; Via
Pelliccia 9; s €55-120, d €70-170, apt €112-240;
❄ @ 🛜) Overlooking the main corso, this
delightful B&B has retained a tangible sense
of history with its carefully selected antiques,
canopy beds and terracotta tiled floors. There's
also a self-catering apartment perfectly
positioned on the cliff overlooking the sea, and a
chatty parrot in reception.

🛏 Residenza il Barone   B&B €€

(☎0963 60 71 81; www.residenzailbarone.
it; Largo Barone; ste €70-200; ❄ @ 🛜) This
graceful palazzo has six suites decorated in
masculine neutrals and tobacco browns, with
dramatic modern paintings by the owner's
brother adding pizzazz to the walls. There's
a computer in each suite and you can eat
breakfast on the small roof terrace with views
over the old city and out to sea.

Gerace ➓

✗ Ristorante a Squella   Calabrian €

(☎0964 35 60 86; Viale della Resistenza 8;
meals €20-25; ☺12.30-2.30pm & 7.30-11pm)
For a taste of traditional Calabrian cooking,
modest, welcoming Ristorante a Squella makes
for a great lunchtime stop. It serves reliably
good dishes, specialising in seafood and pizzas.
Afterwards you can wander down the road and
admire the views.

🛏 La Casa di Gianna   Hotel €€

(☎0964 35 50 18; www.lacasadigianna.it; Via
Paola Frascà 4; d €110-130; ❄ 🛜) Halfway
between mountains and sea in the heart of

Gerace, this stately four-star has eight simple
rooms, decorated with elegant, antique-style
furniture and old prints. It also boasts an
excellent in-house restaurant serving both meat
and seafood with aplomb.

Gambarie ⓮

🛏 Hotel Miramonti   Hotel €

(☎0965 74 31 90; www.
hotelmiramontigambarie.it; Via degli Sci 10; d
€80-90; ❄ @ 🛜 🏊) A few hundred metres
uphill from the main square, the Miramonti
provides all the necessary comforts, steps from
the ski lifts. Rooms are modest and basically
furnished, and the restaurant serves hearty
mountain fare, including soups and stews,
mountain-grown meats, and first-rate local
cheeses.

Reggio Calabria ⓯

✗ Cèsare   Gelateria €

(Piazza Indipendenza 2; gelato from €2.40;
☺6am-1am) The most popular gelateria in
town is in a modest green kiosk at the end of
the lungomare (seafront promenade). Try the
Kinder Egg flavour.

✗ La Cantina del
Macellaio   Trattoria €€

(☎0965 2 39 32; www.lacantinadelmacellaio.
com; Via Arcovito 26; meals from €25; ☺7.30-
11.30pm Mon-Sat, noon-3pm & 8-11pm Sun)
One of the best restaurants in Calabria with
epic risotto (with apple and almonds!), ragù
(meat-and-tomato sauce) and grilled veal. The
mostly Calabrian wines are equally impressive,
as is the service.

🛏 B&B Casa Blanca   B&B €

(☎347 945 92 10; www.bbcasablanca.it; Via
Arcovito 24; s €45-60, d €65-90, apt €90-120;
🅿 ❄ 🛜) A little gem in Reggio's heart, this
19th-century palazzo has spacious rooms
gracefully furnished with romantic white-on-
white decor. There's a self-serve breakfast
nook, a small breakfast table in each room and
two apartments available. Great choice.

Wonders of Ancient Sicily

36

More than a trip around la bella Sicilia, this is also a journey through time, from spare Greek temples to Norman churches decked out with Arab and Byzantine finery.

TRIP HIGHLIGHTS

82 km

Segesta
A huge 5th-century-BC Greek temple amidst desolate mountains

664 km

Taormina
Marvel at the ancient Greek theatre suspended between sea and sky

318 km

Agrigento
Pay homage to this extraordinary complex of five Doric temples

545 km

Syracuse
Extraordinary tapestry of Greek ruins, baroque piazzas and medieval lanes

---

12–14 DAYS
664KM / 412 MILES

GREAT FOR...

BEST TIME TO GO

Spring and autumn are best. Avoid the heat and crowds of high summer.

ESSENTIAL PHOTO

Mt Etna from Taormina's Greek theatre.

BEST FOR HISTORY

Explore layer upon layer of Sicily's past in glorious Syracuse.

---

esta Ruins of the Doric temple

Classic Trip

36 Wonders of Ancient Sicily

A Mediterranean crossroads for 25 centuries, Sicily is heir to an unparalleled cultural legacy, from the temples of Magna Graecia to Norman churches made kaleidoscopic by Byzantine and Arab craftsmen. This trip takes you from exotic, palm-fanned Palermo to the baroque splendours of Syracuse and Catania. On the way, you'll also experience Sicily's startlingly diverse landscape, including bucolic farmland, smouldering volcanoes and long stretches of aquamarine coastline.

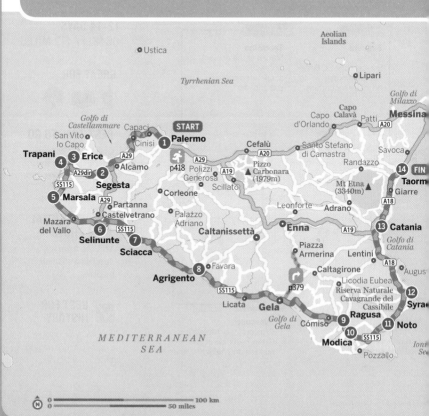

① Palermo

Palermo is a fascinating conglomeration of splendour and decay. Unlike Florence or Rome, many of its treasures are hidden rather than scrubbed up for endless streams of tourists. The evocative history of the city infuses its daily life, lending its dusty backstreet markets a distinct Middle Eastern feel and its architecture a unique East-meets-West look.

A trading port since Phoenician times, the city, which is best explored on foot (p418), first came to prominence as capital of Arab Sicily in the 9th century AD. When the Normans rode into town in the 11th century, they used Arab know-how to turn it into Christendom's richest and most sophisti-

LINK YOUR TRIP

35 The Calabrian Wilderness

To experience the wild peaks of the Pollino head via Messina to Reggio Calabria on the mainland.

37 Sicilian Baroque

Branch off at Ragusa to join this tour of Sicily's Unesco-listed baroque towns.

cated city. The **Cappella Palatina** (Palatine Chapel; www.federicosecondo.org; Piazza Indipendenza; adult/reduced Fri-Mon €8.50/6.50, Tue-Thu €7/5; ☻9am-5pm Mon-Sat, 8.30-9.40am & 11.15am-1pm Sun) is the perfect expression of this marriage, with its gold-inflected Byzantine mosaics crowned by a honeycomb *muqarnas* ceiling – a masterpiece of Arab craftsmanship.

For an insight into Sicily's long and turbulent past, the **Museo Archeologico Regionale** (☎091 611 68 07; www.regione.sicilia.it/beniculturali/salinas; Piazza Olivella 24; ☻9.30am-6.30pm Tue-Fri, to 1pm Sat & Sun) houses some of the island's most valuable Greek and Roman artefacts.

✗ 🛏 p384

The Drive » From Palermo the 82km trip to Segesta starts along the fast-moving A29 as it skirts the mountains west of Palermo, then runs along agricultural plains until you reach the hills of Segesta. The Greek ruins lie just off the A29dir.

TRIP HIGHLIGHT

② Segesta

Set on the edge of a deep canyon in the midst of desolate mountains, the 5th-century-BC ruins of **Segesta** (☎0924 95 23 56; adult/reduced €6/3; ☻9am-7.30pm Apr-Sep, 9am-1hr before sunset Oct-Mar) are a magical site. The city, founded by

the ancient Elymians, was in constant conflict with Selinunte, whose destruction it sought with dogged determination and singular success. Time, however, has done to Segesta what violence inflicted on Selinunte; little remains now, save the theatre and the never-completed Doric temple. The latter dates from around 430 BC and is remarkably well preserved. On windy days its 36 giant columns are said to act like an organ, producing mysterious notes.

The Drive » Keep heading along A29dir through a patchwork of green and ochre fields and follow signs for the 40km to Trapani. As you reach its outskirts, you'll head up the very windy SP3 to Erice, with great views of countryside and sea.

③ Erice

A spectacular hill town, Erice combines medieval charm with astounding 360-degree views from atop the legendary **Mt Eryx** (750m) – on a clear day, you can see as far as Cape Bon in Tunisia. Wander the medieval streets interspersed with churches, forts and tiny cobbled piazzas. Little remains from its ancient past, though as a centre for the cult of Venus, it has a seductive history.

The best views can be had from the **Giardino del Balio**, which

Classic Trip

overlooks the rugged turrets and wooded hillsides down to the saltpans of Trapani and the sea. Adjacent to the gardens is the Norman **Castello di Venere** (☎366 6712832; www.fondazioneericearte. org/castellodivenere.php; Via Castello di Venere; adult/reduced €4/2; ⏱10am-1hr before sunset daily Apr-Oct, 10am-4pm Sat, Sun & holidays Nov-Mar), built in the 12th and 13th centuries over the ancient Temple of Venus.

🛏p384

The Drive ⟩⟩ For the 12km to Trapani, it's back down the switchbacks of the SP3.

- - - - - - - - - -

❹ Trapani

Once a key link in a powerful trading network that stretched from Carthage to Venice, Trapani occupies a sickle-shaped spit of land that hugs its ancient harbour. Although Trapani's industrial outskirts are rather bleak, its historic centre is filled with atmospheric pedestrian streets and some lovely churches and baroque buildings. The narrow network of streets remains a Moorish labyrinth, although it takes much of its character from the fabulous 18th-century baroque of the Spanish period.

🍴 p384

The Drive ⟩⟩ For the 33km trip from Trapani to Marsala, head south on the SS115. Small towns alternate with farmland until you reach Marsala on Sicily's west coast.

- - - - - - - - - -

❺ Marsala

Best known for its eponymous sweet dessert wines, Marsala is an elegant town of stately baroque buildings within a perfect square of city walls. Founded by Phoenicians escaping Roman attacks, the city still has remnants of the 7m-thick ramparts they built, ensuring that it was the last Punic settlement to fall to the Romans.

Marsala's finest treasure is the partially reconstructed remains of a Carthaginian _liburna_ (warship) – the only remaining physical evidence of the Phoenicians' seafaring superiority in the 3rd century BC. You can visit it at the **Museo Archeologico Baglio Anselmi** (☎0923 95 25 35; Lungomare Boeo 30; adult/reduced €4/2; ⏱9am-7.30pm Tue-Sat, to 1.30pm Sun & Mon).

🍴 p384

The Drive ⟩⟩ For this 52km leg, once again head down the SS115, passing through farmland and scattered towns until you reach the A29. Continue on the autostrada to Castelvetrano, then follow the SS115 and SS115dir for the last leg through orchards and fields to seaside Selinunte.

❻ Selinunte

Built on a promontory overlooking the sea, the Greek **ruins of Selinunte** (☎0924 4 62 77; adult/reduced €6/3; ⏱9am-6pm Apr-Oct, to 5pm Nov-Mar) are among the most impressive in Sicily, dating to around the 7th century BC. There are few historical records of the city, which was once one of the world's most powerful, and even the names of the various temples have been forgotten and are now identified by letters. The most impressive, **Temple E**, has been partially rebuilt, its columns pieced together from their fragments with part of its tympanum. Many of the carvings, which are on a par with the Parthenon marbles, particularly those from **Temple C**, are now in Palermo's archaeological museum.

The Drive ⟩⟩ Head back up to the SS115 and past a series of hills and plains for the 37km trip to Sciacca.

- - - - - - - - - -

❼ Sciacca

Seaside Sciacca was founded in the 5th century BC as a thermal resort for nearby Selinunte. Its healing waters still attract visitors, who come to wallow in the sulphurous vapours and mineral-rich mud. Spas and thermal cures apart, it's a laid-back town with an attractive medieval core and some excellent seafood restaurants.

The Drive » Continue eastwards on the SS115 as it follows the southern coast onto Porto Empedocle and then, 10km inland, Agrigento's hilltop centre. In all, it's about 62km.

8 Agrigento

Seen from a distance, Agrigento's unsightly apartment blocks loom incongruously on the hillside, distracting attention from the splendid Valley of Temples below. In the Valley, the mesmerising **ruins** (Valle dei Templi; www.parcovalledeitempli.it; adult/reduced €10/5, incl Museo Archeologico €13.50/7; ☺8.30am-7pm year-round, plus 7.30-9.30pm Mon-Fri, 7.30-11.30pm Sat & Sun Jul–early Sep) of ancient Akragas boast the best-preserved Doric temples outside of Greece.

The ruins are spread over a 1300-hectare site which is divided into eastern and western halves. Head first to the eastern zone, where you'll find the three best temples: the **Tempio di Hera** (aka the Tempio di Giunone), **Tempio di Ercole** and, most spectacularly, the **Tempio della Concordia** (Temple of Concord). This, the only temple to survive relatively intact, was built around 440 BC and was converted into a Christian church in the 6th century.

Uphill from the ruins, Agrigento's **medieval cen-**tre also has its charms, with a 14th-century cathedral and a number of medieval and baroque buildings.

 p384

The Drive » For this 133km leg head back to the SS115, which veers from inland farmland to brief encounters with the sea. Past the town of Gela, you will head into more hilly country, including a steep climb past Comiso, followed by a straight shot along the SP52 to Ragusa.

9 Ragusa

Set amid the rocky peaks northwest of Modica, Ragusa has two faces. Atop the hill sits **Ragusa Superiore**, a busy town with all the trappings of a modern provincial capital, while etched into the hillside is **Ragusa Ibla**. This sloping area of tangled alleyways, grey stone houses and baroque *palazzi* (mansions) is Ragusa's magnificent historic centre.

Like other towns in the region, Ragusa Ibla collapsed after the 1693 earthquake. But the aristocracy, ever impractical, rebuilt their homes on exactly the same spot. Grand baroque churches and *palazzi* line the twisting, narrow lanes, which then open suddenly onto sun-drenched piazzas. Palm-planted Piazza del Duomo, the centre of town, is dominated by the 18th-century baroque **Cattedrale di San Giorgio** (Piazza Duomo; ☺10am-12.30pm & 4-7pm Jun-Sep, reduced hours rest of year), with its magnificent neoclassical dome and stained-glass windows.

p393

The Drive » Follow the SS115 for this winding, up-and-down 15km drive through rock-littered hilltops to Modica.

DETOUR: VILLA ROMANA DEL CASALE

Start: 8 Agrigento

Near the town of Piazza Armerina in central Sicily, the stunning 3rd-century Roman **Villa Romana del Casale** (☎0935 68 00 36; www.villaromanadelcasale.it; adult/reduced €10/5; ☺9am-6pm Apr-Oct, to 4pm Nov-Mar) is thought to have been the country retreat of Diocletian's co-emperor Marcus Aurelius Maximianus. Buried under mud in a 12th-century flood, the villa remained hidden for 700 years before its floor mosaics – considered some of the finest in existence – were discovered in the 1950s. They cover almost the entire villa floor and are considered unique for their natural, narrative style.

Classic Trip

WHY THIS IS A CLASSIC TRIP
DUNCAN GARWOOD, WRITER

Sicily boasts some of the most spectacular artistic and archaeological treasures you've never heard of. The great Greek ruins of Agrigento and Syracuse might be on many travellers' radars but what about Palermo's Cappella Palatina or Noto's flamboyant baroque streets? These masterpieces are all the more rewarding for being so unexpected, and go to make this round-island trip an amazing and unforgettable experience.

Top: Looking from Trapani across the Tyrrhenian Sea to Mt Eryx and the hilltop town of Erice
Left: Porta Reale, Corso Vittorio Emanuele, Noto
Right: Chiesa di San Giorgio, Modica

IMAGESEF/SHUTTERSTOCK ©

⑩ Modica

Modica is a wonderfully atmospheric town with medieval buildings climbing steeply up either side of a deep gorge. But unlike some of the other Unesco-listed cities in the area, it doesn't package its treasures into a single easy-to-see street or central piazza: rather, they are spread around the town and take some discovering. The highlight has to be the baroque **Chiesa di San Giorgio** (Corso San Giorgio, Modica Alta; ⊘ 8am-12.30pm & 3.30-6.30pm), which stands in isolated splendour atop a majestic 250-step staircase.

Corso Umberto I is the place to lap up the lively local atmosphere. A wide avenue flanked by graceful palaces, churches, restaurants, bars and boutiques, it is where the locals come to parade during the *passeggiata* (evening stroll). Originally a raging river flowed through town, but after major flood damage in 1902 it was dammed and Corso Umberto was built over it.

🛏 p385, p393

The Drive » Head back onto the SS115, which becomes quite twisty as you close in on Noto, 40km away.

⑪ Noto

Flattened in 1693 by an earthquake, Noto was rebuilt quickly and grandly, and its golden-hued sandstone buildings make it the finest baroque town in Sicily, especially impressive at night when illuminations accentuate its intricately carved facades. The *pièce de résistance* is **Corso Vittorio Emanuele**, an elegantly manicured walkway flanked by thrilling baroque *palazzi* and churches.

Just off Corso Vittorio Emanuele, **Palazzo Nicolaci di Villadorata** (☎338 7427022; www.comune.noto.sr.it/palazzo-nicolaci; Via Corrado Nicolaci; €4; ☉10am-1.30pm & 2.30-7pm) reveals the luxury to which

THE 1693 EARTHQUAKE

On 11 January 1693, a devastating, 7.4-magnitude earthquake hit southeastern Sicily, destroying buildings from Catania to Ragusa. The destruction was terrible, but it also created a blank palette for architects to rebuild the region's cities and towns out of whole cloth, in the latest style and according to rational urban planning – a phenomenon practically unheard of since ancient times. In fact, the earthquake ushered in an entirely new architectural style known as Sicilian baroque, defined by its seductive curves and elaborate detail, which you can see on display in Ragusa, Modica, Catania and many other cities in the region.

the local nobility were accustomed. The decor is as opulent as the facade, with heavy glass chandeliers, frescoed ceilings and crafty wall paintings designed to look like brocaded wallpaper.

✕ p385, p393

The Drive ≫ The 39km drive to Syracuse from Noto takes you down the SP59 and then northeast on the A18, past the majestic Riserva Naturale Cavagrande del Cassibile as you parallel Sicily's eastern coast.

TRIP HIGHLIGHT

⑫ Syracuse

Encapsulating Sicily's timeless beauty, Syracuse is a dense tapestry of overlapping cultures and civilisations. Ancient Greek ruins rise out of lush citrus orchards, cafe tables spill out onto baroque piazzas, and medieval lanes meander to the sea. Your visit, like the city itself, can be split into two easy parts: one

dedicated to the archaeological site, the other to Ortygia, the ancient island neighbourhood connected to the modern town by bridge.

It's difficult to imagine now but in its heyday Syracuse was the largest city in the ancient world, bigger even than Athens and Corinth. The **Parco Archeologico della Neapolis** (☎0931 6 62 06; Viale Paradiso 14; adult/reduced €10/5, incl Museo Archeologico €13.50/7; ☉8.30am-1.45pm Mon, last entry 12.45pm, 8.30am-7.30pm Tue-Sun, last entry 6pm) is home to a staggering number of well-preserved Greek (and Roman) remains, with the remarkably intact 5th-century-BC **Teatro Greco** as the main attraction. In the grounds of Villa Landolina, about 500m east of the archaeological park, is the **Museo Archeologico Paolo Orsi** (☎0931 48 95 11; www.regione.sicilia.it/beniculturali/museopaoloorsi; Viale Teocrito 66; adult/reduced €8/4, incl Parco Archeologico €13.50/7; ☉9am-6pm Tue-Sat, to 1pm Sun).

Despite the labyrinthine streets, it is hard to get lost on **Ortygia**, since it measures less than 1 sq km. And yet it also manages to encompass 25 centuries of history. At its heart, the city's 7th-century **Duomo** (Piazza del Duomo; adult/reduced €2/1; ☉9am-6.30pm Mon-Sat Apr-Oct, to 5.30pm Nov-Mar) lords it over Piazza del Duomo, one of Sicily's loveliest public spaces. The cathedral was built over a pre-existing 5th-century-BC Greek temple, incorporating most of the original Doric columns in its three-aisled structure. The sumptuous baroque facade was added in the 18th century.

✗ 🛏 p385, p393

The Drive ›› From Syracuse to Catania, it is a 66km drive north along the A18. This is orange-growing country and you will see many orchards, which can be gorgeously fragrant when in bloom.

⓭ Catania

Catania is a true city of the volcano, much of it constructed from the lava that poured down on it during a 1669 eruption. The baroque centre is lava-black in colour, as if a fine dusting of soot permanently covers its elegant buildings, most of which are the work of Giovanni Vaccarini. The 18th-century architect almost single-handedly re-

built the civic centre into an elegant, modern city of spacious boulevards and set-piece piazzas.

Long buried under lava, the **Graeco-Roman Theatre & Odeon** (📞095 715 05 08; Via Vittorio Emanuele II 262; adult/reduced incl Casa Liberti €6/3; 🕑9am-7pm Mon-Sat, to 1.30pm Sun) remind you that the city's history goes back much further. Picturesquely sited in a crumbling residential area, the ruins are occasionally brightened by laundry flapping on the rooftops of vine-covered buildings that appear to have sprouted organically from the half-submerged stage.

✗ p385, p393

The Drive ›› The 53km drive to Taormina along the A18 is a coast-hugging northern run, taking in more orange groves as well as glimpses of the sparkling Ionian Sea.

TRIP HIGHLIGHT

⓮ Taormina

Over the centuries, Taormina has seduced

an exhaustive line of writers and artists, from Goethe to DH Lawrence. The main reason for their swooning? The perfect horseshoe-shaped **Teatro Greco** (📞0942 2 32 20; Via Teatro Greco; adult/reduced €10/5; 🕑9am-1hr before sunset), suspended between sea and sky, with glorious views to brooding Mt Etna through the broken columns. Built in the 3rd century BC, the *teatro* is the most dramatically situated Greek theatre in the world and the second largest in Sicily (after Syracuse).

The 9th-century capital of Byzantine Sicily, Taormina also boasts a well-preserved, if touristy, medieval town – and gorgeous views up and down the Strait of Messina.

✗ 🛏 p385

Eating & Sleeping

Palermo ❶

🍴 Trattoria Ai Cascinari   Sicilian €

(☎091 651 98 04; Via d'Ossuna 43/45; meals €20-25; ⏰12.30-2.30pm Tue-Sun, plus 8-10.30pm Wed-Sat) Yes, it's a bit out of the way, but Ai Cascinari, 1km north of the Cappella Palatina, is a long-standing Palermitan favourite, and deservedly so. It's especially enjoyable on Sunday afternoons, when locals pack the labyrinth of back rooms and waiters perambulate non-stop with plates of scrumptious seasonal antipasti, fresh seafood and desserts from Palermo's beloved Cappello and Scimone *pasticcerie* (pastry shops).

🛏 Butera 28   Apartment €€

(☎333 3165432; www.butera28.it; Via Butera 28; apt per day €60-200, per week €400-1320; ✻🛜) Delightful multilingual owner Nicoletta rents 11 comfortable apartments in the 18th-century Palazzo Lanzi Tomasi, the last home of Giuseppe Tomasi di Lampedusa, author of *The Leopard*. Units range from 30 to 180 sq metres, most sleeping a family of four or more. Four apartments face the sea, most have laundry facilities and all have well-equipped kitchens.

Erice ❸

🛏 Hotel Elimo   Hotel €€

(☎0923 86 93 77; www.hotelelimo.it; Via Vittorio Emanuele 75; s €80-110, d €90-130, ste €150-170; ✻🛜) Communal spaces at this atmospheric historic house are filled with tiled beams, marble fireplaces, intriguing art, knick-knacks and antiques. The bedrooms are more mainstream, although many (along with the hotel terrace and restaurant) have breathtaking vistas south and west towards the Saline di Trapani, the Egadi Islands and the shimmering sea.

Trapani ❹

🍴 Osteria La Bettolaccia   Sicilian €€

(☎0923 2 16 95; www.labettolaccia.it; Via Enrico Fardella 25; meals €35-45; ⏰12.45-3pm Mon-Fri, plus 7.45-11pm Mon-Sat) Unwaveringly authentic, this Slow Food favourite just two blocks from the ferry terminal is the perfect place to try *cous cous con zuppa di mare* (couscous with mixed seafood in a spicy fish sauce, with tomatoes, garlic and parsley). Even with its newly expanded dining room, it can still fill up, so book ahead.

Marsala ❺

🍴 Il Gallo e l'Innamorata   Sicilian €€

(☎0923 195 44 46; www.osteriailgalloelinnamorata.com; Via Bilardello 18; meals €25-35; ⏰12.30-2.30pm & 7.30-10.30pm Tue-Sun) Warm-orange walls and arched stone doorways lend an artsy, convivial atmosphere to this Slow Food–acclaimed eatery. The à la carte menu features a few well-chosen dishes each day, including the classic *scaloppine al Marsala* (veal cooked with Marsala wine and lemon).

Agrigento ❽

🍴 Kalòs   Modern Sicilian €€

(☎0922 2 63 89; www.facebook.com/ristorante.kalos; Piazzetta San Calogero; meals €30-45; ⏰12.30-3pm & 7-11pm Tue-Sun) For fine dining, head to this 'smart' restaurant just outside the historic centre. Five cute tables on little balconies offer a delightful setting to enjoy homemade pasta *all'agrigentina* (with fresh tomatoes, basil and almonds), citrus shrimp or *spada gratinata* (baked swordfish covered in breadcrumbs). Superb desserts, including homemade *cannoli* (pastry shells with a sweet filling) and almond *semifreddi*, round out the menu.

🛏 PortAtenea   B&B €

(☎349 0937492; www.portatenea.com; Via Atenea, cnr Via C Battisti; s €35-50, d €50-75, tr

€70-95; ❄ 📶) This five-room B&B wins plaudits for its panoramic roof terrace overlooking the Valley of the Temples, and its convenient location at the entrance to the old town, five minutes' walk from the train and bus stations. Best of all is the generous advice about Agrigento offered by hosts Sandra and Filippo (witness Filippo's amazing Google Earth tour of nearby beaches!).

Modica ⑩ see also p393

🛏 Villa Quartarella   Agriturismo €

(📞360 654829; www.quartarella.com; Contrada Quartarella Passo Cane 1; s €40, d €75-80, tr €85-100, q €90-120; 🅿 ❄ 📶 ♿) Spacious rooms, welcoming hosts and ample breakfasts make this converted villa in the countryside south of Modica an appealing choice for anyone travelling by car. Owners Francesco and Francesca are generous in sharing their love and encyclopedic knowledge of local history, flora and fauna and can suggest a multitude of driving itineraries.

Noto ⑪ see also p393

🍴 Ristorante Il Cantuccio   Modern Sicilian €€

(📞0931 83 74 64; www.ristoranteilcantuccio. it; Via Cavour 12; meals €32-36; 🕐12.30-2pm & 7.45-10.30pm Tue-Sun) Tucked into the courtyard of a former noble's palace, this inviting restaurant combines familiar Sicilian ingredients in inspired ways. Perennial favourites such as the exquisite *gnocchi al pesto del Cantuccio* (ricotta-potato dumplings with basil, parsley, mint, capers, toasted almonds and cherry tomatoes) are complemented by seasonally changing specials such as lemon-stuffed bass with orange-fennel salad or white-wine-stewed rabbit with *caponata*.

Syracuse ⑫ see also p393

🍴 Bistrot Bella Vita   Italian €€

(📞0931 46 49 38; Via Gargallo 60; sweets €1.50, meals €25; 🕐 cafe 7.30am-midnight, restaurant noon-2.30pm & 7-10.45pm Tue-Sun) This casually elegant cafe-restaurant is one of Ortygia's rising stars. Stop by for good coffee (soy milk available) and made-from-scratch *cornetti, biscotti* and pastries (try the sour orange-and-almond tart). Or book a table in the intimate back dining room, where local, organic produce drives beautifully textured, technically impressive dishes.

🛏 Villa dei Papiri   Agriturismo €

(📞0931 72 13 21; www.villadeipapiri.it; Traversa Cozzo Pantano Testa Pisima 2/c; d €48-108, 2-person ste €68-128, 4-person ste €98-158; 🅿 ❄ 📶) Immersed in an Eden of orange groves and papyrus reeds 8km outside Syracuse, this lovely *agriturismo* sits next to the Fonte Ciana spring immortalised in Ovid's *Metamorphosis*. Eight suites are housed in a beautifully converted 19th-century farmhouse, with 16 double rooms dotted around the lush grounds. Breakfast is an extra €7.50 and served in a baronial stone-walled hall.

Catania ⑬ see also p393

🍴 Trattoria di De Fiore   Trattoria €

(📞095 31 62 83; Via Coppola 24/26; meals €15-25; 🕐7pm-12.30am Mon, 1pm-12.30am Tue-Sun) For over 50 years, septuagenarian chef Rosanna has been recreating her great-grandmother's recipes, including the best *pasta alla Norma* you'll taste anywhere in Sicily. Service can be excruciatingly slow, but for patient souls this is a rare chance to experience classic Catanian cooking from a bygone era. Don't miss Rosanna's trademark *zeppoline* (sugar-sprinkled ricotta-lemon fritters) at dessert time.

Taormina ⑭

🍴 Osteria Nero D'Avola   Sicilian €€

(📞0942 62 88 74; www.osterianerodavola. it; Piazza San Domenico 2b; meals €32-47; 🕐12.30-3pm & 7-11pm Tue-Sun Sep-Jun, 7pm-midnight Jul & Aug) Not only does affable owner Turi Siligato fish, hunt and forage for his smart *osteria*, he'll probably share anecdotes about the day's bounty and play a few tunes on the piano. Here, seasonality, local producers and passion underscore dishes like the signature *cannolo di limone Interdonato* (thinly sliced Interdonato lemon with roe, tuna, tomato and chives).

🛏 Hotel Villa Belvedere   Hotel €€€

(📞0942 2 37 91; www.villabelvedere.it; Via Bagnoli Croce 79; s €70-280, d €80-380, ste €120-450; 🕐Mar–late-Nov; ❄ @ 📶 ♿) Built in 1902, Villa Belvedere was one of Taormina's original grand hotels. Well-positioned with fabulous views and luxuriant gardens, its highlights include a swimming pool complete with century-old palm. Rooms offer neutral hues and understated style. Parking is an extra €16 per day.

Sicilian Baroque

37

From the sparkling blue waters of the Ionian Sea to the hills and gorges of the interior, this trip stars a series of Unesco-listed towns that showcase Sicily's version of baroque grandeur.

TRIP HIGHLIGHTS

56 km

Syracuse
Besides Greek ruins, Syracuse features masterly baroque town planning

77 km

Modica
Ancient buildings climb up either side of a deep gorge

FINISH

Ragusa
Labyrinthine lanes, rock-grey *palazzi* and sun-drenched piazzas

213 km

Noto
Sicily's finest baroque town, carved from golden sandstone

138 km

5 DAYS
213KM / 132 MILES

GREAT FOR...

BEST TIME TO GO

Spring and autumn bring fewer crowds and better weather for hiking in the hillsides of the Monti Iblei.

ESSENTIAL PHOTO

A night-time shot of Noto's Corso Vittorio Emanuele.

BEST FOR HISTORY

Wander the labyrinthine lanes of Ragusa Ibla.

Sicilian Baroque

Dominated by the Monti Iblei hills, this journey through Sicily's southeast takes you to some of the island's most beautiful towns. Shattered by a devastating earthquake in 1693, they were rebuilt in Sicily's own brand of baroque, lending the region a rare, honey-coloured cohesion and collective beauty. The towns sit delightfully amid a region of rich citrus and olive groves, and checkerboard fields shot through with limestone cliffs and rocky gorges.

❶ Catania

Though surrounded by ugly urban sprawl, Sicily's second-largest city is a thriving metropolis with a large university and a beautiful, Unesco-listed centre. Brooding on the horizon, snow-capped Mt Etna is a powerful presence, adding a thrilling edge – and a beautiful backdrop – to local life.

Catania is a true city of the volcano and much of its historic core was constructed from lava that poured down Etna's slopes during a massive eruption in 1669. Many of the elegant baroque *palazzi* (mansions) that line its grand set-piece piazzas and spacious boulevards – most of which were designed by architect Giovanni Vaccarini – are a distinctive black and grey colour. The city's grand showpiece square is **Piazza del Duomo**, a striking space centred on a smiling elephant fountain, the **Fontana dell'Elefante**, and overlooked by the city's majestic **Cattedrale di Sant'Agata** (📞095 32 00 44; Piazza del Duomo; ⏰7am-noon & 4-7pm Mon-Sat, 7.30am-12.30pm & 4.30-7pm Sun).

A short hop away, Catania's exuberant fish market, **La Pescheria** (Via Pardo; ⏰7am-2pm Mon-Sat) offers the best show in town as theatrical

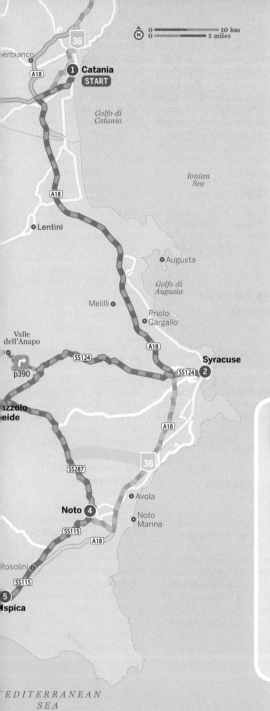

vendors raucously hawk their wares in Sicilian dialect.

 p385, p393

The Drive » From Catania to Syracuse, it is a 66km drive down the A18 autostrada. This is orange-growing country and you'll see many orchards, which are gorgeously fragrant when in bloom. Exit onto the SS124 for the last 4km into central Syracuse.

SOUTHERN ITALY **37** SICILIAN BAROQUE

TRIP HIGHLIGHT

❷ Syracuse

Settled by colonists from Corinth in 734 BC, Syracuse was considered the most beautiful city of the ancient world, rivalling Athens in power and prestige. You can still explore the city's ancient heart at the extraordinary **Parco Archeologico**

LINK YOUR TRIP

Shadow of Vesuvius

From Palermo sail up to Naples, the starting point for this exploration of the Bay of Naples, Vesuvius and Pompeii.

36 **Wonders of Ancient Sicily**

In Catania, you can join the grand tour of Ancient Sicily, which begins in Arab-inflected Palermo and ends at Taormina's spectacular Greek theatre.

della Neapolis (📞0931
6 62 06; Viale Paradiso 14;
adult/reduced €10/5, incl
Museo Archeologico €13.50/7;
⏰8.30am-1.45pm Mon, last
entry 12.45pm, 8.30am-7.30pm
Tue-Sun, last entry 6pm), the
star attraction of which
is the huge 5th-century-
BC Greek theatre.

In the wake of the 1693
earthquake, Syracuse,
like most cities in the
region, got a baroque
facelift. You can see
a number of baroque
paintings at the **Galleria
Regionale di Palazzo Bel-
lomo** (📞0931 6 95 11; www.
regione.sicilia.it/beniculturali/
palazzobellomo; Via Capodieci
16; adult/reduced €8/4;
⏰9am-7pm Tue-Sat, to 1pm
Sun) but the city's real
baroque masterpiece
is **Piazza del Duomo**, a
marvel of 17th-century
town planning. Look
beneath the baroque
veneer, though, and you
can still see traces of the

city's Greek origins. The
Duomo (Piazza del Duomo;
adult/reduced €2/1; ⏰9am-
6.30pm Mon-Sat Apr-Oct, to
5.30pm Nov-Mar), for example, is gloriously baroque
in style with its sumptu-
ous columned facade, but
built into its structure
are several columns from
a 5th-century-BC temple
to Athena.

✖ 🛏 p385, p393

The Drive » From Syracuse,
head through rolling and
unspoilt countryside along the
SS124 for 42km to Palazzolo
Acreide.

---

❸ Palazzolo Acreide

A charming town of
baroque architecture
and ancient ruins,
Palazzolo Acreide's
focal point is **Piazza
del Popolo**, a striking
square dominated by the
ornate bulk of the **Chiesa**

di San Sebastiano and
Palazzo Municipale, an
impressive town hall. A
20-minute uphill walk
from Piazza del Popolo
leads to the archaeologi-
cal park of **Akrai** (📞0931
87 66 02; Colle dell'Acromonte;
€4; ⏰9am-6.30pm Apr-Oct,
to 3.30pm Mon-Sat Nov-Mar),
once a thriving Greek
colony and one of the
area's best-kept secrets.
You'll discover an ancient
Greek theatre and Chris-
tian burial chambers
with exquisitely carved
reliefs.

The Drive » Head southeast
along the SS287 for a 30km
drive through more beautiful
countryside. The road will grow
curvier as you head into Noto.

TRIP HIGHLIGHT

❹ Noto

Rebuilt after being flat-
tened by the 1693 earth-
quake, Noto boasts one
of Sicily's most beautiful
baroque centres. The
golden-hued standstone
buildings and churches
that flank **Corso Vit-
torio Emanuele**, many
designed by local archi-
tect Rosario Gagliardi,
are especially impressive
in the early evening light
(when they seem to glow
with a soft inner light)
and at night (when illu-
minations accentuate the
beauty of their intricately
carved facades).

Particularly eye catch-
ing is the **Cattedrale di
San Nicolò** (Piazza Municipio; ⏰8am-1pm & 4-8pm), a
late baroque beauty with

↱ DETOUR: VALLE DELL'ANAPO

Start: ❷ Syracuse (p389)

For some beautifully wild and unspoilt countryside,
turn off the SS124 between Syracuse and Palazzolo
Acreide and head down into the beautiful Valle
dell'Anapo – a deep limestone gorge. Follow signs
to **Ferla**, with its small but lovely baroque centre.
Another 11km past Ferla, you'll find the **Necropoli di
Pantalica** (Via Pantalica) an important Iron and Bronze
Age necropolis. Dating from the 13th to the 8th
century BC, it is an extensive area of limestone rocks
honeycombed by more than 5000 tombs. There's no
ticket office – just a car park at the end of the long,
winding road down from Ferla.

Catania La Pescheria fish market

its elaborate 18th-century facade and distinctive dome.

To see how the baroque aristocracy lived, head for **Palazzo Nicolaci di Villadorata** (☎338 7427022; www.comune.noto.sr.it/palazzo-nicolaci; Via Corrado Nicolaci; €4; ⏰10am-1.30pm & 2.30-7pm), once a private palace. Its decor is as opulent as the facade, with heavy glass chandeliers, frescoed ceilings, and wall paintings designed to look like brocaded wallpaper.

✗ p385, p393

The Drive ›› Head southwest 22km along SS115 through more fields and orchards, passing through the town of Rosolini. Hilltop Ispica will rise up in front of you. Catch the sharply winding SP47 to the town centre.

- - - - - - - - - - -

⑤ Ispica

Between Noto and Modica, this hilltop town boasts a number of fine baroque buildings. However, the real reason to stop is to peer into the **Cava d'Ispica** (☎0932 77 16 67; adult/reduced €4/2; ⏰9am-6.30pm Apr–mid-Oct, to 1.15pm Mon-Sat mid-Oct–Dec), a verdant, 13km-long gorge studded with thousands of natural caves and grottoes. Evidence of human habitation here dates to about 2000 BC, and over the millennia the caves have served as Neolithic tombs, early Christian catacombs and medieval dwellings.

The Drive ›› Start this 17km leg on the SS115 through relatively flat agricultural land. As you reach the suburbs of Modica, follow signs to Modica Centro and then to Corso Umberto I, the town's main drag.

- - - - - - - - - - -

TRIP HIGHLIGHT

⑥ Modica

With its steeply stacked medieval centre and lively central strip (Corso Umberto I), Modica is

LOCAL KNOWLEDGE: HITTING THE HIGH NOTE

Catania's most famous native son, Vincenzo Bellini (1801–35), was the quintessential composer of *bel canto* opera. Hugely successful in his lifetime, he was known for his inimitable ability to combine sensuality with melodic clarity and his works still woo audiences today. The **Museo Belliniano** (📞095 715 05 35; Piazza San Francesco 3; adult/reduced €5/2; ⏰9am-7pm Mon-Sat, to 1pm Sun), in the composer's former Catania home, has an interesting collection of his memorabilia. Catania's lavish, 19th-century **Teatro Massimo Bellini** (📞095 730 61 11; www.teatromassimobellini.it; Via Perrotta 12) is the place to hear *I Puritani, Norma* and his other masterworks.

one of southern Sicily's most atmospheric towns. But its treasures are spread around the town and take some discovering. The highlight is the **Chiesa di San Giorgio** (Corso San Giorgio, Modica Alta; ⏰8am-12.30pm & 3.30-6.30pm), a spectacular baroque church considered architect Rosario Gagliardi's great masterpiece. It stands in isolated splendour atop a majestic 250-step staircase in Modica Alta, the high part of town.

As well as impressive churches, Modica is also famous for its chocolate. And there's no better place to sample it than **Dolceria Bona-juto** (📞0932 94 12 25; www.bonajuto.it; Corso Umberto I 159, Modica Bassa; ⏰9am-8.30pm, to midnight Aug), Sicily's oldest chocolate factory.

🛏 p385, p393

The Drive » From Modica to Scicli, wind your way southwest along the SP54 for 10km through the rugged, rocky countryside.

❼ Scicli

This pleasant country town boasts a small but charming baroque centre, including the pretty, palm-fringed **Piazza Italia**. Overlooking everything is a rocky peak topped by an abandoned church, the **Chiesa di San Matteo**. The 10-minute walk up rewards you with fine views over the town.

The Drive » The first half of this 26km stretch winds north on SP94, passing along the rim of a pretty canyon typical of the region. Then catch the winding SS115 as it heads up to Ragusa. Across a small canyon, you will see the old, hillside historic centre of Ragusa rising grandly.

TRIP HIGHLIGHT

❽ Ragusa

Set amid rocky peaks, **Ragusa Ibla** – Ragusa's historic centre – is a joy to wander, with its labyrinthine lanes weaving through rock-grey *palazzi,* then opening suddenly onto beautiful, sun-drenched piazzas. After the 1693 earthquake, the aristocracy, ever optimistic, rebuilt Ragusa on exactly the same spot. It's easy to get lost but you can never go too far wrong, and sooner or later you'll end up at **Piazza Duomo**, Ragusa's sublime central space. At the top end of the sloping square is the town's pride and joy, the 1744 **Cattedrale di San Giorgio** (Piazza Duomo; ⏰10am-12.30pm & 4-7pm Jun-Sep, reduced hours rest of year), set high on a grand staircase. It's one of Rosario Gagliardi's finest accomplishments; the extravagant convex facade rises like a three-tiered wedding cake supported by gradually narrowing Corinthian columns.

Up the hill from Ragusa Ibla is **Ragusa Superiore**, the town's modern and less attractive half.

🍴 p393

Eating & Sleeping

Catania ❶ see also p385

✕ Mè Cumpari Turiddu — Sicilian €€

(☎095 715 01 42; Piazza Santo Spirito 36-38; meals €22-30; ☺bistro 11am-1am, restaurant noon-12.30am; ☎) Old chandeliers, recycled furniture and vintage mirrors exude a nostalgic air at this quirky bistro-restaurant-providore, where tradition and modernity meet to impressive effect. Small producers and Slow Food sensibilities underline sophisticated, classically inspired dishes like ricotta-and-marjoram ravioli in a pork sauce, soothing Ustica lentil stew or a playful 'deconstructed' *cannolo*. There's also a great selection of Sicilian cheeses.

▙ B&B Crociferi — B&B €

(☎095 715 22 66; www.bbcrociferi.it; Via Crociferi 81; d €75-85, tr €100-110, apt €120-130; ❂❀☎) Perfectly positioned on pedestrianised Via Crociferi, this B&B in a beautifully decorated family home affords easy access to Catania's historic centre. Three palatial rooms (each with private bathroom across the hall) feature high ceilings, antique tiles, frescoes and artistic accoutrements from the owners' travels. The B&B also houses two apartments, the largest with a leafy panoramic terrace. Book ahead.

Syracuse ❷ see also p385

✕ Don Camillo — Modern Sicilian €€€

(☎0931 6 71 33; www.ristorantedoncamillo.it; Via Maestranza 96; degustation menus €35-70; ☺12.30-2.30pm & 8-10.30pm Mon-Sat; ☎✦) One of Ortygia's most elegant restaurants, Don Camillo specialises in innovative Sicilian cuisine. Pique the appetite with mixed shellfish in a thick soup of Noto almonds, swoon over the swordfish with orange-blossom honey and sweet-and-sour vegetables, or an outstanding *tagliata di tonno* (tuna steak) with red-pepper 'marmalade'. A must for Slow Food gourmands.

▙ Hotel Gutkowski — Hotel €€

(☎0931 46 58 61; www.guthotel.it; Lungomare Vittorini 26; s €60-80, d €75-140; ❂@☎) Book well in advance for the sea-view rooms at this stylish, eclectic hotel on the Ortygia waterfront. Divided between two buildings, its rooms are simple yet chic, with pretty tiled floors,

walls in teals, greys, blues and browns, and a mix of vintage and industrial details.

Noto ❹ see also p385

✕ Ristorante Crocifisso — Sicilian €€

(☎0931 57 11 51; www.ristorantecrocifisso.it; Via Principe Umberto 48; meals €30-40; ☺12.30-2.15pm Thu-Tue, plus 7.30-10pm Tue & Thu-Sat) Up in Noto Alta, this Slow Food–acclaimed restaurant with an extensive wine list is widely regarded as Noto's best. Sicilian classics such as *macco di fave* (broad bean purée with ricotta and toasted breadcrumbs) and *casarecce alla palermitana* (short handmade pasta with sardines and wild fennel) are complemented by juicy roast lamb, Marsala-glazed pork and pistachio- and sesame-crusted tuna.

Modica ❻ see also p385

▙ Casa Gelsomino — Apartment €€

(www.casedisicilia.com; Via Raccomandata, Modica Bassa; per night €130-190, per week €820-1195; ❀☎) It's easy to pretend you're a holidaying celebrity in this stunning abode, its balconies and private terrace serving up commanding views over Modica. Incorporating an airy lounge, fully equipped kitchen, stone-walled bathroom, laundry room, sitting room and separate bedroom, its combination of vaulted ceilings, antique floor-tiles, original artworks and plush furnishings take self-catering to sophisticated highs.

Ragusa ❽

✕ Ristorante Duomo — Modern Sicilian €€€

(☎0932 65 12 65; www.cicciosultano.it; Via Capitano Bocchieri 31; lunch menus €45-59, dinner tasting menus €125-190; ☺12.30-4pm Tue-Sat, plus 7.30-11pm Mon-Sat) Widely regarded as one of Sicily's finest restaurants, Duomo sets a suitably romantic ambience for chef Ciccio Sultano's refined creations. The menu abounds in classic Sicilian ingredients such as pistachios, fennel, almonds and Nero d'Avola wine, combined in imaginative and unconventional ways. Reservations essential.

Sardinia's South Coast

38

Sardinia's less-trodden southern coast reveals all its glory on this trip from Cagliari to Iglesias. En route, you'll encounter spectacular scenery, dreamy beaches and intriguing archaeological finds.

TRIP HIGHLIGHTS

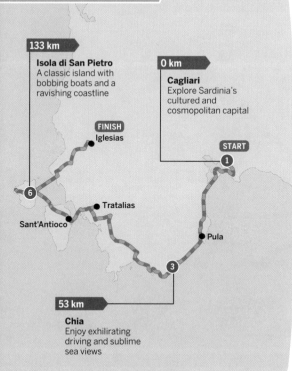

133 km

Isola di San Pietro
A classic island with bobbing boats and a ravishing coastline

0 km

Cagliari
Explore Sardinia's cultured and cosmopolitan capital

FINISH
Iglesias

START
1

6

Tratalias

Sant'Antioco

Pula

3

53 km

Chia
Enjoy exhilirating driving and sublime sea views

4–5 DAYS
168KM / 104 MILES

GREAT FOR...

BEST TIME TO GO

June and September mean perfect beach weather without the August crowds.

ESSENTIAL PHOTO

Isola di San Pietro's coastline from Capo Sandalo.

BEST FOR FAMILIES

Splashing about on the beaches at Chia.

38 Sardinia's South Coast

From Cagliari's cultural gems to ancient ruins and stunning stretches of coastline, this trip is a real eye-opener. Outside of the peak months of August and July, the roads are quiet and you'll be able to concentrate on the natural spectacle as it unfurls before you: spectacular coastal vistas on the Costa del Sud; searing Mediterranean colours on the Isola di San Pietro; melancholy woods and *macchia*-clad hills around Iglesias.

TRIP HIGHLIGHT

❶ Cagliari

Rising from the sea in a helter-skelter of golden-hued *palazzi*, domes and facades, Cagliari is Sardinia's regional capital and most cosmopolitan city. As a working port it exudes an infectious energy, particularly down by the waterfront where Vespas buzz down wide boulevards, locals stop by busy cafes and diners crowd into popular trattorias.

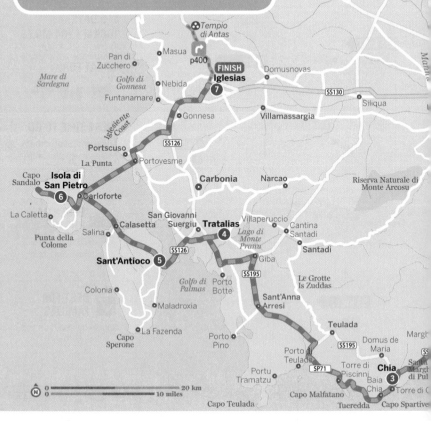

The big trophy sights are huddled in the **Castello** district, the hilltop citadel that rises above the city's sturdy battlements. Up here you'll find the graceful 13th-century **Cattedrale di Santa Maria** (www.duomodicagliari. it; Piazza Palazzo 4; ⊘8am-noon & 4-8pm Mon-Sat, 8am-1pm & 4.30-8.30pm Sun), and Cagliari's premier museum, the **Museo Archeologico Nazionale** (www.archeocaor.beniculturali. it; Piazza dell'Arsenale; adult/reduced €5/2.50; ⊘9am-8pm Tue-Sun), whose collection casts light on Sardinia's ancient and mysterious nuraghic culture. For stunning views, head down to the **Bastione San Remy**, a monumental viewing platform.

A short hop east of the city, **Poetto beach** is the hub of summer life with its limpid waters and upbeat party scene.

✕ 🛏 p401

The Drive ›› Once you've cleared central Cagliari, it's a straightforward 32km drive along the SS195 to Pula. From Pula, the archaeological site of Nora is signposted, 4km away to the southwest. As you approach it, look out for pink flamingos in the nearby lagoon.

- - - - - - - - - -

❷ Pula

The village of Pula makes a good base for exploring the southern beaches and the nearby archaeological site of Nora. There's little to see in the village itself but in summer visitors throng its vibrant cafes and various restaurants lending it a bubbly holiday atmosphere.

A short drive out of Pula, the ruins of **Nora** (⌕070 920 91 38; adult/reduced €7.50/4.50; ⊘10am-sunset) are all that remain of what was once one of Sardinia's most powerful cities. Highlights include a beautifully preserved Roman theatre and an ancient baths complex, the **Terme al Mare**.

Just before you get to the site, keep an eye out for the beachside **Chiesa di Sant'Efisio**, a 12th-century Romanesque church that plays a star-ring role in Cagliari's big 1 May festival, the **Festa di Sant'Efisio**.

The Drive ›› From Pula, push on along the SS195 for the 18km drive to Chia, which is signposted off to the left shortly after Santa Margherita di Pula. For much of the way the road is curtained off by trees and foliage but don't worry as there are plenty of views to be had on the next leg.

- - - - - - - - - -

TRIP HIGHLIGHT

❸ Chia

Extending from Chia to Porto di Teulada, the

START
Cagliari
❶

73km to Dolianova

Monastir

San Sperate

Sestu Sinnai
Settimo

Elmas

Stagno di Cagliari

terra

Golfo degli Angeli

195

Sarroch
Genniauri

Pula

Capo di Pula
ra

MEDITERRANEAN SEA

🔗 **LINK YOUR TRIP**

39 **Emerald Coast**
From Cagliari take the SS131 up to Alghero, 250km away, to join up with this tour of Sardinia's gorgeous, wind-whipped north coast.

40 **Historic Sardinia**
About 100km along the SS131 from Cagliari, Oristano is the start point for this compelling drive through Sardinia's wild and mysterious hinterland.

Costa del Sud is one of southern Sardinia's most beautiful coastal stretches.

At its eastern end, Chia is a hugely popular summer hangout. More a collection of hotels, holiday homes and campsites than a traditional village, it boasts two ravishing beaches – to the west, the **Spiaggia Sa Colonia**, and to the east, the smaller **Spiaggia Su Portu**.

Running the length of the Costa, the **Strada Panoramica della Costa del Sud** is a stunning drive, with dreamy views at every turn and a succession of bays capped by Spanish-era watchtowers.

The Drive » This 56km drive is the most spectacular leg of the trip. From Chia, the SP71, aka the Strada Panoramica della Costa del Sud, snakes along the coast, offering ever more beautiful views as it winds on to Porto di Teulada. Shortly before Porto, turn inland towards Teulada and pick up the northbound SS195 to Tratalias.

ALXPIN/GETTY IMAGES ©

④ Tratalias

Now a sleepy backwater, Tratalias was once a major religious centre. When the town of Sant'Antioco was abandoned in the 13th century, the local Sulcis archdiocese was transferred to Tratalias and the impressive **Chiesa di Santa Maria** (Piazza Chiesa; admission incl Museo del Territorio Tratialese €2.50; ⊙9am-1pm & 3-5pm Wed-Sun winter, longer hr summer) was built. A prime example of Sardinia's Romanesque-Pisan architecture, the church today presides over the town's lovingly renovated *borgo antico,* a medieval quarter that was abandoned in the 1950s after water from the nearby Lago di Monte Pranu started seeping into the subsoil.

The Drive » From Tratalias, it's a short 14km haul over to the Isola di Sant'Antioco via the SS126 which runs over the road bridge to the island's main settlement, Sant'Antioco.

⑤ Sant'Antioco

The **Isola di Sant'Antioco** is the larger and more developed of the two islands off Sardinia's southwestern coast.

Cagliari Bastione San Remy

Unlike many Mediterranean islands it's not dramatically beautiful – although it's by no means ugly – and it exudes no sense of isolation. Instead it feels very much part of Sardinia, both in character and look.

The animated main town, Sant'Antioco, was established by the Phoenicians in the 8th century BC. Evidence of its early history lies all around and the town's small centre is riddled with Phoenician necropolises and fascinating archaeological litter. Just outside the centre, the **Museo Archeologico** (www.archeotur.it; €6, incl tophet €7; ◷9am-7pm) is one of the best museums in this part of southern Sardinia. It has a fascinating collection of local archaeological finds, as well as models of nuraghic houses and Sant'Antioco as it would have looked in the 4th century BC.

✖ ⊨ p401

The Drive ›» To get to the neighbouring island of San Pietro requires a ferry crossing (up to 16 daily, 45 minutes, per adult/car €4.50/9.60) from Calasetta, 10km northwest of

DETOUR: TEMPIO DI ANTAS

Start: ❼ Iglesias

From Iglesias the SS126 twists and turns for 17km through wooded hills up to the **Tempio di Antas** (www.startuno.it; adult/reduced €4/3; ☺9.30pm-7.30pm daily summer, to 5.30pm daily spring & autumn, to 4.30pm Tue-Sun winter), an impressive 3rd-century Roman temple set in lush bucolic greenery.

Built by the emperor Caracalla, the temple was constructed over a 6th-century BC Punic sanctuary, which was itself set over an earlier nuraghic settlement. It lay abandoned for centuries until it was discovered in 1836 and extensively restored in 1967. Most impressively, the original Ionic columns were excavated and re-erected.

From the site several paths branch off into the surrounding countryside. One of them, the **Strada Romana**, leads from near the ticket office to what little remains of the original nuraghic settlement and on to the **Grotta di Su Mannau** (☎0781 58 04 11; www.sumannau.it; adult/reduced €10/6; ☺9.30am-5.30pm Easter-Jun, to 6.30pm Jul-Oct), 2.5km away.

Sant'Antioco on the island's north coast. There are not many roads to choose from, so just head north and follow the signs through the green, rugged interior.

- - - - - - - - - - - - - -

TRIP HIGHLIGHT

❻ Isola di San Pietro

Boasting an elegant main town and some magnificent coastal scenery, the Isola di San Pietro is a hugely popular summer destination.

The island's principal port of call is **Carloforte**, a refined town with an elegant waterfront, graceful *palazzi* and a reputation for excellent seafood – tuna is a local speciality. There are no must-see sights as such, but a slow wander through the quaint, cobbled streets makes for a pleasant prelude to an aperitif and a fine restaurant meal.

Over on the island's west coast, **Capo Sandalo** is well worth searching out. A superb vantage point, it commands breathtaking coastal views and offers some relaxed walking. From the car park near the lighthouse, marked trails head through the rocky, red scrubland that carpets the cliffs.

✕ ⊨ p401

The Drive » Once the ferry (up to 17 daily, one hour; adult/car €4.90/11.90) from Carloforte has docked at Portovesme, head northeast towards Gonnesa to pick up the SS126 for the final run in to Iglesias. The 35km route is not the most scenic but there is something atmospheric about the dark, *macchia*-cloaked hills of Sardinia's traditional mining heartland south of Iglesias.

- - - - - - - - - - - - -

❼ Iglesias

Surrounded by the skeletons of Sardinia's once-thriving mining industry, Iglesias is a historic town that bubbles in the summer and slumbers in the colder months. Its historic centre, an appealing ensemble of lived-in piazzas, sun-bleached buildings and Aragonese-style wrought-iron balconies, creates an atmosphere that's as much Iberian as Sardinian – a vestige of its time as a Spanish colony.

In the heart of the *centro storico* (historic centre), the 13th-century **Cattedrale di Santa Chiara** (Duomo; Piazza del Municipio; ☺8am-6.30pm) is the most impressive of the city's many churches with its Pisan-flavoured facade and chequerboard stone bell tower.

✕ ⊨ p401

Eating & Sleeping

Cagliari ❶

✕ Martinelli's Italian €€
(📞070 65 42 20; www.martinellis.it; Via Principe Amedeo 18; meals from €35; ☺8.30pm-midnight Mon-Sat) Simplicity is the ethos underpinning this intimate, subtly lit bistro in the heart of the Marina district. Service is friendly without being overbearing, and the menu plays up seasonal, winningly fresh seafood along the lines of *fregola* (semolina pasta) with clams and sea bass cooked in *vernaccia* wine and olives.

🛏 Il Cagliarese B&B €
(📞339 6544083; www.ilcagliarese.it; Via Vittorio Porcile 19; s €45-70, d €60-90; ✻ @ 🛜) Bang in the heart of Marina district, this snug B&B is a find. Mauro bends over backwards to please and his sister, Titziana, plays the cake fairy at breakfast with her scrumptious pastries and tiramisu. The immaculate rooms sport homey touches such as embroidered fabrics and carved wooden furnishings.

Sant'Antioco ❺

✕ Rubiu Pizza €
(📞346 7234605; www.rubiubirra.it; Via Bologna; pizzas €5-11.50; ☺7pm-1am) This upbeat and contemporary microbrewery has an easygoing vibe and a terrific selection of home-brewed beers and ales. It also whips up tasty salads, platters of local cheese, and creative pizzas with toppings such as smoked *muggine* (mullet) and *bottarga* (mullet roe).

🛏 Hotel Moderno Hotel €
(📞0781 8 31 05; www.hotel-moderno-sant-antioco.it; Via Nazionale 82; s €45-60, d €70-110, tr €80-135, q €95-145; ✻ 🛜) A bright, welcoming hotel on the main road into Sant'Antioco town. Rooms are agreeable with orange-salmon colours and big, comfy beds. Downstairs, the seafood restaurant, **Ristorante da Achille** (open June to September; tasting menus €40 to €60), has an excellent local reputation.

Isola di San Pietro ❻

✕ Osteria Della Tonnara da Andrea Seafood €€
(📞0781 85 57 34; www.ristorantedaandrea.it; Corso Battellieri 36; meals €40; ☺12.30-2.30pm & 8-10.30pm Thu-Tue, closed mid-Jan–early Mar) Located at the waterfront's southern end, this charming restaurant is one of the best places to taste the local tuna (though it's only available in the tuna-fishing season). Signature dishes include *lasagnetta di tonno con gocce di pesto* (tuna and pesto lasagne) and *tonno arrosto alla carlofortina* (roast tuna with tomato sauce). Booking recommended in summer.

🛏 Hotel Riviera Hotel €€
(📞0781 85 32 34; www.hotelriviera-carloforte. com; Corso Battellieri 26, Carloforte; d €89-184, ste €124-209; ✻ 🛜) Housed in a red seafront villa, this swank but relaxed four-star exudes Mediterranean chic. The rooms are cool and light, with tiled floors, understated furniture and marble-clad bathrooms. Some also have sea views and balconies, though these cost extra.

Iglesias ❼

✕ Trattoria Pintadera Trattoria €€
(📞346 6770183; Via Manno 22; meals €30-35; ☺12.30-2pm & 7.30-11pm) A welcoming family run eatery in the *centro storico,* Pintadera is the sort of place that gives Italian trattorias a good name. In a rustic stone *palazzo* you sit down to hearty local pastas – try the ravioli stuffed with potato and mint – and buttery chargrilled steaks. Great food, a warm atmosphere and excellent value for money; it's a top choice.

🛏 B&B Mare Monti Miniere B&B €
(📞348 3310585, 0781 4 17 65; www. maremontiminiere-bb.it; Via Trento 10; s €30-35, d €45-50, tr €60-65; ✻ 🛜) A warm welcome awaits at this cracking B&B. Situated in a quiet side street near the historic centre, it has three cheery and immaculately kept rooms with above-par touches like DVD players and bathrobes. Independent of the main house, there's also a smart studio flat with its own kitchen facilities. Extras include beach towels and free bike hire.

Emerald Coast

39

This journey takes you around Sardinia's extraordinary northern coast, a land of wind-carved rocks, pearly white beaches and emerald-green seas that entertain divers and dolphins alike.

TRIP HIGHLIGHTS

29 km

Cannigione
Fantastic opportunities for diving, snorkelling and boat excursions

42 kms

Isola della Maddalena
A pink-granite island with striking seascapes

⑥ ⑦ ⑤ ②

Olbia
START

FINISH
Alghero

136 km

Castelsardo
A medieval town huddled picturesquely atop a seaside promontory

Santa Teresa di Gallura
Prime seafront position with a distinct local character

66 km

**5–7 DAYS
253KM / 157 MILES**

GREAT FOR...

BEST TIME TO GO

May, June, September and October, for beach weather without huge crowds.

ESSENTIAL PHOTO

The bizarre shapes of Capo Testa's natural sculpture garden.

BEST FOR OUTDOORS

Dive into the crystalline waters of the Maddalena Archipelago.

39 Emerald Coast

From unassuming Olbia, this trip rockets you into the dazzling coastline that the Aga Khan turned into a playground for oligarchs and their bikini-clad admirers. Head further north, however, and the coast grows wilder, with rocky coves washed by the startlingly blue waters of La Maddalena marine reserve. Rounding Sardinia's northwest corner, popular resorts alternate with timelessly silent stretches of coast, until finally you arrive at lovely, Spanish-inflected Alghero.

① Olbia

Scratch Olbia's industrial outskirts and find a fetching city with a *centro storico* (historic centre) crammed with boutiques, wine bars and cafe-rimmed piazzas. Olbia is also a refreshingly authentic and affordable alternative to the purpose-built resorts stretching to the north and south.

To get a feel of old Olbia, head south of Corso Umberto to the tightly packed warren of streets that represents the original fishing village. You'll find it has a special charm, particularly in the evening when the cafes and trattorias fill with hungry locals.

✗ ⊨ p409

The Drive » Heading north on the SS125 and then the SP13 for this 29km leg, you'll pass through a rocky, sun-bleached landscape that alternates with patchwork farmland.

TRIP HIGHLIGHT

② Cannigione

Cannigione sits on the western side of the Golfo di Arzachena, the largest *ria* (inlet) along this coast. Originally a fishing village established in 1800 to supply the Maddalena islands with food, it is now a prosperous, and reasonably priced, tourist town. Down at the port, various operators offer excursions to the Arcipelago di La Maddalena, plus fantastic opportunities for diving, snorkelling and boat trips that nose around the gorgeous and complex shoreline.

The operators here include **Consorzio del Golfo** (☎ 335 7742392, 0789 8 84 18; www.consorziodelgolfo.it)

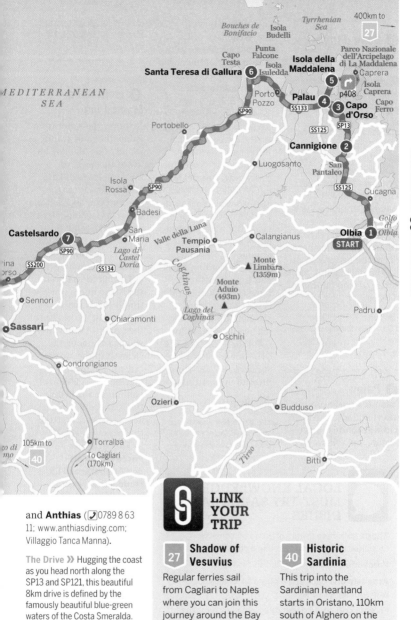

and **Anthias** (☎0789 8 63
11; www.anthiasdiving.com;
Villaggio Tanca Manna).

The Drive » Hugging the coast
as you head north along the
SP13 and SP121, this beautiful
8km drive is defined by the
famously beautiful blue-green
waters of the Costa Smeralda.
Near the village of Le Saline,
you'll see the inlet on which the
Capo d'Orso sits.

LINK YOUR TRIP

27 Shadow of Vesuvius

Regular ferries sail
from Cagliari to Naples
where you can join this
journey around the Bay
of Naples.

40 Historic Sardinia

This trip into the
Sardinian heartland
starts in Oristano, 110km
south of Alghero on the
SS292.

❸ Capo d'Orso

Watching over the strait that separates Sardinia from the Isola della Maddalena, Capo d'Orso (Cape Bear) owes its name to a giant granite rock that, over the millennia, has been modelled by wind and rain to resemble a rather ferocious-looking bear. The ursine lookout commands a dramatic view that, in a single sweep of the eye, takes in Sardinia's rugged northern coast, the Arcipelago di La Maddalena and, to the north, the mountains of Corsica.

The Drive » From Capo d'Orso, head northwest along the SP121 to Palau, just 5km away.

❹ Palau

Palau is a lively summer resort and also the main gateway to the granite islands and jewel-coloured waters of the Arcipelago di La Maddalena. Three kilometres west of town, you can tour the **Fortezza di Monte Altura** (adult/reduced €3/2; ⊙ guided tours 9am-noon & 5-8pm Jun-Aug, 10am-noon & 3-6pm Apr-May & Sep–mid-Oct), a 19th-century sentinel standing guard over the rocky crag. **Dea del Mare** (☑334 788 29 93, 349 490 92 60; www.deadelmare.com; Via Fonte Vecchia 76; day trips €65-110; ⊙ office 9am-5pm) offers boat excursions around the Maddalena islands, including lunch and time to swim on famous beaches. If diving is your thing, there's excellent diving in the marine park. **Nautilus** (☑340 6339006, 0789 70 90 58; www.divesardegna.com; Piazza Fresi 8, Palau) runs dives to up to 40 sites.

✕ 🛏 p409

The Drive » Actually, it's a sail. From Palau, there are at least hourly passenger and car ferry services to Isola della Maddalena. The journey takes 15 minutes.

TRIP HIGHLIGHT

❺ Isola della Maddalena

Just over the water from Palau, the pink-granite island of La Maddalena lies at the heart of the Arcipelago di La Maddalena. From the moment you dock at **Cala Gavetta** (La Maddalena's main port), you'll be in the thrall of its cobbled piazzas and infectious holiday atmosphere.

Beyond the harbour, the island offers startlingly lovely seascapes. Divers sing the praises of the sapphire waters here, which are among the cleanest in the Mediterranean and teem with marine life. A 20km panoramic road circles the island, allowing easy access to several attractive bays.

The ravishing **Parco Nazionale dell'Arcipelago di La Maddalena** (www.lamaddalenapark.it) consists of seven main islands, including La Maddalena, and 40 granite islets, plus several small islands to the south. They form the high points of an underwater valley that once joined Sardinia and Corsica. Over the centuries, the *maestrale* (northwesterly wind) has moulded the granite

LOCAL KNOWLEDGE: MUST-TRY SARDINIAN DISHES

Zuppa gallurese Layers of bread and cheese drenched in broth and baked to a crispy crust.

Porceddu Suckling pig, often spit roasted.

Aragosta alla catalana Alghero's lobster speciality, with tomato and onion.

Fregola con cozze e vongole Sardinian semolina pasta (similar to couscous) with mussels and clams.

Seadas Light pastry turnovers filled with ricotta and lemon zest and drizzled with honey.

Isola della Maddalena Piazza Umberto I

into bizarre natural sculptures. But the great delight lies in its crystalline waters, which are rich in marine life and also assume priceless shades of emerald, aquamarine and sapphire.

To explore the archipelago and some of the smaller, lesser-known islands, **Elena Tour Navigazioni** (☑380 3032664; www.elenatournavigazioni.com; Via Eleonora d'Arborea 24) is one of various outfits offering boat cruises. Costing around €40 per person, these generally include lunch and plenty of opportunities for glorious swimming.

📖 p409

The Drive ›› Hop on the ferry back to Palau, then head northwest on the SS133, which will veer off as the SS133bis. Along the 24km, mostly inland, journey you'll pass Mediterranean scrub and granite boulders, with a brief seaside encounter at Porto Pozzo.

TRIP HIGHLIGHT

6 Santa Teresa di Gallura

Bright, breezy and relaxed, Santa Teresa di Gallura bags a prime seafront position on Gallura's north coast. The resort gets extremely busy in high season, yet somehow retains a distinct local character. When not on the beach, most people hang out at cafe-lined **Piazza Vittorio Emanuele**. Otherwise, you can wander up to the 16th-century **Torre di Longonsardo**, a defensive tower near the entrance to **Spiaggia Rena Bianca**, the town's idyllic (but crowded) beach.

Well worth the 4km hike west of Santa Teresa, the small peninsula known as **Capo Testa** resembles a bizarre sculpture garden. Giant boulders lay strewn about the grassy slopes,

DETOUR:
ISOLA CAPRERA

Start: ❺ Isola della Maddalena (p406)

Just over a causeway from the Isola della Maddalena, Isola Caprera was once Giuseppe Garibaldi's 'Eden' – a wild, wonderfully serene island, covered in green pines which look stunning against the ever-present seascape and ragged granite cliffs. The green, shady Caprera is ideal for walking, and there are plenty of trails weaving through the pines. The island's rugged coast is indented with several tempting coves. You can also tour the **Compendio Garibaldino** (www.compendiogaribaldino.it; adult/reduced €6/3; ☉9am-8pm Tue-Sun), the serene compound the Italian revolutionary built for himself here. Note, however, that guided visits are in Italian only.

their weird and wonderful forms the result of centuries of wind erosion. The walk itself is also stunning, passing through boulder-strewn scrub and affording magnificent views of rocky coves and the cobalt Mediterranean. Stop en route for a swim and to admire the views of not-so-distant Corsica.

✖ 🛏 p409

The Drive ≫ It's rugged, hilly terrain on this 70km southwestern route along the SP90, with a brief stint along the winding SS134 to Castelsardo and the sea.

TRIP HIGHLIGHT

❼ Castelsardo

Medieval Castelsardo huddles atop a high, promontory that juts picturesquely into the Mediterranean. Originally designed as a defensive fort in the 12th-century, the dramatic, hilltop *cen-*

tro storico is an ensemble of dark alleyways and medieval buildings seemingly melded into the rocky grey peak.

The Drive ≫ Hug Sardinia's rugged northern coastline as you head west to Porto Torres along the SS200 and SP81. Then turn inland into desolately beautiful country to Stintino, 63km from Castelsardo, on the SP34.

❽ Stintino

With its saltpans and hard-scrabble landscape, the northwest corner of Sardinia has a particularly desolate feel, especially when the *maestrale* wind blows in, whipping the *macchia* (Mediterranean scrub) and bleak rocks. But it also shelters the welcoming and laid-back resort town of Stintino, gateway to the **Isola dell'Asinara**, formerly home to one of Italy's toughest prisons. Nearby, the fabulous

Spiaggia della Pelosa is one of Sardinia's most celebrated beaches.

The Drive ≫ For this 54km drive, head back down south along the SP34 to the coastal SP57, followed by the SP69. Soon you will reach the flat agricultural plain just north of Alghero, then it's a straight shot on the SS291 into Alghero itself.

❾ Alghero

For many people a trip to Sardinia means a trip to Alghero, the main resort in the northwest and an easy flight from many European cities. Although largely given over to tourism, the town has managed to avoid many of its worst excesses, and it retains a proud and independent spirit.

The main focus is the picturesque *centro storico,* one of the best preserved in Sardinia. Enclosed by robust, honey-coloured seawalls, this is a tightly knit enclave of shady cobbled lanes, Spanish Gothic *palazzi* (mansions) and cafe-lined squares. Below, yachts crowd the marina and long, sandy beaches curve away to the north. Hanging over everything is a palpably Spanish atmosphere, a leftover of the city's past as a Catalan colony. Even today, more than three centuries after the Iberians left, the Catalan tongue is still spoken and street signs and menus are often in both languages.

✖ 🛏 p409

Eating & Sleeping

Olbia ❶

✘ Agriturismo Agrisole   Sardinian €€

(📞349 084 81 63; www.agriturismo-agrisole. com; Via Sole Ruiu 7, Località Casagliana; menu incl drinks €30; ⏰dinner daily by reservation Apr-Sep) Tucked away in the countryside around 10km north of Olbia, this Gallurese farmhouse dishes up a feast of home cooking: antipasti, *fregola* (granular pasta), *porceddu* (roast suckling pig) and ricotta sweets. From Olbia, take the SS125 towards Arzachena/Palau, turning left at the signs at Km 327.800.

🛏 Hotel Panorama   Hotel €€

(📞0789 2 66 56; www.hotelpanoramaolbia.it; Via Giuseppe Mazzini 7; s €60-155, d €74-269, tr €110-279; 🅿 ❄ 🛜) The name says it all: the roof terrace at this friendly, central hotel has peerless views over the rooftops of Olbia to the sea and Monte Limbara. The rooms are fresh and elegant, and there's a whirlpool and sauna for quiet moments.

Palau ❹

✘ C'era una Volta   Italian €€€

(📞0789 70 83 59; www. ristoranteceraunavoltapalau.it; Piazza del Molo 22; meals €45; ⏰noon-2.30pm & 7-11pm) On the road down to the harbour, C'era una Volta offers a good buzz and warm welcome, and the food is some of Palau's best – follow fresh pasta with the catch of the day, simply grilled, and homemade desserts.

🛏 L'Orso e Il Mare   B&B €

(📞331 2222000; www.orsoeilmare.com; Vicolo Diaz 1, Palau; d €50-115, tr €80-145; ❄) Pietro gives his guests a genuinely warm welcome at this B&B, just steps from Piazza Fresi. The spacious rooms sport cool blue-and-white colour schemes. Breakfast is a fine spread of cakes, biscuits and fresh fruit salad.

Isola della Maddalena ❺

🛏 B&B Petite Maison   B&B €

(📞340 6463722, 0789 73 84 32; www. lapetitmaison.net; Via Livenza 7, La Maddalena;

d €80-120; 🛜) Liberally sprinkled with paintings and art-deco furnishings, this B&B is a five-minute amble from the main square. Miriam's artistically presented breakfasts, with fresh homemade goodies, are served in a bougainvillea-draped garden.

Santa Teresa di Gallura ❻

✘ Agriturismo Saltara   Sardinian €€

(📞0789 75 55 97; www.agriturismosaltara. it; Località Saltara; meals €38-48; ⏰7-11pm) At this *agriturismo*, 10km south of town off the SP90 (follow the signs up a dirt track), tables are scenically positioned under the trees for a home-cooked feast. Wood-fired bread and garden vegetable antipasti are a delicious lead to dishes like *pulilgioni* (ricotta-filled ravioli with orange zest) and roast suckling pig or wild boar. Vegetarian menus are also available on request.

🛏 B&B Domus de Janas   B&B €€

(📞338 4990221; www.bbdomusdejanas.it; Via Carlo Felice 20a; s €45-100, d €60-140, q €110-170; ❄ 🛜) Daria and Simon are your affable hosts at this sweet B&B in the centre of town. There are cracking sea views from the terrace and the three colourful rooms are cheery, scattered with art and knick-knacks.

Alghero ❾

✘ La Botteghina   Sardinian €€

(📞079 973 83 75; www.labotteghina.biz; Via Principe Umberto 63; meals €35; ⏰12.30-2.30pm & 7.30-10.45pm Fri-Wed) La Botteghina specialises in simple dishes prepared with seasonal ingredients bought from small local producers. Steaks of *bue rosso* beef, cured meats and Sardinian cheese star on the menu alongside 50cm pizzas and fresh seafood, typically served with *fregola* (semolina pasta similar to couscous).

🛏 Angedras Hotel   Hotel €€

(📞079 973 50 34; www.angedras.it; Via Frank 2; s €44-110, d €49-111; 🅿 ❄ 🛜) A model of whitewashed Mediterranean elegance, the Angedras offers cool, white rooms decorated in an understated Sardinian style. There's also an airy terrace good for iced drinks on hot summer evenings. Note that the hotel is a 15-minute walk from the historic centre.

Historic Sardinia

40

Head straight into the wild heart of Sardinia, a strange and haunting landscape littered with Bronze Age nuraghic ruins and isolated mountain towns legendary for feuding and banditry.

TRIP HIGHLIGHTS

218 km

Orosei
An intriguing seaside town surrounded by extraordinary Bronze Age ruins

Nuoro
An isolated hilltop village with a rich bohemian past

76 km

Oristano
START

58 km

Laconi
A bucolic hilltown with a fine archeological museum

Dorgali
FINISH

150 km

Orgosolo
Former stronghold of mountain banditry now awash in vibrant murals

7 DAYS
239KM / 148 MILES

GREAT FOR...

BEST TIME TO GO

March to May for wildflowers and green hillsides.

ESSENTIAL PHOTO

The spectacular coastal scenery on the Golfo di Orosei.

BEST FOR OUTDOORS

Great hikes abound around Dorgali.

tano A costumed rider races during the city's carnival

This trip immerses you in Sardinia's strange and captivating hinterlands. You will discover remnants of the prehistoric *nuraghi* (Bronze Age fortified settlements) and the lonesome villages of the Barbagia, which are still steeped in bandit legend. You'll end up in the wilds of the eastern coast, where limestone mountains and deep canyons roll down to the aquamarine waves of the Golfo di Orosei.

❶ Oristano

One of Sardinia's most important medieval cities, Oristano has a historic centre that retains traces of its former greatness, most notably the 13th century **Torre di Mariano II**. The centre is a pleasant place to wander, with its elegant shopping streets, ornate central square – **Piazza Eleonora d'Arborea** – and crowded cafes.

The region around Oristano was an important centre of the Bronze Age nuraghic people, and the **Museo Antiquarium Arborense** (☏0783 79 12 62; www.antiquariumarbo rense.it; Piazza Corrias; adult/reduced €5/2.50; ⊘9am-8pm Mon-Fri, 9am-2pm & 3-8pm Sat & Sun) is home to one of Sardinia's major archaeological collections.

Located 3km south of town, the 12th-century **Basilica di Santa Giusta** – one of Sardinia's finest Tuscan-style Romanesque churches – is worth seeking out.

✕ ⨾ p417

The Drive » Your main routes on the 58km drive to Laconi will be the meandering SP35 and SS442. You'll traverse a widely varied land of patchwork farms, small towns, rocky crags and wooded slopes.

TRIP HIGHLIGHT

❷ Laconi

Laconi is a charismatic mountain town with a blissfully slow pace of life and bucolic views of rolling green countryside. Its cobbled lanes hide some genuine attractions, including an intriguing archaeological museum, the **Museo delle Statue Menhir** (http://menhir museum.it; Via Amsicora; adult/reduced €5/3; ⊘10am-1pm & 3.30-7pm Tue-Sun

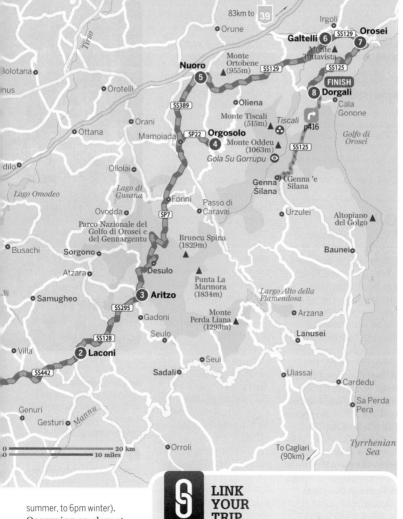

summer, to 6pm winter).
Occupying an elegant
19th-century *palazzo*
(mansion), this museum
beautifully exhibits a collection of 40 menhirs –
stark anthropomorphic
slabs probably connected
with prehistoric funerary
rites.

Just outside town, the
Parco Aymerich (⏱8am-

LINK YOUR TRIP

38 **Sardinia's South Coast**

Some 97km southeast
of Oristano on the SS131
Cagliari is the startpoint
for this visually stunning
tour of the island's south
coast.

39 **Emerald Coast**

Starting 90km
up the coast from
Orosei, this trip reveals
Sardinia's wind-carved
northern coast.

8pm summer, to 4pm winter) is a gorgeous 22-hectare park with exotic trees, lakes, grottoes, great views and the remains of 11th-century **Castello Aymerich**.

The Drive » For this 27km leg, you'll head northeast along the SS128 and then the SS295 as you enter a wilder, more barren landscape, eventually reaching the pine-covered slopes around Aritzo.

❸ Aritzo

With its cool climate and Alpine character, this vivacious mountain resort (elevation 796m) has been attracting visitors since the 19th century, when it caught the imagination of boar-hunting Piedmontese nobility. But long before tourism took off, the village flourished thanks to its lucrative trade in snow gathering. For five centuries, Aritzo supplied the whole of Sardinia with ice, and snow farmers, known as *niargios,* collected the white stuff from the slopes of **Punta di Funtana Cungiada** (1458m) and stored it in straw-lined wooden chests before sending it off to the high tables of Cagliari.

The Drive » Heading northeast along Via Marginigola, turn onto the sharply curving SP7 for the 65km to Orgosolo through the deserted mountains and valleys of central Sardinia. At the town of Mamoiada, take

the winding SP22 for the last 10km up to Orgosolo.

TRIP HIGHLIGHT

❹ Orgosolo

High in the brooding mountains, Orgosolo is Sardinia's most notorious town, its name long a byword for the banditry and bloody feuds that once blighted this region. Between 1901 and 1950, the village was averaging a murder every two months as rival families feuded over disputed inheritances. In the 1950s and '60s, feuding gave way to more lucrative kidnapping, led by the village's most infamous son, Graziano Mesina, nicknamed the Scarlet Pimpernel.

The problem of violence now largely resolved, Orgosolo is drawing visitors with the vibrant graffiti-style murals that adorn its town centre. Like satirical caricatures, they depict all the big political events of the 20th century and are often very moving. But in the evening, the villagers reclaim their streets – the old boys staring at anyone they don't recognise and the lads with crew cuts racing up and down in their mud-splattered cars.

✖ p417

The Drive » For the 26km to Nuoro, head back down the SP22 to Mamoiada, and take

the SS389 northeast through a particularly sun-bleached landscape of cacti and *macchia*.

TRIP HIGHLIGHT

❺ Nuoro

Once an isolated hilltop village synonymous with banditry, Nuoro had its cultural renaissance in the 19th and early 20th centuries, attracting a hotbed of artistic talent, from author Grazia Deledda to sculptor Francesco Ciusa. This legacy is reflected in the fine **Museo d'Arte** (MAN; www.museoman.it; Via S Satta 27; adult/reduced €3/2; ⊙10am-8pm Tue-Sun summer,

REALY EASY STAR/MASSIMO PIACENTINO/ALAMY STOCK PHOTO ©

Laconi Parco Aymerich

10am-1pm & 3-7pm Tue-Sun winter). The only serious contemporary art gallery in Sardinia, it displays more than 400 works by the island's top 20th-century painters. Nuoro is also home to the **Museo Etnografico Sardo** (www.isresardegna.it; Via Antonio Mereu 56; adult/reduced €5/3; ☉10am-1pm & 3-8pm Tue-Sun summer, to 7pm winter), a peerless collection of Sardinian arts and crafts, from filigree jewellery and rich embroidery to weapons and masks.

The city's spectacular backdrop is the granite peak of **Monte Ortobene**

(955m). Capped by a 7m-high bronze statue of the *Redentore* (Christ the Redeemer), it makes for good hiking.

🍴 🛏 p417

The Drive ≫ Head 33km east along SS129 as mountains give way to a green-and-ochre checkerboard of farmland.

- - - - - - - - - -

6 Galtelli

Crouched at the foot of **Monte Tuttavista** and hemmed in by olive groves, vineyards and sheep-nibbled pastures, Galtelli is quite the village idyll. Its tiny medieval centre is a joy

to wander, with narrow lanes twisting to old stone houses and sun-dappled piazzas. If you fancy tiptoeing off the map for a while, this is the place.

The Drive ≫ It's a quick and relatively straight 9km jaunt along SS129 to Orosei, as rugged limestone peaks rear up again on your right.

- - - - - - - - - -

TRIP HIGHLIGHT

7 Orosei

Scenically positioned at the northernmost point of the Golfo di Orosei and surrounded by marble quarries and fruit orchards, Orosei

DETOUR: GOLA SU GORROPU & TISCALI

Start: ❽ Dorgali

Dubbed the 'Grand Canyon of Europe', the **Gola Su Gorropu** (📱328 897 65 63; www.gorropu.info; adult/reduced €5/3.50; ⊙10.30am-5.30pm) is a spectacular gorge flanked by vertical 400m rock walls that, at their narrowest point, stand just 4m apart. The hike down to and through the canyon floor takes you into a strangely silent world of gnarled holm oaks, sheer limestone slopes and pockmarked cliffs. There are two main approach routes. The shorter and more dramatic begins from the car park opposite Hotel Silana at the **Genna 'e Silana** pass on the SS125 at kilometre 183. The easier, but longer, route is via the **Sa Barva bridge** over the Rio Flumineddu, about 15km from Dorgali.

Also at the Sa Barva bridge is the trailhead for the walk to one of Sardinia's archaeological highlights. Hidden in a mountaintop cave deep in the Valle Lanaittu is the nuraghic village of **Tiscali** (adult/reduced €5/2; ⊙9am-7pm daily summer, to 5pm winter). The hike up to the village is part of the pleasure, as you strike into the heart of the limestone Supramonte highlands. You'll need sturdy footwear for some rock hopping, but most of the path is easygoing, and canopies of juniper and cork oaks afford shady respite. Allow five hours for the return hike, including breaks and time for visiting Tiscali.

is an unsung treasure. Over the centuries the silting of the Cedrino river – plus malaria, pirate raids and Spanish neglect – took their toll on the town, once an important Pisan port. However, its demise left behind an atmospheric historic centre laced with cobbled lanes, pretty stone-built houses, medi-eval churches and leafy piazzas.

🍴 p417

The Drive >> From the plains around Orosei, head southwest on the SS125 for 21km. Expect glimpses of both mountains and sea as you wind your way to Dorgali.

❽ Dorgali

Nestled at the foot of **Monte Bardia** and framed by vineyards and olive groves, Dorgali is a down-to-earth town with a grandiose backdrop. Limestone peaks rear above the centre's pastel-coloured houses and steep, narrow streets, luring hikers and climbers to their summits. For more outdoor escapades, the dramatic **Golfo di Orosei** and spectacularly rugged **Supramonte** mountain range are within easy striking distance.

Just south of town lies one of Sardinia's most dramatically sited *nuraghe*. Follow signs along the Dorgali–Cala Gonone road to the **Nuraghe Mannu** (adult/reduced €3/2; ⊙9am-noon & 5-8pm summer, 9am-noon & 4-7pm Apr-Jun & Sep, 10am-1pm & 3-6pm Apr & Oct). First inhabited around 1600 BC, the tower is a modest ruin but it more than makes up for this by offering spectacular views of the gulf. The site captured ancient Roman imaginations too, and you can see the rectilinear remnants of their constructions alongside the elliptical shapes of earlier buildings.

🍴🛏 p417

Eating & Sleeping

Oristano ❶

✖ Trattoria Gino   Trattoria €€
(☎0783 7 14 28; Via Tirso 13; meals €30;
⏰12.30-3pm & 7.30-11pm Mon-Sat) For excellent
food and a bustling, authentic vibe, head to this
old-school trattoria. Gino's has been on the
go since the 1930s and today both locals and
visitors squeeze into the single dining room
to feast on tasty seafood and classic pastas.
Particularly good is the seafood antipasto and
the butter-soft roast *seppie* (cuttlefish).

🛏 Eleonora B&B   B&B €
(☎347 4817976, 0783 7 04 35; www.eleonora-
bed-and-breakfast.com; Piazza Eleonora
d'Arborea 12; s €40-60, d €60-80, tr €75-110;
❄ 🛜) This charming B&B scores on all counts:
location – it's in a medieval *palazzo* on Oristano's
central piazza; decor – rooms are tastefully
decorated with a mix of antique furniture,
exposed brick walls, and gorgeous old tiles; and
hospitality. And it's excellent value for money.

Orgosolo ❹

✖ Il Portico   Pizza €
(☎0784 40 29 29; Via Giovanni XXIII 34; pizza
€4-7, meals €16-20; ⏰noon-2pm & 7-11pm)
An excellent pizzeria-cum-restaurant serving
flavoursome, pizzas and superb local vegetables
and meats, such as *cinghiale in umido* (wild
boar stew) with olives. The airy dining room and
friendly, smiley service add to the pleasure.

Nuoro ❺

✖ La Locanda Pili Monica   Trattoria €
(☎0784 3 10 32; Via Brofferio 31; meals €20;
⏰12.30-2.45pm & 8.30-10.30pm Mon-Sat) It's
all about the food at this friendly, down-to-earth
trattoria, and the €9.20 set lunch is a bargain.
Bag a table and you're in for a treat – think fresh
pastas, mains of grilled steak or seafood, and
highly quaffable house wine.

✖ Il Portico   Sardinian €€
(☎0784 23 29 09; www.ilporticonuoro.it; Via
Monsignor Bua 13; meals €40; ⏰12.30-2.30pm
& 8-11pm Thu-Tue) You'll receive a heartfelt
welcome at this restaurant, where abstract
paintings grace the walls and jazzy music plays.
Behind the scenes, a talented husband-and-wife
team rustle up a feast of local fare like *spaghetti
ai ricci* (spaghetti with sea urchins) and fresh
gnocchi with lamb *ragù*. Save room for the
delectable caramel-nougat semifreddo.

🛏 Silvia e Paolo   B&B €
(☎0784 3 12 80; www.silviaepaolo.it; Corso
Garibaldi 58; r €55-65; ❄ 🛜) Silvia and Paolo run
this sweet B&B in the historic centre. Cheerful
decor makes you feel right at home in the bright,
spacious rooms, while there's a roof terrace for
observing the action on Corso Garibaldi by day
and stargazing by night. Note that two of the
three guest rooms share a bathroom.

Orosei ❼

✖ S'Hostera   Sardinian €€
(☎380 701 43 55; Via Grazia Deledda 56; meals
€35-40; ⏰7.30-11pm) A simple trattoria on the
face of it, S'Hostera stands head and shoulders
above most restaurants in Orosei when it comes
to food. The carpaccio, homemade pasta, freshly
grilled fish and specialities like *zuppa di pesce* (a
rich shellfish stew) and *orata alla vernaccia* (sea
bass cooked in white wine) are big on flavour and
served with a smile.

Dorgali ❽

✖ Ristorante Colibrì   Sardinian €€
(☎0784 9 60 54; Via Gramsci 14; meals €30;
⏰12.30-2.30pm & 7-10.30pm daily Jul & Aug,
closed Sun rest of year) Squirreled away in a
residential area (follow the numerous signs), this
lemon-walled restaurant is the real McCoy for
meat eaters. Stars of the menu include *cinghiale
al rosmarino* (wild boar with rosemary), *capra alla
selvatiza* (goat with thyme) and *porceddu*.

🛏 Sa Corte Antica   B&B €
(☎349 8401371; www.sacorteantica.it; Via Mannu
17; d €50-60, tr €75-90; ❄ 🛜) Gathered around
an old stone courtyard, this B&B housed in an
18th-century townhouse oozes charm from every
brick and beam. The rooms are traditional and
peaceful, with reed ceilings and wrought-iron
bedsteads.

STRETCH YOUR LEGS
PALERMO

Start/Finish: Palazzo dei Normanni

Distance: 2.8km

Duration: Three hours

Take in the complex warp and weave of Sicily's capital, from baroque fountains and dazzling Arab-Norman mosaics, to the vivid sights and sounds of its sprawling outdoor markets – all in just a few hours. Park your car at Piazzale Ungheria and then continue on foot.

Take this walk on Trip

36

Palazzo dei Normanni

This austere palace, once the seat of a magnificent court, today houses Sicily's parliament. In addition to political haggling, the palace holds Palermo's greatest treasure, the **Cappella Palatina** (Palatine Chapel; www.federico secondo.org; Piazza Indipendenza; adult/reduced Fri-Mon €8.50/6.50, Tue-Thu €7/5; ⊙9am-5pm Mon-Sat, 8.30-9.40am & 11.15am-1pm Sun). Designed by Norman king Roger II in 1130, this mosaic-clad chapel swarms with figures in glittering gold.

The Walk ≫ The short walk to the cathedral takes you along Corso Vittorio Emanuele, the city's main east–west thoroughfare, and through the baroque Porta Nuova, once the city's main gate.

Cattedrale

A feast of geometric patterns, ziggurat crenulations and majolica cupolas, Palermo's **cathedral** (☎091 33 43 73; www.cattedrale.palermo.it; Corso Vittorio Emanuele; cathedral free, tombs €1.50, treasury & crypt €2, roof adult/reduced €5/3, all-inclusive ticket adult/reduced €7/5; ⊙ cathedral 7am-7pm Mon-Sat, 8am-7pm Sun, royal tombs, treasury & roof 9.30am-5pm) is an extraordinary example of Sicily's unique Arab-Norman architecture. The 18th-century interior, while impressive in scale, is essentially a marble shell whose most interesting features are the royal Norman tombs and treasury.

The Walk ≫ Head straight down Corso Vittorio Emanuele and admire the decaying splendour of its elaborate baroque facades.

Quattro Canti

The intersection of Corso Vittorio Emanuele and Via Maqueda forms the civic heart of Palermo. Built in the early 17th century, the crossroads is adorned with four elaborate facades. The intersection represents one of Europe's first coordinated efforts at urban planning since ancient times.

The Walk >> Just beyond the Quattro Canti you'll see stairs on the right. Take these and you'll emerge on Piazza Pretoria.

Fontana Pretoria

This huge and ornate fountain originally graced a garden in Florence, but was bought by Palermo in 1573. However, the flagrant nudity of the provocative nymphs proved too much for the local church-goers, and it was prudishly dubbed the Fountain of Shame.

The Walk >> Exiting the piazza onto Via Maqueda, you will find the next two churches just a few steps to the south.

Chiesa Capitolare di San Cataldo & La Martorana

With its cubic simplicity, Arabic dome and delicate tracery, the 12th-century **Chiesa Capitolare di San Cataldo** (Piazza Bellini 3; €2.50; ☻9.30am-12.30pm & 3-6pm) is one of Palermo's most striking buildings. Disappointingly, it's almost bare inside. That's not the case for the adjacent **La Martorana** (Chiesa di Santa Maria dell'Ammiraglio; ☎345 8288231; Piazza Bellini 3; adult/reduced €2/1; ☻9.30am-1pm & 3.30-5.30pm Mon-Sat, 9-10.30am Sun), a luminously beautiful 12th-century church adorned with magnificent Byzantine mosaics. Its interior is best appreciated in the morning sunlight.

The Walk >> On the right just a few steps down Via Maqueda, look for Via del Ponticello, which leads directly into the Mercato di Ballarò.

Mercato di Ballarò

Snaking for several city blocks east of Palazzo dei Normanni is Palermo's busiest street market, which throbs with activity well into the early evening. It's a fascinating mix of noises, smells and street life, and the cheapest place for everything from Chinese padded bras to fresh produce, fish and cheese.

The Walk >> Head along Via Porta di Castro. Eventually the walls of the Palazzo dei Normanni will loom up on your right.

ROAD TRIP ESSENTIALS

Italy Driving Guide

Italy's stunning natural scenery, comprehensive road network and passion for cars makes it a wonderful road-trip destination.

DRIVING LICENCE & DOCUMENTS

➡ All EU driving licences are recognised in Italy.

➡ Travellers from other countries should obtain an International Driving Permit (IDP) through their national automobile association. This should be carried with your licence; it is not a substitute for it.

When driving in Italy you are required to carry with you:

➡ The vehicle registration document

➡ Your driving licence

➡ Proof of third-party liability insurance

INSURANCE

➡ Third-party liability insurance is mandatory for all vehicles in Italy, including cars brought in from abroad.

➡ If driving an EU-registered vehicle, your home country insurance is sufficient. Ask your insurer for a European Accident Statement (EAS) form, which can simplify matters in the event of an accident.

➡ Residents of non-EU countries should contact their insurance company to see if they need a green card international insurance certificate.

➡ Hire agencies provide the minimum legal insurance, but you can supplement it if you choose.

HIRING A CAR

Car-hire agencies are widespread in Italy but pre-booking on the internet is often cheaper. Online booking agency Rental-cars.com (www.rentalcars.com) compares the rates of numerous car-rental companies.

Considerations before renting:

➡ Bear in mind that a car is generally more hassle than it's worth in cities, so only hire one for the time you'll be on the open road.

➡ Consider vehicle size carefully. High fuel prices, extremely narrow streets and tight parking conditions mean that smaller is often better.

➡ Road signs can be iffy in remote areas, so consider booking and paying for GPS/sat nav.

Standard regulations:

➡ Many agencies have a minimum rental age of 25 and a maximum of 79. You can sometimes

---

Driving Fast Facts

➡ **Right or left?** Drive on the right

➡ **Manual or automatic?** Mostly manual

➡ **Legal driving age** 18

➡ **Top speed limit** 130km/h to 150km/h (on autostradas)

➡ **Signature car** Flaming red Ferrari or Fiat 500

hire if you're over 21 but supplements will apply.

➡ To rent you'll need a credit card, valid driver's licence (with IDP if necessary) and passport or photo ID. Note that some companies require that you've had your licence for at least a year.

➡ Hire cars come with the minimum legal insurance, which you can supplement by purchasing additional coverage.

➡ Check with your credit-card company to see if it offers a Collision Damage Waiver, which covers you for additional damage if you use that card to pay for the car.

The following companies have pick-up locations throughout Italy:

Auto Europe (www.autoeurope.com)
Avis (www.avis.com)
Budget (www.budget.com)
Europcar (www.europcar.com)
Hertz (www.hertz.it)
Italy by Car (http://italybycar.it)

Road-Trip Websites

AUTOMOBILE ASSOCIATIONS
Automobile Club d'Italia (www.aci.it) Has a comprehensive online guide to motoring in Italy. Provides 24-hour roadside assistance.

CONDITIONS & TRAFFIC
Autostrade (www.autostrade.it) Route planner, weather forecasts and the traffic situation in real time. Also lists service stations, petrol prices and toll costs.

CCISS (www.cciss.it) Italian-language site with updates on road works and real time traffic flows.

MAPS
Michelin (www.viamichelin.it) Online road-trip planner.

Tutto Città (www.tuttocitta.it) Good for detailed town and city maps.

Mappy (https://en.mappy.com) Online mapping tool.

Maggiore (www.maggiore.it)
Sixt (www.sixt.com)

Motorcycles

Agencies throughout Italy rent motorbikes, ranging from small Vespas to larger touring bikes. Prices start at around €35/150 per day/week for a 50cc scooter, or upwards of €80/400 per day/week for a 650cc motorcycle.

BRINGING YOUR OWN VEHICLE

➡ All foreign vehicles entering Italy must display a sticker or licence plate identifying its country of registration.

➡ If you're driving a left-hand-drive UK vehicle you'll have to adjust its headlights to avoid dazzling oncoming traffic.

➡ You'll need snow chains if travelling in mountainous areas between 15 October and 15 April.

MAPS

We recommend you purchase a good road map for your trip. The best driving maps are produced by the **Touring Club Italiano** (www.touringclub.com), Italy's largest map publisher. They are available at bookstores across Italy or online at the following:

Stanfords (www.stanfords.co.uk) Excellent UK-based shop that stocks many useful maps.

Omni Resources (www.omnimap.com) US-based online retailer with an impressive selection of Italian maps.

ROADS & CONDITIONS

Italy's extensive road network covers the entire peninsula and with enough patience you'll be able to get just about anywhere. Road quality varies – the autostradas are generally excellent but smaller roads, particularly in rural areas, are not always great. Heavy rain can cause axle-busting potholes to form and road surfaces to crumble.

Traffic in and around the main cities is bad during morning and evening rush hours. Coastal roads get very busy on summer weekends. As a rule, traffic is quietest between 2pm and 4pm.

Local Expert: Driving Tips

A representative of the Automobile Club d'Italia (ACI) offers these pearls to ease your way on Italian roads:

➡ Pay particular attention to the weather. In summer it gets very hot, but, in winter, watch out for ice, snow and fog.

➡ On the extra-urban roads and autostradas, cars must have their headlights on even during the day.

➡ Watch out for signs at the autostrada toll booths – the lanes marked 'Telepass' are for cars that pay through an automatic electronic system without stopping.

➡ Watch out in the cities – big and small – for the Limited Traffic Zones (ZTL) and pay parking. There is no universal system for indicating these or their hours.

Road Categories

Autostradas Italy boasts an extensive network of autostradas, represented on road signs by a white 'A' followed by a number on a green background. The main north–south link is the Autostrada del Sole (the 'Motorway of the Sun'), which runs from Milan (Milano) to Reggio di Calabria. It's called the A1 from Milan to Rome (Roma), the A2 from Rome to Naples (Napoli), and the A3 from Naples to Reggio di Calabria. There are tolls on most motorways, payable by cash or credit card as you exit. To calculate the toll price for any given journey, use the route planner on www.autostrade.it.

Strade statali State highways; represented on maps by 'S' or 'SS'. Vary from four-lane highways to two-lane main roads. The latter can be extremely slow, especially in mountainous regions.

Strade regionali Regional highways. Coded 'SR' or 'R'.

Strade provinciali Provincial highways; coded 'SP' or 'P'.

Strade locali Often not even paved or mapped.

Along with their A or SS number, some Italian roads are labelled with an E number – for example, the A4 autostrada is also shown as the E64 on maps and signs. This E number refers to the road's designation on the Europe-wide E-road network. E routes, which often cross national boundaries, are generally made up of major national roads strung together. The E70, for example, traverses 10 countries and includes the Italian A4, A21 and A32 autostradas, as it runs from northern Spain to Georgia.

Limited Traffic Zones

Many town and city centres are off-limits to unauthorised traffic at certain times. If you drive past a sign with the wording *Zona a Traffico Limitato* you are entering a Limited Traffic Zone (ZTL) and risk being caught on camera and fined. Being in a hire car will not exempt you from this rule.

If you think your hotel might be in a ZTL, contact it beforehand to ask about access arrangements.

ROAD RULES

➡ Cars drive on the right side of the road and overtake on the left. Unless otherwise indicated, always give way to cars entering an intersection from a road on your right.

➡ Seatbelt use (front and rear) is required by law; violators are subject to an on-the-spot fine. Helmets are required on all two-wheeled vehicles.

➡ Day and night, it is compulsory to drive with your headlights on outside built-up areas.

➡ It's obligatory to carry a warning triangle and fluorescent waistcoat in case of breakdown. Recommended accessories include a first-aid kit, spare-bulb kit and fire extinguisher.

Coins

Always try to keep some coins to hand. They come in very useful for parking meters.

Driving Problem-Buster

I can't speak Italian, will that be a problem? When at a petrol station you might have to ask the attendant for your fill-up. Ask for the amount you want, so *venti euro* for €20 or *pieno* for full. Always specify *benzina senza piombo* for unleaded petrol or *gasolio* for diesel.

What should I do if my car breaks down? Call the service number of your car-hire company. The Automobile Club d'Italia (ACI) provides a 24-hour roadside emergency service – call 803 116 from an Italian landline or mobile, or 800 116 800 from a foreign mobile phone. Foreigners do not have to join but instead pay a per-incident fee. Note that in the event of a breakdown, a warning triangle is compulsory, as is use of an approved yellow or orange safety vest if you leave your vehicle.

What if I have an accident? For minor accidents there's no need to call the police. Fill in an accident report – *Constatazione Amichevole di Incidente* (CAI; Agreed Motor Accident Statement) – through your car-hire firm or insurance company.

What should I do if I get stopped by the police? The police will want to see your passport (or photo ID), licence, car registration papers and proof of insurance.

Will I need to pay tolls in advance? No. When you join an autostrada you have to pick up a ticket at the barrier. When you exit you pay based on the distance you've covered. Pay by cash or credit card.

Are the road signs easy to understand? Most signs are fairly obvious but it helps to know that town/city centres are indicated by the word *centro* and a kind of black-and-white bullseye sign; *divieto fermata* means 'no stopping'; and *tutte le direzione* means 'all directions'.See the inside back cover of this book for some of the most common road signs.

Will I be able to find ATMs along the road? Some autostrada service stations have ATMs (known as *bancomat* in Italian). Otherwise they are widely available in towns and cities.

➡ A licence is required to ride a scooter – a car licence will do for bikes up to 125cc; for anything over 125cc you'll need a motorcycle licence.

➡ Motorbikes can enter most restricted traffic areas in Italian cities, and traffic police generally turn a blind eye to motorcycles or scooters parked on footpaths.

➡ The blood alcohol limit is 0.05%; it's zero for drivers under 21 and those who have had their licence for less than three years.

Unless otherwise indicated, speed limits are as follows:

➡ 130km/h on autostradas

➡ 110km/h on all main, non-urban roads

➡ 90km/h on secondary, non-urban roads

➡ 50km/h in built-up areas

Road Etiquette

➡ Italian drivers are fast, aggressive and skillful. Lane hopping and late braking are the norm and it's not uncommon to see cars tailgating at 130km/h. Don't expect cars to slow down for you or let you out. As soon as you see a gap, go for it. Italians expect the unexpected and react swiftly, but they're not used to ditherers, so be decisive.

➡ Headlight flashing is common on the roads and has several meanings. If a car behind you flashes it means: 'Get out of the way' or 'Don't pull out, I'm not stopping'. But if an approaching car flashes you, it's warning you that there's a police check ahead.

➡ Use of the car horn is widespread. It might be a warning but it might equally be an expression of frustration at slow-moving traffic or celebration that the traffic light's just turned green.

PARKING

➡ Parking can be a major headache. Space is at a premium in towns and cities and Italy's traffic wardens are annoyingly efficient.

➡ Parking spaces outlined in blue are designated for paid parking – get a ticket from the nearest meter (coins only) or *tabaccaio* (tobacconist) and display it on your dashboard. Note that charges often don't apply overnight, typically between 8pm and 8am.

➡ White or yellow lines almost always indicate that residential permits are needed.

➡ Traffic police generally turn a blind eye to motorcycles or scooters that are parked on footpaths.

FUEL

➡ You'll find filling stations all over, but smaller ones tend to close between about 1pm and 3.30pm and on Sunday afternoons.

➡ Many have *fai da te* (self-service) pumps that you can use any time. Simply insert a bank note into the payment machine and press the number of the pump you want.

➡ Italy's petrol prices are among the highest in Europe and vary from one service station (*benzinaio, stazione di servizio*) to another. At the time of research, unleaded petrol (*benzina senza piombo*) was averaging €1.49 per litre and diesel (*gasolio*) €1.33 per litre.

➡ At petrol stations, it costs slightly less to fill up yourself rather than have an assistant do it for you.

➡ Fuel costs most at austostrada service stations.

Road Distances (KM)

Note

Distances between Palermo and mainland towns do not take into account the ferry from Reggio di Calabria to Messina. Add an extra hour to your journey time to allow for this crossing.

	Bari	Bologna	Florence	Genoa	Milan	Naples	Palermo	Perugia	Reggio di Calabria	Rome	Siena	Trento	Trieste	Turin	Venice
Bologna	681														
Florence	784	106													
Genoa	996	285	268												
Milan	899	218	324	156											
Naples	322	640	534	758	858										
Palermo	734	1415	1345	1569	1633	811									
Perugia	612	270	164	432	488	408	1219								
Reggio di Calabria	490	1171	1101	1325	1389	567	272	816							
Rome	482	408	302	526	626	232	1043	170	664						
Siena	714	176	70	296	394	464	1275	103	867	232					
Trento	892	233	339	341	218	874	1626	459	1222	641	375				
Trieste	995	308	414	336	420	948	1689	543	1445	715	484	279			
Turin	1019	338	442	174	139	932	1743	545	1307	702	460	349	551		
Venice	806	269	265	387	284	899	799	394	1296	567	335	167	165	415	
Verona	808	141	247	282	164	781	1534	377	1139	549	293	97	250	295	120

Italy Playlist

Nessun Dorma Puccini

O sole mio Traditional

Tu vuoi fare l'americano Renato Carsone

Vieni via con me Paolo Conte

Volare Domenico Modugno

Four Seasons Vivaldi

SAFETY

➡ The main safety threat to motorists is theft. Hire cars and foreign vehicles are a target for robbers and although you're unlikely to have a problem, thefts do occur.

➡ As a general rule, always lock your car and never leave anything showing, particularly valuables, and certainly not overnight. If at all possible, avoid leaving luggage in an unattended car.

➡ It's a good idea to pay extra to leave your car in supervised car parks.

RADIO

RAI, Italy's state broadcaster, operates three national radio stations – Radio 1, 2 and 3 – offering news, current affairs, classical and commercial music. Isoradio, another RAI station, provides regular news and traffic bulletins. There are also thousands of commercial radio stations, many broadcasting locally. Major ones include Radio Capital, good for modern hits; Radio Deejay, aimed at a younger audience; and Radio 24, which airs news and talk shows.

Italy Travel Guide

GETTING THERE & AWAY

AIR

Italy's main international airports:

Rome Leonardo da Vinci (www.adr.it/fiu micino) Often referred to as Fiumicino airport.

Rome Ciampino (www.adr.it/ciampino) Hub for Ryanair flights to Rome.

Milan Malpensa (www.milanomalpensa-airport.com)

Milan Linate (www.milanolinate-airport.com) Milan's second airport.

Venice Marco Polo (www.veniceairport.it)

Pisa International (www.pisa-airport.com) Main international gateway for Tuscany.

Naples International (www.aeroportodi napoli.it)

Catania Fontanarossa (www.aeroporto.catania.it) Sicily's busiest airport.

Bergamo Orio al Serio (www.orioaero porto.it)

Turin (turin-airport.com)

Bologna Guglielmo Marconi (www.bologna-airport.it)

Bari Palese (www.aeroportidipuglia.it)

Palermo Falcone-Borsellino (www.gesap.it)

Cagliari Elmas (www.cagliariairport.it) Main gateway for Sardinia

Car hire is available at all these airports.

CAR & MOTORCYCLE

Driving into Italy is fairly straightforward – thanks to the Schengen Agreement, there are no customs checks when driving in from neighbours France, Switzerland, Austria and Slovenia.

Aside from the coast roads linking Italy with France and Slovenia, border crossings into Italy mostly involve tunnels through the Alps (open year-round) or mountain passes (seasonally closed or requiring snow chains). The list below outlines the major points of entry.

Austria From Innsbruck to Bolzano via A22/E45 (Brenner Pass); Villach to Tarvisio via A23/E55.

France From Nice to Ventimiglia via A10/E80; Modane to Turin (Torino) via A32/E70 (Fréjus Tunnel); Chamonix to Courmayeur via A5/E25 (Mont Blanc Tunnel).

Slovenia From Sežana to Trieste via SR58/E61.

Switzerland From Martigny to Aosta via SS27/E27 (Grand St Bernard Tunnel); Lugano to Como via A9/E35.

SEA

International car ferries sail to Italy from Albania, Croatia, Greece, Malta, Montenegro, Morocco, Slovenia, Spain and Tunisia. Many routes only operate in summer, when ticket prices rise. Prices for vehicles vary according to their size. Car hire is not always available at ports, so check beforehand.

The website www.directferries.co.uk allows you to search routes and compare prices between the numerous international ferry companies serving Italy.

Principal operators:

Adria Ferries (www.adriaferries.com) Albania to Bari (nine to 10 hours), Ancona (14 hours), Trieste (12 hours).

Anek Lines (www.anekitalia.com) Greece to Bari (8 to 18½ hours), Ancona (15½ to 22 hours), Venice (21 hours).

GNV (Grandi Navi Veloci; www.gnv.it) Spain to Genoa (18 hours).

Grimaldi Lines (www.grimaldi-lines.com) Spain to Civitavecchia (18 hours), Livorno (20½ hours).

Jadrolinija (www.jadrolinija.hr) Croatia to Ancona (from nine hours), Bari (10 hours).

Minoan Lines (www.minoan.it) Greece to Ancona (16 to 22 hours), Trieste (22½ to 28½ hours).

Montenegro Lines (www.montenegrolines. net) Bar to Bari (nine hours).

Superfast (www.superfast.com) Greece to Bari (11 to 16 hours), Ancona (16 to 22 hours), Venice (26½ to 33 hours).

TRAIN

Regular trains on two western lines connect Italy with France (one along the coast and the other from Turin into the French

Alps). Trains from Milan head north into Switzerland and on towards the Benelux countries. Further east, two lines connect with Central and Eastern Europe.

Car hire is generally available at principal city stations.

DIRECTORY A–Z

ACCOMMODATION

From dreamy villas to chic boutique hotels, historic hideaways and ravishing farmstays, Italy offers accommodation to suit every taste and budget.

Seasons & Rates

➡ Hotel rates fluctuate enormously from high to low season, and even from day to day depending on demand, season and booking method (online, through an agency etc).

➡ As a rule, peak rates apply at Easter, in summer (July and August) and over the Christmas/New Year period. But there are exceptions – in the mountains, high season means the ski season (December to late March). Also, August is high season on the coast but low season in many cities where hotels offer discounts.

➡ Southern Italy is generally cheaper than the north.

Reservations

➡ Always book ahead in peak season, even if it's only for the first night or two.

➡ In the off-season, it always pays to call ahead to check that your hotel is open. Many coastal hotels close for winter, typically opening from late March to late October.

➡ Hotels usually require that reservations be confirmed with a credit-card number. No-shows will be docked a night's accommodation.

B&Bs

B&Bs are a burgeoning sector of the Italian accommodation market and can be found throughout the country in both urban and rural settings. Options include everything from restored farmhouses, city *palazzi* (mansions) and seaside bungalows to rooms in family houses. Tariffs for a double room cover a wide range, from around €60 to €140.

Book Your Stay Online

For more accommodation reviews by Lonely Planet authors, check out http://hotels.lonelyplanet.com. You'll find independent reviews, as well as recommendations on the best places to stay. Best of all, you can book online.

Lists of B&Bs across the country are available online at the following sites:

BBItalia.it (www.bbitalia.it)

Bed-and-Breakfast.it (www.bed-and-breakfast.it)

Hotels & Pensioni

While the difference between an *albergo* (hotel) and a *pensione* is often minimal, a *pensione* will generally be of one- to three-star quality while an *albergo* can be awarded up to five stars. *Locande* (inns) long fell into much the same category as *pensioni*, but the term has become a trendy one in some parts and reveals little about the quality of a place. *Affittacamere* are simple rooms for rent in private houses.

All hotels are rated from one to five stars:

➡ One-star hotels and *pensioni* tend to be basic and often do not offer private bathrooms.

➡ Two-star places are similar but rooms will generally have a private bathroom.

➡ Three-star hotel rooms will come with a hairdryer, minibar (or fridge), safe and air-con.

➡ Four- and five-star hotels offer facilities such as room service, laundry and dry-cleaning.

Tourist offices usually have booklets with local accommodation listings. Many hotels are also signing up with online accommodation-booking services.

Agriturismi

From rustic country houses to luxurious estates and fully functioning farms, Italian farmstays, known as *agriturismi* (singular – *agriturismo*) are hugely popular. Comfort levels, facilities and prices vary but the best will offer swimming pools and top-class accommodation. Many also operate restaurants specialising in traditional local cuisine.

For listings and further details, check the following:

Agriturismo.it (www.agriturismo.it)

Agriturismo.net (www.agriturismo.net)

Agriturismo.com (www.agriturismo.com)

Agriturismo-Italia.net (www.agriturismo-italia.net)

Other Options

Camping A popular summer option. Most campsites are big, summer-only complexes with swimming pools, restaurants and supermarkets. Many have space for RVs and offer bungalows or simple, self-contained flats. Minimum stays sometimes apply in high season. Check out www.campeggi.com and www.camping.it.

Hostels Official HI hostels and a growing contingent of independent hostels offer dorm beds and private rooms. Breakfast is usually included in rates and dinner is sometimes available for about €10. For listings and further details, see www.aighostels.com or www.hostelworld.com.

Convents & Monasteries Some convents and monasteries provide basic accommodation. Expect curfews, few frills and value for money. Useful resources include www.monasterystays.com, www.initaly.com/agri/convents.htm and www.santasusanna.org/index.php/resources/convent-accomodations.

Refuges Mountain huts with rooms sleeping anything from two to a dozen or more people. Many also offer hot meals and/or communal

---

Sleeping Price Ranges

The following price ranges refer to a double room with private bathroom (breakfast included) in high season.

€ less than €110

€€ €110-200

€€€ more than €200

Room Tax

Italy's *tassa di soggiorno* (accommodation tax) sees visitors charged an extra €1 to €7 per night as a 'room occupancy tax'.

Exactly how much you're charged depends on the type of accommodation (campground, guesthouse, hotel), a hotel's star rating, and the number of people under your booking.

Our listings do not include the hotel tax, although it's always a good idea to confirm whether taxes are included when booking.

cooking facilities. Generally open from June to late September.

Villas Villas and *fattorie* (farmhouses) can be rented in their entirety or sometimes by the room. Many have swimming pools.

ELECTRICITY

230V/50Hz

230V/50Hz

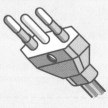

FOOD

A full Italian meal consists of an *antipasto* (appetiser), *primo* (first course, usually a pasta, risotto or polenta), *secondo* (second course, meat or fish) with *contorno* (vegetable side dish) or *insalata* (salad), and *dolce* (dessert) and/or fruit. When eating out it's perfectly OK to mix and match and order, say, a *primo* followed by an *insalata* or *contorno*.

Where to Eat

➡ **Ristorante (Restaurant)** Formal service and refined dishes. Reservations generally required for popular and top-end places.

➡ **Trattoria** Cheaper than a restaurant, with more-relaxed service and regional food and wine. Some newer-wave trattorias offer more creative fare. Generally cheap to mid-range.

➡ **Wine Bar** At an *enoteca* you can drink wine by the glass and eat snacks such as cheese, cold meats, bruschette and *crostini* (little toasts) to accompany your tipple. Some also serve hot dishes.

➡ **Agriturismo** A farmhouse offering food made with farm-grown produce. Booking generally required.

➡ **Pizzeria** Alongside pizza, many pizzerias also offer *antipasti*, pastas, meat and vegetable

230V/50Hz

dishes. They're often only open in the evening. The best have a wood-oven (*forno a legna*).

➡ **Bar & Cafe** Italians often breakfast on a *cornetto* (Italian croissant) and cappuccino at a bar or cafe. Many places sell *panini* (bread rolls with simple fillers) at lunchtime and serve a buffet of hot and cold dishes during the early evening *aperitivo* (aperitif) hour.

➡ **Market** Most towns and cities have morning produce markets where you can stock up on picnic provisions.

HEALTH

➡ Italy has a public health system that is legally bound to provide emergency care to everyone.

➡ EU nationals are entitled to reduced-cost, sometimes free, medical care with a European Health Insurance Card (EHIC), available from your home health authority.

➡ Non-EU citizens should take out medical insurance.

➡ For emergency treatment, go to the *pronto soccorso* (casualty) section of an *ospedale* (public hospital), though be prepared for a long wait.

➡ Pharmacists can give advice and sell over-the-counter medication for minor illnesses. Pharmacies generally keep the same hours as other shops, closing at night and on Sundays. A handful remain open on a rotation basis (*farmacie di turno*) for emergency purposes. These are usually listed in newspapers. Closed pharmacies display a list of the nearest ones open.

Eating Price Ranges

The following price ranges refer to a two-course meal with a glass of house wine and *coperto* (cover charge).

€ less than €25

€€ €25–€45

€€€ more than €45

Note that most eating establishments add a *coperto* of around €2 to €3. Some also include a service charge (*servizio*) of 10% to 15%.

Italian Wine Classifications

Italian wines are classified according to strict quality-control standards and carry one of four denominations:

DOCG (Denominazione di Origine Controllata e Garantita) Italy's best wines; made in specific areas according to stringent production rules.

DOC (Denominazione di Origine Controllata) Quality wines produced in defined regional areas.

IGT (Indicazione di Geografica Tipica) Wines typical of a certain region. Technically, also includes the high-quality Super Tuscan wines.

VdT (Vino da Tavola) Wines for everyday drinking; often served as house wine in trattorias.

➡ In major cities you are likely to find English-speaking doctors or a translator service available.

➡ Italian tap water is fine to drink.

➡ No vaccinations are required for travel to Italy.

INTERNET ACCESS

➡ Numerous Italian cities and towns offer public wi-fi hotspots, including Rome, Bologna and Venice. To use them, you will need to register online using a credit card or an Italian mobile number. An easier option (no need for a local mobile number) is to head to a cafe or bar offering free wi-fi.

➡ Most hotels, B&Bs, hostels and *agriturismi* offer free wi-fi to guests, though signals can vary in quality. There will sometimes be a computer for guest use.

LGBT TRAVELLERS

➡ Homosexuality is legal in Italy and well tolerated in the major cities. However, overt displays of affection by homosexual couples could attract a negative response, especially in smaller towns.

➡ There are gay venues in Rome, Milan and Bologna, and a handful in places such as Florence and Naples. Some coastal towns and resorts (such as the Tuscan town of Viareggio or Taormina in Sicily) have much more action in summer.

Online resources include the following Italian-language websites:

Arcigay (www.arcigay.it) Bologna-based national organisation for the LGBTI community.

Gay.it (www.gay.it) Website featuring LGBT news, feature articles and gossip.

Pride (www.prideonline.it) National monthly magazine of art, music, politics and gay culture.

MONEY

Italy uses the euro. Euro notes come in denominations of €500, €200, €100, €50, €20, €10 and €5; coins come in denominations of €2 and €1, and 50, 20, 10, five, two and one cents.

For the latest exchange rates, check out www.xe.com.

Admission Prices

➡ State museums and galleries offer free admission to under-18s and discounted entry to 18-25 year-olds.

➡ You'll need photo ID to claim reduced entry.

➡ State museums are free on the first Sunday of the month.

Tipping Guide

Taxis Optional, but most people round up to the nearest euro.

Hotels Tip porters about €4 at high-end hotels.

Restaurants Service (servizio) is generally included in restaurants – if it's not, a euro or two is fine in pizzerias, 10% in restaurants.

Bars Optional, though many Italians leave small change on the bar when ordering coffee. If drinks are brought to your table, a small tip is generally appreciated.

ATMs & Credit Cards

➡ ATMs (known as *bancomat*) are widely available throughout Italy and most will accept cards tied into the Visa, MasterCard, Cirrus and Maestro systems.

➡ Credit cards are good for payment in most hotels, restaurants, shops, supermarkets and tollbooths. Major cards such as Visa, MasterCard, Eurocard, Cirrus and Eurocheques are widely accepted. Amex is also recognised, though less common.

➡ Let your bank know when you are going abroad, in case they block your card when payments from unusual locations appear.

➡ Check any charges with your bank. Most banks charge a foreign exchange fee (usually around 1% to 3%) as well as a transaction charge of around 1%. ATM withdrawals can attract a further fee, usually around 1.5%.

➡ If your card is lost, stolen or swallowed by an ATM, call to have it blocked:

Amex ☏06 729 00 347

Diners Club ☏800 39 39 39

MasterCard ☏800 870 866

Visa ☏800 819 014

Moneychangers

You can change money in banks, at post offices or in a *cambio* (exchange office). Post offices and banks tend to offer the best rates; exchange offices keep longer hours; but watch for high commissions and inferior rates.

Have your passport or some form of photo ID available when exchanging money.

OPENING HOURS

Opening hours vary throughout the year. We've provided high-season opening hours; hours will generally decrease in the shoulder and low seasons. 'Summer' times generally refer to the period from April to September or October, while 'winter' times generally run from October or November to March.

Banks 8.30am-1.30pm & 2.45-3.45 or 4.30pm Monday to Friday

Restaurants noon–2.30pm & 7.30–11pm or midnight

Cafes 7.30am–8pm

Bars and clubs 10pm–4am or 5am

Shops 9am–1pm & 4–8pm Monday to Saturday, some also open Sunday

---

PUBLIC HOLIDAYS

Individual towns have public holidays to celebrate the feasts of their patron saints. National public holidays:

Capodanno (New Year's Day) 1 January

Epifania (Epiphany) 6 January

Pasquetta (Easter Monday) March/April

Giorno della Liberazione (Liberation Day) 25 April

Festa del Lavoro (Labour Day) 1 May

Festa della Repubblica (Republic Day) 2 June

Ferragosto (Feast of the Assumption) 15 August

Festa di Ognisanti (All Saints' Day) 1 November

Festa dell'Immacolata Concezione (Feast of the Immaculate Conception) 8 December

Natale (Christmas Day) 25 December

Festa di Santo Stefano (Boxing Day) 26 December

SAFE TRAVEL

Italy is a safe country but petty theft can be a problem. There's no need for paranoia but be aware that thieves and pickpockets operate in touristy areas, so watch out when exploring the sights in Rome, Florence, Venice and Naples.

Cars, particularly those with foreign number plates or rental-company stickers, provide rich pickings for thieves.

In case of theft or loss, report the incident to the police within 24 hours and ask for a statement.

➜ Keep essentials in a money belt but carry your day's spending money in a separate wallet.

➜ Wear your bag/camera strap across your body and away from the road – thieves on mopeds can swipe a bag and be gone in seconds.

➜ Never drape your bag over an empty chair at a street-side cafe or put it where you can't see it.

➜ Always check your change to see you haven't been short changed.

TELEPHONE

Domestic Calls

➜ Italian telephone area codes all begin with ✐0 and consist of up to four digits. Area codes are an integral part of all Italian phone numbers and must be dialled even when calling locally.

➜ Mobile-phone numbers are nine or 10 digits and have a three-digit prefix starting with a ✐3.

➜ Toll-free (free-phone) numbers are known as *numeri verdi* and usually start with ✐800.

➜ Non-geographical special rate and service numbers often start with ✐840, 848 or 199.

➜ Some six-digit national rate numbers are also in use (such as those for Alitalia, rail and postal information).

International Calls

➜ To call Italy from abroad, call your international access number, then Italy's country code (✐39) and the area code of the location you want, including the leading 0.

➜ Avoid making international calls from a hotel, as rates are high.

➜ The cheapest options are free or low-cost computer programs/smartphone apps such as Skype and Viber.

➜ Another cheap option is to call from a private call centre, or from a payphone with an international calling card. These are commonly sold at newsstands and tobacconists.

Mobile Phones (Cell Phones)

➜ Italian mobile phones operate on the GSM 900/1800 network, which is compatible with the rest of Europe and Australia but not always with the North American GSM or CDMA systems – check with your service provider.

➜ Most smartphones are multiband, meaning that they are compatible with a variety of international networks. Before bringing your own phone to Italy, check with your service provider to make sure it is compatible, and beware of calls being routed internationally (very expensive for a 'local' call).

➜ If you have a GSM dual-, tri- or quad-band phone that you can unlock (check with your service provider), it can cost as little as €10 to activate a prepaid (*prepagato*) SIM card in Italy. TIM (Telecom Italia Mobile; www.tim.it), Wind

Important Numbers

Italy country code (☏39)

International access code (☏00)

Police (☏113)

Carabinieri (☏112)

Ambulance (☏118)

Fire (☏115)

Roadside assistance (☏803 116 from an Italian landline or mobile phone; ☏800 116 800 from a foreign mobile phone)

(www.wind.it) and Vodafone (www.vodafone.it) all offer SIM cards and have retail outlets across town. All SIM cards must be registered in Italy, so make sure you have a passport or ID card with you when you buy one.

➡ You can easily top up your Italian SIM with a recharge card (*ricarica*), available from most tobacconists, some bars, supermarkets and banks.

Payphones & Phonecards

➡ You can still find payphones around Italy. Most take phonecards (*schede telefoniche*), although some accept credit cards.

➡ You can buy phonecards at post offices, tobacconists and news stands.

TOILETS

➡ Public toilets are thin on the ground in Italy. You'll find them in autostrada service stations (generally free) and in main train stations (usually with a €1 fee).

➡ Often, the best thing is to nip into a cafe or bar, although you'll probably have to order a quick drink first.

➡ Keep tissues to hand as loo paper is rare.

TOURIST INFORMATION

Practically every village, town and city in Italy has a tourist office of sorts. These operate under a variety of names: *Azienda di Promozione Turistica* (APT), *Azienda Autonoma di Soggiorno e Turismo* (AAST), *Informazione e Assistenza ai Turisti* (IAT) and *Pro Loco*. All deal directly with the public and most will respond to written and telephone requests for information.

Tourist offices can usually provide a city map, accommodation lists and information on local sights. In larger towns and major tourist areas, English is usually spoken.

Main offices are generally open Monday to Friday; some also open on weekends, especially in urban areas and in peak summer season. Info booths (at train stations and airports, for example) may keep slightly different hours.

Tourist Authorities

The **Italian National Tourist Office** (www.enit.it) maintains offices in 21 cities on five continents. Contact information for all offices can be found on its website.

Regional tourist authorities are more concerned with planning, marketing and promotion than with offering a public information service. However, most offer useful websites:

Abruzzo (www.abruzzoturismo.it)

Basilicata (www.aptbasilicata.it)

Calabria (www.turiscalabria.it)

Campania (www.regione.campania.it/it/tematiche/magazine-turismo-e-cultura)

Emilia-Romagna (www.emiliaromagna turismo.it)

Friuli Venezia Giulia (www.turismofvg.it)

Lazio (www.visitlazio.com)

Le Marche (www.turismo.marche.it)

Liguria (www.turismoinliguria.it)

Lombardy (www.in-lombardia.it)

Molise (www.moliseturismo.eu)

Piedmont (www.piemonteitalia.eu)

Puglia (www.viaggiareinpuglia.it)

Sardinia (www.sardegnaturismo.it)

Sicily (www.regione.sicilia.it/turismo)

Trentino-Alto Adige (www.visittrentino.it)

Tuscany (www.turismo.intoscana.it)

Umbria (www.umbriatourism.it)

Valle d'Aosta (www.lovevda.it)

Veneto (www.veneto.eu)

Another useful website is www.italia.it.

TRAVELLERS WITH DISABILITIES

➡ Italy is not an easy country for travellers with disabilities and getting around can be a problem for wheelchair users. Even a short journey in a city or town can become a major expedition if cobblestone streets have to be negotiated. Although many buildings have lifts, they are not always wide enough for wheelchairs. Not an awful lot has been done to make life for the hearing/vision impaired easier.

➡ The Italian National Tourist Office in your country may be able to provide advice on Italian associations for travellers with disabilities and information on what help is available.

➡ Airline companies should be able to arrange assistance at airports if you notify them of your needs in advance. Alternatively, contact ADR Assistance (www.adrassistance.it) for assistance at Fiumicino or Ciampino airports.

➡ Some taxis are equipped to carry passengers in wheelchairs; ask for a taxi for a *sedia a rotelle* (wheelchair).

➡ Italy's official tourism website (www.italia. it) offers a number of links for travellers with disabilities. Another online resource is Lonely Planet's Travel for All community on Google+, worth joining for information sharing and networking.

Accessible Travel Guide

Lonely Planet's free Accessible Travel guide can be downloaded here: http://lptravel.to/AccessibleTravel.

VISAS

➡ Italy is one of the 26 countries that comprise the Schengen area. Within the Schengen area there are no internal border controls.

➡ EU and Swiss citizens do not need a visa for Italy.

➡ Nationals of some other countries, including Australia, Canada, Israel, Japan, New Zealand and the USA, do not need a tourist visa for stays of up to 90 days. However, passports must be valid for at least three months after the planned date of departure from the Schengen area.

➡ For full details of Italy's visa requirements check http://vistoperitalia.esteri.it/home/en.

➡ The standard tourist visa for a Schengen country is valid for 90 days. You must apply for it in your country of residence. For further details see www.schengenvisainfo.com.

Language

Italian sounds can all be found in English. If you read our coloured pronunciation guides as if they were English, you'll be understood. Note that ai is pronounced as in 'aisle', ay as in 'say', ow as in 'how', dz as the 'ds' in 'lids', and that r is strong and rolled. If the consonant is written as a double letter, it's pronounced a little stronger, eg *sonno son*·no (sleep) versus *sono so*·no (I am). The stressed syllables are indicated with italics.

BASICS

Hello.	*Buongiorno.*	bwon·*jor*·no
Goodbye.	*Arrivederci.*	a·ree·ve·*der*·chee
Yes./No.	*Sì./No.*	see/no
Excuse me.	*Mi scusi.*	mee *skoo*·zee
Sorry.	*Mi dispiace.*	mee dees·*pya*·che
Please.	*Per favore.*	per fa·*vo*·re
Thank you.	*Grazie.*	*gra*·tsye

You're welcome.
Prego.   *pre*·go

Do you speak English?
Parli inglese?   *par*·lee een·*gle*·ze

I don't understand.
Non capisco.   non ka·*pee*·sko

How much is this?
Quanto costa questo?   *kwan*·to *kos*·ta *kwe*·sto

ACCOMMODATION

Do you have a room?
Avete una camera?   a·*ve*·te *oo*·na *ka*·me·ra

Want More?

For in-depth language information and handy phrases, check out Lonely Planet's *Italian Phrasebook*. You'll find it at **shop.lonelyplanet.com**, or you can buy Lonely Planet's iPhone phrasebooks at the Apple App Store.

How much is it per night/person?
Quanto costa per una notte/persona?   *kwan*·to *kos*·ta per *oo*·na *no*·te/per·*so*·na

DIRECTIONS

Where's ...?
Dov'è ...?   do·*ve* ...

Can you show me (on the map)?
Può mostrarmi (sulla pianta)?   pwo mos·*trar*·mee (*soo*·la *pyan*·ta)

EATING & DRINKING

What would you recommend?
Cosa mi consiglia?   *ko*·za mee kon·*see*·lya

I'd like ..., please.
Vorrei ..., per favore.   vo·*ray* ... per fa·*vo*·re

I don't eat (meat).
Non mangio (carne).   non *man*·jo (*kar*·ne)

Please bring the bill.
Mi porta il conto, per favore?   mee *por*·ta eel *kon*·to per fa·*vo*·re

EMERGENCIES

Help!
Aiuto!   a·*yoo*·to

I'm lost.
Mi sono perso/a. (m/f)   mee *so*·no *per*·so/a

I'm ill.
Mi sento male.   mee *sen*·to *ma*·le

Call the police!
Chiami la polizia!   *kya*·mee la po·lee·*tsee*·a

Call a doctor!
Chiami un medico!   *kya*·mee oon *me*·dee·ko

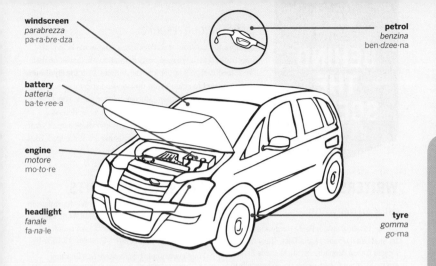

windscreen
parabrezza
pa·ra·bre·dza

petrol
benzina
ben·dzee·na

battery
batteria
ba·te·ree·a

engine
motore
mo·to·re

headlight
fanale
fa·na·le

tyre
gomma
go·ma

ON THE ROAD

I'd like to hire a/an ...	*Vorrei noleggiare ...*	vo·ray no·le·ja·re ...
4WD	*un fuoristrada*	oon fwo·ree·stra·da
automatic/ manual	*una macchina automatica/ manuale*	oo·na ma·kee·na ow·to·ma·tee·ka/ ma·noo·a·le
motorbike	*una moto*	oo·na mo·to

How much is it ...?	*Quanto costa ...?*	kwan·to kos·ta ...
daily	*al giorno*	al jor·no
weekly	*alla settimana*	a·la se·tee·ma·na

Does that include insurance?
E' compresa l'assicurazione?
e kom·pre·sa la·see·koo·ra·tsyo·ne

Signs

Alt	Stop
Dare la Precedenza	Give Way
Deviazione	Detour
Divieto di Accesso	No Entry
Entrata	Entrance
Pedaggio	Toll
Senso Unico	One Way
Uscita	Exit

Does that include mileage?
E' compreso il chilometraggio?
e kom·pre·so eel kee·lo·me·tra·jo

What's the city/country speed limit?
Qual'è il limite di velocità in città/campagna?
kwa·le eel lee·mee·te dee ve·lo·chee·ta een chee·ta/kam·pa·nya

Is this the road to (Venice)?
Questa strada porta a (Venezia)?
kwe·sta stra·da por·ta a (ve·ne·tsya)

(How long) Can I park here?
(Per quanto tempo) Posso parcheggiare qui?
(per kwan·to tem·po) po·so par·ke·ja·re kwee

Where's a service station?
Dov'è una stazione di servizio?
do·ve oo·na sta·tsyo·ne dee ser·vee·tsyo

Please fill it up.
Il pieno, per favore.
eel pye·no per fa·vo·re

I'd like (30) litres.
Vorrei (trenta) litri.
vo·ray (tren·ta) lee·tree

Please check the oil/water.
Può controllare l'olio/ l'acqua, per favore?
pwo kon·tro·la·re lo·lyo/ la·kwa per fa·vo·re

I need a mechanic.
Ho bisogno di un meccanico.
o bee·zo·nyo dee oon me·ka·nee·ko

The car/motorbike has broken down.
La macchina/moto si è guastata.
la ma·kee·na/mo·to see e gwas·ta·ta

I had an accident.
Ho avuto un incidente.
o a·voo·to oon een·chee·den·te

437

BEHIND THE SCENES

SEND US YOUR FEEDBACK

We love to hear from travellers – your comments help make our books better. We read every word, and we guarantee that your feedback goes straight to the authors. Visit **lonelyplanet. com/contact** to submit your updates and suggestions.

Note: We may edit, reproduce and incorporate your comments in Lonely Planet products such as guidebooks, websites and digital products, so let us know if you don't want your comments reproduced or your name acknowledged. For a copy of our privacy policy visit lonelyplanet.com/privacy.

WRITERS' THANKS

DUNCAN GARWOOD

Thanks to fellow author Paula Hardy and all the team at Lonely Planet: Anna Tyler, Tracy Whitmey, Angela Tinson, Monique Perrin, Michelle Bennett, Darren O'Connell. And, as always, *grazie mille* to Lidia, Ben and Nick.

PAULA HARDY

I'd like to thank the following people for sharing the best of northern Italy: Claudio Bonasera, Mario Pietraccetta, Francesca at Villa Rosmarino, Alessandro Manzana, Contessa Caroline di Levetzow Lantieri Piccolomini, Lorenzo Bagnara, the staff at Rosa Alpina and Francesca Giubilei. Also thanks to co-author Duncan Garwood, and Anna Tyler for the commission.

ACKNOWLEDGMENTS

Climate map data adapted from Peel MC, Finlayson BL & McMahon TA (2007) 'Updated World Map of the Köppen-Geiger Climate Classification', *Hydrology and Earth System Sciences*, 11, 163344.

Front cover photographs: (top) San Giovanni church, Ranui, Dolomites, Francesco Riccardo Iacomino/AWL©; (left) Vintage Fiat 500 on the road, Naples, Elis Koro/Alamy©; (right) Duomo, Florence, Tuscany, Pietro Canali/4Corners©

Back cover photograph: Cinque Terre, Anna Omelchenko/Shutterstock©

THIS BOOK

This 2nd edition of Lonely Planet's *Italy's Best Trips* guidebook was researched and written by Duncan Garwood and Paula Hardy. The previous edition was written by Duncan Garwood, Paula Hardy and Robert Landon. This guidebook was produced by the following:

Destination Editor Anna Tyler

Product Editor Tracy Whitmey

Senior Cartographer Anthony Phelan

Book Designer Mazzy Prinsep

Assistant Editors Michelle Bennett, Bruce Evans, Paul Harding, Jodie Martire, Monique Perrin

Cover Researcher Naomi Parker

Thanks to Will Chaplin, Andi Jones, Indra Kilfoyle, Virginia Moreno, Wayne Murphy, Kirsten Rawlings, Jessica Rose, Dianne Schallmeiner, James Smart, Luna Soo, Stefania Spitaleri, John Taufa, Angela Tinson, Tony Wheeler, Juan Winata, Dora Whitaker

INDEX

W

INDEX V-W

OUR WRITERS

OUR STORY

A beat-up old car, a few dollars in the pocket and a sense of adventure. In 1972 that's all Tony and Maureen Wheeler needed for the trip of a lifetime – across Europe and Asia overland to Australia. It took several months, and at the end – broke but inspired – they sat at their kitchen table writing and stapling together their first travel guide, *Across Asia on the Cheap*. Within a week they'd sold 1500 copies. Lonely Planet was born.

Today, Lonely Planet has offices in Franklin, London, Melbourne, Oakland, Dublin, Beijing and Delhi, with more than 600 staff and writers. We share Tony's belief that 'a great guidebook should do three things: inform, educate and amuse'.

DUNCAN GARWOOD

A Brit travel writer based in the Castelli Romani hills just outside Rome, Duncan has clocked up tens of thousands of kilometres driving through Italy and exploring its far-flung reaches. He's co-author of the *Rome* city guide and has contributed to a host of Lonely Planet guidebooks including *Italy, Piedmont, Sicily, Sardinia,* and *Naples and the Amalfi Coast*. He has also written on Italy for newspapers, websites and magazines.

Read more about Duncan at: https://auth. lonelyplanet.com/profiles/duncangarwood

PAULA HARDY

From the slopes of Valpolicella to the shores of Lake Como and the spritz-fuelled bars of Venice and Milan, Paula has been contributing to Lonely Planet Italian guides for over 15 years, including previous editions of *Venice & the Veneto, Pocket Milan, The Italian Lakes, Sicily, Sardinia, Puglia & Basilicata* and *Italy*. When she's not scooting around the *bel paese,* she writes for a variety of travel publications and websites. Currently she divides her time between London, Italy and Morocco, and tweets her finds @paula6hardy.

Read more about Paula at: https://auth. lonelyplanet.com/profiles/paulahardy

Published by Lonely Planet Global Limited
CRN 554153
2nd edition – March 2017
ISBN 978 1 78657 321 6
© Lonely Planet 2017
Photographs © as indicated 2017
10 9 8 7 6 5 4 3 2 1
Printed in China

MIX
Paper from responsible sources
FSC™ C021741

Paper in this book is certified against the Forest Stewardship Council™ standards. FSC™ promotes environmentally responsible, socially beneficial and economically viable management of the world's forests.